From the Library of
LAWRENCE R. TAYLOR, Ph.D.

# Dramatic Comedy

Edited by
Harry H. Schanker

WEBSTER DIVISION
McGRAW-HILL BOOK COMPANY

New York   St. Louis   Dallas
San Francisco   Atlanta

# ACKNOWLEDGMENTS

*Arsenic and Old Lace*
Copyright 1941 and renewed 1969 by Charlotte Kesselring. Reprinted from *Arsenic and Old Lace*, by Joseph Kesselring, by permission of Random House, Inc.

*Candida*
Reprinted by permission of The Society of Authors, on behalf of the Bernard Shaw Estate.


Library of Congress Cataloging in Publication Data

Schanker, Harry H     comp.
    Dramatic comedy.

    (Patterns in literary art series)
    CONTENTS: Shakespeare, W. Twelfth night.—Goldsmith, O. She stoops to conquer.—Wilde, O. The importance of being earnest. [etc.]
    1. English drama (Comedy) [1. Plays—Collections] I. Title.
[PR1248.S3]      822'.052      72-8878
ISBN 0-07-055140-5

---

Copyright © 1973 by McGraw-Hill, Inc. All Rights Reserved. Printed in the United States of America. No part of this publication may be reproduced, stored in a retrieval system, or transmitted in any form or by any means, electronic, mechanical, photocopying, recording, or otherwise, without the prior written permission of the publisher.

Editorial Development, Susan Gelles; Editing and Styling, Joan Rosen; Design, John Keithley; Production, Peter Guilmette

# CONTENTS

GENERAL INTRODUCTION .......................... *vi*

TWELFTH NIGHT
    William Shakespeare ........................... *1*

SHE STOOPS TO CONQUER
    Oliver Goldsmith ............................... *85*

THE IMPORTANCE OF BEING EARNEST
    Oscar Wilde ................................... *155*

CANDIDA
    George Bernard Shaw .......................... *215*

ARSENIC AND OLD LACE
    Joseph Kesselring ............................. *279*

APPENDIX: HOW TO READ A COMEDY ............... *367*

SUGGESTED READING LIST .......................... *370*

# GENERAL INTRODUCTION

*Man is the only animal that laughs and weeps; for he is the only animal that is struck with the difference between what things are, and what they ought to be.*

*Hazlitt*

What makes man laugh? What provokes a smile rather than a tear? For 2500 years man has tried to define the comic spirit—that inherent, but unique impulse that prompts man to react with amusement. Humor is one of the strangest of human emotions. What might cause a person to laugh today could make him cry tomorrow. Consequently, there is a close relationship between humor and pathos and, in a greater sense, between comedy and tragedy. How a person responds is determined by his "mental set"—the attitude or point of view through which he perceives a particular situation. This mental set may vary according to the time of day or how a person feels emotionally or physically at the moment.

Laughter is essential to the mental well-being of man. It relieves tensions, provides an acceptable escape from daily life, and eases the embarrassment of human mistakes. In order to maintain his mental stability, a person has to release the pressures of life, and the quickest and most effective release he has found is laughter. Some comedies are built upon the complete obliteration of an unpleasant situation or overwhelming predicament. In our Space Age, the need to forget troubles, to relax, and to change direction or attitudes is still being met by humor.

WHAT IS COMEDY? Comedies are usually light in tone. The characters in them find themselves in complicated situations which they solve by their wits, their bumblings, or by a pleasant twist of chance. The comic characters are often people much like ourselves. However, they always have a character fault or weakness which is the primary cause of their problems and the basis for our laughter. In fact, we quite frequently laugh at these characters in order that the pathos of their struggles does not force us to cry. The intent of comedy is to laugh at life's problems.

Comedy may be contrasted with tragedy in that the final outcome in a comedy is rarely inevitable or fixed while in a tragedy the final outcome is really never in doubt. Most comedies employ *discovery*, the disclosure or awareness of identity or concealed fact, and *reversal*, the changing of the expected outcome, sometimes with an ironic twist. In tragedy, discovery and reversal bring about an awareness that leads directly to the climax and subsequent catastrophe. In comedy, the catastrophic threat which seems imminent is turned aside by amusing solutions. The comic hero may even be threatened with death or failure, but is saved from this fate, frequently at the last moment. Even if death or failure should befall the comic hero it is usually exaggerated to a point where it provokes a comic response. Both comedies and tragedies begin with a conflict, but the comic hero emerges as the controller and unifier whereas the tragic protagonist ends up controlled or destroyed.

Of course both comedy and tragedy, like all written works, reflect the society in which the author lived. But comedy and comic characters almost always reflect the manners and mores of a society, while tragedy and, more specifically, tragic heroes are concerned with the individual within the larger context of a society.

Much of what is comic, then, is based on the styles, manners, and customs of a society at a particular period. With the passing of time an audience may fail to catch all of the humor in a comedy. Yet the comic spirit is timeless and universal for it is based on human nature. Although particular situations in societies may change, human nature remains essentially the same. So the things man laughs at do not really change. The greatest comedies are based on ageless truths, and all great comedies have something serious to say beneath the comic lines and action.

Because comedy is generally concerned with the larger aspects of man in society and not with the personal or individual response, it requires an objective evaluation and demands a thinking response before the laughter. With the exception of low comedy, the primary appeal of comedy is to the intellect.

Comedy is built upon *character, situation,* and *dialogue.* Unusual character types are always interesting and can be most amusing, but the *stock characters* of comedy are those which have delighted audiences for centuries. Heroes and heroines are usually less interesting than the characters around them. The *ingenue* is the romantic female lead. The *villain* is the stock antagonist. He can be anything from the handlebar-mustached scoundrel of the "mellerdramer" to a crafty magician, a sorcerer or a tyrant king. The *rogue* is the mischief-maker, a clever scamp who delights the audience so much by his pranks (which are never too serious) that he is forgiven for his devious ways. The *parasite*

v

is the leech, fawner, or flatterer who gains his strength or success at the expense of someone else—his king, master, or friend. The *clown* or *jester* is the professional fool, whose role in life is to make others laugh. Frequently his humor is piercing, and his clever tongue strikes close to man's own shallowness. The *pedant* is the psuedo-intellectual whose knowledge is strictly bookish and never practical. He never understands the people around him or human feelings. He is often a scientist or philosopher. The *braggart* is an egotistical character. He sets himself up for a fall because he talks of deeds he has never attempted or accomplished. The *fop* or *coxcomb* is an affected dandy, overdone in manners, clothes, and speech. He is an offensive character because of his excesses, and his humiliation or defeat seems justified to the audience. The *dowager* might be considered a female fop. She is usually an older woman of wealth or prestige whose affectations or shallowness of mind make her blind to the realities of life. The *shrew* is a vixenish woman who is difficult to tame, a temperamental creature who is unfit for marriage or, if married, impossible to live with. She usually is loudmouthed like a fishwife, coarse in speech and manners. The *dunce* or *gull* is the poor fellow who blunders along because of a lack of wit or intelligence. He is the "sucker" P. T. Barnum spoke of, for he is a victim of con men, circumstances, and his own stupidity. The *eccentric* can be a character amusing for his peculiar idiosyncrasies, a pleasant lunatic whose mild insanity gives him the opportunity to perceive life's core in a way sane persons could not. The extreme eccentric may be a madman, but he is always comic and never truly frightening. Of course the preceding types are stock characters, and in any comedy a character may combine the characteristics of several of these types. For instance, Algernon in *The Importance of Being Earnest* is a combination of the parasite and the fop.

Clever *dialogue* is essential to all comedy and most especially to what is called *high comedy*. Wordplay, including puns, misunderstood terms, and multiple meanings, is amusing to discerning audiences. So, too, is the rapid exchange of witty lines called *repartee*. The comic success of dialogue depends greatly upon the actual delivery of the lines on stage. Therefore, when you read a play you must imagine the emphasis, pace, pitch, level, and, above all, the timing of the line as it would be delivered by the actor playing the role. Proper timing is probably the most important delivery skill needed to draw a laugh from an audience and a factor often overlooked when a play is read.

*Situation* is a term that refers to the humorous predicaments in which characters find themselves. The protagonist of course, seeks to overcome obstacles between himself and his goals, but any character in a comedy may find himself involved in an amusing situation. Sometimes the circumstances are already established when the play begins, and the characters seem to be tossed helplessly into troubles. At other times, the characters seem to bring about perplexing conditions by their own acts. Audiences greatly enjoy situations which they know must come about sooner or later. Such inevitable occurrences as the meeting of separated twins have been referred to as *obligatory scenes*. The audience knows that the twins will meet before the play ends, yet the comic effect is heightened each time their identities are confused or the two nearly cross paths.

*Situation* may also mean the total plot—the initial problem that builds to a hilarious climax before being resolved. However, comic situations are not necessarily synonymous with plot; they are more often a series of individual predicaments that face the characters one right after another. In most comedies there are several major situations that form the basis for the overall plot structure.

TYPES OF COMEDIES  Comedies may be classified by type. *Low comedy* is usually coarse or obscene and in most instances is built around sexual allusions. There are few plays built primarily on low comedy which remain perennially popular. *Farce* involves almost anything done strictly for laughs. It is fast-paced, based upon highly contrived situations, and contains a considerable amount of physical action such as beatings, pushing and shoving, and chases. The farce depends heavily on a broad form of humor called *slapstick*: pies in the face, clowning, practical jokes, and other physical acts. Many of the so-called higher types of comedy include sprinklings of farce.

*Burlesque* imitates people or ideas which are easily recognized by the audience. It exaggerates minor faults or idiosyncrasies in such a way that those weaknesses are amusing to the audience. One of the most common forms of burlesque is the *parody*. A parody may be simply the imitation of a literary work. This imitation may be one of form, in which the style, pattern, rhyme, or any other readily identifiable structural characteristic is precisely matched to the original. "To be or not to be, that is the question" becomes something like "To flee or not to flee, what's your suggestion?" A second form of parody is the parody of idea, in which the goal of the imitation is to get the audience to recognize the ideology, categorical style, or genre being burlesqued. Famous political speeches, instruction manuals, and even Victorian melodramas can be parodied by idea. The third type of parody is one which imitates both form and idea.

Closely related to parody is *caricature*—the mimicry of real or literary figures by the exaggeration of a physical characteristic, speech pattern, manner of dress, etc. A form of burlesque related to parody is the *travesty*. A travesty takes an elevated or noble topic and treats it on a trivial level. On the other hand, the *mock heroic* or *mock epic* takes a lowly person or topic and seeks to elevate it. This approach is commonly seen in the would-be hero who accidentally performs great deeds, often much to his own surprise. Humor results from the great acclaim and rewards he receives for his "successful mistake."

*Sentimental comedy* appeals at least as much to the "heart" as to the "head." Tears may flow freely as man's benevolent nature wins out over his evil side. Repentances and virtues are extolled and weaknesses pardoned as goodness prevails. Since most characters are from the middle class, there is little farce and even less wit.

*Romantic comedies* are fanciful plays dealing with strange and imaginary realms. Romanticism is a philosophical concept based upon belief in the inherent good of the individual. This goodness enables the characters to work their way out of improbable situations by escapes into forests, never-never lands, and mystical islands.

The *Comedy of Manners* is a sophisticated social comedy that laughs at the follies of man. The dialogue is clever, sometimes bristling in its attack on the social customs and the weaknesses of the people of a given time and place. Molière developed the style in France, but it reached its peak during the Restoration period in England. The style was continued in the eighteenth century with, for example, Oliver Goldsmith's *She Stoops to Conquer*. In the nineteenth century Oscar Wilde wrote several comedies of manners including *Lady Windermere's Fan* and *The Importance of Being Earnest*.

The highest form of comedy is *satire*. It is a direct, scornful attack on human weakness. As the epitome of high comedy, satire ridicules accepted notions and identifiable conventions including self-identification. Most satire is subtle, but irony, invectives, and even sarcasm may be used to arouse contempt for the object of the attack. The clever satirist's wit is like a razor-sharp rapier which might "pepper" its victim (the spectator) dozens of times before the victim discovers it is he who has been slashed to shreds. Most satirists believe that man will correct his mistakes after having them pointed out through satirical ridicule. However, there is little evidence to support the satirist's dreams.

CAUSES OF LAUGHTER  It is difficult to analyze what amuses people or causes them to laugh out loud. A line or action might prompt a laugh in one situation and complete silence in another. It has already been noted how closely related laughter and tears may be, but the horror, the pain, and the shock of laughter-provoking situations is baffling to the student of the comic spirit. The comedian may say he knows *what* makes people laugh but not *why* they laugh.

The first catalyst of laughter seems to be *exaggeration*. Although comedy deals with everyday life, people laugh at things obviously bigger than life. The overstatement or hyperbole may be found in line, character, or situation. The opposite of the hyperbole is the understatement which is a negative exaggeration or exaggeration in reverse: "Yesterday, my house was robbed, my wife fell down the well, the hens stopped laying, the transmission fell out of the car, and I ripped the seat out of my best pair of pants. It was not the luckiest day of my life."

A second cause of laughter is what we may call the *incongruous*—that which seems out of place, out of time, or out of character. The basis for laughing at incongruity is man's sense of appropriateness. The sweet, highly respected Brewster sisters in *Arsenic and Old Lace* who murder lonely old men out of kindness jars the audience's sense of appropriateness and evokes a kind of unbelieving laughter. The juxtaposition of their "kindness" to the maniacal homicides of their nephew adds to the incongruity.

Another type of incongruity is found in the *grotesque*. The grotesque may be shocking, frightening, pathetic, or humorous depending on how the character sees himself or others, or how the audience sees him. The grotesque sometimes combines incongruity and exaggeration. In *Twelfth Night* Sir Andrew Aguecheek's puffed up swaggering and absurd desire to marry Olivia are humorous until the audience sees how manipulated and abused he is by Sir Toby Belch. The grotesque often takes the form of unnatural action or nonhuman characters. The scarecrow and tin woodman of Oz are examples of nonhuman characters. In fact, almost any unnatural movements or sounds may make the audience laugh if performed with comic intent.

The *unexpected* is another form of incongruity. The pattern we anticipate is illogically reversed. Surprise endings are pleasing when "impossible" situations turn out as we hoped they would. Reversal is similar to the unexpected twist in that the "tables are turned," but with reversal the incongruity centers upon a complete turnabout—the weak overcoming the powerful, the lowly supplanting the elite, or misfortune turning into happiness and success.

*Anticipation* is at the heart of many comic situations. The audience's reaction is often in proportion to how much it is "in the know." Much depends upon the *plant*. The plant is an idea, line, or action that is emphasized early in the play in order to be used later as the basis for laughter. As you read a comedy, remember that it usually takes at least three exposures to get the maximum anticipatory effect. The first exposure, the plant, *alerts* the audience that this particular element may be used later. The second use *establishes* the element; this assures the audience that the line or business is going to be "milked" for laughs. The third exposure *clinches*—this is the big laugh, the payoff for the anticipation the audience has built up. From then on, every repetition continues to draw laughs. That repetition can bring many laughs has been shown by television characters built solely on idiosyncrasies which the audience has learned to anticipate.

*Incompletion* is a variation of anticipation that depends upon man's sense of order. A line or bit of action is begun but never finished. The audience either immediately responds with laughter or pauses to think about the completion of the idea and then laughs. Similar to this is the *anticlimax*. A situation is built up and up and up and then, suddenly, the bubble bursts and an expressionless line or action follows which does not fulfill the anticipation of the buildup. One common form of the anticlimax is the *letdown* or *flat line*. Uttered with little emotion, the flat line always comes after a sequence of rapid-fire or highly stressed dialogue.

*Recognition* and *relief* are other causes of laughter. Recognition involves the audience's making a discovery and drawing a conclusion before laughing. When they know the character's motivation, they can laugh more readily at his dialogue and actions, especially when these are confusing to the other characters. Audiences are also amused when they discover what is going to happen before it happens. Delayed recognition on the part of a character is also amusing to the audience. *Relief* brings about laughter because it releases tensions or pressures. For instance, a scene is built up to a point where the audience feels it can stand no more and then something is said or done that allows the pressure to explode in a huge laugh.

*Ambiguity* or double-meaning comedy is a major cause of laughter. It is also the nucleus of all wordplay, discussed earlier, which is used extensively in high comedy, although puns, mistaken identities, and misinterpretations leading to comic situations are found in all types of comedy. The success of double-meaning comedy is contingent upon one of two things: either the character has a choice of interpretations and chooses the wrong one, or the audience is given a choice of interpretation and without fail takes that which is least likely, but which, of course, is the most humorous. Repartee and risqué humor depend greatly upon the use of double meanings.

The last element of comedy to be discussed here is one of the most important—*protection*. The protection factor depends upon a knowledge of two things: first, the audience knows that a play is not real, consequently, what happens on stage is not real; and second, the events are happening to someone else. Thus, we are protected by the knowledge that the violent, grotesque, and punitive acts which occur on stage do

x

not really harm the characters. If those painful experiences were real, we would share the pain and respond with pathos, but the protection factor shields us from emphathic fear and as a result we can laugh freely, safe in the knowledge that it is the character in the play who is beaten, harrassed, or tempted and not us.

The comedies that people have enjoyed in the past give valuable indications of what they have found amusing, and therefore bearable, in the human condition. The plays that follow reveal a great deal about the people who saw them. They also remind us of some of the more enduring characteristics of humankind—traits that run like an unbroken thread from earliest times to the present.

# Twelfth Night

# WILLIAM SHAKESPEARE

## Introduction

*Twelfth Night* is a comedy of love and lightheartedness, as indicated by the subtitle, *What You Will*. Placing his characters in the imaginary land of Illyria, Shakespeare effectively weaves three plots together. The first scene introduces Duke Orsino, who fancies himself in love with the Countess Olivia. The second scene brings Viola into the first plot and initiates the second plot. Viola has just been rescued from a shipwreck, and, thinking her twin brother drowned, seeks her fortune in a man's world by donning man's clothing, taking the name Cesario, and joining Orsino's court as a page.

The next scene involves the third set of characters, the household of Olivia, which includes her uncle, Toby Belch; his friend, Sir Andrew Aguecheek; her steward, Malvolio; her lady-in-waiting, Maria; her clown, Feste; and another servant, Fabian. It is Feste who provides the link between the three plots.

Viola (Cesario) becomes the Duke's envoy to Olivia, who, saddened by the death of her brother, has refused to see anyone outside her own gates. As Cesario, Viola stirs the affections of Olivia. At about this time, Shakespeare reveals to the audience that Sebastian, Viola's twin brother, has survived the shipwreck after all. Not only do Viola and Sebastian look alike, but, by dramatic coincidence, they are dressed alike. We know that brother and sister must eventually reunite, but until that happens, we may anticipate some comic scenes of mistaken identity.

One of the most humorous scenes of mistaken identity occurs when Viola (Cesario) is tricked into facing the cowardly Sir Andrew by Fabian and the prankish Sir Toby. Each of the duelists would like to

1

turn and run, but both are saved by the providential entrance of the sea captain, Antonio, who mistakes Viola for Sebastian, whom he is seeking. The confusion of the twins from this moment on leads to the series of humorous predicaments in which all three plots are resolved. Sebastian, mistaken for Cesario, is summoned to Olivia's house where he accepts Olivia's invitation to dinner and enthusiastically takes the bethrothal vows with her. He also encounters Sir Andrew, who, mistaking him for the timid Cesario, engages him in a fight, much to Sir Andrew's disadvantage. This turn of events carries Olivia out of her grief and into real love, and at the same time frees Cesario to become Viola, the soon-to-be wife of Orsino.

*Twelfth Night* treats the subject of love with humorous melancholy. Although Olivia is in love with her mourning, she still becomes the object of love for several suitors—desired or undesired—Orsino, Sir Andrew, Malvolio, and Sebastian. Sir Toby is above all a pleasure-seeker. But he loves Maria for her shrewdness and her physical beauty. Deluded into thinking he could really compete with Orsino, the foolish Sir Andrew hardly has enough sense to love anyone besides himself. Feste possesses both a love for his mistress and his companions as well as a personal vanity which is stung by Malvolio. Viola has the capacity for a sacrificial all-giving love which establishes her as one of Shakespeare's great women. She is sensible. She mourns her brother, but not to the point of self-isolation or distraction. Instead, she turns her affections to the living. The play ends, as it opened, on a note of musical melancholy, as Feste sings a plaintive song.

## Characters

ORSINO, *Duke of Illyria*
SEBASTIAN, *brother to Viola*
ANTONIO, *a sea captain, friend to Sebastian*
A SEA CAPTAIN, *friend to Viola*
VALENTINE,
CURIO, } *gentlemen attending the Duke*
SIR TOBY BELCH, *uncle to Olivia*
SIR ANDREW AGUECHEEK
MALVOLIO, *steward to Olivia*

FABIAN,  } servants to Olivia
FESTE, *a Clown,*

OLIVIA, *a countess*
VIOLA, *sister to Sebastian*
MARIA, *attendant to Olivia*

Lords, a Priest, Sailors, Officers, Musicians, and Attendants

SCENE: A city in Illyria, and the nearby seacoast

# ACT I

### SCENE 1. The Duke's Palace.

[*Enter* ORSINO, *Duke of Illyria;* CURIO *and other Lords; Musicians attending.*]

DUKE. If music be the food of love, play on;
    Give me excess of it, that, surfeiting,[1]
    The appetite may sicken, and so die.
    That strain again!  It had a dying fall;[2]
    O, it came o'er my ear like the sweet sound         5
    That breathes upon a bank of violets,
    Stealing and giving odor!  Enough, no more!
    'Tis not so sweet now as it was before.
    O spirit of love, how quick and fresh art thou,
    That, notwithstanding thy capacity         10
    Receiveth as the sea, naught enters there,
    Of what validity and pitch soe'er,
    But falls into abatement and low price
    Even in a minute!  So full of shapes[3] is fancy[4]
    That it alone is high fantastical.[5]         15
CUR. Will you go hunt, my lord?
DUKE.                 What, Curio?
CUR. The hart.[6]

---

1. *surfeiting:* eating or drinking to excess; being overfull.
2. *a dying fall:* a lowering of the voice or note; a musical term.
3. *shapes:* imagination.     4. *fancy:* love.     5. *high fantastical:* wholly imaginative.
6. *The hart:* the stag.

DUKE. Why, so I do, the noblest that I have.[7]
    O, when mine eyes did see Olivia first,
    Methought she purged the air of pestilence![8]     20
    That instant was I turned into a hart,
    And my desires, like fell[9] and cruel hounds,
    E'er since pursue me.[10]

[*Enter* VALENTINE.]

                How now? What news from her?
VAL. So please my lord, I might not be admitted.     25
    But from her handmaid do return this answer:
    The element[11] itself, till seven years' heat,[12]
    Shall not behold her face at ample view;
    But like a cloistress[13] she will veiled walk,
    And water once a day her chamber round     30
    With eye-offending brine:[14] all this to season
    A brother's dead love, which she would keep fresh
    And lasting in her sad remembrance.
DUKE. O, she that hath a heart of that fine frame
    To pay this debt of love but to a brother,
    How will she love when the rich golden shaft[15]     35
    Hath killed the flock of all affections else
    That live in her; when liver, brain, and heart,[16]
    These sovereign thrones, are all supplied, and filled,
    Her sweet perfections, with one self king![17]     40
    Away before me to sweet beds of flowers!
    Love-thoughts lie rich when canopied with bowers.

[*Exeunt.*]

7. Orsino refers, of course, to his heart, not a hart.
8. *purged . . . pestilence!* She rid the very heavens of all impurity.
9. *fell:* fierce, savage.
10. Orsino's tale is a variation of the story of Actaeon, a familiar tale in Shakespeare's day. Actaeon, while hunting with his hounds, accidentally came upon the goddess Diana bathing. As punishment she turned him into a stag, and he was pursued and torn to pieces by his own dogs.
11. *The element:* the sky.     12. *till . . . heat:* until seven years have passed.
13. *a cloistress:* a nun.     14. *eye-offending brine:* tears.
15. *the rich golden shaft:* the golden arrow of Cupid which was held to inspire love in the person struck.
16. *liver, brain, and heart:* the centers, respectively, of the passions, judgment, and sentiment.
17. *and filled . . . king:* Olivia will be made perfect by her marriage to the Duke. It was a common belief that women were only made perfect through marriage.

## SCENE 2. The seacoast.

[*Enter* VIOLA, *a* CAPTAIN, *and Sailors.*]

VIO. What country, friends, is this?
CAPT. This is Illyria,[1] lady.
VIO. And what should I do in Illyria?
    My brother he is in Elysium.[2]
    Perchance he is not drowned: what think you, sailors? 5
CAPT. It is perchance that you yourself were saved.
VIO. O my poor brother! and so perchance may he be.
CAPT. True, madam; and, to comfort you with chance,
    Assure yourself, after our ship did split,
    When you, and those poor number saved with you, 10
    Hung on our driving boat,[3] I saw your brother,
    Most provident in peril, bind himself
    (Courage and hope both teaching him the practice)
    To a strong mast that lived upon the sea;
    Where, like Arion[4] on the dolphin's back, 15
    I saw him hold acquaintance with the waves
    So long as I could see.
VIO. For saying so, there's gold.
    Mine own escape unfoldeth to my hope,
    Whereto thy speech serves for authority, 20
    The like of him. Knowst thou this country?
CAPT. Ay, madam, well, for I was bred and born
    Not three hours' travel from this very place.
VIO. Who governs here?
CAPT. A noble duke,[5] in nature as in name. 25
VIO. What is his name?
CAPT. Orsino.
VIO. Orsino! I have heard my father name him.
    He was a bachelor then.
CAPT. And so is now, or was so very late; 30

---

1. *Illyria:* The play is supposed to take place in a city of the Venetian Republic. In its tone, however, and in many of its references, it is thoroughly English. Orsino is the ruler of Illyria.   2. *Elysium:* heaven.
3. *driving boat:* boat driven by the wind.
4. *Arion:* a bard (poet or singer) who was saved from drowning in the sea by a dolphin.
5. *A noble duke:* Orsino is sometimes referred to as a *duke* and sometimes as a *count*.

Twelfth Night

> For but a month ago I went from hence,
> And then 'twas fresh in murmur (as you know
> What great ones do, the less will prattle of)
> That he did seek the love of fair Olivia.

VIO. What's she? 35

CAPT. A virtuous maid, the daughter of a count
> That died some twelvemonth since; then leaving her
> In the protection of his son, her brother,
> Who shortly also died; for whose dear love,
> They say, she hath abjured the sight 40
> And company of men.

VIO.                O that I served that lady,
> And might not be delivered to the world,
> Till I had made mine own occasion mellow,
> What my estate is![6]

CAPT.             That were hard to compass,
> Because she will admit no kind of suit; 45
> No, not the Duke's.

VIO. There is a fair behavior in thee, Captain;
> And though that nature with a beauteous wall
> Doth oft close in pollution,[7] yet of thee
> I will believe thou hast a mind that suits 50
> With this thy fair and outward character.
> I prithee (and I'll pay thee bounteously)
> Conceal me what I am, and be my aid
> For such disguise as haply shall become
> The form of my intent. I'll serve this duke. 55
> Thou shalt present me as an eunuch[8] to him;
> It may be worth thy pains. For I can sing,
> And speak to him in many sorts of music
> That will allow me very worth his service.
> What else may hap, to time I will commit; 60
> Only shape thou thy silence to my wit.

---

6. *might not be delivered ... estate is!* Olivia wishes that her identity be not disclosed until the proper time for revealing her name and station.
7. *oft close in pollution:* often conceals evil. Nature often hides impurity behind a fair face.
8. *an eunuch:* a castrated male. Eunuchs were often valued as singers for their soprano voices.

CAPT. Be you his eunuch, and your mute I'll be.
  When my tongue blabs, then let mine eyes not see.
VIO. I thank thee. Lead me on.

[*Exeunt.*]

### SCENE 3. Olivia's house.

[*Enter* SIR TOBY *and* MARIA.]

TO. What a plague means my niece to take the death of her brother thus? I am sure care's an enemy to life.
MAR. By my troth, Sir Toby, you must come in earlier o' nights. Your cousin, my lady, takes great exceptions to your ill hours.
TO. Why, let her except before excepted![1]
MAR. Ay, but you must confine yourself within the modest limits of order.
TO. Confine? I'll confine myself no finer than I am. These clothes are good enough to drink in, and so be these boots too. An[2] they be not, let them hang themselves in their own straps.
MAR. That quaffing and drinking will undo you. I heard my lady talk of it yesterday; and of a foolish knight that you brought in one night here to be her wooer.
TO. Who? Sir Andrew Aguecheek?
MAR. Ay, he.
TO. He's as tall[3] a man as any's in Illyria.
MAR. What's that to the purpose?
TO. Why, he has three thousand ducats a year.
MAR. Ay, but he'll have but a year in all these ducats. He's a very fool and a prodigal.
TO. Fie that you'll say so! He plays o' the viol de gamboys,[4] and speaks three or four languages word for word without book, and hath all the good gifts of nature.
MAR. He hath, indeed, almost natural![5] for, besides that he's a fool,

---

1. *except before excepted:* a play upon a legal term; Sir Toby means that Olivia should tell him of her displeasure herself.   2. *An:* if.   3. *tall:* great, well-to-do.
4. *the viol de gamboys:* a base-viol. This instrument was considered a necessary part of a fashionable dwelling, and the ability to play upon it was thought to be a necessary accomplishment in a fashionable person.
5. *almost natural:* a misprint for *all, most natural.* Maria means that Sir Andrew possesses his gifts as a natural (an idiot).

he's a great quarreler; and but that he hath the gift of a coward to allay the gust he hath in quarreling, 'tis thought among the prudent he would quickly have the gift of a grave.
TO. By this hand, they are scoundrels and substractors[6] that say so of him. Who are they?
MAR. They that add, moreover, he's drunk nightly in your company.
TO. With drinking healths to my niece. I'll drink to her as long as there is a passage in my throat and drink in Illyria. He's a coward and a coistrel[7] that will not drink to my niece till his brains turn o' the toe like a parish top.[8] What, wench! Castiliano vulgo![9] for here comes Sir Andrew Agueface.

[*Enter* SIR ANDREW.]

AND. Sir Toby Belch! How now, Sir Toby Belch?
TO. Sweet Sir Andrew!
AND. Bless you, fair shrew.[10]
MAR. And you too, sir.
TO. Accost, Sir Andrew, accost.
AND. What's that?
TO. My niece's chambermaid.[11]
AND. Good Mistress Accost, I desire better acquaintance.
MAR. My name is Mary, sir.
AND. Good Mistress Mary Accost—
TO. You mistake, knight. "Accost" is front her, board her, woo her, assail her.
AND. By my troth, I would not undertake her in this company. Is that the meaning of "accost"?
MAR. Fare you well, gentlemen.
TO. An thou let part[12] so, Sir Andrew, would thou mightst never draw sword again!
AND. An you part so, mistress, I would I might never draw sword again! Fair lady, do you think you have fools in hand?

6. *substractors:* detractors.   7. *a coistrel:* a base fellow, knave.
8. *a parish top:* a spinning top kept in villages so that (presumably) the poor could keep warm in the winter by exercising with it.
9. *Castiliano vulgo:* The meaning of this expression is not known. It may have been a pun easily understood by an Elizabethan audience, or a common exclamation among drinkers, or a bit of nonsense invented by Sir Toby. He may have been telling Maria to put on her Spanish face (a grave, polite face) to greet Sir Andrew.
10. *Bless . . . shrew:* a common form of familiar address.
11. *chambermaid:* companion, gentlewoman.   12. *let part:* allow her to leave.

MAR. Sir, I have not you by the hand. 55
AND. Marry,[13] but you shall have! and here's my hand.
MAR. Now, sir, thought is free. I pray you, bring your hand to the buttery bar[14] and let it drink.
AND. Wherefore, sweetheart? What's your metaphor?
MAR. It's[15] dry, sir. 60
AND. Why, I think so. I am not such an ass but I can keep my hand dry.[16] But what's your jest?
MAR. A dry[17] jest, sir.
AND. Are you full of them?
MAR. Ay, sir, I have them at my fingers' ends. Marry, now I let go 65 your hand, I am barren.[18]

[*Exit.*]

TO. O knight, thou lackst a cup of canary![19] When did I see thee so put down?
AND. Never in your life, I think, unless you see canary put me down. Methinks sometimes I have no more wit than a Christian or an 70 ordinary man has. But I am a great eater of beef,[20] and I believe that does harm to my wit.
TO. No question.
AND. An I thought that, I'd forswear it. I'll ride home tomorrow, Sir Toby. 75
TO. *Pourquoi*,[21] my dear knight?
AND. What is "*pourquoi*"? Do, or not do? I would I had bestowed that time in the tongues[22] that I have in fencing, dancing, and bear-baiting. O, had I but followed the arts!
TO. Then hadst thou had an excellent head of hair. 80
AND. Why, would that have mended my hair?
TO. Past question, for thou seest it will not curl by nature.[23]

13. *Marry:* an exclamation of surprise or indignation; in answer to a question it often means *why, to be sure.*
14. *buttery bar:* the ledge or shelf on the half-door leading to the storeroom. It was used as a serving counter.
15. *It's:* Sir Andrew's hand. A dry hand was supposed to show a stingy, loveless nature.   16. *keep my hand dry:* come in out of the rain.   17. *dry:* stupid, boring.
18. *barren:* witless.   19. *canary:* a wine from the Canary Islands.
20. *eater of beef:* eating beef was commonly held to cause melancholy or dull-wittedness.   21. *Pourquoi:* French for *why.*   22. *tongues:* languages.
23. *it . . . by nature:* Sir Andrew's hair will not curl naturally. His hair would have to be curled with tongs. The word *tongs* was pronounced *tongues*—Sir Toby puns upon Sir Andrew's use of the word *tongues* for languages.

Twelfth Night    9

AND. But it becomes me well enough, does't not?

TO. Excellent. It hangs like flax on a distaff;[24] and I hope to see a housewife take thee between her legs and spin it off.

AND. Faith, I'll home tomorrow, Sir Toby. Your niece will not be seen; or if she be, it's four to one she'll none of me.[25] The Count himself here hard by[26] woos her.

TO. She'll none o' the Count. She'll not match above her degree, neither in estate, years, nor wit; I have heard her swear't. Tut, there's life in't,[27] man.

AND. I'll stay a month longer. I am a fellow o' the strangest mind i' the world. I delight in masques and revels sometimes altogether.

TO. Art thou good at these kickshawses,[28] knight?

AND. As any man in Illyria, whatsoever he be, under the degree of my betters; and yet I will not compare with an old man.

TO. What is thy excellence in a galliard,[29] knight?

AND. Faith, I can cut a caper.

TO. And I can cut the mutton to't.[30]

AND. And I think I have the back-trick[31] simply as strong as any man in Illyria.

TO. Wherefore are these things hid? Wherefore have these gifts a curtain before 'em? Are they like to take dust, like Mistress Mall's picture?[32] Why dost thou not go to church in a galliard and come home in a coranto?[33] My very walk should be a jig.[34] I would not so much as make water but in a sink-a-pace.[35] What dost thou mean? Is it a world to hide virtues in? I did think, by the excellent constitution of thy leg, it was formed under the star of a galliard.

AND. Ay, 'tis strong, and it does indifferent well in a flame-colored stock.[36] Shall we set about some revels?

---

24. *flax on a distaff:* straight.
25. *she'll none of me:* she'll have nothing to do with me.
26. *hard by:* nearby, close.   27. *there's life in't:* there's still hope.
28. *kickshawses:* toys, trifles; a corruption of the French *Quelque chose*.
29. *a galliard:* a lively dance. The galliard consisted of five steps or positions and a leap, or caper.   30. *cut the mutton to't:* play the woman's part.
31. *the back-trick:* the galliard in reverse; the steps were performed in reverse to return the dancers to their starting positions. This obviously required much skill.
32. *Mistress Mall's picture:* the meaning of this phrase is not known.
33. *a coranto:* a running dance, livelier than the galliard.
34. *a jig:* a faster dance than either the galliard or the coranto.
35. *a sink-a-pace:* literally, five steps. Another name for the galliard.
36. *stock:* stocking.

TO. What shall we do else? Were we not born under Taurus?
AND. Taurus?[37] That's sides and heart.
TO. No, sir; it is legs and thighs.[38] Let me see thee caper. [SIR ANDREW *dances*.] Ha, higher! Ha, ha, excellent!

[*Exeunt.*]

SCENE 4. The Duke's Palace.

[*Enter* VALENTINE, *and* VIOLA *in man's attire.*]

VAL. If the Duke continue these favors towards you, Cesario, you are like to be much advanced. He hath known you but three days, and already you are no stranger.
VIO. You either fear his humor[1] or my negligence, that you call in question the continuance of his love. Is he inconstant, sir, in his favors?
VAL. No, believe me.

[*Enter* DUKE, CURIO, *and Attendants.*]

VIO. I thank you. Here comes the Count.
DUKE. Who saw Cesario, ho?
VIO. On your attendance, my lord, here.
DUKE. Stand you awhile aloof.—Cesario,
Thou knowst no less but all. I have unclasped
To thee the book even of my secret soul.
Therefore, good youth, address thy gait unto her;
Be not denied access, stand at her doors,
And tell them there thy fixed foot shall grow
Till thou have audience.
VIO.                    Sure, my noble lord,
If she be so abandoned to her sorrow
As it is spoke, she never will admit me.
DUKE. Be clamorous and leap all civil bounds
Rather than make unprofited return.
VIO. Say I do speak with her, my lord, what then?

---

37. *Taurus:* The constellations were thought to control parts of the body.
38. *legs and thighs:* the almanacs of Shakespeare's time indicate that Taurus governed the neck and throat.

1. *humor:* whim.

DUKE. O, then unfold the passion of my love;
　　　Surprise her with discourse of my dear faith!
　　　It shall become thee well to act my woes.　　　　　　　　25
　　　She will attend it better in thy youth
　　　Then in a nuncio's² of more grave aspect.
VIO. I think not so, my lord.
DUKE.　　　　　　　　Dear lad, believe it;
　　　For they shall yet belie thy happy years
　　　That say thou art a man.　Diana's³ lip　　　　　　　　　30
　　　Is not more smooth and rubious;⁴ thy small pipe⁵
　　　Is as the maiden's organ, shrill and sound,
　　　And all is semblative⁶ a woman's part.
　　　I know thy constellation⁷ is right apt
　　　For this affair.　Some four or five attend him—　　　　35
　　　All, if you will; for I myself am best
　　　When least in company.　Prosper well in this,
　　　And thou shalt live as freely as thy lord
　　　To call his fortunes thine.
VIO.　　　　　　　　　I'll do my best
　　　To woo your lady. [*Aside.*]　Yet a barful strife!⁸　　　40
　　　Whoe'er I woo, myself would be his wife.

[*Exeunt.*]

### SCENE 5. Olivia's house.

[*Enter* MARIA *and* CLOWN.¹]

MAR. Nay, either tell me where thou hast been, or I will not open my lips so wide as a bristle may enter in way of thy excuse. My lady will hang thee for thy absence.

CLOWN. Let her hang me! He that is well hanged in this world needs to fear no colors.²　　　　　　　　　　　　　　　　　　　　5

---

2. *nuncio's:* messenger's.
3. *Diana's:* Diana, a goddess never kissed by man, represents purity.
4. *rubious:* red.　　5. *pipe:* voice.　　6. *semblative:* like.
7. *thy constellation:* the sign of the zodiac under which Cesario (Viola) was born.
8. *barful strife:* struggle filled with impediments.

1. *Clown:* Feste, a hired (professional) fool in Olivia's service.
2. *He that is well hanged . . . colors:* a pun on color and collar (a hangman's noose). This pun was common, but so old that Maria had not heard it.

MAR. Make that good.³

CLOWN. He shall see none to fear.

MAR. A good lenten⁴ answer. I can tell thee where that saying was born, of "I fear no colors."⁵

CLOWN. Where, good Mistress Mary?

MAR. In the wars; and that may you be bold to say in your foolery.

CLOWN. Well, God give them wisdom that have it; and those that are fools, let them use their talents.

MAR. Yet you will be hanged for being so long absent, or to be turned away—is not that as good as a hanging to you?

CLOWN. Many a good hanging prevents a bad marriage; and for turning away, let summer bear it out.⁶

MAR. You are resolute then?

CLOWN. Not so, neither; but I am resolved on two points.

MAR. That if one break, the other will hold;⁷ or if both break, your gaskins⁸ fall.

CLOWN. Apt, in good faith; very apt. Well, go thy way! If Sir Toby would leave drinking, thou wert as witty a piece of Eve's flesh as any in Illyria.

MAR. Peace, you rogue; no more o' that. Here comes my lady. Make your excuse wisely, you were best.

[*Exit.*]

[*Enter* LADY OLIVIA *with* MALVOLIO *and Attendants.*]

CLOWN. Wit, an't be thy will, put me into good fooling! Those wits that think they have thee do very oft prove fools; and I that am sure I lack thee may pass for a wise man. For what says Quinapalus?⁹ "Better a witty fool than a foolish wit."—God bless thee, lady!

OLI. Take the fool away.

CLOWN. Do you not hear, fellows? Take away the lady.

---

3. *Make that good:* explain that.   4. *lenten:* short and spare, as food is in Lent.
5. *colors:* flags.
6. *let summer . . . out:* running away is easier in summer when the weather is warm.
7. *if one . . . hold:* although Feste is apparently resolved upon two points of the argument, Maria refers to the points of his clothing. Such points were the metal-tipped strings which, fastened to the doublet, held up the stockings.
8. *gaskins:* a type of hose.
9. *Quinapalus:* an imaginary person; one of the leaders of the imaginary Vapians.

**Twelfth Night**

OLI. Go to, y'are a dry[10] fool! I'll no more of you. Besides, you grow dishonest.

CLOWN. Two faults, madonna, that drink and good counsel will amend. For give the dry fool drink, then is the fool not dry. Bid the dishonest man mend himself: if he mend, he is no longer dishonest; if he cannot, let the botcher[11] mend him. Anything that's mended is but patched; virtue that transgresses is but patched with sin, and sin that amends is but patched with virtue. If that this simple syllogism[12] will serve, so; if it will not, what remedy? As there is no true cuckold but calamity, so beauty's a flower.[13] The lady bade take away the fool; therefore, I say again, take her away.

OLI. Sir, I bade them take away you.

CLOWN. Misprision[14] in the highest degree! Lady, *cucullus non facit monachum*.[15] That's as much to say as, I wear not motley[16] in my brain. Good madonna, give me leave to prove you a fool.

OLI. Can you do it?

CLOWN. Dexteriously, good madonna.

OLI. Make your proof.

CLOWN. I must catechize you for it, madonna. Good my mouse of virtue,[17] answer me.

OLI. Well, sir, for want of other idleness, I'll bide[18] your proof.

CLOWN. Good madonna, why mournest thou?

OLI. Good fool, for my brother's death.

CLOWN. I think his soul is in hell, madonna.

OLI. I know his soul is in heaven, fool.

CLOWN. The more fool, madonna, to mourn for your brother's soul being in heaven. Take away the fool, gentlemen.

OLI. What think you of this fool, Malvolio? Doth he not mend?[19]

MAL. Yes, and shall do till the pangs of death shake him. Infirmity, that decays the wise, doth ever make the better fool.

---

10. *dry:* tedious, boring.   11. *botcher:* one who mended old clothes.
12. *syllogism:* in logic, a formal argument presented in a particular set form.
13. Feste is purposefully rattling off confusing nonsense to delay his punishment.
14. *Misprision:* literally, mistake. The Clown may have meant also that Olivia had offended against his "majesty."
15. *cucullus non facit monachum:* the cowl makes not the monk; a proverb.
16. *motley:* the parti-colored costume of the professional fool.
17. *Good . . . virtue:* a term of endearment.   18. *bide:* await.
19. *mend:* make amends. Malvolio understands her to mean *improve*.

CLOWN. God send you, sir, a speedy infirmity, for the better increasing your folly! Sir Toby will be sworn that I am no fox; but he will not pass his word for twopence that you are no fool.
OLI. How say you to that, Malvolio?
MAL. I marvel your ladyship takes delight in such a barren[20] rascal. I saw him put down the other day with an ordinary fool that has no more brain than a stone. Look you now, he's out of his guard[21] already. Unless you laugh and minister occasion to him,[22] he is gagged. I protest I take these wise men that crow so at these set kind of fools no better than the fools' zanies.[23]
OLI. O, you are sick of self-love, Malvolio, and taste with a distempered appetite. To be generous, guiltless, and of free disposition, is to take those things for bird bolts[24] that you deem cannon bullets. There is no slander in an allowed[25] fool, though he do nothing but rail; nor no railing in a known discreet man, though he do nothing but reprove.
CLOWN. Now Mercury[26] indue[27] thee with leasing,[28] for thou speakest well of fools!

[*Enter* MARIA.]

MAR. Madam, there is at the gate a young gentleman much desires to speak with you.
OLI. From the Count Orsino, is it?
MAR. I know not, madam. 'Tis a fair young man, and well attended.
OLI. Who of my people hold him in delay?
MAR. Sir Toby, madam, your kinsman.
OLI. Fetch him off, I pray you. He speaks nothing but madman. Fie on him! [*Exit* MARIA.] Go you, Malvolio. If it be a suit from the Count, I am sick, or not at home. What you will, to dismiss it. [*Exit* MALVOLIO.] Now you see, sir, how your fooling grows old, and people dislike it.
CLOWN. Thou hast spoke for us, madonna, as if thy eldest son should be a fool; whose skull Jove cram with brains!

---

20. *barren:* witless.   21. *out of his guard:* had run out of defense.
22. *minister occasion to him:* feed him a line.
23. *the fools' zanies:* the fool's attendants and imitators.
24. *bird bolts:* small blunt arrows for killing birds.   25. *allowed:* licensed.
26. *Mercury:* the god of lies.   27. *indue:* endow.
28. *with leasing:* with the gift of lying.

[*Enter* SIR TOBY.]

for—here he comes—one of thy kin has a most weak *pia mater*.²⁹
OLI. By mine honor, half drunk! What is he at the gate, cousin?
TO. A gentleman.
OLI. A gentleman? What gentleman?
TO. 'Tis a gentleman here. [*Hiccups.*] A plague o' these pickle- 100
herring! How now, sot?
CLOWN. Good Sir Toby!
OLI. Cousin, cousin, how have you come so early by this lethargy?³⁰
TO. Lechery?³¹ I defy lechery. There's one at the gate.
OLI. Ay, marry, what is he? 105
TO. Let him be the Devil an he will, I care not! Give me faith, say I.
Well, it's all one.

[*Exit.*]

OLI. What's a drunken man like, fool?
CLOWN. Like a drowned man, a fool, and a madman. One draught
above heat makes him a fool, the second mads him, and a third 110
drowns him.
OLI. Go thou and seek the crowner,³² and let him sit o' my coz;³³ for
he's in the third degree of drink—he's drowned. Go look after
him.
CLOWN. He is but mad yet, madonna, and the fool shall look to the 115
madman.

[*Exit.*]

[*Enter* MALVOLIO.]

MAL. Madam, yond young fellow swears he will speak with you. I
told him you were sick: he takes on him to understand so much,
and therefore comes to speak with you. I told him you were
asleep: he seems to have a foreknowledge of that too, and there- 120
fore comes to speak with you. What is to be said to him, lady?
He's fortified against any denial.

---

29. *pia mater:* in Elizabethan medicine, one of the membranes of the brain; here used to mean simply *brain.*     30. *lethargy:* lack of sense, drunkenness.
31. *Lechery:* lewdness.     32. *the crowner:* the coroner.
33. *coz:* cousin, kinsman. Used of any kinsman. In Shakespeare it is used most often in the uncle-nephew relationship.

OLI. Tell him he shall not speak with me.
MAL. Has been told so; and he says he'll stand at your door like a sheriff's post,[34] and be the supporter to a bench, but he'll speak with you. 125
OLI. What kind o' man is he?
MAL. Why, of mankind.
OLI. What manner of man?
MAL. Of very ill manner. He'll speak with you, will you or no. 130
OLI. Of what personage and years is he?
MAL. Not yet old enough for a man nor young enough for a boy; as a squash[35] is before 'tis a peasecod,[36] or a codling[37] when 'tis almost an apple. 'Tis with him in standing water,[38] between boy and man. He is very well-favored[39] and he speaks very shrew- 135 ishly.[40] One would think his mother's milk were scarce out of him.
OLI. Let him approach. Call in my gentlewoman.
MAL. Gentlewoman, my lady calls.

[*Exit.*]

[*Enter* MARIA.]

OLI. Give me my veil; come, throw it o'er my face. We'll once more 140 hear Orsino's embassy.

[*Enter* VIOLA.]

VIO. The honorable lady of the house, which is she?
OLI. Speak to me; I shall answer for her. Your will?
VIO. Most radiant, exquisite, and unmatchable beauty—I pray you tell me if this be the lady of the house, for I never saw her. I 145 would be loath to cast away my speech; for, besides that it is excellently well penned, I have taken great pains to con[41] it. Good beauties, let me sustain no scorn. I am very comptible,[42] even to the least sinister usage.
OLI. Whence came you, sir? 150

---

34. *a sheriff's post:* a post erected before the house of a mayor or sheriff as a sign of office.   35. *a squash:* an unripe pea pod.   36. *a peasecod:* a pea pod.
37. *a codling:* an unripe, half-grown apple.
38. *in standing water:* in the condition of standing water.
39. *well-favored:* good looking.   40. *shrewishly:* in a high voice, like a woman.
41. *con:* memorize.   42. *comptible:* susceptible, sensitive.

VIO. I can say little more than I have studied, and that question's out of my part. Good gentle one, give me modest assurance if you be the lady of the house, that I may proceed in my speech.

OLI. Are you a comedian?[43]

VIO. No, my profound heart; and yet (by the very fangs of malice I swear) I am not that I play. Are you the lady of the house?

OLI. If I do not usurp[44] myself, I am.

VIO. Most certain, if you are she, you do usurp yourself; for what is yours to bestow is not yours to reserve. But this is from my commission.[45] I will on with my speech in your praise and then show you the heart of my message.

OLI. Come to what is important in't. I forgive you the praise.

VIO. Alas, I took great pains to study it, and 'tis poetical.

OLI. It is the more like to be feigned; I pray you keep it in. I heard you were saucy at my gates; and allowed your approach rather to wonder at you than to hear you. If you be not mad, be gone; if you have reason, be brief. 'Tis not that time of moon with me[46] to make one in so skipping[47] a dialogue.

MAR. Will you hoist sail, sir? Here lies your way.[48]

VIO. No, good swabber;[49] I am to hull[50] here a little longer. Some mollification for your giant,[51] sweet lady!

OLI. Tell me your mind.

VIO. I am a messenger.

OLI. Sure you have some hideous matter to deliver, when the courtesy of it is so fearful. Speak your office.

VIO. It alone concerns your ear. I bring no overture of war, no taxation of homage.[52] I hold the olive in my hand. My words are as full of peace as matter.

OLI. Yet you began rudely. What are you? What would you?

---

43. *comedian:* an insult; socially speaking, comedians were considered to be very low.
44. *usurp:* counterfeit.
45. *this is from my commission:* this is getting ahead of my instructions.
46. *'Tis not . . . me:* the various phases or positions of the moon were believed to influence human behavior.   47. *skipping:* wild, mad.
48. *Here . . . way:* Maria urges Viola to leave.
49. Viola responds to Maria's metaphor with a series of nautical expressions.
50. *to hull:* to be driven by the wind on the hull alone, without sails.
51. *your giant:* Maria. Ladies in romances were customarily guarded by giants. Viola draws attention to Maria's efforts to protect her mistress and to the chambermaid's small size.   52. *taxation of homage:* demand for submission.

VIO. The rudeness that hath appeared in me have I learned from my    180
    entertainment.⁵³   What I am, and what I would, are as secret
    as maidenhead:⁵⁴ to your ears, divinity; to any other's, profana-
    tion.
OLI. Give us the place alone; we will hear this divinity. [*Exit* MARIA.]
    Now, sir, what is your text?    185
VIO. Most sweet lady—
OLI. A comfortable⁵⁵ doctrine, and much may be said of it.  Where
    lies your text?
VIO. In Orsino's bosom.
OLI. In his bosom?  In what chapter of his bosom?    190
VIO. To answer by the method,⁵⁶ in the first of his heart.
OLI. O, I have read it! it is heresy.  Have you no more to say?
VIO. Good madam, let me see your face.
OLI. Have you any commission from your lord to negotiate with my
    face?  You are now out of your text.  But we will draw the cur-    195
    tain and show you the picture.  [*Unveils.*]  Look you, sir, such
    a one I was this present. Is't not well done?⁵⁷
VIO. Excellently done, if God did all.⁵⁸
OLI. 'Tis in grain,⁵⁹ sir; 'twill endure wind and weather.
VIO. 'Tis beauty truly blent, whose red and white    200
    Nature's own sweet and cunning hand laid on.
    Lady, you are the cruel'st she alive
    If you will lead these graces to the grave,
    And leave the world no copy.⁶⁰
OLI. O, sir, I will not be so hard-hearted.  I will give out divers    205
    schedules⁶¹ of my beauty.  It shall be inventoried, and every
    particle and utensil labeled to my will:⁶²—as, item, two lips, in-
    different red; item, two grey eyes, with lids to them; item, one neck,
    one chin, and so forth.  Were you sent hither to praise⁶³ me?

---

53. *entertainment:* reception.
54. *as secret as maidenhead:* as sacred as maidenhood.
55. *comfortable:* comforting.
56. *by the method:* in the same biblical metaphor used by Olivia.
57. *Look . . . done?*  Olivia comments upon herself as one might upon a painting.
58. *if God did all:* if you have not used any artificial aids to beauty.
59. *in grain:* dyed in the wool; permanent; that is, natural.    60. *copy:* child.
61. *schedules:* catalogs, inventories.
62. *labeled to my will:* added to Olivia's will, as in a codicil, or perhaps explained in her will.    63. *praise:* appraise.

VIO. I see you what you are—you are too proud; 210
But if you were the Devil, you are fair.
My lord and master loves you. O, such love
Could be but recompensed though you were crowned
The nonpareil[64] of beauty!
OLI. How does he love me?
VIO. With adorations, fertile[65] tears, 215
With groans that thunder love, with sighs of fire.
OLI. Your lord does know my mind; I cannot love him.
Yet I suppose him virtuous, know him noble,
Of great estate, of fresh and stainless youth;
In voices well divulged,[66] free, learned, and valiant, 220
And in dimension and the shape of nature
A gracious person. But yet I cannot love him.
He might have took his answer long ago.
VIO. If I did love you in my master's flame,
With such a suff'ring, such a deadly life, 225
In your denial I would find no sense;
I would not understand it.
OLI. Why, what would you?[67]
VIO. Make me a willow cabin at your gate
And call upon my soul within the house;
Write loyal cantons[68] of contemned[69] love 230
And sing them loud even in the dead of night;
Halloa your name to the reverberate hills
And make the babbling gossip of the air
Cry out "Olivia!" O, you should not rest
Between the elements of air and earth 235
But you should pity me!
OLI. You might do much. What is your parentage?
VIO. Above my fortunes, yet my state is well.
I am a gentleman.
OLI. Get you to your lord.
I cannot love him. Let him send no more, 240

64. *nonpareil:* one without equal.   65. *fertile:* copious.
66. *In voices well divulged:* publicly spoken of as.
67. *what would you?* What would you do?
68. *cantons:* cantos, songs.   69. *contemned:* despised.

       Unless, perchance, you come to me again
       To tell me how he takes it.   Fare you well.
       I thank you for your pains.   Spend this for me.
VIO. I am no fee'd post,[70] lady; keep your purse;
       My master, not myself, lacks recompense.                      245
       Love make his heart of flint that you shall love;
       And let your fervor, like my master's, be
       Placed in contempt!   Farewell, fair cruelty.

[*Exit.*]

OLI. "What is your parentage?"
       "Above my fortunes, yet my state is well.                      250
       I am a gentleman." I'll be sworn thou[71] art.
       Thy tongue, thy face, thy limbs, actions, and spirit
       Do give thee fivefold blazon.[72] Not too fast! soft, soft!
       Unless the master were the man.   How now?
       Even so quickly may one catch the plague?                    255
       Methinks I feel this youth's perfections
       With an invisible and subtle stealth
       To creep in at mine eyes.   Well, let it be.
       What ho, Malvolio!

[*Enter* MALVOLIO.]

MAL.                 Here, madam, at your service.
OLI. Run after that same peevish messenger,                    260
       The County's[73] man.   He left this ring behind him,
       Would I or not.   Tell him I'll none of it.
       Desire him not to flatter with his lord
       Nor hold him up with hopes.   I am not for him.
       If that the youth will come this way tomorrow,        265
       I'll give him reasons for't.   Hie thee,[74] Malvolio.
MAL. Madam, I will.

[*Exit.*]

70. *fee'd post:* paid messenger.
71. *thou:* Olivia here uses the familiar, affectionate *thou* instead of the more formal *you.*
72. *Do . . . blazon:* proclaim Cesario a gentleman as would a coat of arms.
73. *County's:* Count's.    74. *Hie thee:* haste you, make haste.

Twelfth Night    21

OLI. I do I know not what, and fear to find
Mine eye too great a flatterer for my mind.⁷⁵
Fate, show thy force!  Ourselves we do not owe.⁷⁶ 270
What is decreed must be—and be this so!

[*Exit.*]

# ACT II

## SCENE 1. The seacoast.

[*Enter* ANTONIO *and* SEBASTIAN.]

ANT. Will you stay no longer? nor will you not that I go with you?
SEB. By your patience, no. My stars shine darkly over me; the malignancy of my fate might perhaps distemper¹ yours. Therefore I shall crave of you your leave, that I may bear my evils alone. It were a bad recompense for your love to lay any of them on you. 5
ANT. Let me yet know of you whither you are bound.
SEB. No, sooth,² sir. My determinate voyage is mere extravagancy.³ But I perceive in you so excellent a touch of modesty that you will not extort from me what I am willing to keep in; therefore 10 it charges me in manners the rather to express myself.⁴ You must know of me then, Antonio, my name is Sebastian, which I called Roderigo. My father was that Sebastian of Messaline⁵ whom I know you have heard of. He left behind him myself and a sister, both born in an hour.⁶ If the heavens had been 15 pleased, would we had so ended! But you, sir, altered that, for some hour before you took me from the breach of the sea was my sister drowned.
ANT. Alas the day!
SEB. A lady, sir, though it was said she much resembled me, was yet 20

---

75. *Mine . . . mind:* my mind will not be able to resist the impression of my eyes.
76. *owe:* own, possess.

1. *distemper:* disturb, infect.    2. *sooth:* in sooth (truth), truly.
3. *My . . . extravagancy:* my travel plan is mere wandering.
4. *express myself:* reveal myself.    5. Messaline is unknown to geographers.
6. *both born in an hour:* the same hour; they were twins.

of many accounted beautiful. But though I could not with such
estimable wonder overfar believe that,[7] yet thus far I will boldly
publish[8] her: she bore a mind that envy could not but call fair.
She is drowned already, sir, with salt water, though I seem to
drown her remembrance again with more.

ANT. Pardon me, sir, your bad entertainment.[9]
SEB. O good Antonio, forgive me your trouble!
ANT. If you will not murder me for my love,[10] let me be your servant.
SEB. If you will not undo what you have done, that is, kill him whom
you have recovered, desire it not. Fare ye well at once. My
bosom is full of kindness;[11] and I am yet so near the manners of
my mother[12] that, upon the least occasion more, mine eyes will
tell tales of me. I am bound to the Count Orsino's court. Farewell.

[*Exit.*]

ANT. The gentleness of all the gods go with thee!
   I have many enemies in Orisino's court,
   Else would I very shortly see thee there.
   But come what may, I do adore thee so
   That danger shall seem sport, and I will go.

[*Exit.*]

### SCENE 2. A street.

[*Enter* VIOLA *and* MALVOLIO *at several doors.*]

MAL. Were not you even now with the Countess Olivia?
VIO. Even now, sir. On a moderate pace I have since arrived but
hither.
MAL. She returns this ring to you, sir. You might have saved me my
pains, to have taken it away yourself. She adds, moreover, that
you should put your lord into a desperate[1] assurance she will
none of him. And one thing more, that you be never so hardy to

---

7. *I could not . . . believe that:* in modesty (as he is her twin) Sebastian cannot believe his sister beautiful.   8. *boldly publish:* proclaim.
9. *Pardon . . . entertainment:* Forgive me for my poor hospitality.
10. *If . . . love:* Do not kill me for my love by leaving me.
11. *kindness:* tenderness.   12. *so near . . . mother:* so close to weeping.

1. *desperate:* definite.

come again in his affairs, unless it be to report your lord's taking of this.  Receive it so.

VIO. She took the ring of me.  I'll none of it. 10

MAL. Come, sir, you peevishly threw it to her; and her will is, it should be so returned.  If it be worth stooping for, there it lies, in your eye;² if not, be it his that finds it.

[*Exit.*]

VIO. I left no ring with her.  What means this lady?
Fortune forbid my outside have not charmed her! 15
She made good view of me;³ indeed, so much
That methought her eyes had lost her tongue,
For she did speak in starts distractedly.
She loves me sure; the cunning of her passion
Invites me in this churlish messenger. 20
None of my lord's ring?  Why, he sent her none!
I am the man.  If it be so—as 'tis—
Poor lady, she were better love a dream!
Disguise, I see thou art a wickedness
Wherein the pregnant enemy⁴ does much. 25
How easy is it for the proper-false⁵
In women's waxen hearts to set their forms!
Alas, our frailty is the cause, not we!
For such as we are made of, such we be.
How will this fadge?⁶  My master loves her dearly; 30
And I (poor monster⁷) fond⁸ as much on him;
And she (mistaken) seems to dote on me.
What will become of this?  As I am man,
My state is desperate for my master's love.
As I am woman (now alas the day!), 35
What thriftless⁹ sighs shall poor Olivia breathe!
O Time, thou must untangle this, not I;
It is too hard a knot for me t'untie!

[*Exit.*]

2. *in your eye:* in your sight.   3. *made good view of me:* looked at me closely.
4. *the pregnant enemy:* possibly the devil.
5. *the proper-false:* the handsome, deceitful ones.   6. *fadge:* succeed, come off.
7. *monster:* neither man nor woman.   8. *fond:* dote.
9. *thriftless:* pointless, useless.

SCENE 3. Olivia's house.

[*Enter* SIR TOBY *and* SIR ANDREW.]

TO. Approach, Sir Andrew. Not to be abed after midnight is to be up betimes; and *diluculo surgere*,[1] thou knowst—
AND. Nay, by my troth,[2] I know not; but I know to be up late is to be up late.
TO. A false conclusion! I hate it as an unfilled can. To be up after midnight, and to go to bed then, is early; so that to go to bed after midnight is to go to bed betimes. Does not our life consist of the four elements?[3]
AND. Faith, so they say; but I think it rather consists of eating and drinking.
TO. Th'art a scholar! Let us therefore eat and drink. Marian[4] I say! a stoup[5] of wine!

[*Enter* CLOWN.]

AND. Here comes the fool, i' faith.
CLOWN. How now, my hearts? Did you never see the picture of We Three?[6]
TO. Welcome, ass.[7] Now let's have a catch.[8]
AND. By my troth, the fool has an excellent breast.[9] I had rather than forty shillings I had such a leg, and so sweet a breath to sing, as the fool has. In sooth, thou wast in very gracious fooling last night, when thou spokest of Pigrogromitus, of the Vapians passing the equinoctial of Queubus.[10] 'Twas very good, i' faith. I sent thee sixpence for thy leman.[11] Hadst it?
CLOWN. I did impeticos thy gratillity;[12] for Malvolio's nose is no whip-

---

1. *diluculo surgere:* From *diluculo surgere saluberrimum est,* to get up at dawn is most healthy. An adage (proverb).  2. *troth:* pledged word.
3. *the four elements:* earth, water, fire, and air.  4. *Marian:* Maria.
5. *a stoup:* a cup, tankard.
6. *the picture of We Three:* A picture of two fools with the inscription *We Three*. The spectator, of course, was the third fool.
7. *ass:* Sir Toby refers to another version of the picture, in which there were two asses instead of two fools.
8. *a catch:* a round in which one singer "catches" comically at the words of another.
9. *breast:* singing voice.
10. *Pigrogromitus . . . Queubus:* probably nonsense names invented by the Clown.
11. *leman:* sweetheart.  12. *I . . . gratillity:* I put your tiny tip in my pocket.

Twelfth Night    25

stock.¹³ My lady has a white hand, and the Myrmidons are no bottle-ale houses.¹⁴
AND. Excellent! Why, this is the best fooling, when all is done. Now a song!
TO. Come on! there is sixpence for you. Let's have a song.
AND. There's a testril¹⁵ of me too. If one knight give a—
CLOWN. Would you have a love song, or a song of good life?
TO. A love song, a love song.
AND. Ay, ay! I care not for good life.

[CLOWN *sings*.]

> O mistress mine, where are you roaming?
> O, stay and hear! your truelove's coming,
>   That can sing both high and low.
> Trip no further, pretty sweeting;
> Journeys end in lovers meeting,
>   Every wise man's son doth know.

AND. Excellent good, i' faith!
TO. Good, good!

[CLOWN *sings*.]

> What is love? 'Tis not hereafter;
> Present mirth hath present laughter;
>   What's to come is still unsure:
> In delay there lies no plenty;
> Then come kiss me, sweet and twenty!
>   Youth's a stuff will not endure.

AND. A mellifluous¹⁶ voice, as I am true knight.
TO. A contagious breath.¹⁷
AND. Very sweet and contagious, i' faith.

---

13. *for . . . whipstock:* Malvolio will smell out any missing wine. The whipstock is the handle of the whip.
14. *My lady . . . houses:* My sweetheart does not condescend to common drink and the tavern we usually go to (the Myrmidons) is not cheap.
15. *a testril:* a coin worth sixpence.    16. *mellifluous:* sweet as honey.
17. *A contagious breath:* a "catchy" song; another of Sir Toby's puns.

TO. To hear by the nose, it is dulcet in contagion.[18] But shall we make the welkin dance[19] indeed? Shall we rouse the night owl in a catch that will draw three souls out of one weaver?[20] Shall we do that?

AND. An you love me, let's do't! I am dog[21] at a catch.

CLOWN. By'r Lady,[22] sir, and some dogs will catch well.

AND. Most certain. Let our catch be "Thou knave."

CLOWN. "Hold thy peace, thou knave," knight? I shall be constrained in't to call thee knave, knight.

AND. 'Tis not the first time I have constrained one to call me knave. Begin, fool. It begins, "Hold thy peace."

CLOWN. I shall never begin if I hold my peace.

AND. Good, i' faith! Come, begin.

[*Catch sung. Enter* MARIA.]

MAR. What a caterwauling do you keep here! If my lady have not called up her steward Malvolio and bid him turn you out of doors, never trust me.

TO. My lady's a Cataian,[23] we are politicians,[24] Malvolio's a Peg-a-Ramsey,[25] and [*Sings.*] "Three merry men be we." Am not I consanguineous?[26] Am I not of her blood? Tilly-vally,[27] lady! [*Sings.*] "There dwelt a man in Babylon, lady, lady!"

CLOWN. Beshrew me,[28] the knight's in admirable fooling.

AND. Ay, he does well enough if he be disposed, and so do I too. He does it with a better grace, but I do it more natural.[29]

TO. [*Sings.*] "O' the twelfth day of December"—

MAR. For the love o' God, peace!

---

18. *To hear . . . contagion:* Since Sir Andrew has missed Sir Toby's pun on *contagious* and *catchy,* Sir Toby says that if a song really is contagious it must be caught in the nose, like any other contagion.   19. *the welkin dance:* the sky spin.   20. *Shall we rouse . . . weaver?* A humorous comment on the power of music, heightened by the fact that weavers were known as psalm-singers, not lovers of drinking songs.   21. *dog:* expert.   22. *By'r Lady:* By Our Lady, an oath.
23. *a Cataian:* The meaning of this term is not clear. It apparently was meant to be insulting. It meant perhaps a thief or one who promises more than he can deliver.   24. *politicians:* for Shakespeare, a derogatory term.
25. *a Peg-a-Ramsey:* apparently no one but Sir Toby knows what he meant by this.
26. *consanguineous:* a blood relative (of Olivia).
27. *Tilly-vally:* a nonsense interjection corresponding to *fiddle faddle.*
28. *Beshrew me:* may ill luck take me, or may mischief befall me.
29. *I . . . natural:* an unintentional pun on Sir Andrew's part. He has just said that he fools as an idiot **would.**

Twelfth Night

[*Enter* MALVOLIO.]

MAL. My masters, are you mad? or what are you? Have you no wit, manners, nor honesty, but to gabble like tinkers at this time of night? Do ye make an alehouse of my lady's house, that ye squeak out your coziers'[30] catches without any mitigation or remorse of voice? Is there no respect of place, persons, nor time[31] in you?

TO. We did keep time,[32] sir, in our catches. Sneck up![33]

MAL. Sir Toby, I must be round[34] with you. My lady bade me tell you that, though she harbors you as her kinsman, she's nothing allied to your disorders. If you can separate yourself and your misdemeanors, you are welcome to the house. If not, and it would please you to take leave of her, she is very willing to bid you farewell.

TO. [*Sings.*] "Farewell, dear heart, since I must needs be gone."

MAR. Nay, good Sir Toby!

CLOWN. [*Sings.*] "His eyes do show his days are almost done."

MAL. Is't even so?

TO. "But I will never die."

CLOWN. Sir Toby, there you lie.

MAL. This is much credit to you!

TO. "Shall I bid him go?"

CLOWN. "What an if you do?"

TO. "Shall I bid him go, and spare not?"

CLOWN. "O, no, no, no, no, you dare not!"

TO. Out o' tune, sir?[35] Ye lie.[36] Art any more than a steward? Dost thou think, because thou art virtuous, there shall be no more cakes and ale?[37]

CLOWN. Yes, by Saint Anne! and ginger[38] shall be hot i' the mouth too.

TO. Th'art i' the right.—Go, sir, rub your chain with crumbs.[39] A stoup of wine, Maria!

MAL. Mistress Mary, if you prized my lady's favor at anything more

---

30. *coziers'*: cobblers'.   31. *time*: time of night.   32. *time*: in the musical sense.
33. *Sneck up!* Begone!   34. *round*: to the point, plain spoken.
35. *Out . . . sir?* Addressed to Feste, who has added one *no* too many.
36. *Ye lie*: when you say I dare not bid him go.
37. *Art any . . . ale?* Addressed to Malvolio. Cakes and ale were served in honor of saints' days, a custom disapproved of by the Puritans.
38. *ginger*: ginger was thought to be an aphrodisiac.
39. *rub . . . crumbs*: rub your chain of office (as a steward) to clean it.

than contempt, you would not give means for this uncivil rule.[40] She shall know of it, by this hand.

[*Exit.*]

MAR. Go shake your ears!

AND. 'Twere as good a deed as to drink when a man's ahungry,[41] to challenge him the field,[42] and then to break promise with him and make a fool of him.

TO. Do't, knight. I'll write thee a challenge; or I'll deliver thy indignation to him by word of mouth.

MAR. Sweet Sir Toby, be patient for tonight. Since the youth of the Count's was today with my lady, she is much out of quiet. For Monsieur Malvolio, let me alone with him. If I do not gull him into a nay-word,[43] and make him a common recreation,[44] do not think I have wit enough to lie straight in my bed. I know I can do it.

TO. Possess us,[45] possess us! Tell us something of him.

MAR. Marry, sir, sometimes he is a kind of Puritan.

AND. O, if I thought that, I'd beat him like a dog!

TO. What, for being a Puritan? Thy exquisite reason, dear knight?

AND. I have no exquisite reason for't, but I have reason good enough.

MAR. The devil a Puritan that he is, or anything constantly but a time-pleaser;[46] an affectioned ass, that cons state without book[47] and utters it by great swarths; the best persuaded of himself;[48] so crammed, as he thinks, with excellencies that it is his grounds of faith that all that look on him love him; and on that vice in him will my revenge find notable cause to work.

TO. What wilt thou do?

MAR. I will drop in his way some obscure epistles of love, wherein by the color of his beard, the shape of his leg, the manner of his gait, the expressure of his eye, forehead, and complexion, he shall find himself most feelingly personated.[49] I can write very like

---

40. *uncivil rule:* misbehavior, revel.    41. *ahungry:* thirsty.
42. *to challenge him the field:* challenge him to a duel.
43. *a nayword:* a laughingstock, a byeword.
44. *common recreation:* object of laughter.    45. *Possess us:* tell us.
46. *a time-pleaser:* a timeserver, a parasite.
47. *cons state without book:* learns polite conversation by heart.
48. *the best persuaded of himself:* he has the highest opinion of himself.
49. *feelingly personated:* exactly described.

my lady your niece; on a forgotten matter we can hardly make distinction of our hands.

TO. Excellent! I smell a device.

AND. I have't in my nose too.

TO. He shall think by the letters that thou wilt drop that they come from my niece, and that she's in love with him. 140

MAR. My purpose is indeed a horse of that color.

AND. And your horse now would make him an ass.

MAR. Ass, I doubt not.

AND. O, 'twill be admirable! 145

MAR. Sport royal, I warrant you. I know my physic will work with him. I will plant you two, and let the fool make a third, where he shall find the letter. Observe his construction of it. For this night, to bed, and dream on the event. Farewell.

[*Exit.*]

TO. Good night, Penthesilea.[50] 150

AND. Before me, she's a good wench.

TO. She's a beagle true-bred,[51] and one that adores me. What o' that?

AND. I was adored once too.

TO. Let's to bed, knight. Thou hadst need send for more money. 155

AND. If I cannot recover[52] your niece, I am a foul way out.

TO. Send for money, knight. If thou hast her not i' the end, call me Cut.[53]

AND. If I do not, never trust me, take it how you will.

TO. Come, come; I'll go burn some sack.[54] 'Tis too late to go to bed now. Come, knight; come, knight. 160

[*Exeunt.*]

SCENE 4. The Duke's Palace.

[*Enter* DUKE, VIOLA, CURIO, *and others.*]

DUKE. Give me some music. Now good morrow, friends.
Now, good Cesario, but that piece of song,
That old and antique song we heard last night.

---

50. *Penthesilea:* the Queen of the Amazons.
51. *a beagle true-bred:* a complement to Maria for her keenness and shrewdness.
52. *recover:* win.  53. *Cut:* a contemptuous term; the meaning is obscure.
54. *burn some sack:* heat some wine.

Methought it did relieve my passion[1] much,
More than light airs and recollected terms[2]
Of these most brisk and giddy-paced times.
Come, but one verse.

CUR. He is not here, so please your lordship, that should sing it.
DUKE. Who was it?
CUR. Feste the jester, my lord, a fool that the Lady Olivia's father took much delight in. He is about the house.
DUKE. Seek him out. [*Exit* CURIO.] And play the tune the while.

[*Music plays.*]

Come hither, boy. If ever thou shalt love,
In the sweet pangs of it remember me;
For such as I am all true lovers are,
Unstaid and skittish in all motions else
Save in the constant image of the creature
That is beloved. How dost thou like this tune?

VIO. It gives a very echo to the seat
Where Love is throned.[3]

DUKE.                Thou dost speak masterly.
My life upon't, young though thou art, thine eye
Hath stayed upon some favor[4] that it loves.
Hath it not, boy?

VIO.            A little, by your favor.

DUKE. What kind of woman is't?

VIO.            Of your complexion.

DUKE. She is not worth thee then. What years, i' faith?
VIO. About your years, my lord.
DUKE. Too old, by heaven! Let still[5] the woman take
An elder than herself: so wears she to him,
So sways she level in her husband's heart;
For, boy, however we do praise ourselves,
Our fancies are more giddy and unfirm,
More longing, wavering, sooner lost and won,
Than women's are.

VIO.            I think it well, my lord.

---

1. *passion:* suffering.   2. *recollected terms:* artifical, studied phrases.
3. *It . . . throned:* It echoes the emotions of the heart.   4. *favor:* face, countenance.
5. *still:* always.

**Twelfth Night**

DUKE. Then let thy love be younger than thyself,
    Or thy affection cannot hold the bent;⁶     35
    For women are as roses, whose fair flower,
    Being once displayed, doth fall that very hour.
VIO. And so they are; alas, that they are so!
    To die, even when they to perfection grow!

[*Enter* CURIO *and* CLOWN.]

DUKE. O, fellow, come, the song we had last night.     40
    Mark it, Cesario; it is old and plain.
    The spinsters and the knitters in the sun,
    And the free maids that weave their thread with bones,⁷
    Do use to chant it. It is silly sooth,⁸
    And dallies with the innocence of love,     45
    Like the old age.⁹
CLOWN. Are you ready, sir?
DUKE. Ay; prithee sing.

[*Music plays.*]

[CLOWN *sings.*]

    Come away, come away, death,
        And in sad cypress¹⁰ let me be laid.     50
    Fly away, fly away, breath;
        I am slain by a fair cruel maid.
    My shroud of white, stuck all with yew,
        O, prepare it!
    My part of death, no one so true     55
        Did share it.

    Not a flower, not a flower sweet,
        On my black coffin let there be strown;
    Not a friend, not a friend greet
        My poor corpse, where by bones shall be thrown.     60

---

6. *hold the bent:* the tension, as of a drawn bow.
7. *the free maids . . . bones:* the lace makers.     8. *silly sooth:* plain, simple truth.
9. *the old age:* the former age, the simple past.
10. *sad cypress:* either a coffin made of cypress or a shroud made of the material called cypress.

> A thousand thousand sighs to save,
> > Lay me, O, where
> Sad true lover never find my grave,
> > To weep there!

DUKE. There's for thy pains. 65
CLOWN. No pains, sir. I take pleasure in singing, sir.
DUKE. I'll pay thy pleasure then.
CLOWN. Truly, sir, and pleasure will be paid[11] one time or another.
DUKE. Give me now leave to leave thee.[12]
CLOWN. Now the melancholy god protect thee, and the tailor make 70 thy doublet of changeable taffeta, for thy mind is a very opal![13] I would have men of such constancy put to sea, that their business might be everything, and their intent everywhere; for that's it that always makes a good voyage of nothing. Farewell.

[*Exit.*]

DUKE. Let all the rest give place.

[*Exeunt* CURIO *and Attendants.*]

> > > Once more, Cesario, 75
> Get thee to yond same sovereign cruelty.
> Tell her, my love, more noble than the world,
> Prizes not quantity of dirty lands.
> The parts that Fortune hath bestowed upon her,
> Tell her I hold as giddily as Fortune;[14] 80
> But 'tis that miracle and queen of gems
> That nature pranks her in,[15] attracts my soul.

VIO. But if she cannot love you, sir—
DUKE. I cannot be so answered.
VIO. > > > Sooth, but you must.
> Say that some lady, as perhaps there is, 85
> Hath for your love as great a pang of heart
> As you have for Olivia: You cannot love her;
> You tell her so. Must she not then be answered?

---

11. *pleasure will be paid:* with pain.  12. *Give . . . thee:* a command to withdraw.
13. *the tailor . . . opal!* Both taffeta and opals change color; they are used here to comment on the Duke's changeable mood.
14. *as giddily as Fortune:* as carelessly as Fortune holds them.
15. *pranks her in:* adorns her with (the miracle, of course, is her beauty).

**Twelfth Night**

DUKE. There is no woman's sides
    Can bide the beating of so strong a passion
    As love doth give my heart; no woman's heart
    So big to hold so much; they lack retention.
    Alas, their love may be called appetite—
    No motion of the liver,[16] but the palate—
    That suffers surfeit, cloyment, and revolt;
    But mine[17] is all as hungry as the sea
    And can digest as much. Make no compare
    Between that love a woman can bear me
    And that I owe Olivia.
VIO.                 Ay, but I know—
DUKE. What dost thou know?
VIO. Too well what love women to men may owe.
    In faith, they are as true of heart as we.
    My father had a daughter loved a man
    As it might be perhaps, were I a woman,
    I should your lordship.
DUKE.               And what's her history?
VIO. A blank, my lord. She never told her love,
    But let concealment, like a worm i' the bud,
    Feed on her damask[18] cheek. She pined in thought;
    And, with a green and yellow melancholy,
    She sat like Patience on a monument,[19]
    Smiling at grief. Was not this love indeed?
    We men may say more, swear more; but indeed
    Our shows are more than will; for still we prove
    Much in our vows but little in our love.
DUKE. But died thy sister of her love, my boy?
VIO. I am all the daughters of my father's house,
    And all the brothers too—and yet I know not.
    Sir, shall I do this lady?
DUKE.               Ay, that's the theme.
    To her in haste! Give her this jewel. Say
    My love can give no place, bide no denay.[20]

[*Exeunt.*]

16. *no motion of the liver:* no true passion; the liver was believed to be the seat of love and courage.    17. *mine:* my love.    18. *damask:* a pink or pale red rose.
19. *like Patience on a monument:* like a statue of Patience.
20. *denay:* denial.

SCENE 5. Olivia's garden.

[*Enter* SIR TOBY, SIR ANDREW, *and* FABIAN.]

TO. Come thy ways, Signior Fabian.
FAB. Nay, I'll come. If I lose a scruple[1] of this sport, let me be boiled to death with melancholy.
TO. Wouldst thou not be glad to have the niggardly rascally sheep-biter[2] come by some notable shame?
FAB. I would exult, man. You know he brought me out o' favor with my lady about a bear-baiting here.
TO. To anger him we'll have the bear again; and we will fool him black and blue. Shall we not, Sir Andrew?
AND. An we do not, it is pity of our lives.

[*Enter* MARIA.]

TO. Here comes the little villain. How now, my metal of India?[3]
MAR. Get ye all three into the box tree.[4] Malvolio's coming down this walk. He has been yonder i' the sun practicing behavior to his own shadow this half hour. Observe him, for the love of mockery; for I know this letter will make a contemplative idiot[5] of him. Close, in the name of jesting! Lie thou there [*Throws down a letter.*]; for here comes the trout that must be caught with tickling.[6]

[*Exit.*]

[*Enter* MALVOLIO.]

MAL. 'Tis but fortune; all is fortune. Maria once told me she[7] did affect[8] me; and I have heard herself come thus near, that, should she fancy,[9] it should be one of my complexion. Besides, she uses me with a more exalted respect than anyone else that follows her. What should I think on't?
TO. Here's an overweening[10] rogue!

1. *a scruple:* a small part, the least bit.
2. *sheepbiter:* a sheep dog who took to biting the sheep, thus becoming worthless. Such a dog was considered incorrigible and was killed.
3. *metal of India:* girl of gold, precious girl.    4. *the box tree:* the hedge.
5. *contemplative idiot:* pompous fool.
6. *tickling:* Poachers tickled trout about the gills to quiet them so that they could be caught by hand. The word *trout* was used figuratively to mean anyone who could be easily caught.    7. *she:* Olivia.    8. *affect:* like.    9. *fancy:* love.
10. *overweening:* proud.

Twelfth Night    35

FAB. O, peace! Contemplation makes a rare turkey cock of him. How he jets[11] under his advanced plumes!
AND. 'Slight,[12] I could so beat the rogue!
FAB. Peace, I say.
MAL. To be Count Malvolio!
TO. Ah, rogue!
AND. Pistol him, pistol him!
FAB. Peace, peace!
MAL. There is example[13] for't. The Lady of the Strachy married the yeoman of the wardrobe.[14]
AND. Fie on him, Jezebel![15]
FAB. O, peace! Now he's deeply in. Look how imagination blows him.
MAL. Having been three months married to her, sitting in my state—[16]
TO. O for a stonebow,[17] to hit him in the eye!
MAL. Calling my officers about me, in my branched[18] velvet gown; having come from a day bed,[19] where I have left Olivia sleeping—
TO. Fire and brimstone!
FAB. O, peace, peace!
MAL. And then to have the humor of state;[20] and after a demure travel of regard[21]—telling them I know my place, as I would they should do theirs—to ask for my kinsman Toby—
TO. Bolts and shackles!
FAB. O, peace, peace, peace! Now, now.
MAL. Seven of my people, with an obedient start, make out for him. I frown the while, and perchance wind up my watch, or play with my—some rich jewel. Toby approaches; curtsies[22] there to me—
TO. Shall this fellow live?

11. *jets:* struts.    12. *'Slight:* By this light; an oath.    13. *example:* precedent.
14. *The Lady ... wardrobe:* These persons, if indeed they ever existed, are not known to us.
15. *Jezebel!* Jezebel represented shameless impudence. Sir Andrew is a bit confused over the sex.    16. *my state:* my chair of state.
17. *a stonebow:* a crossbow which shot stones.
18. *branched:* ornamented with patterns of leaves and branches.
19. *day bed:* couch.    20. *the humor of State:* high airs.
21. *after ... regard:* after looking at each of my officers gravely.
22. *curtsies:* makes a gesture of reverence. Curtsies were customarily performed by both men and women.

FAB. Though our silence be drawn from us with cars, yet peace![23]
MAL. I extend my hand to him thus, quenching my familiar smile with an austere regard of control—
TO. And does not Toby take you a blow o' the lips then?
MAL. Saying, "Cousin Toby, my fortunes having cast me on your niece, give me this prerogative[24] of speech." 60
TO. What, what?
MAL. "You must amend your drunkenness."
TO. Out, scab!
FAB. Nay, patience, or we break the sinews of our plot. 65
MAL. "Besides, you waste the treasure of your time with a foolish knight"—
AND. That's me, I warrant you.
MAL. "One Sir Andrew"—
AND. I knew 'twas I, for many do call me fool. 70
MAL. What employment have we here?[25]

[Picks up letter.]

FAB. Now is the woodcock[26] near the gin.[27]
TO. O, peace! and the spirit of humors intimate reading aloud to him!
MAL. By my life, this is my lady's hand! These be her very C's, her U's, and her T's; and thus makes she her great P's. It is, in contempt of question,[28] her hand. 75
AND. Her C's, her U's, and her T's? Why that?
MAL. [Reads.] "To the unknown beloved, this, and my good wishes." Her very phrases! By your leave, wax.[29] Soft! and the impressure[30] her Lucrece, with which she uses to seal! 'Tis my lady. To whom should this be? 80
FAB. This wins him, liver and all.
MAL. [Reads.]

"Jove knows I love—
  But who?
Lips, do not move; 85
  No man must know."

23. *Though . . . peace!* Though the greatest pressure be placed upon us, we must be still.    24. *prerogative:* privilege.    25. *What . . . here?* What is this?
26. *the woodcock:* a stupid bird, easily snared.    27. *gin:* trap.
28. *in contempt of question:* doubtless.    29. *wax:* the letter is sealed with wax.
30. *the impressure:* the imprint of.

Twelfth Night    37

"No man must know." What follows? The numbers altered! "No man must know." If this should be thee, Malvolio?

TO. Marry, hang thee, brock!³¹

MAL. [*Reads.*]

"I may command where I adore;                              90
    But silence, like a Lucrece knife,³²
With bloodless stroke my heart doth gore.
    M. O. A. I. doth sway my life."

FAB. A fustian riddle!³³

TO. Excellent wench, say I.                                  95

MAL. "M. O. A. I. doth sway my life." Nay, but first, let me see, let me see, let me see.

FAB. What dish o' poison has she dressed him!

TO. And with what wing the staniel³⁴ checks³⁵ at it!

MAL. "I may command where I adore." Why, she may command   100
me: I serve her; she is my lady. Why, this is evident to any formal capacity. There is no obstruction in this. And the end—what should that alphabetical position portend? If I could make that resemble something in me! Softly! M. O. A. I.

TO. O, ay, make up that! He is now at a cold scent.³⁶       105

FAB. Sowter³⁷ will cry upon't for all this, though it be as rank as a fox.

MAL. M.—Malvolio. M.—Why, that begins my name!

FAB. Did not I say he would work it out? The cur is excellent at faults.³⁸

MAL. M.—But then there is no consonancy in the sequel. That  110
suffers under probation.³⁹ A should follow, but O does.

FAB. And O shall end, I hope.

TO. Ay, or I'll cudgel him, and make him cry O!

MAL. And then I comes behind.

FAB. Ay, an you had any eye behind you, you might see more detrac-  115
tion at your heels than fortunes before you.

---

31. *brock:* badger, a common term of contempt.
32. *a Lucrece knife:* the knife used by Lucrece to stab herself.
33. *fustian:* ridiculous, pompous.   34. *the staniel:* an inferior type of hawk.
35. *checks:* to check is to turn aside from one's prey after a lesser prey which crosses one's path.   36. *a cold scent:* a scent that will baffle him.
37. *Sowter:* quite possibly a common name for a hunting dog, or hound.
38. *faults:* breaks in a line of scent; a hunting term.
39. *suffers under probation:* fails when tested.

MAL. M, O, A, I. This simulation is not as the former;[40] and yet, to crush[41] this a little, it would bow to me, for every one of these letters are in my name.[42] Soft! here follows prose. [*Reads.*]

"If this fall into thy hand, revolve.[43] In my stars[44] I am above thee; but be not afraid of greatness. Some are born great, some achieve greatness, and some have greatness thrust upon 'em. Thy Fates open their hands; let thy blood and spirit embrace them; and to inure thyself[45] to what thou are like to be, cast thy humble slough[46] and appear fresh. Be opposite[47] with a kinsman, surly with servants. Let thy tongue tang[48] arguments of state; put thyself into the trick of singularity.[49] She thus advises thee that sighs for thee. Remember who commended thy yellow stockings and wished to see thee ever cross-gartered.[50] I say, remember. Go to, thou art made, if thou desirest to be so. If not, let me see thee a steward still, the fellow of servants, and not worthy to touch Fortune's fingers. Farewell. She that would alter services with thee,

"THE FORTUNATE UNHAPPY."

Daylight and champian[51] discovers[52] not more. This is open. I will be proud, I will read politic authors,[53] I will baffle[54] Sir Toby, I will wash off gross acquaintance, I will be point-device the very man.[55] I do not now fool myself, to let imagination jade[56] me; for every reason excites to this, that my lady loves me. She did commend my yellow stockings of late, she did praise my leg being cross-gartered; and in this she manifests herself to my

---

40. *This . . . former:* This hidden meaning is not as easy to figure out as the earlier part of the letter.     41. *crush:* force.
42. The meaning of these mysterious letters has never been satisfactorily worked out.
43. *revolve:* think about it, consider.     44. *in my stars:* in the fortunes of my birth.
45. *inure thyself:* accustom thyself.
46. *cast . . . slough:* cast off your humility as a snake sheds its skin.
47. *opposite:* antagonistic.     48. *tang:* utter with a ringing tone.
49. *singularity:* eccentricity.
50. *cross-gartered:* In cross-gartering the garter was brought from beneath the knee and tied in a bow above it after passing behind the leg. Both yellow stockings and cross-gartering were probably out of fashion by the time Shakespeare wrote *Twelfth Night*.     51. *daylight and champian:* broad day and open country.
52. *discovers:* reveals.     53. *politic authors:* authors of books on strategy.
54. *baffle:* publicly disgrace.
55. *I . . . man:* I will be the very man in every particular.     56. *jade:* trick, deceive.

love, and with a kind of injunction drives me to these habits of her liking. I thank my stars, I am happy. I will be strange,⁵⁷ stout,⁵⁸ in yellow stockings, and cross-gartered, even with the swiftness of putting on. Jove and my stars be praised! Here is yet a postscript. [*Reads.*] "Thou canst not choose but know who I am. If thou entertainst my love, let it appear in thy smiling. Thy smiles become thee well. Therefore in my presence still smile, dear my sweet, I prithee."

Jove, I thank thee. I will smile; I will do everything that thou wilt have me.

[*Exit.*]

FAB. I will not give my part of this sport for a pension of thousands to be paid from the Sophy.⁵⁹
TO. I could marry this wench⁶⁰ for this device—
AND. So could I too.
TO. And ask no other dowry with her but such another just.

[*Enter* MARIA.]

AND. Nor I neither.
FAB. Here comes my noble gull-catcher.⁶¹
TO. Wilt thou set thy foot o' my neck?
AND. Or o' mine either?
TO. Shall I play my freedom at tray-trip⁶² and become thy bondslave?
AND. I' faith, or I either?
TO. Why, thou hast put him in such a dream that, when the image of it leaves him, he must run mad.
MAR. Nay, but say true, does it work upon him?
TO. Like aqua vitae⁶³ with a midwife.
MAR. If you will, then, see the fruits of the sport mark his first approach before my lady. He will come to her in yellow stockings, and 'tis a color she abhors, and cross-gartered, a fashion she detests; and he will smile upon her, which will now be so unsuitable to her disposition, being addicted to a melancholy as she

---

57. *strange:* distant.    58. *stout:* haughty, overbearing.
59. *the Sophy:* the Shah of Persia.    60. *this wench:* Maria.
61. *gull-catcher:* trickster; a gull was a person who was easily fooled.
62. *tray-trip:* a game of cards, played with dice as well, in which winning depended upon throwing trays (threes).    63. *aqua vitae:* strong waters, perhaps brandy.

is, that it cannot but turn him into a notable contempt. If you will see it, follow me.

TO. To the gates of Tartar,⁶⁴ thou most excellent devil of wit!

AND. I'll make one too. 175

[*Exeunt.*]

# ACT III

### SCENE 1. Olivia's garden.

[*Enter* VIOLA, *and* CLOWN *with a tabor and pipe.*¹]

VIO. Save thee,² friend, and thy music! Dost thou live by³ thy tabor?

CLOWN. No, sir, I live by the church.

VIO. Art thou a churchman?

CLOWN. No such matter, sir. I do live by the church; for I do live at my house, and my house doth stand by the church. 5

VIO. So thou mayst say, the king lies by a beggar, if a beggar dwell near him; or, the church stands by⁴ thy tabor, if thy tabor stand by the church.

CLOWN. You have said, sir. To see this age! A sentence is but a chev'ril glove⁵ to a good wit. How quickly the wrong side may 10 be turned outward!

VIO. Nay, that's certain. They that dally nicely⁶ with words may quickly make them wanton.⁷

CLOWN. I would therefore my sister had had no name, sir.

VIO. Why, man? 15

CLOWN. Why, sir, her name's a word, and to dally with that word might make my sister wanton.⁸ But indeed words are very rascals since bonds disgraced them.

VIO. Thy reason, man?

---

64. *the gates of Tartar:* the gates of hell.

1. *tabor and pipe:* the tabor (a small drum) and the pipe were traditional properties of the fool.   2. *Save thee:* God save thee.
3. *live by:* earn your living by.
4. *stands by:* the double meaning here is (1) stands near and (2) is upheld by.
5. *a chev'ril glove:* a kid glove. Such gloves were easily stretched and could easily and quickly be turned inside out.   6. *dally nicely:* play, trifle idly.
7. *make them wanton:* give them a double meaning.   8. *wanton:* lascivious, lewd.

CLOWN. Troth, sir, I can yield you none without words, and words 20
are grown so false I am loath to prove reason with them.
VIO. I warrant thou are a merry fellow and carest for nothing.
CLOWN. Not so, sir; I do care for something; but in my conscience, sir, I do not care for you. If that be to care for nothing, sir, I would it would make you invisible. 25
VIO. Art not thou the Lady Olivia's fool?
CLOWN. No, indeed, sir. The Lady Olivia has no folly. She will keep no fool, sir, till she be married; and fools are as like husbands as pilchards[9] are to herrings—the husband's the bigger. I am indeed not her fool, but her corrupter of words. 30
VIO. I saw thee late at the Count Orsino's.
CLOWN. Foolery, sir, does walk about the orb like the sun; it shines everywhere. I would be sorry, sir, but the fool should be as oft with your master as with my mistress. I think I saw your wisdom[10] there. 35
VIO. Nay, an thou pass upon[11] me, I'll no more with thee. Hold, there's expenses for thee. [*Gives a piece of money.*]
CLOWN. Now Jove, in his next commodity[12] of hair, send thee a beard!
VIO. By my troth, I'll tell thee, I am almost sick for one, though I 40
would not have it grow on my chin. Is thy lady within?
CLOWN. Would not a pair of these have bred,[13] sir?
VIO. Yes, being kept together and put to use.
CLOWN. I would play Lord Pandarus of Phrygia,[14] sir, to bring a Cressida to this Troilus. 45
VIO. I understand you, sir. 'Tis well begged.
CLOWN. The matter, I hope, is not great, sir, begging but a beggar: Cressida was a beggar. [VIOLA *tosses him another coin.*] My lady is within, sir. I will conster[15] to them whence you come. Who you are and what you would are out of my welkin[16]—I 50
might say "element," but the word is over-worn.[17]

9. *pilchards:* small fish, very much like herring.
10. *your wisdom:* your worship (Feste is being sarcastic).
11. *pass upon:* make a pass, as in fencing.  12. *commodity:* shipment, cargo.
13. *Would . . . bred:* Wouldn't a pair of these coins breed more money?
14. *Lord Pandarus of Phrygia:* a go-between; Pandarus brought Troilus and Cressida together.  15. *conster:* explain, unfold.  16. *welkin:* literally, heavens or sky.
17. *I might . . . over-worn:* Shakespeare may be making fun of another play in which a character constantly used the word *element* for *sky.*

[*Exit.*]

VIO. This fellow is wise enough to play the fool,
And to do that well craves[18] a kind of wit.
He must observe their mood on whom he jests,
The quality of persons, and the time;  55
Not, like the haggard,[19] check at[20] every feather
That comes before his eye. This is a practice
As full of labor as a wise man's art;
For folly that he wisely shows, is fit;[21]
But wise men, folly-fall'n, quite taint their wit.[22]  60

[*Enter* SIR TOBY *and* SIR ANDREW.]

TO. Save you, gentleman!
VIO. And you, sir.
AND. *Dieu vous garde, monsieur.*[23]
VIO. *Et vous aussi; votre serviteur.*[24]
AND. I hope, sir, you are, and I am yours.  65
TO. Will you encounter[25] the house? My niece is desirous you should enter, if your trade[26] be to her.
VIO. I am bound to your niece, sir. I mean, she is the list[27] of my voyage.
TO. Taste your legs, sir; put them to motion.  70
VIO. My legs do better understand me, sir, than I understand what you mean by bidding me taste my legs.
TO. I mean, to go, sir, to enter.
VIO. I will answer you with gait and entrance. But we are prevented.[28]  75

[*Enter* OLIVIA *and the Gentlewoman* MARIA.]

Most excellent accomplished lady, the heavens rain odors on you!
AND. [*Aside.*] That youth's a rare courtier. "Rain odors"—well!

---

18. *craves:* requires.  19. *the haggard:* the wild hawk.  20. *check at:* pursue.
21. *fit:* skillful.  22. *taint their wit:* call their wit into question.
23. *Dieu vous garde, monsieur:* French; God keep you, sir.
24. *Et vous aussi; votre serviteur:* And you, too, I am your servant.
25. *encounter:* enter. Sir Toby uses extravagant language to ridicule Viola, but she gives as good as she gets.  26. *trade:* business.  27. *the list:* the end, limit.
28. *prevented:* forestalled, anticipated.

VIO. My matter hath no voice, lady, but to your own most pregnant[29] and vouchsafed ear.
AND. [*Aside.*] "Odors," "pregnant," and "vouchsafed"—I'll get 'em all three all ready.
OLI. Let the garden door be shut, and leave me to my hearing.

[*Exeunt* SIR TOBY, SIR ANDREW, *and* MARIA.]

    Give me your hand, sir.
VIO. My duty, madam, and most humble service.
OLI. What is your name?
VIO. Cesario is your servant's name, fair princess.
OLI. My servant, sir? 'Twas never merry world
Since lowly feigning[30] was called compliment.
Y'are servant to the Count Orsino, youth.
VIO. And he is yours, and his[31] must needs be yours.
Your servant's servant is your servant, madam.
OLI. For him, I think not on him; for his thoughts,
Would they were blanks, rather than filled with me!
VIO. Madam, I come to whet your gentle thoughts
On his behalf,
OLI.           O, by your leave, I pray you!
I bade you never speak again of him;
But, would you undertake another suit,
I had rather hear you to solicit that
Than music from the spheres.[32]
VIO.                 Dear lady—
OLI. Give me leave, beseech you. I did send,
After the last enchantment you did here,
A ring in chase of you. So did I abuse[33]
Myself, my servant, and, I fear me, you.
Under your hard construction[34] must I sit,

---

29. *pregnant:* ready.
30. *lowly feigning:* Olivia does not feel that Viola is inferior to her.
31. *his:* his servants.
32. *music from the spheres:* Plato explains in his *Republic* that the earth is surrounded by eight spheres, fitted one within another like casks. The stars and planets are attached to these spheres, which are in motion. A siren sits upon each sphere; each siren sings one note, and the harmonious sound produced is called the music of the spheres.    33. *abuse:* impose upon.
34. *hard construction:* interpretation, critical attitude.

   To force that on you in a shameful cunning   105
   Which you knew none of yours. What might you think?
   Have you not set mine honor at the stake[35]
   And baited[36] it with all the unmuzzled thoughts
   That tyrannous heart can think? To one of your receiving[37]
   Enough is shown; a cypress,[38] not a bosom,   110
   Hides my heart. So, let me hear you speak.
VIO. I pity you.
OLI.     That's a degree[39] to love.
VIO. No, not a grise;[40] for 'tis a vulgar proof[41]
   That very oft we pity enemies.
OLI. Why then, methinks 'tis time to smile again.   115
   O world, how apt the poor are to be proud!
   If one should be a prey, how much the better
   To fall before the lion than the wolf!

[*Clock strikes.*]

   The clock upbraids me with the waste of time.
   Be not afraid, good youth, I will not have you;   120
   And yet, when wit and youth is come to harvest,[42]
   Your wife is like to reap a proper[43] man.
   There lies your way, due west.
VIO.         Then westward ho![44]
   Grace and good disposition attend your ladyship!
   You'll nothing, madam, to my lord by me?   125
OLI. Stay.
   I prithee tell me what thou thinkst of me.
VIO. That you do think you are not what you are.
OLI. If I think so, I think the same of you.
VIO. Then think you right. I am not what I am.   130
OLI. I would you were as I would have you be!
VIO. Would it be better, madam, than I am?
   I wish it might; for now I am your fool.

---

35. *set . . . stake:* like a bear.   36. *baited:* tormented, teased.
37. *receiving:* understanding.
38. *a cypress:* a kerchief made of a fine, gauze-like material.
39. *degree:* step.   40. *grise:* a whole flight of steps.
41. *vulgar proof:* common, everyday experience.
42. *when wit . . . harvest:* when you have matured.   43. *proper:* handsome.
44. *westward ho!* The call of a west-bound boatman on the river Thames in England.

OLI. O, what a deal of scorn looks beautiful
 In the contempt and anger of his lip! 135
 A murd'rous guilt shows not itself more soon
 Than love that would seem hid: love's night is noon.
 Cesario, by the roses of the spring,
 By maidhood, honor, truth, and everything,
 I love thee so that, maugre[45] all thy pride, 140
 Nor wit nor reason can my passion hide.
 Do not extort thy reasons from this clause,
 For that I woo, thou therefore hast no cause;
 But rather reason thus with reason fetter:
 Love sought is good, but given unsought is better. 145
VIO. By innocence I swear, and by my youth,
 I have one heart, one bosom, and one truth,
 And that no woman has; nor never none
 Shall mistress be of it, save I alone.
 And so adieu, good madam. Never more 150
 Will I my master's tears to you deplore.
OLI. Yet come again; for thou perhaps mayst move
 That heart which now abhors to like his love.

[*Exeunt.*]

### SCENE 2. Olivia's house.

[*Enter* SIR TOBY, SIR ANDREW, *and* FABIAN.]

AND. No, faith, I'll not stay a jot longer.
TO. Thy reason, dear venom;[1] give thy reason.
FAB. You must needs yield your reason, Sir Andrew.
AND. Marry, I saw your niece do more favors to the Count's serving-
 man than ever she bestowed upon me. I saw't i' the orchard. 5
TO. Did she see thee the while,[2] old boy? Tell me that.
AND. As plain as I see you now.
FAB. This was a great argument of love in her toward you.
AND. 'Slight! will you make an ass o' me?

---

45. *maugre:* despite, in spite of.

1. *venom:* a possible reference to Sir Andrew's jealous (poisonous) anger.
2. *the while:* during that time.

FAB. I will prove it legitimate,³ sir, upon the oaths of judgment and reason.⁴

TO. And they have been grand-jurymen⁵ since before Noah was a sailor.

FAB. She did show favor to the youth in your sight only to exasperate you, to awake your dormouse⁶ valor, to put fire in your heart and brimstone in your liver. You should then have accosted her; and with some excellent jests, fire-new from the mint,⁷ you should have banged the youth into dumbness. This was looked for at your hand, and this was balked. The double gilt⁸ of this opportunity you let time wash off, and you are now sailed into the North⁹ of my lady's opinion, where you will hang like an icicle on a Dutchman's beard unless you do redeem it by some laudable attempt either of valor or policy.

AND. An't be any way, it must be with valor; for policy I hate. I had as lief¹⁰ be a Brownist¹¹ as a politician.

TO. Why then, build me thy fortunes upon the basis of valor. Challenge me the Count's youth to fight with him; hurt him in eleven places. My niece shall¹² take note of it; and assure thyself there is no love-broker in the world can more prevail in man's commendation with woman than report of valor.

FAB. There is no way but this, Sir Andrew.

AND. Will either of you bear me a challenge to him?

TO. Go, write it in a martial hand. Be curst¹³ and brief; it is no matter how witty, so it be eloquent and full of invention. Taunt him with the license of ink.¹⁴ If thou thou'st him¹⁵ some thrice,

---

3. *legitimate:* legally, as in a court.
4. *upon . . . reason:* Fabian will call judgment and reason as witnesses. Their oaths will prove his case, as, in English law, the oaths of witnesses proved matters at issue.
5. *grand-jurymen:* This is an apparent error. It was the witness, not the grand juror, whose oath was proof.
6. *dormouse:* a small rodent reknowned for its hibernation.
7. *fire-new from the mint:* like new-coined money.
8. *double gilt:* The best gold plate was dipped twice.  9. *the North:* the cold area.
10. *lief:* soon.
11. *Brownist:* a follower of Robert Brown. The Brownists were separatists from the Church of England, their principal objections to that church lying in the areas of discipline and church government. They seem to be popular objects of satire in Elizabethan plays.
12. *shall:* must.  13. *curst:* unpleasant.
14. *the license of ink:* the freedom which pen and ink give.
15. To address a stranger by the familiar form *thou* was an affront.

it shall not be amiss; and as many lies as will lie in thy sheet of paper, although the sheet were big enough for the bed of Ware[16] in England, set 'em down. Go, about it! Let there be gall enough in thy ink, though thou write with a goose-pen, no matter. About it!

AND. Where shall I find you?
TO. We'll call thee at the cubiculo.[17] Go.

[*Exit* SIR ANDREW.]

FAB. This is a dear manikin[18] to you, Sir Toby.
TO. I have been dear[19] to him, lad—some two thousand strong, or so.
FAB. We shall have a rare letter from him—but you'll not deliver't?
TO. Never trust me then; and by all means stir on the youth to an answer. I think oxen and wainropes[20] cannot hale[21] them together. For Andrew, if he were opened, and you find so much blood in his liver as will clog the foot of a flea, I'll eat the rest of the anatomy.
FAB. And his opposite, the youth, bears in his visage no great presage[22] of cruelty.

[*Enter* MARIA.]

TO. Look where the youngest wren[23] of mine comes.
MAR. If you desire the spleen,[24] and will laugh yourselves into stitches, follow me. Yond gull Malvolio is turned heathen, a very renegado;[25] for there is no Christian that means to be saved by believing rightly can ever believe such impossible passages of grossness.[26] He's in yellow stockings!
TO. And cross-gartered?
MAR. Most villainously; like a pedant[27] that keeps a school i' the church. I have dogged him like his murderer. He does obey

---

16. *the bed of Ware:* a famous bed so large it could hold four couples.
17. *the cubiculo:* this may mean a bed-chamber or private apartment, or it may have been the name of a particular room in Olivia's house.
18. *manikin:* plaything, puppet.     19. *dear:* expensive, costly.
20. *wainropes:* wagon ropes.     21. *hale:* draw or pull.     22. *presage:* prediction.
23. *wren:* a small, vivacious bird.     24. *the spleen:* considered the seat of mirth.
25. *renegado:* one who forsakes a religious faith, particularly a Christian who becomes a Mohammedan.     26. *passages of grossness:* absurd acts.
27. *pedant:* schoolmaster.

every point of the letter that I dropped to betray him. He does smile his face into more lines than is in the new map with the augmentation of the Indies.²⁸ You have not seen such a thing as 'tis. I can hardly forbear hurling things at him. I know my lady will strike him. If she do, he'll smile, and take't for a great favor. 65
TO. Come bring us, bring us where he is!

[*Exeunt.*]

SCENE 3. A street.

[*Enter* SEBASTIAN *and* ANTONIO.]

SEB. I would not by my will have troubled you;
   But since you make your pleasure of your pains,
   I will no further chide you.
ANT. I could not stay behind you. My desire,
   More sharp than filed steel, did spur me forth; 5
   And not all love to see you (though so much
   As might have drawn one to a longer voyage)
   But jealousy¹ what might befall your travel,
   Being skilless in these parts; which to a stranger,
   Unguided and unfriended, often prove 10
   Rough and unhospitable. My willing love,
   The rather by these arguments of fear,
   Set forth in your pursuit.
SEB.                My kind Antonio,
   I can no other answer make but thanks,
   And thanks, and ever thanks; for oft good turns 15
   Are shuffled off with such uncurrent² pay.
   But, were my worth³ as is my conscience⁴ firm,
   You should find better dealing. What's to do?
   Shall we go see the relics of this town?

---

28. *new . . . Indies:* Maria refers to a map which was probably published in 1599. It was prepared on a new projection and was augmented by showing all of the East Indies, including Japan, and showing these more accurately and in greater detail than had previous maps.

1. *jealousy:* apprehension, fear.   2. *uncurrent:* counterfeit.   3. *worth:* wealth.
4. *conscience:* consciousness of what I owe you.

Twelfth Night    49

ANT. Tomorrow, sir; best first go see your lodging.
SEB. I am not weary, and 'tis long to night.
  I pray you let us satisfy our eyes
  With the memorials and the things of fame
  That do renown this city.
ANT.                   Would you'ld pardon me.
  I do not without danger walk these streets.
  Once in a sea-fight 'gainst the Count his galleys
  I did some service; of such note indeed
  That, were I ta'en here, it would scarce be answered.[5]
SEB. Belike you slew great number of his people?
ANT. The offense is not of such a bloody nature,
  Albeit[6] the quality of the time and quarrel
  Might well have given us bloody argument.[7]
  It might have since been answered[8] in repaying
  What we took from them, which for traffic's sake[9]
  Most of our city did. Only myself stood out;
  For which, if I be lapsed[10] in this place,
  I shall pay dear.
SEB.            Do not then walk too open.
ANT. It doth not fit me. Hold, sir, here's my purse.
  In the south suburbs at the Elephant[11]
  Is best to lodge. I will bespeak our diet,[12]
  Whiles you beguile the time and feed your knowledge
  With viewing of the town. There shall you have me.
SEB. Why I your purse?
ANT. Haply your eye shall light upon some toy
  You have desire to purchase; and your store
  I think is not for idle markets, sir.
SEB. I'll be your purse-bearer, and leave you for
  An hour.
ANT.       To the Elephant.
SEB.                I do remember.

[*Exeunt.*]

---

5. *answered:* defended.    6. *Albeit:* although.    7. *argument:* reason.
8. *answered:* made up for.    9. *traffic's sake:* the sake of trade.
10. *be lapsed:* caught unawares, surprised.
11. *the Elephant:* an inn (actually an English inn).    12. *diet:* daily fare.

SCENE 4. Olivia's garden.

[*Enter* OLIVIA *and* MARIA.]

OLI. I have sent after him; he says he'll come.[1]
How shall I feast him? what bestow of[2] him?
For youth is bought more oft than begged or borrowed.
I speak too loud.
Where is Malvolio?  He is sad and civil,[3]  5
And suits well for a servant with my fortunes.
Where is Malvolio?
MAR. He's coming, madam; but in very strange manner.  He is sure possessed, madam.
OLI. Why, what's the matter?  Does he rave?  10
MAR. No, madam, he does nothing but smile.  Your ladyship were best to have some guard about you if he come, for sure the man is tainted in's wits.
OLI. Go call him hither. [*Exit* MARIA.]  I am as mad as he,
If sad and merry madness equal be.  15

[*Enter* MARIA, *with* MALVOLIO.]

How now, Malvolio?
MAL. Sweet lady, ho, ho!
OLI. Smilest thou?
I sent for thee upon a sad occasion.
MAL. Sad, lady?  I could be sad.  This does make some obstruction  20
in the blood, this cross-gartering; but what of that?  If it please the eye of one, it is with me as the very true sonnet is, "Please one, and please all."[4]
OLI. Why, how dost thou, man?  What is the matter with thee?
MAL. Not black in my mind, though yellow in my legs.  It did come  25
to his hands, and commands shall be executed.  I think we do know the sweet Roman hand.[5]
OLI. Wilt thou go to bed, Malvolio?
MAL. To bed?  Ay, sweetheart; and I'll come to thee.

1. *he says . . . come:* suppose he says he'll come.   2. *of:* on.
3. *sad and civil:* solemn and grave.
4. *"Please one, and please all."*  A popular ballad.
5. *the sweet Roman hand:* the Italian (Roman) style of handwriting, which was becoming popular in Shakespeare's time.

Twelfth Night

OLI. God comfort thee! Why dost thou smile so, and kiss thy hand[6] 30
so oft?
MAR. How do you, Malvolio?
MAL. At your request? Yes, nightingales answer daws![7]
MAR. Why appear you with this ridiculous boldness before my lady?
MAL. "Be not afraid of greatness." 'Twas well writ. 35
OLI. What meanst thou by that, Malvolio?
MAL. "Some are born great"—
OLI. Ha?
MAL. "Some achieve greatness"—
OLI. What sayst thou? 40
MAL. "And some have greatness thrust upon them."
OLI. Heaven restore thee!
MAL. "Remember who commended thy yellow stockings"—
OLI. Thy yellow stockings?
MAL. "And wished to see thee cross-gartered." 45
OLI. Cross-gartered?
MAL. "Go to, thou art made, if thou desirest to be so"—
OLI. Am I made?
MAL. "If not, let me see thee a servant still."
OLI. Why, this is very midsummer madness.[8] 50

[*Enter* SERVANT.]

SER. Madam, the young gentleman of the Count Orsino's is returned. I could hardly entreat him back. He attends your ladyship's pleasure.
OLI. I'll come to him. [*Exit* SERVANT.] Good Maria, let this fellow be looked to. Where's my cousin Toby? Let some of my people 55 have a special care of him. I would not have him miscarry[9] for the half of my dowry.

[*Exit* OLIVIA; *then* MARIA.]

MAL. O ho! do you come near[10] me now? No worse man than Sir Toby to look to me! This concurs directly with the letter. She sends him on purpose, that I may appear stubborn to him; for she 60

---

6. *kiss thy hand:* Malvolio believes he is displaying courtly manners by kissing his fingers.   7. *At . . . daws!* Addressed to Maria.
8. *midsummer madness:* midsummer was considered the season of madness.
9. *miscarry:* come to grief.   10. *come near:* understand.

52                                                                                          Act III, 4

incites me to that in the letter. "Cast thy humble slough," says she; "be opposite with a kinsman, surly with servants; let thy tongue tang with arguments of state; put thyself into the trick of singularity";—and consequently sets down the manner how: as, a sad face, a reverend carriage, a slow tongue, in the habit of some sir of note,[11] and so forth. I have limed her;[12] but it is Jove's doing, and Jove make me thankful! And when she went away now, "Let this fellow be looked to." "Fellow!"[13] not "Malvolio," nor after my degree, but "fellow." Why, everything adheres together, that no dram[14] of a scruple,[15] no scruple[16] of a scruple, no obstacle, no incredulous or unsafe circumstance—What can be said? Nothing that can be can come between me and the full prospect of my hopes. Well, Jove, not I, is the doer of this, and he is to be thanked.

[*Enter* SIR TOBY, FABIAN, *and* MARIA.]

TO. Which way is he, in the name of sanctity? If all the devils of hell be drawn in little, and Legion[17] himself possessed him, yet I'll speak to him.

FAB. Here he is, here he is! How is't with you, sir? How is't with you, man?

MAL. Go off; I discard you. Let me enjoy my private.[18] Go off.

MAR. Lo, how hollow the fiend speaks within him! Did not I tell you? Sir Toby, my lady prays you to have a care of him.

MAL. Aha! does she so?

TO. Go to, go to; peace, peace! We must deal gently with him. Let me alone. How do you, Malvolio? How is't with you? What, man! defy the devil! Consider, he's an enemy to mankind.

MAL. Do you know what you say?

MAR. La you, an you speak ill of the devil, how he takes it at heart! Pray God he be not bewitched!

FAB. Carry his water to the wise woman.[19]

---

11. *some sir of note:* some man of importance.
12. *limed her:* caught her, as a bird is caught in birdlime.
13. *"Fellow!"* Companion.   14. *dram:* a measure, ⅛ fluid ounce.
15. *scruple:* doubt or uncertainty.   16. *scruple:* a unit of weight, ¹⁄₂₄ ounce.
17. *Legion:* In *Mark, V*, when Jesus asked the unclean spirit his name, he replied "My name is Legion; for we are many."   18. *private:* privacy.
19. *Carry . . . woman:* so that she may diagnose his case. This practice, of course, was a form of divination rather than medicine.

**Twelfth Night**

MAR. Marry, and it shall be done tomorrow morning if I live. My lady would not lose him for more than I'll say.

MAL. How now, mistress?

MAR. O Lord!

TO. Prithee hold thy peace. This is not the way. Do you not see you move him? Let me alone with him.

FAB. No way but gentleness; gently, gently. The fiend is rough and will not be roughly used.

TO. Why, how now, my bawcock?[20] How dost thou, chuck?[21]

MAL. Sir!

TO. Ay, biddy, come with me.[22] What, man! 'tis not for gravity to play at cherry-pit[23] with Satan. Hang him, foul collier![24]

MAR. Get him to say his prayers. Good Sir Toby, get him to pray.

MAL. My prayers, minx?[25]

MAR. No, I warrant you, he will not hear of godliness.

MAL. Go hang yourselves all! You are idle shallow things; I am not of your element. You shall know more hereafter.

[*Exit.*]

TO. Is't possible?

FAB. If this were played upon a stage now, I could condemn it as an improbable fiction.

TO. His very genius[26] hath taken the infection of the device, man.

MAR. Nay, pursue him now, lest the device take air and taint.[27]

FAB. Why, we shall make him mad indeed.

MAR. The house will be the quieter.

TO. Come, we'll have him in a dark room and bound.[28] My niece is already in the belief that he's mad. We may carry it thus, for our pleasure and his penance, till our very pastime, tired out of breath, prompt us to have mercy on him; at which time we will bring the device to the bar[29] and crown thee for a finder of madmen.[30] But see, but see!

20. *bawcock:* a burlesque term of affection.   21. *chuck:* chick.
22. *Ay . . . me:* this may possibly be a scrap of an old song.
23. *cherry-pit:* a game in which cherry pits were tossed into a small hole.
24. *foul collier:* the devil. The devil was frequently called a collier (a coal miner) because of his supposed blackness.   25. *minx:* giggle, flirt.
26. *genius:* innermost being, spiritual nature.   27. *taint:* spoil.
28. *we'll have . . . bound:* a customary treatment for madness.
29. *to the bar:* to court.
30. *a finder of madmen:* one who acted under a writ which directed him to find out whether the person charged was a lunatic.

[*Enter* SIR ANDREW.]

FAB. More matter for a May morning.[31]

AND. Here's the challenge; read it. I warrant there's vinegar and pepper in't.

FAB. Is't so saucy?

AND. Ay, is't, I warrant him.[32] Do not read.

TO. Give me. [*Reads.*] "Youth, whatsoever thou art, thou art but a scurvy fellow."

FAB. Good, and valiant.

TO. [*Reads.*] "Wonder not nor admire not[33] in thy mind why I do call thee so, for I will show thee no reason for't."

FAB. A good note! That keeps you from the blow of the law.

TO. [*Reads.*] "Thou comest to the Lady Olivia, and in my sight she uses thee kindly. But thou liest in thy throat;[34] that is not the matter I challenge thee for."

FAB. Very brief, and to exceeding good sense—less.

TO. [*Reads.*] "I will waylay thee going home; where if it be thy chance to kill me"—

FAB. Good.

TO. [*Reads.*] "Thou killst me like a rogue and a villain."

FAB. Still you keep o' the windy side[35] of the law. Good.

TO. [*Reads.*] "Fare thee well, and God have mercy upon one of our souls! He may have mercy upon mine, but my hope is better; and so look to thyself. Thy friend, as thou usest him, and thy sworn enemy,

"ANDREW AGUECHEEK."

If this letter move him not, his legs cannot. I'll give't him.

MAR. You may have very fit occasion for't. He is now in some commerce with my lady and will by-and-by depart.

TO. Go, Sir Andrew! Scout me for him at the corner of the orchard like a bum-baily.[36] So soon as ever thou seest him, draw; and as thou drawst, swear horrible; for it comes to pass oft that a terrible oath, with a swaggering accent sharply twanged off,

---

31. *matter for a May morning:* material suitable for the fun and games of an English May Day celebration.   32. *I warrant him:* I challenge him.
33. *admire not:* be not amazed.
34. *thou liest in thy throat:* a stronger accusation than the simple "Thou liest."
35. *the windy side:* the safe side; the term is derived from the practice of the hunting dog in keeping downwind from the game.
36. *a bum-baily:* a bumbailiff; a minor bailiff (sheriff's deputy) charged with such lowly jobs as arrests.

Twelfth Night

gives manhood more approbation than ever proof itself would have earned him. Away!

AND. Nay, let me alone for swearing. 155

[*Exit.*]

TO. Now will not I deliver his letter; for the behavior of the young gentleman gives him out to be of good capacity and breeding; his employment between his lord and my niece confirms no less. Therefore this letter, being so excellently ignorant, will breed no terror in the youth. He will find it comes from a clodpoll.³⁷ 160 But, sir, I will deliver his challenge by word of mouth, set upon Aguecheek a notable report of valor, and drive the gentleman (as I know his youth will aptly receive it) into a most hideous opinion of his rage, skill, fury, and impetuosity. This will so fright them both that they will kill one another by the look, like 165 cockatrices.³⁸

[*Enter* OLIVIA *and* VIOLA.]

FAB. Here he comes with your niece. Give them way till he take leave, and presently after him.

TO. I will meditate the while upon some horrid message for a challenge. 170

[*Exeunt* SIR TOBY, FABIAN, *and* MARIA.]

OLI. I have said too much unto a heart of stone
And laid mine honor too unchary³⁹ out.
There's something in me that reproves my fault;
But such a headstrong potent fault it is
That it but mocks reproof. 175

VIO. With the same 'havior that your passion bears
Goes on my master's grief.

OLI. Here, wear this jewel⁴⁰ for me; 'tis my picture.
Refuse it not; it hath no tongue to vex you.
And I beseech you come again tomorrow. 180

37. *a clodpoll:* a blockhead.
38. *cockatrices:* fabled serpents (the Basilisks) whose very glance supposedly could kill.   39. *unchary:* generously, lavishly.
40. *jewel:* any valuable ornament; not confined to gems.

> What shall you ask of me that I'll deny,
> That honor, saved, may upon asking give?

VIO. Nothing but this—your true love for my master.

OLI. How with mine honor may I give him that
> Which I have given to you?

VIO.                      I will acquit[41] you.        185

OLI. Well, come again tomorrow. Fare thee well.
> A fiend like thee might bear my soul to hell.

[*Exit.*]

[*Enter* SIR TOBY *and* FABIAN.]

TO. Gentleman, God save thee!

VIO. And you, sir.

TO. That defense thou hast, betake thee to't. Of what nature the wrongs are thou hast done him, I know not; but thy intercepter, full of despite,[42] bloody as the hunter, attends thee at the orchard end. Dismount thy tuck,[43] be yare[44] in thy preparation; for thy assailant is quick, skillful, and deadly.

VIO. You mistake, sir. I am sure no man hath any quarrel to[45] me. My remembrance is very free and clear from any image of offense done to any man.

TO. You'll find it otherwise, I assure you. Therefore, if you hold your life at any price, betake you to your guard; for your opposite hath in him what youth, strength, skill, and wrath can furnish man withal.

VIO. I pray you, sir, what is he?

TO. He is knight, dubbed with unhatched[46] rapier and on carpet consideration;[47] but he is a devil in private brawl. Souls and bodies hath he divorced three; and his incensement at this moment is so implacable that satisfaction can be none but by pangs of death and sepulcher. "Hob, nob" is his word; "give't or take't."

VIO. I will return again into the house and desire some conduct[48] of the lady. I am no fighter. I have heard of some kind of men

---

41. *acquit:* release.    42. *despite:* outrage, injury.
43. *Dismount thy tuck:* Draw your sword.    44. *yare:* quick, ready.
45. *to:* against.    46. *unhatched:* not dented from battle, unhacked.
47. *on carpet consideration:* the implication is that Sir Andrew purchased his knighthood.    48. *conduct:* guide.

# Twelfth Night

that put quarrels purposely on others to taste their valor. Belike 210
this is a man of that quirk.⁴⁹

TO. Sir, no. His indignation derives itself out of a very competent⁵⁰ injury; therefore get you on and give him his desire. Back you shall not to the house, unless you undertake that with me which with as much safety you might answer him. Therefore on! or 215 strip your sword stark naked; for meddle you must, that's certain, or forswear to wear iron about you.

VIO. This is as uncivil as strange. I beseech you do me this courteous office, as to know of the knight what my offense to him is. It is something of my negligence, nothing of my purpose. 220

TO. I will do so. Signior Fabian, stay you by this gentleman till my return.

[*Exit.*]

VIO. Pray you, sir, do you know of this matter?

FAB. I know the knight is incensed against you, even to a mortal arbitrament;⁵¹ but nothing of the circumstance more. 225

VIO. I beseech you, what manner of man is he?

FAB. Nothing of that wonderful promise, to read him by his form, as you are like to find him in the proof of his valor. He is indeed, sir, the most skillful, bloody, and fatal opposite that you could possibly have found in any part of Illyria. Will you walk 230 towards him? I will make your peace with him if I can.

VIO. I shall be much bound to you for't. I am one that had rather go with sir priest than sir knight. I care not who knows so much of my mettle.

[*Exeunt.*]

[*Enter* SIR TOBY *and* SIR ANDREW.]

TO. Why, man, he's a very devil; I have not seen such a virago.⁵² I 235 had a pass with him, rapier, scabbard, and all, and he gives me the stuck⁵³ in with such a mortal⁵⁴ motion that it is inevitable;

---

49. *quirk:* whim, caprice.   50. *competent:* sufficient.
51. *a mortal arbitrament:* a decision by a fight to the death.
52. *virago:* a term used ordinarily for a heroic, vigorous, man-like woman; it was rarely applied to a man. As it is used here it suggests a man who was ferocious and furious as well as heroic and vigorous.
53. *the stuck:* the stoccata, or thrust; a fencing term.   54. *mortal:* deadly.

and on the answer[55] he pays you[56] as surely as your feet hit the ground they step on. They say he has been fencer to the Sophy.

AND. Pox on't, I'll not meddle with him.

TO. Ay, but he will not now be pacified. Fabian can scarce hold him yonder.

AND. Plague on't, an I thought he had been valiant, and so cunning in fence, I'd have seen him damned ere I'd have challenged him. Let him let the matter slip, and I'll give him my horse, grey Capilet.

TO. I'll make the motion. Stand here; make a good show on't. This shall end without the perdition of souls. [*Aside.*] Marry, I'll ride your horse as well as I ride you.

[*Enter* FABIAN *and* VIOLA.]

I have his horse to take up[57] the quarrel. I have persuaded him the youth's a devil.

FAB. He is as horribly conceited of him;[58] and pants and looks pale, as if a bear were at his heels.

TO. There's no remedy, sir; he will fight with you for's oath sake. Marry, he hath better bethought him of his quarrel, and he finds that now scarce to be worth talking of. Therefore draw for the supportance of his vow. He protests he will not hurt you.

VIO. [*Aside.*] Pray God defend me! A little thing would make me tell them how much I lack of a man.

FAB. Give ground if you see him furious.

TO. Come, Sir Andrew, there's no remedy. The gentlemen will for his honor's sake have one bout with you; he cannot by the duello[59] avoid it; but he has promised me, as he is a gentleman and a soldier, he will not hurt you. Come on, to't!

AND. Pray God he keep his oath! [*Draws.*]

[*Enter* ANTONIO.]

VIO. I do assure you 'tis against my will. [*Draws.*]

ANT. Put up your sword. If this young gentleman
   Have done offense, I take the fault on me;
   If you offend him, I for him defy you.

55. *the answer:* the return hit; a fencing term.   56. *he pays you:* he hits you.
57. *take up:* resolve.
58. *is as horribly conceited of him:* has just as horrible a conception of him.
59. *the duello:* the duelling code.

Twelfth Night    59

TO. You, sir? Why, what are you? 270
ANT. [*Draws.*] One, sir, that for his love dares yet do more
   Than you have heard him brag to you he will.
TO. Nay, if you be an undertaker,⁶⁰ I am for you. [*Draws.*]

[*Enter* OFFICERS.]

FAB. O good Sir Toby, hold! Here come the officers.
TO. I'll be with you anon.⁶¹ 275
VIO. Pray, sir, put your sword up, if you please.
AND. Marry, will I, sir; and for that I promise you,⁶² I'll be as good
   as my word. He will bear you easily, and reins well.
1. OFF. This is the man; do thy office.
2. OFF. Antonio, I arrest thee at the suit 280
   Of Count Orsino.
ANT.            You do mistake me, sir.
1. OFF. No, sir, no jot. I know your favor⁶³ well,
   Though now you have no sea-cap on your head.
   Take him away. He knows I know him well.
ANT. I must obey. [*To* VIOLA.] This comes with seeking you. 285
   But there's no remedy; I shall answer it.
   What will you do, now my necessity
   Makes me to ask you for my purse? It grieves me
   Much more for what I cannot do for you
   Than what befalls myself. You stand amazed, 290
   But be of comfort.
2. OFF. Come, sir, away.
ANT. I must entreat of you some of that money.
VIO. What money, sir?
   For the fair kindness you have showed me here, 295
   And part being prompted by your present trouble,
   Out of my lean and low ability
   I'll lend you something. My having is not much.
   I'll make division of my present⁶⁴ with you.
   Hold, there's half my coffer.⁶⁵
ANT.            Will you deny me now? 300

---

60. *an undertaker:* an invidious name in the early seventeenth century. It is
intended as an insult.   61. *anon:* at once.   62. *that I promised you:* the horse.
63. *favor:* face.   64. *present:* possession.   65. *coffer:* treasure.

Act III, 4

>             Is't possible that my deserts to you
>             Can lack persuasion?  Do not tempt my misery,
>             Lest that it make me so unsound a man
>             As to upbraid you with those kindnesses
>             That I have done for you.
> VIO.                      I know of none, 305
>             Nor know I you by voice or any feature.
>             I hate ingratitude more in a man
>             Than lying, vainness, babbling drunkenness,
>             Or any taint of vice whose strong corruption
>             Inhabits our frail blood.
> ANT.                   O heavens themselves! 310
> 2. OFF. Come, sir, I pray you go.
> ANT. Let me speak a little.  This youth that you see here
>             I snatched one half out of the jaws of death;
>             Relieved him with such sanctity of love,
>             And to his image, which methought did promise 315
>             Most venerable worth, did I devotion.
> 1. OFF. What's that to us?  The time goes by.  Away!
> ANT. But, O, how vile an idol proves this god!
>             Thou hast, Sebastian, done good feature, shame.
>             In nature there's no blemish but the mind; 320
>             None can be called deformed but the unkind.[66]
>             Virtue is beauty; but the beauteous evil
>             Are empty trunks, o'erflourished by the devil.
> 1. OFF. The man grows mad.  Away with him!  Come, come, sir.
> ANT. Lead me on. 325
>
> [*Exit with* OFFICERS.]
>
> VIO. Methinks his words do from such passion fly
>             That he believes himself; so do not I.
>             Prove true, imagination, O, prove true,
>             That I, dear brother, be now ta'en for you!
> TO. Come hither, knight; come hither, Fabian.  We'll whisper o'er a 330
>             couplet or two of most sage saws.[67]
> VIO. He named Sebastian.  I my brother know

66. *unkind:* unnatural.
67. *sage saws:* wise sayings; Sir Toby is ridiculing Antonio's moralizing.

Twelfth Night  61

  Yet living in my glass.⁶⁸ Even such and so
  In favor was my brother, and he went
  Still in this fashion, color, ornament,         335
  For him I imitate. O, if it prove,⁶⁹
  Tempests are kind, and salt waves fresh in love!

[*Exit.*]

TO. A very dishonest paltry boy, and more a coward than a hare.
  His dishonesty appears in leaving his friend here in necessity and
  denying him; and for his cowardship, ask Fabian.   340
FAB. A coward, a most devout coward; religious in it.⁷⁰
AND. 'Slid,⁷¹ I'll after him again and beat him!
TO. Do; cuff him soundly, but never draw thy sword.
AND. An I do not—

[*Exit.*]

FAB. Come, let's see the event.            345
TO. I dare lay any money 'twill be nothing yet.

[*Exeunt.*]

# ACT IV

### SCENE 1. Before Olivia's house.

[*Enter* SEBASTIAN *and* CLOWN.]

CLOWN. Will you make me believe that I am not sent for you?
SEB. Go to, go to,¹ thou art a foolish fellow. Let me be clear of thee.
CLOWN. Well held out, i' faith! No, I do not know you; nor I am not
  sent to you by my lady, to bid you come speak with her; nor
  your name is not Master Cesario; nor this is not my nose neither.  5
  Nothing that is so is so.

---

68. *glass:* looking glass, mirror.   69. *if it prove:* if it prove to be so.
70. *religious in it:* practicing cowardice religiously.   71. *'Slid:* a petty oath.

1. *Go to, go to:* an expression of impatience.

SEB. I prithee vent thy folly somewhere else. Thou knowst not me.
CLOWN. Vent my folly! He has heard that word of some great man, and now applies it to a fool.² Vent my folly! I am afraid this great lubber, the world, will prove a cockney.³ I prithee now, ungird thy strangeness, and tell me what I shall vent to my lady. Shall I vent to her that thou art coming?
SEB. I prithee, foolish Greek,⁴ depart from me. There's money for thee. If you tarry longer, I shall give worse payment.
CLOWN. By my troth, thou hast an open hand. These wise men that give fools money get themselves a good report—after fourteen years' purchase.⁵

[*Enter* SIR ANDREW, SIR TOBY, *and* FABIAN.]

AND. Now, sir, have I met you again? There's for you! [*Striking* SEBASTIAN.]
SEB. Why, there's for thee, and there, and there! [*Returning the blow.*]
Are all the people mad?
TO. Hold, sir, or I'll throw your dagger o'er the house.
CLOWN. This will I tell my lady straight.⁶ I would not be in some of your coats for twopence.

[*Exit.*]

TO. Come on, sir; hold!
AND. Nay, let him alone. I'll go another way to work with him. I'll have an action of battery against him, if there be any law in Illyria. Though I stroke⁷ him first, yet it's no matter for that.⁸
SEB. Let go thy hand.
TO. Come, sir, I will not let you go.⁹ Come, my young soldier, put up your iron. You are well fleshed.¹⁰ Come on.

---

2. *He has . . . fool:* Feste is commenting on what he considers affected, effeminate expression.   3. *cockney:* a milksop, an effeminate man.
4. *Greek:* a common Elizabethan meaning of this term was a merry, jocular fellow. It may, on the other hand, have signified a procurer (Feste after all, was trying to get Sebastian to visit his mistress).   5. *fourteen years' purchase:* a very high price.
6. *strait:* immediately.   7. *stroke:* struck.
8. *Though . . . that:* Sir Andrew could hardly bring an action for battery if he himself struck the first blow.   9. *Come . . . go:* Addressed to Sebastian.
10. *Come . . . fleshed:* Addressed to Sir Andrew.

Twelfth Night

SEB. I will be free from thee. What wouldst thou now? [*Draws.*]
    If thou darest tempt me further, draw thy sword.
TO. What, what? Nay then, I must have an ounce or two of this
    malapert[11] blood from you. [*Draws.*]

[*Enter* OLIVIA.]

OLI. Hold, Toby! On thy life I charge thee hold!                35
TO. Madam!
OLI. Will it be ever thus? Ungracious wretch,
    Fit for the mountains and the barbarous caves,
    Where manners ne'er were preached! Out of my sight!
    Be not offended, dear Cesario.                               40
    Rudesby,[12] be gone!

[*Exeunt* SIR TOBY, SIR ANDREW, *and* FABIAN.]

                    I prithee, gentle friend,
    Let thy fair wisdom, not thy passion, sway
    In this uncivil and unjust extent[13]
    Against thy peace. Go with me to my house,
    And hear thou there how many fruitless pranks               45
    This ruffian hath botched up,[14] that thou thereby
    Mayst smile at this. Thou shalt not choose but go;
    Do not deny. Beshrew his soul for me!
    He started[15] one poor heart of mine, in thee.
SEB. What relish is in this?[16] How runs the stream?            50
    Or I am mad, or else this is a dream.
    Let fancy still my sense in Lethe[17] steep;
    If it be thus to dream, still let me sleep!
OLI. Nay, come, I prithee. Would thou'dst be ruled by me!
SEB. Madam, I will.
OLI.            O, say so, and so be!                            55

[*Exeunt.*]

---

11. *malapert:* saucy, knavish.    12. *Rudesby:* an unmannerly, disorderly fellow.
13. *extent:* attack, violence.    14. *botched up:* put together ineptly.
15. *started:* a hunting expression. To start an animal was to cause it to move
suddenly.    16. *What . . . this?* What am I to make of this?
17. *Lethe:* the river of forgetfulness in Hades.

SCENE 2. Olivia's house.

[*Enter* MARIA *and* CLOWN.]

MAR. Nay, I prithee put on this gown and this beard; make him believe thou art Sir Topas the curate; do it quickly. I'll call Sir Toby the whilst. [*Exit.*]
CLOWN. Well, I'll put it on, and I will dissemble myself in't, and I would I were the first that ever dissembled in such a gown. I am not tall[1] enough to become the function well, nor lean enough to be thought a good student; but to be said[2] an honest man and a good housekeeper goes as fairly as to say a careful man and a great scholar. The competitors[3] enter.

[*Enter* SIR TOBY *and* MARIA.]

TO. Jove bless thee, Master Parson.
CLOWN. *Bonos dies,* Sir Toby; for, as the old hermit of Prague, that never saw pen and ink, very wittily said to a niece of King Gorboduc,[4] "That that is is"; so I, being Master Parson, am Master Parson; for what is "that" but "that," and "is" but "is"?
TO. To him, Sir Topas.
CLOWN. What ho, I say. Peace in this prison!
TO. The knave counterfeits well; a good knave.

[MALVOLIO *within.*]

MAL. Who calls there?
CLOWN. Sir Topas the curate, who comes to visit Malvolio the lunatic.
MAL. Sir Topas, Sir Topas, good Sir Topas, go to my lady.
CLOWN. Out, hyperbolical[5] fiend! How vexest thou this man! Talkest thou nothing but of ladies?
TO. Well said, Master Parson.
MAL. Sir Topas, never was man thus wronged. Good Sir Topas, do not think I am mad. They have laid me here in hideous darkness.
CLOWN. Fie, thou dishonest Satan! I call thee by the most modest

1. *tall:* stout portly.   2. *to be said:* to be called.   3. *competitors:* confederates.
4. *as . . . King Gorboduc:* more nonsensical "learning" by the Clown.
5. *hyperbolical:* a term used in rhetoric (the study of the rules of composition of ancient critics) to mean exaggerated or extravagant.

terms; for I am one of those gentle ones that will use the Devil himself with courtesy. Sayst thou that house[6] is dark?[7]

MAL. As hell, Sir Topas.

CLOWN. Why, it hath bay windows transparent as barricadoes,[8] and the clerestories[9] toward the south north are as lustrous as ebony; and yet complainest thou of obstruction?

MAL. I am not mad, Sir Topas. I say to you this house is dark.

CLOWN. Madman, thou errest. I say there is no darkness but ignorance, in which thou art more puzzled than the Egyptians in their fog.[10]

MAL. I say this house is as dark as ignorance, though ignorance were as dark as hell; and I say there was never man thus abused. I am no more mad than you are. Make the trial of it in any constant question.[11]

CLOWN. What is the opinion of Pythagoras[12] concerning wild fowl?

MAL. That the soul of our grandam might happily inhabit a bird.[13]

CLOWN. What thinkst thou of his opinion?

MAL. I think nobly of the soul and no way approve his opinion.

CLOWN. Fare thee well. Remain thou still in darkness. Thou shalt hold the opinion of Pythagoras ere I will allow of thy wits, and fear to kill a woodcock, lest thou dispossess the soul of thy grandam. Fare thee well.

MAL. Sir Topas, Sir Topas!

TO. My most exquisite Sir Topas!

CLOWN. Nay, I am for all waters.[14]

MAR. Thou mightst have done this without thy beard and gown. He sees thee not.

---

6. *that house:* the small room in which Malvolio lies. Feste is outside, looking in through the door or window.
7. *dark:* Madmen were treated by being placed in a darkened room, often called a *dark house.*    8. *barricadoes:* barricades.
9. *clerestories:* the upper parts of large churches containing windows whose function was to admit light to the central part of the building.
10. *the Egyptians in their fog:* the thick darkness ("a darkness to be felt") which came over the land of Egypt when Moses stretched out his hand toward heaven. *Exodus, X, 21–23.*    11. *constant question:* formal discussion.
12. *Pythagoras:* a Greek philosopher who is credited with originating the doctrine of the transmigration of souls between human beings and between human beings and animals.
13. *That . . . bird:* It was believed in Elizabethan times that one who could recall the previous habitation of his soul could not possibly be insane.
14. *I . . . waters:* I can do anything.

TO. To him in thine own voice, and bring me word how thou findst    55
him.  I would we were well rid of this knavery.  If he may be
conveniently delivered, I would he were; for I am now so far in
offense with my niece that I cannot pursue with any safety this
sport to the upshot.[15]  Come by-and-by to my chamber.

[*Exit with* MARIA.]

CLOWN. [*Singing.*]
"Hey, Robin, jolly Robin,                                          60
   Tell me how thy lady does."
MAL. Fool!
CLOWN. "My lady is unkind, perdie!"[16]
MAL. Fool!
CLOWN. "Alas, why is she so?"                                      65
MAL. Fool, I say!
CLOWN. "She loves another"—Who calls, ha?
MAL. Good fool, as ever thou wilt deserve well at my hand, help me
to a candle, and pen, ink, and paper.  As I am a gentleman,
I will live to be thankful to thee for't.                          70
CLOWN. Master Malvolio?
MAL. Ay, good fool.
CLOWN. Alas, sir, how fell you besides[17] your five wits?[18]
MAL. Fool, there was never man so notoriously abused.  I am as
well in my wits, fool, as thou art.                                75
CLOWN. But as well?[19]  Then you are mad indeed, if you be no better
in your wits than a fool.
MAL. They have here propertied me;[20] keep me in darkness, send
ministers to me, asses, and do all they can to face me[21] out of
my wits.                                                           80
CLOWN. Advise you what you say.  The minister is here.—Malvolio,
Malvolio, thy wits the heavens restore!  Endeavor thyself to
sleep[22] and leave thy vain bibble babble.

---

15. *the upshot:* the conclusion; in archery the upshot was the decisive shot.
16. *perdie:* by God; a corruption of the French *par Dieu.*    17. *besides:* out of.
18. *five wits:* The five wits have been listed as estimation, fantasy, memory, imagination, and common wit.    19. *But as well?* But only as well?
20. *They . . . me:* Either (1) they have treated me like a piece of property, or (2) they have, in shutting me in this small dark room (like the storage room for stage properties), treated me like a stage property.    21. *face me:* cheat me.
22. *Endeavor . . . sleep:* try to sleep.

Twelfth Night

MAL. Sir Topas!

CLOWN. Maintain no words with him, good fellow.[23]—Who, I, sir? Not I, sir. God be wi' you, good Sir Topas!—Marry, amen.—I will, sir, I will.

MAL. Fool, fool, fool, I say!

CLOWN. Alas, sir, be patient. What say you, sir? I am shent[24] for speaking to you.

MAL. Good fool, help me to some light and some paper. I tell thee, I am as well in my wits as any man in Illyria.

CLOWN. Well-a-day[25] that you were, sir!

MAL. By this hand, I am. Good fool, some ink, paper, and light; and convey what I will set down to my lady. It shall advantage thee more than ever the bearing of letter did.

CLOWN. I will help you to't. But tell me true, are you not mad indeed? or do you but counterfeit?

MAL. Believe me, I am not. I tell thee true.

CLOWN. Nay, I'll ne'er believe a madman till I see his brains. I will fetch you light and paper and ink.

MAL. Fool, I'll requite it in the highest degree. I prithee be gone.

CLOWN. [*Singing.*]

> I am gone, sir;
> And anon, sir,
> I'll be with you again,
>   In a trice,[26]
>   Like to the old Vice,[27]
> Your need to sustain;
> Who, with dagger of lath,[28]
> In his rage and his wrath,
>   Cries "aha!" to the Devil.

---

23. Feste here begins a conversation with himself, playing both Sir Topas and himself. Malvolio, of course, can't see him.   24. *shent:* reproved, scolded.
25. *Well-a-day:* alas.   26. *a trice:* an instant.
27. *the old Vice:* a stock comic character which first appears in English plays during the Reformation. He was usually dressed in the same fashion as the fool, and gradually merged with that character. It was customary for the Vice to carry a wooden dagger with which he belabored the Devil. At the close of plays in which the Vice appeared, he was carried into hell by the Devil, or else fled there on his own.
28. *lath:* a thin, narrow piece of wood.

                Like a mad lad,
            "Pare thy nails, dad."²⁹
                Adieu, goodman Devil.

[*Exit.*]

### SCENE 3. Olivia's garden.

[*Enter* SEBASTIAN.]

SEB. This is the air; that is the glorious sun;
    This pearl she gave me, I do feel't and see't;
    And though 'tis wonder that enwraps me thus,
    Yet 'tis not madness.  Where's Antonio then?
    I could not find him at the Elephant;                   5
    Yet there he was; and there I found this credit,¹
    That he did range the town to seek me out.
    His counsel now might do me golden service;
    For though my soul disputes well with my sense
    That this may be some error, but no madness,           10
    Yet doth this accident and flood of fortune
    So far exceed all instance,² all discourse,³
    That I am ready to distrust mine eyes
    And wrangle with my reason, that persuades me
    To any other trust but that I am mad,                  15
    Or else the lady's mad.  Yet, if 'twere so,
    She could not sway her house, command her followers,
    Take and give back affairs and their dispatch
    With such a smooth, discreet, and stable bearing
    As I perceive she does.  There's something in't        20
    That is deceivable.⁴  But here the lady comes.

[*Enter* OLIVIA *and* PRIEST.]

OLI. Blame not this haste of mine.  If you mean well,
    Now go with me and with this holy man

---

29. *"Pare thy nails, dad."* An insult, directed at the Devil. The Devil was supposed to grow his nails long by choice.

1. *credit:* belief.    2. *instance:* example.    3. *discourse:* reason, rationality.
4. *deceivable:* deceptive.

Twelfth Night      69

Into the chantry by.⁵  There, before him,
And underneath that consecrated roof,                          25
Plight⁶ me the full assurance of your faith,⁷
That my most jealous and too doubtful soul
May live at peace.  He shall conceal it
Whiles⁸ you are willing it shall come to note,
What time we will our celebration⁹ keep                        30
According to my birth.  What do you say?
SEB. I'll follow this good man and go with you
And having sworn truth, ever will be true.
OLI. Then lead the way, good father; and heavens so shine
That they may fairly note this act of mine!                    35

[*Exeunt.*]


## ACT V

### SCENE 1.  Before Olivia's house.

[*Enter* CLOWN *and* FABIAN.]

FAB. Now as thou lovest me, let me see his letter.
CLOWN. Good Master Fabian, grant me another request.
FAB. Anything.
CLOWN. Do not desire to see this letter.
FAB. This is to give a dog, and in recompense desire my dog again.¹   5

[*Enter* DUKE, VIOLA, CURIO, *and Lords.*]

DUKE. Belong you to the Lady Olivia, friends?
CLOWN. Ay, sir, we are some of her trappings.²

---

5. *the chantry by:* the nearby chapel.    6. *Plight:* pledge, engage.
7. *the full assurance of your faith:* this is the betrothal, or marriage engagement.
8. *Whiles:* until.    9. *celebration:* marriage ceremony.

1. *This . . . again:* Queen Elizabeth is said to have asked a kinsman to grant her one wish, and in return he could have whatever he wanted.  She then demanded that he give her his beloved dog.  When he had done so, he reminded her of her promise to give him whatever he wanted, and asked for his dog again.
2. *trappings:* trifling ornaments.

DUKE. I know thee well. How dost thou, my good fellow?
CLOWN. Truly, sir, the better for my foes, and the worse for my friends.
DUKE. Just the contrary: the better for thy friends.
CLOWN. No, sir, the worse.
DUKE. How can that be?
CLOWN. Marry, sir, they praise me and make an ass of me. Now my foes tell me plainly I am an ass; so that by my foes, sir, I profit in the knowledge of myself, and by my friends I am abused; so that, conclusions to be as kisses,[3] if your four negatives make your two affirmatives, why then, the worse for my friends and the better for my foes.
DUKE. Why, this is excellent.
CLOWN. By my troth, sir, no: though it please you to be one of my friends.
DUKE. Thou shalt not be the worse for me. There's gold.
CLOWN. But that it would be double-dealing, sir, I would you could make it another.
DUKE. O, you give me ill counsel.
CLOWN. Put your grace[4] in your pocket, sir, for this once, and let your flesh and blood obey it.[5]
DUKE. Well, I will be so much a sinner to be a double-dealer. There's another.
CLOWN. *Primo, secundo, tertio* is a good play; and the old saying is "The third pays for all." The triplex,[6] sir, is a good tripping measure; or the bells of Saint Bennet,[7] sir, may put you in mind—one, two, three.
DUKE. You can fool no more money out of me at this throw.[8] If you will let your lady know I am here to speak with her, and bring her along with you, it may awake my bounty further.
CLOWN. Marry, sir, lullaby to your bounty till I come again! I go, sir; but I would not have you to think that my desire of having is the

---

3. *conclusions . . . kisses:* Feste's affirmative conclusions are to follow his negative premises, as kisses often follow refusals.
4. *your grace:* a pun upon *your grace* as (1) the form of address proper to a duke and (2) the spiritual gift of God which (among other things) imparts strength to resist temptation.    5. *it:* the ill counsel.    6. *the triplex:* triple time in music.
7. *the bells of Saint Bennet:* a reference either to an old rhyme or to a church famous for its bells.
8. *throw:* a throw of the dice. *Throw* was also used to mean *time.*

sin of covetousness. But, as you say, sir, let your bounty take a  40
nap; I will awake it anon.

[*Exit.*]

[*Enter* ANTONIO *and* OFFICERS.]

VIO. Here comes the man, sir, that did rescue me.
DUKE. That face of his I do remember well;
    Yet when I saw it last, it was besmeared
    As black as Vulcan[9] in the smoke of war.  45
    A baubling[10] vessel was he captain of,
    For shallow draught and bulk unprizable,[11]
    With which such scathful[12] grapple did he make
    With the most noble bottom[13] of our fleet
    That very envy and the tongue of loss[14]  50
    Cried fame and honor on him. What's the matter?
1. OFF. Orsino, this is that Antonio
    That took the "Phœnix" and her fraught[15] from Candy;[16]
    And this is he that did the "Tiger" board
    When your young nephew Titus lost his leg.  55
    Here in the streets, desperate of[17] shame and state,
    In private brabble[18] did we apprehend him.
VIO. He did me kindness, sir; drew on my side;
    But in conclusion put strange speech upon me.
    I know not what 'twas but distraction.[19]  60
DUKE. Notable pirate, thou salt-water thief!
    What foolish boldness brought thee to their mercies
    Whom thou in terms so bloody and so dear[20]
    Hast made thine enemies?
ANT.             Orsino, noble sir,
    Be pleased that I shake off these names you give me.  65
    Antonio never yet was thief or pirate,
    Though I confess, on base and ground enough,

9. *Vulcan:* the Roman god of fire and metalworking.
10. *baubling:* trifling, insignificant.    11. *unprizable:* without value.
12. *scathful:* destructive.    13. *bottom:* ship.
14. *the tongue of loss:* the cries of those who had lost their ships.
15. *fraught:* freight, cargo.    16. *Candy:* Candia, now the isle of Crete.
17. *desperate of:* careless of, as a desperate man would be.    18. *brabble:* brawl.
19. *distraction:* madness.    20. *dear:* heavy, severe.

  Orsino's enemy. A witchcraft drew me hither.
  That most ingrateful boy there by your side
  From the rude sea's enraged and foamy mouth    70
  Did I redeem. A wrack[21] past hope he was.
  His life I gave him, and did thereto add
  My love without retention or restraint,
  All his in dedication. For his sake
  Did I expose myself (pure[22] for his love)    75
  Into the danger of this adverse town;
  Drew to defend him when he was beset;
  Where being apprehended, his false cunning
  (Not meaning to partake with me in danger)
  Taught him to face me out of his acquaintance,[23]    80
  And grew a twenty years removed thing
  While one would wink; denied me mine own purse,
  Which I had recommended to[24] his use
  Not half an hour before.
VIO.         How can this be?
DUKE. When came he to this town?    85
ANT. Today, my lord; and for three months before,
  No int'rim,[25] not a minute's vacancy,
  Both day and night did we keep company.

[*Enter* OLIVIA *and Attendants.*]

DUKE. Here comes the Countess; now heaven walks on earth.
  But for thee,[26] fellow—fellow, thy words are madness.    90
  Three months this youth hath tended upon me;
  But more of that anon. Take him aside.
OLI. What would my lord, but that he may not have,[27]
  Wherein Olivia may seem serviceable?
  Cesario, you do not keep promise with me.    95
VIO. Madam!
DUKE. Gracious Olivia—
OLI. What do you say, Cesario?—Good my lord—
VIO. My lord would speak; my duty hushes me.

---

21. *wrack:* wreck.    22. *pure:* purely.
23. *face me out of his acquaintance:* impudently deny he knew me.
24. *recommended to:* loaned or given for.    25. *int'rim:* interim.
26. *for thee:* as for thee.    27. *that . . . have:* her love.

**Twelfth Night**

OLI. If it be aught to the old tune, my lord,
 It is as fat and fulsome[28] to mine ear
 As howling after music.
DUKE. Still so cruel?
OLI. Still so constant, lord.
DUKE. What, to perverseness?  You uncivil lady,
 To whose ingrate[29] and unauspicious[30] altars
 My soul the faithful'st off'rings hath breathed out
 That e'er devotion tendered!  What shall I do?
OLI. Even what it please my lord, that shall become him.
DUKE. Why should I not, had I the heart to do it,
 Like to the Egyptian thief at point of death,
 Kill what I love?[31]—a savage jealousy
 That sometime savors nobly.  But hear me this:
 Since you to non-regardance cast my faith,
 And that I partly know the instrument
 That screws me from my true place in your favor,
 Live you the marble-breasted tyrant still.
 But this your minion,[32] whom I know you love,
 And whom, by heaven I swear, I tender[33] dearly,
 Him will I tear out of that cruel eye
 Where he sits crowned in his master's spite.[34]
 Come, boy, with me.  My thoughts are ripe in mischief.
 I'll sacrifice the lamb that I do love
 To spite a raven's heart within a dove.
VIO. And I, most jocund,[35] apt,[36] and willingly,
 To do you rest a thousand death would die.
OLI. Where goes Cesario?
VIO. After him I love
 More than I love these eyes, more than my life,
 More, by all mores, than e'er I shall love wife.

---

28. *fat and fulsome:* too much, sickening, unbearable.   29. *ingrate:* ungrateful.
30. *unauspicious:* unpromising.
31. *Like . . . love?*  In the *Ethiopica* of Heliodorus the Egyptian thief Thyamis, thinking himself upon the point of death, attempted to kill his beloved mistress, Chariclea.  Heliodorus was a Greek writer who lived several centuries after Christ, and this story is the oldest existing Greek romance.  An English translation of the *Etiopica* was a popular Elizabethan book.   32. *minion:* favorite.
33. *tender:* hold.   34. *in his master's spite:* in place of his master.
35. *jocund:* merry.   36. *apt:* ready.

>If I do feign,[37] you witnesses above
>Punish my life for tainting of my love! 130
OLI. Ay me detested![38] how am I beguiled![39]
VIO. Who does beguile you?  Who does do you wrong?
OLI. Hast thou forgot thyself?  Is it so long?
>Call forth the holy father.

[*Exit an Attendant.*]

DUKE. [*To* VIOLA.] Come, away! 135
OLI. Whither, my lord?  Cesario, husband,[40] stay.
DUKE. Husband?
OLI.Ay, husband.  Can he that deny?
DUKE. Her husband, sirrah?[41]
VIO.No, my lord, not I.
OLI. Alas, it is the baseness of thy fear
>That makes thee strangle thy propriety.[42] 140
>Fear not, Cesario; take thy fortunes up;
>Be that thou knowst thou art, and then thou art
>As great as that thou fearest.

[*Enter* PRIEST.]

>O, welcome, father!
>Father, I charge thee by thy reverence
>Here to unfold—though lately we intended 145
>To keep in darkness what occasion now
>Reveals before 'tis ripe—what thou dost know
>Hath newly passed between this youth and me.
PRIEST. A contract of eternal bond of love,[43]
>Confirmed by mutual joinder of your hands, 150
>Attested by the holy close of lips,
>Strengthened by interchangement of your rings;

---

37. *feign:* pretend.
38. *Ay me detested!*  Olivia's cry does not mean only that she feels that she is abhored (detested).  The term means also that one has been cried out against publicly.    39. *beguiled:* cheated.
40. *husband:* Olivia is not yet married, but it was common practice for a woman to address her betrothed as *husband.*
41. *sirrah:* a form of address implying superiority or contempt, or both.
42. *strangle thy propriety:* belie your true identity.
43. *A contract . . . love:* a betrothal, or espousal.  A contract of future marriage.

> And all the ceremony of this compact
> Sealed in my function, by my testimony;
> Since when, my watch hath told me, toward my grave  155
> I have traveled but two hours.

DUKE. O thou dissembling cub! What wilt thou be
  When time hath sowed a grizzle[44] on thy case?[45]
  Or will not else thy craft so quickly grow
  That thine own trip shall be thine overthrow?  160
  Farewell, and take her; but direct thy feet
  Where thou and I, henceforth, may never meet.
VIO. My lord, I do protest—
OLI.                    O, do not swear!
  Hold[46] little faith, though thou hast too much fear.

[*Enter* SIR ANDREW.]

AND. For the love of God, a surgeon! Send one presently to Sir Toby.  165
OLI. What's the matter?
AND. Has broke my head across, and has given Sir Toby a bloody coxcomb[47] too. For the love of God, your help! I had rather than forty pound I were at home.
OLI. Who has done this, Sir Andrew?  170
AND. The Count's gentleman, one Cesario. We took him for a coward, but he's the very Devil incardinate.[48]
DUKE. My gentleman Cesario?
AND. Od's lifelings,[49] here he is! You broke my head for nothing; and that that I did, I was set on to do't by Sir Toby.  175
VIO. Why do you speak to me? I never hurt you.
  You drew your sword upon me without cause,
  But I bespake[50] you fair and hurt you not.

[*Enter* SIR TOBY *and* CLOWN.]

AND. If a bloody coxcomb be a hurt, you have hurt me. I think you set nothing by[51] a bloody coxcomb. Here comes Sir Toby  180 halting[52] you shall hear more. But if he had not been in drink, he would have tickled you othergates[53] than he did.

---

44. *grizzle:* gray hair.   45. *case:* skin.   46. *Hold:* hold a.
47. *coxcomb:* head.   48. *incardinate:* incarnate.
49. *Od's lifelings:* God's little life; a mild oath.   50. *bespake:* addressed.
51. *set nothing by:* do not regard.   52. *halting:* limping.
53. *othergates:* otherwise.

DUKE. How now, gentleman? How is't with you?
TO. That's all one! Has hurt me, and there's the end on't—Sot, didst see Dick Surgeon, sot?
CLOWN. O, he's drunk, Sir Toby, an hour agone. His eyes were set[54] at eight i' the morning.
TO. Then he's a rogue and a passy measures pavin.[55] I hate a drunken rogue.
OLI. Away with him! Who hath made this havoc with them?
AND. I'll help you, Sir Toby, because we'll be dressed together.
TO. Will you help—an ass-head and a coxcomb and a knave—a thin-faced knave, a gull?
OLI. Get him to bed, and let his hurt be looked to.

[*Exeunt* SIR TOBY, SIR ANDREW, CLOWN, *and* FABIAN.]

[*Enter* SEBASTIAN.]

SEB. I am sorry, madam, I have hurt your kinsman;
But had it been the brother of my blood,
I must have done no less with wit and safety.
You throw a strange regard[56] upon me, and by that
I do perceive it hath offended you.
Pardon me, sweet one, even for the vows
We made each other but so late ago.[57]
DUKE. One face, one voice, one habit,[58] and two persons!
A natural perspective,[59] that is and is not!
SEB. Antonio! O my dear Antonio!
How have the hours racked and tortured me
Since I have lost thee!
ANT. Sebastian are you?
SEB.            Fearst thou that, Antonio?
ANT. How have you made division of yourself?
An apple cleft in two is not more twin
Than these two creatures. Which is Sebastian?

54. *set:* glazed, glassy.
55. *a passy measures pavin:* the Passamezzo, a dance. The Passamezzo was a variation on the ordinary pavan. It contains eight bars in each strain, and Sir Toby uses it here in a surprising comparison with the surgeon, who was drunk at eight.    56. *strange regard:* strange look.
57. *so late ago:* such a short time ago.    58. *habit:* clothes.
59. *A natural perspective:* nature's version of the optical illusions produced by a perspective glass. Such glasses were made in a variety of shapes and produced a number of visual distortions.

Twelfth Night

OLI. Most wonderful!
SEB. Do I stand there? I never had a brother;
　　　Nor can there be that deity in my nature
　　　Of here and everywhere.⁶⁰　I had a sister,
　　　Whom the blind⁶¹ waves and surges have devoured.　　215
　　　Of charity, what kin are you to me?
　　　What countryman? what name? what parentage?
VIO. Of⁶² Messaline; Sebastian was my father—
　　　Such a Sebastian was my brother too;
　　　So went he suited⁶³ to his watery tomb.　　　　　　220
　　　If spirits can assume both form and suit,
　　　You come to fright us.
SEB. 　　　　　　　　　A spirit I am indeed,
　　　But am in that dimension grossly clad⁶⁴
　　　Which from the womb I did participate.
　　　Were you a woman, as the rest goes even,⁶⁵　　　　　225
　　　I should my tears let fall upon your cheek
　　　And say, "Thrice welcome, drowned Viola!"
VIO. My father had a mole upon his brow—
SEB. And so had mine.
VIO. And died that day when Viola from her birth　　　　230
　　　Had numbered thirteen years.
SEB. O, that record is lively in my soul!
　　　He finished indeed his mortal act
　　　That day that made my sister thirteen years.
VIO. If nothing lets⁶⁶ to make us happy both　　　　　　235
　　　But this my masculine usurped attire,
　　　Do not embrace me till each circumstance
　　　Of place, time, fortune do cohere and jump⁶⁷
　　　That I am Viola; which to confirm,
　　　I'll bring you to a captain in this town,　　　　　　240
　　　Where lie my maiden weeds;⁶⁸ by whose gentle help
　　　I was preserved to serve this noble Count.
　　　All the occurrence of my fortune since
　　　Hath been between this lady and this lord.

---

60. *deity . . . everywhere:* the attribute of God called *ubiquity* (the ability to be everywhere at once).　　61. *blind:* pitiless.　　62. *Of:* from.　　63. *suited:* dressed.
64. *in that dimension grossly clad:* in that body materially dressed.
65. *as the rest goes even:* all else agreeing.　　66. *lets:* prevents, hinders.
67. *jump:* agree.　　68. *weeds:* clothes.

SEB. [*To* OLIVIA.]  So comes it, lady, you have been mistook.   245
    But nature to her bias drew[69] in that.
    You would have been contracted to a maid;
    Nor are you therein, by my life, deceived:
    You are betrothed both to a maid and man.
DUKE.  Be not amazed; right noble is his blood.   250
    If this be so, as yet the glass seems true,[70]
    I shall have share in this most happy wrack.[71]
    [*To* VIOLA.]  Boy, thou hast said to me a thousand times
    Thou never shouldst love woman like to me.
VIO.  And all those sayings will I over swear,   255
    And all those swearings keep as true in soul
    As doth that orbed continent[72] the fire
    That severs day from night.
DUKE.                               Give me thy hand,
    And let me see thee in thy woman's weeds.
VIO.  The captain that did bring me first on shore   260
    Hath my maid's garments.  He upon some action
    Is now in durance,[73] at Malvolio's suit,
    A gentleman, and follower of my lady's.
OLI.  He shall enlarge him.  Fetch Malvolio hither.
    And yet alas! now I remember me,   265
    They say, poor gentleman, he's much distract.

[*Enter* CLOWN *with a letter, and* FABIAN.]

    A most extracting frenzy of mine own[74]
    From my remembrance clearly banished his.
    How does he, sirrah?
CLOWN.  Truly, madam, he holds Belzebub[75] at the stave's end as well   270
    as a man in his case may do.  Has here writ a letter to you;
    I should have given't you today morning.  [*Offers the letter.*]

---

69. *to her bias drew:* Bias is a bowling term, meaning both an oblique line and the weight which was added to one side of the bowl itself to affect its action. As Sebastian uses the expression here, it means that nature, in her oblique way, has brought an unhappy situation to a happy conclusion.
70. *as yet . . . true:* as the seeming illusion of the glass proves to be the truth—there are two people.
71. *this most happy wrack:* the happy outcome of the shipwreck.
72. *orbed continent:* the sun.    73. *durance:* jail.
74. *A most . . . own:* a frenzy which drew Olivia's mind away from everything but its object, her betrothal.    75. *Belzebub:* Beelzebub; the devil.

# Twelfth Night

But as a madman's epistles are no gospels, so it skills not much[76] when they are delivered.

OLI. Open't and read it.

CLOWN. Look then to be well edified, when the fool delivers[77] the madman. [*Reads loudly.*] "By the Lord, madam"—

OLI. How now? Art thou mad?

CLOWN. No, madam, I do but read madness. An your ladyship will have it as it ought to be, you must allow vox.[78]

OLI. Prithee read i' thy right wits.

CLOWN. So I do, madonna; but to read his right wits is to read thus. Therefore perpend,[79] my princess, and give ear.

OLI. [*To* FABIAN.] Read it you, sirrah.

FAB. [*Reads.*] "By the Lord, madam, you wrong me, and the world shall know it. Though you have put me into darkness, and given your drunken cousin rule over me, yet have I the benefit of my senses as well as your ladyship. I have your own letter that induced me to the semblance I put on; with the which I doubt not but to do myself much right, or you much shame. Think of me as you please. I leave my duty a little unthought of,[80] and speak out of my injury.
"THE MADLY USED MALVOLIO."

OLI. Did he write this?

CLOWN. Ay, madam.

DUKE. This savors not much of distraction.

OLI. See him delivered,[81] Fabian; bring him hither. [*Exit* FABIAN.]
My lord, so please you, these things further thought on,
To think me as well a sister as a wife,
One day shall crown the alliance[82] on't, so please you,
Here at my house and at my proper[83] cost.

DUKE. Madam, I am most apt t'[84] embrace your offer.
[*To* VIOLA.] Your master quits[85] you; and for your service done him,

---

76. *it skills not much:* it makes little difference.   77. *delivers:* utters, pronounces.
78. *vox:* full voice. The Clown must be allowed to continue reading loudly and extravagantly.   79. *perpend:* consider, ponder.
80. *I . . . unthought of:* I depart from the proper dutiful closing of a letter (from an inferior to a superior).   81. *delivered:* freed.
82. *the alliance:* the family alliance which will follow if the Duke marries Viola and Olivia marries Sebastian.
83. *proper:* own.   84. *apt t':* ready to, eager to.   85. *quits:* releases.

      So much against the mettle[86] of your sex,      305
      So far beneath your soft and tender breeding,
      And since you called me master, for so long,
      Here is my hand: you shall from this time be
      Your master's mistress.
OLI.                A sister! you are she.

[*Enter* FABIAN, *with* MALVOLIO.]

DUKE.  Is this the madman?
OLI.                Ay, my lord, this same.      310
      How now, Malvolio?
MAL.            Madam, you have done me wrong,
      Notorious wrong.
OLI.             Have I, Malvolio?  No.
MAL.  Lady, you have.  Pray you peruse that letter.
      You must not now deny it is your hand.
      Write from it[87] if you can, in hand or phrase,    315
      Or say 'tis not your seal, not your invention.
      You can say none of this.  Well, grant it then,
      And tell me, in the modesty of honor,
      Why you have given me such clear lights of favor,
      Bade me come smiling and cross-gartered to you,    320
      To put on yellow stockings, and to frown
      Upon Sir Toby and the lighter[88] people;
      And, acting this in an obedient hope,
      Why have you suffered[89] me to be imprisoned,
      Kept in a dark house, visited by the priest,    325
      And made the most notorious geck[90] and gull[91]
      That e'er invention played on?  Tell me why.
OLI.  Alas, Malvolio, this is not my writing,
      Though I confess much like the character;[92]
      But, out of question, 'tis Maria's hand.    330
      And now I do bethink me, it was she
      First told me thou wast mad.  Thou camest in smiling,
      And in such forms which here were presupposed
      Upon thee in the letter.  Prithee be content.

---

86. *mettle:* disposition.    87. *Write from it:* write differently from it.
88. *lighter:* lesser.    89. *suffered:* allowed.    90. *geck:* fool, ninnyhammer.
91. *gull:* simpleton, dupe.    92. *character:* handwriting.

This practice[93] hath most shrewdly passed upon thee;  335
But when we know the grounds and authors of it,
Thou shalt be both the plaintiff and the judge
Of thine own cause.

FAB.                 Good madam, hear me speak,
And let no quarrel, nor no brawl to come,
Taint the condition of this present hour,  340
Which I have wond'red at. In hope it shall not,
Most freely I confess myself and Toby
Set this device against Malvolio here,
Upon some stubborn and uncourteous parts
We had conceived against him. Maria writ  345
The letter, at Sir Toby's great importance,[94]
In recompense whereof he hath married her.
How with a sportful malice it was followed
May rather pluck on laughter than revenge,
If that the injuries be justly weighed  350
That have on both sides passed.

OLI. Alas poor fool,[95] how have they baffled[96] thee!
CLOWN. Why, "some are born great, some achieve greatness, and some have greatness thrown upon them." I was one, sir, in this interlude—one Sir Topas, sir; but that's all one. "By the Lord, 355 fool, I am not mad!" But do you remember—"Madam, why laugh you at such a barren rascal? An you smile not, he's gagged"? And thus the whirligig[97] of time brings in his revenges.
MAL. I'll be revenged on the whole pack of you! [*Exit.*]  360
OLI. He hath been most notoriously abused.
DUKE. Pursue him and entreat him to a peace.
He hath not told us of the captain yet.
When that is known, and golden time convents,[98]
A solemn combination shall be made  365
Of our dear souls. Meantime, sweet sister,
We will not part from hence. Cesario, come—
For so you shall be while you are a man;

93. *practice*: plot.    94. *great importance*: persistent solicitation.
95. *fool*: in this case, an expression of Olivia's compassion for Malvolio.
96. *baffled*: gulled, hoodwinked.    97. *the whirligig*: the whirling top.
98. *When . . . golden time convents*: when we meet again by summons.

> But when in other habits you are seen,
> Orsino's mistress and his fancy's queen. 370

[*Exeunt all but the* CLOWN.]

[CLOWN *sings.*]

> When that I was and a little tiny boy,
>     With hey, ho, the wind and the rain,
> A foolish thing was but a toy,
>     For the rain it raineth every day.
>
> But when I came to man's estate, 375
>     With hey, ho, the wind and the rain,
> 'Gainst knaves and thieves men shut their gate,
>     For the rain it raineth every day.
>
> But when I came, alas! to wive,
>     With hey, ho, the wind and the rain, 380
> By swaggering could I never thrive,
>     For the rain it raineth every day.
>
> But when I came unto my beds,
>     With hey, ho, the wind and the rain,
> With tosspots[99] still had drunken heads, 385
>     For the rain it raineth every day.
>
> A great while ago the world begun,
>     With hey, ho, the wind and the rain;
> But that's all one, our play is done,
>     And we'll strive to please you every day. 390

[*Exit.*]

---

99. *tosspots:* heavy drinkers.

# She Stoops to Conquer

# OLIVER GOLDSMITH

## Introduction

*She Stoops to Conquer* is an unusual mixture of high comedy and farce, a type of comedy that pleases audiences greatly. The characters are all truly likeable, which is a rarity in comedy. The names of the characters subtly describe their personalities—Hardcastle, Lumpkin, Marlow, Hastings, Constance. Much of the humor of the play is found in the characters themselves rather than in wordplay or wit. However, many comic dialogues emanate from mistaken identities and confusing situations. The incongruity of Marlow is a typical example: he is tongue-tied when with a young woman of his own social class, but articulately amorous in the presence of lower-class females. Mrs. Hardcastle is an exaggerated figure of overindulgence. She fails to see the simple beauty of country life, and apes the affectations of the city in her enormous wig, her concern for fashion, and her foolish vanity. She is equally ludicrous in her attempts to create a love match between her profligate son and her ward, Miss Neville. As a consequence, she pays for both with frustration, pain, and embarrassment.

The great strength of the play, however, is in the farcical situations that are created. It all begins when Sir Charles Marlow arranges a love match for his son with the daughter of his good friend, Hardcastle. Traveling at night, young Marlow and his friend, Hastings, seek directions at a tavern. There they meet Tony Lumpkin, who mischievously tells them that they are far from their destination and that they might spend the night at an inn just down the road. The "inn," of course, is the country estate of the Hardcastles. Marlow, who by his own admission is "one of the most bashful and reserved young fellows in all the world," thinks Hardcastle a presumptuous innkeeper and treats him like a bothersome busybody. However, when Marlow meets Hardcastle's daughter, Kate, he becomes so shy and flustered he stumbles over his tongue and can't even look at her. In the meantime, Hastings has met his sweetheart, Constance Neville, who informs him of the trick played by Tony. Afraid that his plans for an elopement might be upset, Hastings decides not to inform his companion of the truth of the situation. Kate has no desire for a suitor with no backbone and tells her father so. Later, when Kate has changed into the customary about-the-house clothes of a lady of the country, Marlow mistakes her for a servant girl and makes rather liberal romantic advances. Marlow's new personality seems such a strong contrast to that of the shy young man who at their first meeting couldn't even look her in the face, that Kate decides to continue in her mistaken identity; thus, "she stoops to conquer." Both Hardcastle and Sir Charles are fooled by Marlow's strange behavior. In a common scene of comedy —that of the concealed observors— Kate proves to both fathers that her young suitor is not quite what either thinks him to be.

Other hilarious situations are built around the triangle of Tony, Constance, and Hastings. Although his mother has made plans for his marriage, Tony wants to have nothing to do with his attractive cousin. However, in Mrs. Hardcastle's presence, Tony and Constance pretend to be lovers. When Tony thinks Hastings might take Constance off his hands, he eagerly agrees to help Constance obtain her inheritance— a box of jewels. When Mrs. Hardcastle reads a note written by Hastings and intended for Constance, she immediately determines to take Miss Neville away by coach. But Tony has had a bright idea as he departs to escort the coach. With no further explanation, he tells Hastings to meet him at the lower end of the garden in two hours. Tony then leads the coach on a wild night ride about the countryside. The strange irony of both the jewel theft and the coach ride is that each ends right where it started in a farcical merry-go-round.

The play closes with a general unification: the young couples are brought together; Tony is discovered to be legally of age and free to make his own decisions; the two old friends, Sir Charles and Hardcastle, have successfully completed their matchmaking; the foolish Mrs. Hardcastle is a sadder, but hopefully wiser, woman. Most important of all, Kate may have stooped to conquer, but, as a result, Marlow has discovered who and what he really is.

# Characters

SIR CHARLES MARLOW
YOUNG MARLOW, his son
HARDCASTLE
HASTINGS
TONY LUMPKIN
DIGGORY

MRS HARDCASTLE
MISS HARDCASTLE
MISS NEVILLE
MAID
Landlord, Servants, *etc.*

## Prologue

### By David Garrick,[1] Esq.

[*Enter* MR WOODWARD,[2] *dressed in black, and holding a handkerchief to his eyes.*]

> Excuse me, sirs, I pray—I can't yet speak—
>    I'm crying now—and have been all the week.
> 'Tis not alone this mourning suit,' good masters;
>    'I've that within'[3]—for which there are no plasters!
> Pray would you know the reason why I'm crying?    5
>    The comic muse, long sick, is now a-dying!
> And if she goes, my tears will never stop;
>    For as a player, I can't squeeze out one drop:
> I am undone, that's all—shall lose my bread—
>    I'd rather, but that's nothing—lose my head.    10
> When the sweet maid is laid upon the bier,
>    Shuter[4] and I shall be chief mourners here.
> To her a mawkish drab of spurious breed,
>    Who deal in Sentimentals[5] will succeed!

1. *David Garrick:* David Garrick (1717–1779), one of the greatest actors of the English stage, wrote many prologues.
2. *Mr Woodward:* Henry Woodward, one of finest of eighteenth-century comedians, did not appear in *She Stoops to Conquer*; he spoke only the prologue.
3. *'Tis . . . within':* These lines are a parody of Hamlet's speech which begins "'Tis not alone my inky cloak," and concludes "I have that within which passeth show—/These but the trappings and the suits of woe." *Hamlet*, I, 2.
4. *Shuter:* Ned Shuter, a great comic actor, played the role of Hardcastle when the play first opened.
5. *Sentimentals:* Sentimental comedy, comedy depicting lofty morals and fine sentiments, is under attack here. *She Stoops to Conquer* was itself vigorously attacked in turn (by those who favored sentimental comedy) as being "low."

Poor Ned and I are dead to all intents; 15
　　We can as soon speak Greek as Sentiments.
Both nervous grown, to keep our spirits up,
　　We now and then take down a hearty cup.[6]
What shall we do?  If Comedy forsake us!
　　They'll turn us out, and no one else will take us, 20
But, why can't I be moral?  Let me try—
　　My heart thus pressing—fix'd my face and eye—
With a sententious look, that nothing means
　　(Faces are blocks, in sentimental scenes),
Thus I begin—'All is not gold that glitters,[7] 25
　　'Pleasure seems sweet, but proves a glass of bitters.
'When ignorance enters, folly is at hand:
　　'Learning is better far than house and land.
'Let not your virtue trip, who trips may stumble,
　　'And virtue is not virtue, if she tumble.' 30
I give it up—morals won't do for me;
　　To make you laugh, I must play tragedy.
One hope remains—hearing the maid was ill,
　　A Doctor[8] comes this night to show his skill.
To cheer her heart, and give your muscles motion, 35
　　He in Five Draughts[9] prepar'd, presents a potion:
A kind of magic charm—for be assur'd,
　　If you will swallow it, the maid is cur'd.
But desperate the Doctor, and her case is,
　　If you reject the dose, and make wry faces! 40
This truth he boasts, will boast it while he lives,
　　No poisonous drugs are mix'd in what he gives.
Should he succeed, you'll give him his degree;
　　If not, within he will receive no fee!
The college You,[10] must his pretensions back, 45
　　Pronounce him Regular, or dub him Quack.

6. *We ... cup:* This is possibly a reference to Ned Shuter's heavy drinking. It was not unknown for him to appear onstage drunk.
7. *'All is not gold that glitters:* A variation on the line "All, as they say, that glitters is not gold," from Dryden's poem *The Hind and the Panther* (1687).
8. *A Doctor:* Goldsmith himself.  Dr. Goldsmith was at one time a practicing physician.
9. *Five Draughts:* five acts.  A draught was literally a dose of liquid medicine.
10. *The college You:* The audience must act as would the Royal College of Physicians in judging Dr. Goldsmith.

# ACT I

SCENE 1. A chamber in an old-fashioned house.

[*Enter* MRS HARDCASTLE *and* MR HARDCASTLE.]

MRS HARD. I vow, Mr Hardcastle, you're very particular. Is there a creature in the whole country, but ourselves, that does not take a trip to town now and then, to rub off the rust a little? There's the two Miss Hoggs, and our neighbour, Mrs Grigsby, go to take a month's polishing every winter.

HARD. Ay, and bring back vanity and affectation to last them the whole year. I wonder why London cannot keep its own fools at home. In my time, the follies of the town crept slowly among us, but now they travel faster than a stage-coach.[1] Its fopperies come down, not only as inside passengers, but in the very basket.[2]

MRS HARD. Ay, your times were fine times, indeed; you have been telling us of them for many a long year. Here we live in an old rambling mansion, that looks for all the world like an inn, but that we never see company. Our best visitors are old Mrs Oddfish, the curate's wife,[3] and little Cripplegate, the lame dancing-master: and all our entertainment your old stories of Prince Eugene and the Duke of Marlborough.[4] I hate such old-fashioned trumpery.

HARD. And I love it. I love everything that's old: old friends, old times, old manners, old books, old wine; and, I believe, Dorothy [*Taking her hand.*], you'll own I have been pretty fond of an old wife.

MRS HARD. Lord, Mr Hardcastle, you're for ever at your Dorothys and your old wives. You may be a Darby, but I'll be no Joan,[5] I promise

---

1. *faster than a stage-coach:* In the eighteenth century stagecoaches were considered very fast indeed.
2. *basket:* a stagecoach basket was a large wicker basket mounted at the rear of the coach. It was usually used to hold luggage, but passengers occasionally rode there.
3. *the curate's wife:* a curate may be a clergyman in charge of a parish or the pastor's assistant.
4. *Prince Eugene and the Duke of Marlborough:* Prince Eugene of Savoy (1663–1736) was an Austrian general in the service of Emperor Leopold I. During the War of the Spanish Succession, Prince Eugene and the English Duke of Marlborough, working together, fought the battles of Blenheim, Oudenarde, and Malplaquet. John Churchill, 1st Duke of Marlborough (1650–1722), was commander in chief of the armies of England and Holland in the War of the Spanish Succession.
5. *Darby . . . Joan:* originally (in eighteenth-century verses), an old married couple. The names eventually came to be used jokingly of fond married couples, especially those who were elderly and humble.

you. I'm not so old as you'd make me, by more than one good year. Add twenty to twenty, and make money of that.

HARD. Let me see; twenty added to twenty makes just fifty and seven.

MRS HARD. It's false, Mr Hardcastle: I was but twenty when Tony was born, the son of Mr Lumpkin, my first husband; and he's not come to years of discretion yet.

HARD. Nor ever will, I dare answer for him. Ay, you have taught him finely!

MRS HARD. No matter, Tony Lumpkin has a good fortune. My son is not to live by his learning. I don't think a boy wants much learning to spend fifteen hundred a-year.

HARD. Learning, quotha![6] a mere composition of tricks and mischief!

MRS HARD. Humour, my dear: nothing but humour. Come, Mr Hardcastle, you must allow the boy a little humour.

HARD. I'd sooner allow him a horse-pond![7] If burning the footmen's shoes, frightening the maids, and worrying the kittens be humour, he has it. It was but yesterday he fastened my wig to the back of my chair, and when I went to make a bow, I popt my bald head in Mrs Frizzle's face!

MRS HARD. And am I to blame? The poor boy was always too sickly to do any good. A school would be his death. When he comes to be a little stronger, who knows what a year or two's Latin may do for him?

HARD. Latin for him! A cat and fiddle! No, no, the ale-house and the stable are the only schools he'll ever go to.

MRS HARD. Well, we must not snub[8] the poor boy now, for I believe we shan't have him long among us. Anybody that looks in his face may see he's consumptive.

HARD. Ay, if growing too fat be one of the symptoms.

MRS HARD. He coughs sometimes.

HARD. Yes, when his liquor goes the wrong way.

MRS HARD. I'm actually afraid of his lungs.

HARD. And truly, so am I; for he sometimes whoops like a speaking-trumpet

[TONY *hallooing behind the scenes.*]

O, there he goes—a very consumptive figure, truly!

---

6. *quotha!* Indeed! Forsooth!
7. *horse-pond:* The horse-pond was a pond used for watering and washing horses. It was also used for ducking obnoxious people.   8. *snub:* restrain.

[*Enter* TONY, *crossing the stage.*]

MRS HARD. Tony, where are going, my charmer? Won't you give papa and I a little of your company, lovee?

TONY. I'm in haste, mother; I cannot stay.

MRS HARD. You shan't venture out this raw evening, my dear; you look most shockingly.

TONY. I can't stay, I tell you. The Three Pigeons expects me down every moment. There's some fun going forward.

HARD. Ay; the alehouse, the old place: I thought so.

MRS HARD. A low, paltry set of fellows.

TONY. Not so low, neither. There's Dick Muggins the exciseman,[9] Jack Slang the horse doctor, Little Aminadab that grinds the music-box, and Tom Twist that spins the pewter platter.[10]

MRS HARD. Pray, my dear, disappoint them for one night, at least.

TONY. As for disappointing them, I should not so much mind; but I can't abide to disappoint myself!

MRS HARD. [*Detaining him.*] You shan't go.

TONY. I will, I tell you.

MRS HARD. I say you shan't.

TONY. We'll see which is strongest, you or I.

[*Exit, hauling her out.*]

[HARDCASTLE *alone.*]

HARD. Ay, there goes a pair that only spoil each other. But is not the whole age in a combination to drive sense and discretion out of doors? There's my pretty darling Kate! the fashions of the times have almost infected her too. By living a year or two in town, she's as fond of gauze and French frippery as the best of them.

[*Enter* MISS HARDCASTLE.]

HARD. Blessings on my pretty innocence! drest out as usual, my Kate. Goodness! What a quantity of superfluous silk hast thou got about thee, girl! I could never teach the fools of this age, that the indigent world could be clothed out of the trimmings of the vain.

MISS HARD. You know our agreement, sir. You allow me the morning to

---

9. *the exciseman:* the tax collector.
10. *that spins the pewter platter:* A plate spun upon its edges was sometimes used as an accompaniment to song.

receive and pay visits, and to dress in my own manner; and in the evening I put on my housewife's dress to please you.

HARD. Well, remember, I insist on the terms of our agreement; and, by the by, I believe I shall have occasion to try your obedience this very evening.

MISS HARD. I protest, sir, I don't comprehend your meaning.

HARD. Then, to be plain with you, Kate, I expect the young gentleman I have chosen to be your husband from town this very day. I have his father's letter, in which he informs me his son is set out, and that he intends to follow himself shortly after.

MISS HARD. Indeed! I wish I had known something of this before. Bless me, how shall I behave? It's a thousand to one I shan't like him; our meeting will be so formal, and so like a thing of business, that I shall find no room for friendship or esteem.

HARD. Depend upon it, child, I never will control your choice; but Mr Marlow, whom I have pitched upon, is the son of my old friend, Sir Charles Marlow, of whom you have heard me talk so often. The young gentleman has been bred a scholar, and is designed for an employment in the service of his country. I am told he's a man of an excellent understanding.

MISS HARD. Is he?

HARD. Very generous.

MISS HARD. I believe I shall like him.

HARD. Young and brave.

MISS HARD. I am sure I shall like him.

HARD. And very handsome.

MISS HARD. My dear papa, say no more. [*Kissing his hand.*] He's mine, I'll have him.

HARD. And, to crown all, Kate, he's one of the most bashful and reserved young fellows in all the world.

MISS HARD. Eh! you have frozen me to death again. That word *reserved* has undone all the rest of his accomplishments. A reserved lover, it is said, always makes a suspicious husband.

HARD. On the contrary, modesty seldom resides in a breast that is not enriched with nobler virtues. It was the very feature in his character that first struck me.

MISS HARD. He must have more striking features to catch me, I promise you. However, if he be so young, so handsome, and so everything as you mention, I believe he'll do still. I think I'll have him.

HARD. Ay, Kate, but there is still an obstacle. It is more than an even wager, he may not have you.

MISS HARD. My dear papa, why will you mortify one so? Well, if he refuses, instead of breaking my heart at his indifference, I'll only break my glass for its flattery, set my cap to some newer fashion, and look out for some less difficult admirer.

HARD. Bravely resolved! In the meantime I'll go prepare the servants for his reception; as we seldom see company, they want as much training as a company of recruits the first day's muster.

[*Exit.*]

MISS HARD. [*Alone.*] Lud, this news of papa's puts me all in a flutter. Young, handsome; these he put last; but I put them foremost. Sensible, good-natured; I like all that. But then reserved, and sheepish, that's much against him. Yet can't he be cured of his timidity, by being taught to be proud of his wife? Yes, and can't I—but I vow I'm disposing of the husband before I have secured the lover.

[*Enter* MISS NEVILLE.]

MISS HARD. I'm glad you're come, Neville, my dear. Tell me, Constance, how do I look this evening? Is there anything whimsical[11] about me? Is it one of my well-looking days, child? Am I in face to-day?

MISS NEVILLE. Perfectly, my dear. Yet, now I look again—bless me!—sure no accident has happened among the canary birds or the goldfishes? Has your brother or the cat been meddling? Or has the last novel been too moving?

MISS HARD. No; nothing of all this. I have been threatened—I can scarce get it out—I have been threatened with a lover.

MISS NEVILLE. And his name—

MISS HARD. Is Marlow.

MISS NEVILLE. Indeed!

MISS HARD. The son of Sir Charles Marlow.

MISS NEVILLE. As I live, the most intimate friend of Mr Hastings, my admirer. They are never asunder. I believe you must have seen him when we lived in town.

MISS HARD. Never.

11. *whimsical:* out of the ordinary.

MISS NEVILLE. He's a very singular character, I assure you. Among women of reputation he is the modestest man alive; but his acquaintance give him a very different character among creatures of another stamp: you understand me.

MISS HARD. An odd character, indeed. I shall never be able to manage him. What shall I do? Pshaw, think no more of him, but trust to occurrences for success. But how goes on your own affair, my dear? Has my mother been courting you for my brother Tony as usual?

MISS NEVILLE. I have just come from one of our agreeable *tête-à-têtes*. She has been saying a hundred tender things, and setting off her pretty monster as the very pink of perfection.

MISS HARD. And her partiality is such, that she actually thinks him so. A fortune like yours is no small temptation. Besides, as she has the sole management of it, I'm not surprised to see her unwilling to let it go out of the family.

MISS NEVILLE. A fortune like mine, which chiefly consists in jewels, is no such mighty temptation. But at any rate, if my dear Hastings be but constant, I make no doubt to be too hard for her at last. However, I let her suppose that I am in love with her son, and she never once dreams that my affections are fixed upon another.

MISS HARD. My good brother holds out stoutly. I could almost love him for hating you so.

MISS NEVILLE. It is a good-natured creature at bottom, and I'm sure would wish to see me married to anybody but himself. But my aunt's bell rings for our afternoon's walk round the improvements.[12] *Allons.*[13] Courage is necessary, as our affairs are critical.

MISS HARD. Would it were bed-time and all were well.[14]

[*Exeunt.*]


SCENE 2. An alehouse room.

[*Several shabby fellows, with punch and tobacco.* TONY *at the head of the table, a little higher than the rest, a mallet in his hand.*]

OMNES. Hurrea! hurrea! hurrea! bravo!

---

12. *the improvements:* lands improved by cultivation or by buildings.
13. *Allons:* Come on! A French expression.
14. *Would . . . well:* A slight misquotation of a line from one of Shakespeare's historical plays: "I would 'twere bed-time, Hal, and all were well." *I Henry IV,* V, 1.

FIRST FELLOW. Now, gentlemen, silence for a song. The 'squire is going to knock himself down for a song.[1]
OMNES. Ay, a song, a song.
TONY. Then I'll sing you, gentlemen, a song I made upon this alehouse, the Three Pigeons.

    Let school-masters puzzle their brain
        With grammar, and nonsense, and learning;
    Good liquor, I stoutly maintain,
        Gives genius a better discerning,
    Let them brag of their heathenish gods,     5
        Their Lethes,[2] their Styxes,[3] and Stygians;[4]
    Their Quis, and their Quaes, and their Quods,[5]
        They're all but a parcel of pigeons.[6]
            Toroddle, toroddle, toroll!

    When Methodist preachers come down,     10
        A-preaching that drinking is sinful,
    I'll wager the rascals a crown,
        They always preach best with a skinful.
    But when you come down with your pence,
        For a slice of their scurvy religion,     15
    I'll leave it to all men of sense,
        But you, my good friend, are the pigeon.
            Toroddle, toroddle, toroll!

    Then come, put the jorum[7] about,
        And let us be merry and clever,     20
    Our hearts and our liquors are stout,
        Here's the Three Jolly Pigeons for ever.

---

1. *knock . . . song:* call upon himself for a song. Note that Tony has a mallet in his hand, and has apparently been playing the auctioneer.
2. *Lethes:* Lethe was the river of forgetfulness in Hades. Supposedly the souls of those dead who were about to be reincarnated drank of its waters in order to forget their former lives.
3. *Styxes:* The Styx was another river of Hades. The boatman Charon ferried the souls of the dead across it.
4. *Stygians: Stygian* means pertaining to the river Styx or to the infernal regions of Hades.   5. *Quis . . . Quods:* Latin for *who, which, what.*
6. *They're . . . pigeons:* They're all dishonest. A pigeon was one who cheated, gulled, or swindled others at gambling.
7. *the jorum:* a large drinking bowl, especially a bowl of punch.

> Let some cry up woodcock or hare,
>   Your bustards, your ducks, and your widgeons;
> But of all the birds in the air, 25
>   Here's a health to the Three Jolly Pigeons.
>       Toroddle, toroddle, toroll!

OMNES. Bravo, bravo!

FIRST FELLOW. The 'squire has got spunk in him.

SECOND FELLOW. I loves to hear him sing, bekeays he never gives us nothing that's low.[8]

THIRD FELLOW. O damn anything that's low, I cannot bear it.

FOURTH FELLOW. The genteel thing is the genteel thing at any time: if so be that a gentleman bees in a concatenation accordingly.[9]

THIRD FELLOW. I like the maxum of it, Master Muggins. What, though I am obligated to dance a bear, a man may be a gentleman for all that. May this be my poison if my bear ever dances but to the very genteelest of tunes; Water Parted,[10] or the minuet in *Ariadne*.[11]

SECOND FELLOW. What a pity it is the 'squire is not come to his own. It would be well for all the publicans within ten miles round of him.

TONY. Ecod, and so it would, Master Slang. I'd then show what it was to keep choice of company.

SECOND FELLOW. Oh, he takes after his own father for that. To be sure, old 'squire Lumpkin was the finest gentleman I ever set my eyes on. For winding the straight horn, or beating a thicket for a hare, or a wench, he never had his fellow. It was a saying in the place, that he kept the best horses, dogs, and girls, in the whole county.

TONY. Ecod, and when I'm of age I'll be no bastard, I promise you. I have been thinking of Bet Bouncer and the miller's grey mare to begin with. But come, my boys, drink about and be merry, for you pay no reckoning. Well, Stingo, what's the matter?

[*Enter* LANDLORD.]

LANDLORD. There be two gentlemen in a postchaise[12] at the door. They

---

8. *I loves . . . low:* Goldsmith's first play, *The Good-Natur'd Man,* had been severely criticized for being *low,* or not genteel.
9. *if so be . . . accordingly:* the Fourth Fellow is, of course, speaking nonsense.
10. *Water Parted:* A song of this name was part of the 1762 opera *Artaxerxes.*
11. *the minuet in Ariadne:* Handel's opera *Ariadne* (1734) contained a famous minuet (a slow, graceful dance) at the end of the overture.
12. *postchaise:* a closed, four-wheeled carriage which seated two or four people.

have lost their way upo' the forest; and they are talking something about Mr Hardcastle.

TONY. As sure as can be, one of them must be the gentleman that's coming down to court my sister. Do they seem to be Londoners?

LANDLORD. I believe they may. They look woundily[13] like Frenchmen.

TONY. Then desire them to step this way, and I'll set them right in a twinkling. [*Exit* LANDLORD.] Gentlemen, as they mayn't be good enough company for you, step down for a moment, and I'll be with you in the squeezing of a lemon.

[*Exeunt* MOB.]

TONY. [*Alone.*] Father-in-law[14] has been calling me whelp and hound this half-year. Now, if I pleased, I could be so revenged upon the old grumbletonian. But then I'm afraid—afraid of what? I shall soon be worth fifteen hundred a year, and let him frighten me out of that if he can!

[*Enter* LANDLORD, *conducting* MARLOW *and* HASTINGS.]

MARLOW. What a tedious uncomfortable day have we had of it! We were told it was but forty miles across the country, and we have come above threescore!

HASTINGS. And all, Marlow, from that unaccountable reserve of yours that would not let us inquire more frequently on the way.

MARLOW. I own, Hastings, I am unwilling to lay myself under an obligation to everyone I meet, and often stand the chance of an unmannerly answer.

HASTINGS. At present, however, we are not likely to receive any answer.

TONY. No offense, gentlemen. But I'm told you have been inquiring for one Mr Hardcastle in these parts. Do you know what part of the country you are in?

HASTINGS. Not in the least, sir, but should thank you for information.

TONY. Nor the way you came?

HASTINGS. No, sir; but if you can inform us—

TONY. Why, gentlemen, if you know neither the road you are going, nor

---

13. *woundily:* extremely, dreadfully.
14. *Father-in-law:* Tony refers to his stepfather, Mr. Hardcastle.

She Stoops to Conquer

where you are, nor the road you came, the first thing I have to inform you is, that—you have lost your way.

MARLOW. We wanted no ghost to tell us that.[15]

TONY. Pray, gentlemen, may I be so bold as to ask the place from whence you came?

MARLOW. That's not necessary towards directing us where we are to go.

TONY. No offence; but question for question is all fair, you know. Pray, gentlemen, is not this same Hardcastle a cross-grained, old-fashioned, whimsical fellow with an ugly face, a daughter, and a pretty son?

HASTINGS. We have not seen the gentleman; but he has the family you mention.

TONY. The daughter, a tall, trapesing, trolloping, talkative maypole—the son, a pretty, well-bred, agreeable youth, that everybody is fond of?

MARLOW. Our information differs in this. The daughter is said to be well-bred, and beautiful; the son, an awkward booby, reared up and spoiled at his mother's apron-string.

TONY. He-he-hem! Then gentlemen, all I have to tell you is, that you won't reach Mr Hardcastle's house this night, I believe.

HASTINGS. Unfortunate!

TONY. It's a damned long, dark, boggy, dirty, dangerous way. Stingo, tell the gentlemen the way to Mr Hardcastle's. [*Winking upon the* LANDLORD.] Mr Hardcastle's of Quagmire Marsh, you understand me.

LANDLORD. Master Hardcastle's! Lock-a-daisy, my masters, you're come a deadly deal wrong! When you came to the bottom of the hill, you should have crossed down Squash Lane.

MARLOW. Cross down Squash Lane!

LANDLORD. Then you were to keep straight forward, until you came to four roads.

MARLOW. Come to where four roads meet!

TONY. Ay, but you must be sure to take only one of them.

MARLOW. O, sir, you're facetious!

TONY. Then, keeping to the right, you are to go sideways till you come upon Crack-skull common: there you must look sharp for the track of the wheel, and go forward, till you come to Farmer Murrain's barn. Coming to the farmer's barn, you are to turn to the right, and

---

15. *We . . . that:* An echo of Horatio's rebuke to Hamlet: "There needs no ghost, my lord, come from the grave/To tell us this." *Hamlet,* I, 5.

then to the left, and then to the right about again, till you find out the old mill.

MARLOW. Zounds, man! we could as soon find out the longitude![16]

HASTINGS. What's to be done, Marlow?

MARLOW. This house promises but a poor reception; though perhaps the landlord can accommodate us.

LANDLORD. Alack, master, we have but one spare bed in the whole house.

TONY. And to my knowledge, that's taken up by three lodgers already. [*After a pause, in which the rest seem disconcerted.*] I have hit it. Don't you think, Stingo, our landlady could accommodate the gentlemen by the fireside, with—three chairs and a bolster?

HASTINGS. I hate sleeping by the fireside.

MARLOW. And I detest your three chairs and a bolster.

TONY. You do, do you?—then let me see—what if you go on a mile farther, to the Buck's Head; the old Buck's Head on the hill, one of the best inns in the whole country?

HASTINGS. Oho! so we have escaped an adventure for this night, however.

LANDLORD. [*Apart to* TONY.] Sure, you ben't sending them to your father's as an inn, be you?[17]

TONY. Mum, you fool, you. Let them find that out. [*To them.*] You have only to keep on straight forward, till you come to a large old house by the roadside. You'll see a pair of large horns over the door. That's the sign. Drive up the yard, and call stoutly about you.

HASTINGS. Sir, we are obliged to you. The servants can't miss the way?

TONY. No, no: but I tell you, though, the landlord is rich, and going to leave off business; so he wants to be thought a gentleman, saving your presence, he! he! he! He'll be for giving you his company, and, ecod, if you mind him, he'll persuade you that his mother was an alderman, and his aunt a justice of peace!

LANDLORD. A troublesome old blade, to be sure; but 'a keeps as good wines and beds as any in the whole country.

MARLOW. Well, if he supplies us with these, we shall want no further connexion. We are to turn to the right, did you say?

---

16. *we . . . longitude:* In the eighteenth century Parliament offered a reward of twenty thousand pounds to anyone who could discover an accurate means of ascertaining the longitude at sea. Three months after the first presentation of *She Stoops to Conquer* the reward was given to John Harrison.

17. This hoax was based upon an actual experience of Goldsmith's youth.

TONY. No, no; straight forward. I'll just step myself, and show you a piece of the way. [*To the* LANDLORD.] Mum.

LANDLORD. Ah, bless your heart for a sweet, pleasant—damned, mischievous son of a whore.

## ACT II

An old-fashioned house.

[*Enter* HARDCASTLE, *followed by three or four awkward* SERVANTS.]

HARD. Well, I hope you're perfect in the table exercise I have been teaching you these three days. You all know your posts and your places, and can shew that you have been used to good company, without ever stirring from home.

OMNES. Ay, ay.

HARD. When company comes, you are not to pop out and stare, and then run in again, like frightened rabbits in a warren.

OMNES. No, no.

HARD. You, Diggory, whom I have taken from the barn, are to make a shew at the side-table; and you, Roger, whom I have advanced from the plough, are to place yourself behind my chair. But you're not to stand so, with your hands in your pockets. Take your hands from your pockets, Roger; and from your head, you blockhead, you. See how Diggory carries his hands. They're a little too stiff, indeed, but that's no great matter.

DIGGORY. Ay, mind how I hold them. I learned to hold my hands this way, when I was upon drill for the militia. And so being upon drill—

HARD. You must not be so talkative, Diggory. You must be all attention to the guests. You must hear us talk, and not think of talking; you must see us drink, and not think of drinking; you must see us eat, and not think of eating.

DIGGORY. By the laws, your worship, that's parfectly unpossible. Whenever Diggory sees yeating going forward, ecod, he's always wishing for a mouthful himself.

HARD. Blockhead! Is not a bellyful in the kitchen as good as a bellyful in the parlour? Stay your stomach with that reflexion.

DIGGORY. Ecod, I thank your worship, I'll make a shift to stay my stomach with a slice of cold beef in the pantry.

HARD. Diggory, you are too talkative. Then, if I happen to say a good thing, or tell a good story at table, you must not all burst out a-laughing, as if you made part of the company.

DIGGORY. Then, ecod, your worship must not tell the story of old Grouse in the gun-room: I can't help laughing at that—he! he! he!—for the soul of me! We have laughed at that these twenty years—ha! ha! ha!

HARD. Ha! ha! ha! The story is a good one. Well, honest Diggory, you may laugh at that—but still remember to be attentive. Suppose one of the company should call for a glass of wine, how will you behave? A glass of wine, sir, if you please [*To* DIGGORY.]—Eh, why don't you move?

DIGGORY. Ecod, your worship, I never have courage till I see the eatables and drinkables brought upo' the table, and then I'm as bauld as a lion.

HARD. What, will nobody move?

FIRST SERVANT. I'm not to leave this pleace.

SECOND SERVANT. I'm sure it's no pleace of mine.

THIRD SERVANT. Nor mine, for sartain.

DIGGORY. Wauns,[1] and I'm sure it canna be mine.

HARD. You numskulls! and so while, like your betters, you are quarrelling for places, the guests must be starved. O, you dunces! I find I must begin all over again. But don't I hear a coach drive into the yard? To your posts, you blockheads. I'll go in the meantime and give my old friend's son a hearty reception at the gate.

[*Exit* HARDCASTLE.]

DIGGORY. By the elevens, my pleace is gone quite out of my head.

ROGER. I know that my pleace is to be everywhere!

FIRST SERVANT. Where the devil is mine?

SECOND SERVANT. My pleace is to be nowhere at all; and so I'ze go about my business!

[*Exeunt* SERVANTS, *running about as if frighted, different ways.*]

1. *Wauns:* God's wounds; an oath.

[*Enter* SERVANT *with lighted candles, showing in* MARLOW *and* HASTINGS.]

SERVANT. Welcome, gentlemen, very welcome! This way.

HASTINGS. After the disappointments of the day, welcome once more, Charles, to the comforts of a clean room and a good fire. Upon my word, a very well-looking house; antique but creditable.

MARLOW. The usual fate of a large mansion. Having first ruined the master by good house-keeping, it at last comes to levy contributions as an inn.

HASTINGS. As you say, we passengers are to be taxed to pay for all these fineries. I have often seen a good sideboard, or a marble chimney-piece, though not actually put in the bill, inflame a reckoning confoundedly.

MARLOW. Travellers, George, must pay in all places. The only difference is, that in good inns you pay dearly for luxuries, in bad inns, you are fleeced and starved.

HASTINGS. You have lived pretty much among them. In truth, I have been often surprised, that you who have seen so much of the world, with your natural good sense, and your many opportunities, could never yet acquire a requisite share of assurance.

MARLOW. The Englishman's malady. But tell me, George, where could I have learned that assurance you talk of? My life has been chiefly spent in a college or an inn, in seclusion from that lovely part of the creation that chiefly teach men confidence. I don't know that I was ever familiarly acquainted with a single modest woman—except my mother—but among females of another class, you know—

HASTINGS. Ay, among them you are impudent enough of all conscience!

MARLOW. They are of *us*, you know.

HASTINGS. But in the company of women of reputation I never saw such an idiot, such a trembler; you look for all the world as if you wanted an opportunity of stealing out of the room.

MARLOW. Why, man, that's because I do want to steal out of the room. Faith, I have often formed a resolution to break the ice, and rattle away at any rate. But I don't know how, a single glance from a pair of fine eyes has totally overset my resolution. An impudent fellow may counterfeit modesty, but I'll be hanged if a modest man can ever counterfeit impudence.

HASTINGS. If you could but say half the fine things to them, that I have heard you lavish upon the barmaid of an inn, or even a college bed-maker—

MARLOW. Why, George, I can't say fine things to them. They freeze, they petrify me. They may talk of a comet, or a burning mountain, or some such bagatelle;[2] but to me, a modest woman, drest out in all her finery, is the most tremendous object of the whole creation.

HASTINGS. Ha! ha! ha! At this rate, man, how can you ever expect to marry!

MARLOW. Never; unless, as among kings and princes, my bride were to be courted by proxy. If, indeed, like an eastern bridegroom, one were to be introduced to a wife he never saw before, it might be endured. But to go through all the terrors of a formal courtship, together with the episode of aunts, grandmothers, and cousins, and at last to blurt out the broad staring question of, Madam, will you marry me? No, no, that's a strain much above me, I assure you!

HASTINGS. I pity you. But how do you intend behaving to the lady you are come down to visit at the request of your father?

MARLOW. As I behave to all other ladies. Bow very low; answer yes, or no, to all her demands. But for the rest, I don't think I shall venture to look in her face, till I see my father's again.

HASTINGS. I'm surprised that one who is so warm a friend can be so cool a lover.

MARLOW. To be explicit, my dear Hastings, my chief inducement down was to be instrumental in forwarding your happiness, not my own. Miss Neville loves you, the family don't know you; as my friend you are sure of a reception, and let honour do the rest.

HASTINGS. My dear Marlow! But I'll suppress the emotion. Were I a wretch, meanly seeking to carry off a fortune, you should be the last man in the world I would apply to for assistance. But Miss Neville's person is all I ask, and that is mine, both from her deceased father's consent, and her own inclination.

MARLOW. Happy man! You have talents and art to captivate any woman. I'm doomed to adore the sex, and yet to converse with the only part of it I despise. This stammer in my address, and this awkward unprepossessing visage of mine, can never permit me to soar above the reach of a milliner's apprentice, or one of the duchesses of Drury-Lane.[3] Pshaw! this fellow here to interrupt us.

---

2. *bagatelle:* a trifle, a thing of no importance.
3. *the duchesses of Drury-Lane:* The prostitutes of the area near Drury Lane appropriated noble titles.

[*Enter* HARDCASTLE.]

HARD. Gentlemen, once more you are heartily welcome. Which is Mr Marlow? Sir, you're heartily welcome. It's not my way, you see, to receive my friends with my back to the fire. I like to give them a hearty reception in the old style at my gate. I like to see their horses and trunks taken care of.

MARLOW. [*Aside.*] He has got our names from the servants already. [*To him.*] We approve your caution and hospitality, sir. [*To* HASTINGS.] I have been thinking, George, of changing our travelling dresses in the morning. I am grown confoundedly ashamed of mine.

HARD. I beg, Mr Marlow, you'll use no ceremony in this house. [*Both ignore him.*]

HASTINGS. I fancy, George, you're right: the first blow is half the battle. I intend opening the campaign with the white and gold.

HARD. Mr Marlow—Mr Hastings—gentlemen—pray be under no constraint in this house. This is Liberty Hall, gentlemen. You may do just as you please here.

MARLOW. Yet, George, if we open the campaign too fiercely at first, we may want ammunition before it is over. I think to reserve the embroidery to secure a retreat.

HARD. Your talking of a retreat, Mr Marlow, puts me in mind of the Duke of Marlborough, when we went to besiege Denain.[4] He first summoned the garrison—

MARLOW. Don't you think the *ventre d'or*[5] waistcoat will do with the plain brown?

HARD. He first summoned the garrison, which might consist of about five thousand men—

HASTINGS. I think not: brown and yellow mix but very poorly.

HARD. I say, gentlemen, as I was telling you, he summoned the garrison which might consist of about five thousand men—

MARLOW. The girls like finery.

HARD. Which might consist of about five thousand men, well appointed with stores, ammunition, and other implements of war. 'Now,' says the Duke of Marlborough to George Brooks, that stood next to

---

4. *the Duke . . . Denain:* The French Marshal Villars defeated Prince Eugene in battle in the vicinity of the present Denain in 1712. The Duke of Marlborough was not present, however.    5. *ventre d'or:* gold-fronted.

him—you must have heard of George Brooks; 'I'll pawn my Dukedom,' says he, 'but I take that garrison without spilling a drop of blood.' So—

MARLOW. What, my good friend, if you gave us a glass of punch in the meantime, it would help us to carry on the siege with vigour.

HARD. Punch, sir! [*Aside.*] This is the most unaccountable kind of modesty I ever met with.

MARLOW. Yes, sir, punch! A glass of warm punch, after our journey, will be comfortable. This is Liberty Hall, you know.

HARD. Here's a cup, sir.

MARLOW. [*Aside.*] So this fellow, in his Liberty Hall, will only let us have just what he pleases.

HARD. [*Taking the cup.*] I hope you'll find it to your mind. I have prepared it with my own hands, and I believe you'll own the ingredients are tolerable. Will you be so good as to pledge me, sir? Here, Mr Marlow, here is our better acquaintance! [*Drinks.*]

MARLOW. [*Aside.*] A very impudent fellow this! but he's a character, and I'll humour him a little. Sir, my service to you. [*Drinks.*]

HASTINGS. [*Aside.*] I see this fellow wants to give us his company, and forgets that he's an innkeeper, before he has learned to be a gentleman.

MARLOW. From the excellence of your cup, my old friend, I suppose you have a good deal of business in this part of the country. Warm work, now and then, at elections, I suppose?

HARD. No, sir, I have long given that work over. Since our betters have hit upon the expedient of electing each other, there's no business 'for us that sell ale.'[6]

HASTINGS. So, then you have no turn for politics, I find.

HARD. Not in the least. There was a time, indeed, I fretted myself about the mistakes of government, like other people; but, finding myself every day grow more angry, and the government growing no better, I left it to mend itself. Since that, I no more trouble my head about Heyder Ally or Ally Cawn,[7] than about Ally Croaker.[8] Sir, my service to you.

---

6. '*for us that sell ale*': This may mean *for those of us who buy votes with ale.*
7. *Heyder Ally or Ally Cawn:* Haider Ali was a Mohammedan prince of India who made himself maharaja of Mysore and fought against the British (1767–1769). Two Ally Cawns of Bengal are referred to in the *Gentleman's Magazine* of 1761.
8. *Ally Croaker:* a character in a popular Irish song.

HASTINGS. So that, with eating above stairs, and drinking below, with receiving your friends within, and amusing them without, you lead a good pleasant bustling life of it.

HARD. I do stir about a great deal, that's certain. Half the differences of the parish are adjusted in this very parlour.

MARLOW. [*After drinking.*] And you have an argument in your cup, old gentleman, better than any in Westminster Hall.[9]

HARD. Ay, young gentleman, that, and a little philosophy.

MARLOW. [*Aside.*] Well, this is the first time I ever heard of an innkeeper's philosophy.

HASTINGS. So then, like an experienced general, you attack them on every quarter. If you find their reason manageable, you attack it with your philosophy; if you find they have no reason, you attack them with this. Here's your health, my philosopher. [*Drinks.*]

HARD. Good, very good, thank you; ha! ha! Your generalship puts me in mind of Prince Eugene, when he fought the Turks at the battle of Belgrade.[10] You shall hear.

MARLOW. Instead of the battle of Belgrade, I believe it's almost time to talk about supper. What has your philosophy got in the house for supper?

HARD. For supper, sir! [*Aside.*] Was ever such a request to a man in his own house!

MARLOW. Yes, sir, supper, sir; I begin to feel an appetite. I shall make devilish work to-night in the larder, I promise you.

HARD. [*Aside.*] Such a brazen dog sure never my eyes beheld. [*To him.*] Why, really, sir, as for supper I can't well tell. My Dorothy, and the cook-maid, settle these things between them. I leave these kind of things entirely to them.

MARLOW. You do, do you?

HARD. Entirely. By the by, I believe they are in actual consultation upon what's for supper this moment in the kitchen.

MARLOW. Then I beg they'll admit me as one of their privy council. It's a way I have got. When I travel I always choose to regulate my own supper. Let the cook be called. No offence, I hope, sir.

HARD. Oh no, sir, none in the least; yet, I don't know how: our Bridget,

---

9. *Westminster Hall:* the principal seat of justice from the time of Henry III (1207–1272), and the scene of a great many trials.
10. *Prince Eugene ... Belgrade:* Prince Eugene succeeded in taking the city of Belgrade from the invading Turks on April 10, 1717. Goldsmith was supposed to have heard the story often from General Oglethorpe, who was there. Oglethorpe's description of the battle at a dinner party is recorded in Boswell's *Life of Johnson.*

the cook-maid, is not very communicative upon these occasions. Should we send for her, she might scold us all out of the house.

HASTINGS. Let's see your list of the larder, then. I ask it as a favour. I always match my appetite to my bill of fare.

MARLOW. [*To* HARDCASTLE, *who looks at them with surprise.*] Sir, he's very right, and it's my way, too.

HARD. Sir, you have a right to command here. Here, Roger, bring us the bill of fare for to-night's supper. I believe it's drawn out. Your manner, Mr Hastings, puts me in mind of my uncle, Colonel Wallop. It was a saying of his, that no man was sure of his supper till he had eaten it.

HASTINGS. [*Aside.*] All upon the high rope! His uncle a colonel! We shall soon hear of his mother being a justice of peace. [HARDCASTLE *gives the paper to* MARLOW.] But let's hear the bill of fare.

MARLOW. [*Perusing.*] What's here? For the first course; for the second course; for the dessert. The devil, sir, do you think we have brought down the whole Joiners' Company, or the Corporation of Bedford,[11] to eat up such a supper? Two or three little things, clean and comfortable, will do.

HASTINGS. But let's hear it.

MARLOW. [*Reading.*] For the first course at the top, a pig, and pruin sauce.

HASTINGS. Damn your pig, I say!

MARLOW. And damn your pruin sauce, say I!

HARD. And yet, gentlemen, to men that are hungry, pig with pruin sauce is very good eating.

MARLOW. At the bottom a calf's tongue and brains.

HASTINGS. Let your brains be knocked out, my good sir, I don't like them.

MARLOW. Or you may clap them on a plate by themselves. I do.

HARD. [*Aside.*] Their impudence confounds me. [*To them.*] Gentlemen, you are my guests, make what alterations you please. Is there anything else you wish to retrench or alter, gentlemen?

MARLOW. A pork pie, a boiled rabbit and sausages, a Florentine,[12] a shaking pudding,[13] and a dish of tiff—taff—taffety cream![14]

---

11. *the whole . . . Bedford:* Both the town corporation of Bedford and the Joiners' (carpenters') Company were well known for their hearty eating.
12. *a Florentine:* a pie or kind of tart, especially a meat pie.
13. *a shaking pudding:* gelatin.
14. *tiff—taff—taffety cream:* Taffety cream was a dessert so-called because of its resemblance to taffeta.

HASTINGS. Confound your made dishes; I shall be as much at a loss in this house as at a green and yellow dinner at the French ambassador's table, I'm for plain eating.

HARD. I'm sorry, gentlemen, that I have nothing you like, but if there be anything you have a particular fancy to—

MARLOW. Why really, sir, your bill of fare is so exquisite, that any one part of it is full as good as another. And now to see that our beds are aired, and properly taken care of.

HARD. I entreat you'll leave all that to me. You shall not stir a step.

MARLOW. Leave that to you! I protest, sir, you must excuse me, I always look to these things myself.

HARD. I must insist, sir, you'll make yourself easy on that head.

MARLOW. You see I'm resolved on it. [*Aside.*] A very troublesome fellow this, as ever I met with.

HARD. Well, sir, I'm resolved at least to attend you. [*Aside.*] This may be modern modesty, but I never saw anything look so like old-fashioned impudence.

[*Exeunt* MARLOW *and* HARDCASTLE.]

HASTINGS. [*Alone.*] So I find this fellow's civilities begin to grow troublesome. But who can be angry at those assiduities which are meant to please him? Ha! what do I see! Miss Neville, by all that's happy!

[*Enter* MISS NEVILLE.]

MISS NEVILLE. My dear Hastings! To what unexpected good fortune, to what accident, am I to ascribe this happy meeting?

HASTINGS. Rather let me ask the same question, as I could never have hoped to meet my dearest Constance at an inn.

MISS NEVILLE. An inn! sure you mistake: my aunt, my guardian, lives here. What could induce you to think this house an inn?

HASTINGS. My friend, Mr Marlow, with whom I came down, and I, have been sent here as to an inn, I assure you. A young fellow, whom we accidentally met at a house hard by, directed us thither.

MISS NEVILLE. Certainly it must be one of my hopeful cousin's tricks, of whom you have heard me talk so often: ha! ha! ha!

HASTINGS. He whom your aunt intends for you? He of whom I have such just apprehensions?

MISS NEVILLE. You have nothing to fear from him, I assure you. You'd adore him if you knew how heartily he despises me. My aunt knows it, too, and has undertaken to court me for him, and actually begins to think she had made a conquest.

HASTINGS. Thou dear dissembler! You must know, my Constance, I have just seized this happy opportunity of my friend's visit here to get admittance into the family. The horses that carried us down are now fatigued with their journey, but they'll soon be refreshed; and then, if my dearest girl will trust in her faithful Hastings, we shall soon be landed in France, where even among slaves the laws of marriage are respected.[15]

MISS NEVILLE. I have often told you, that though ready to obey you, I yet should leave my little fortune behind with reluctance. The greatest part of it was left me by my uncle, the India Director, and chiefly consists in jewels. I have been for some time persuading my aunt to let me wear them. I fancy I'm very near succeeding. The instant they are put into my possession you shall find me ready to make them and myself yours.

HASTINGS. Perish the baubles! Your person is all I desire. In the meantime, my friend Marlow must not be let into his mistake. I know the strange reserve of his temper is such that, if abruptly informed of it, he would instantly quit the house before our plan was ripe for execution.

MISS NEVILLE. But how shall we keep him in the deception? Miss Hardcastle is just returned from walking; what if we still continue to deceive him? This, this way—[*They confer.*]

[*Enter* MARLOW.]

MARLOW. The assiduities of these good people tease me beyond bearing. My host seems to think it ill manners to leave me alone, and so he claps not only himself, but his old-fashioned wife on my back. They talk of coming to sup with us, too; and then, I suppose, we are to run the gauntlet through all the rest of the family. What have we got here?

HASTINGS. My dear Charles! Let me congratulate you! The most fortunate accident! Who do you think is just alighted?

MARLOW. Cannot guess.

---

15. *in France . . . respected:* possibly a criticism of the Royal Marriage Act of 1772, a restrictive measure concerning the members of the English royal family.

HASTINGS. Our mistresses, boy, Miss Hardcastle and Miss Neville. Give me leave to introduce Miss Constance Neville to your acquaintance. Happening to dine in the neighbourhood, they called, on their return, to take fresh horses here. Miss Hardcastle has just stepped into the next room, and will be back in an instant. Wasn't it lucky? eh!

MARLOW. [*Aside.*] I have just been mortified enough of all conscience, and here comes something to complete my embarrassment.

HASTINGS. Well! but wasn't it the most fortunate thing in the world?

MARLOW. Oh! yes. Very fortunate—a most joyful encounter. But our dresses, George, you know, are in disorder. What if we should postpone the happiness till to-morrow? To-morrow at her own house. It will be every bit as convenient—and rather more respectful. To-morrow let it be. [*Offering to go.*]

MISS NEVILLE. By no means, sir. Your ceremony will displease her. The disorder of your dress will shew the ardour of your impatience. Besides, she knows you are in the house, and will permit you to see her.

MARLOW. Oh! the devil! how shall I support it? Hem! hem! Hastings, you must not go. You are to assist me, you know. I shall be confoundedly ridiculous. Yet, hang it! I'll take courage. Hem!

HASTINGS. Pshaw, man! it's but the first plunge, and all's over. She's but a woman, you know.

MARLOW. And of all women, she that I dread most to encounter!

[*Enter* MISS HARDCASTLE, *as returned from walking.*]

HASTINGS. [*Introducing them.*] Miss Hardcastle. Mr Marlow. I'm proud of bringing two persons of such merit together, that only want to know, to esteem each other.

MISS HARD. [*Aside.*] Now, for meeting my modest gentleman with a demure face, and quite in his own manner. [*After a pause, in which he appears very uneasy and disconcerted.*] I'm glad of your safe arrival, sir—I'm told you had some accidents by the way.

MARLOW. Only a few, madam. Yes, we had some. Yes, madam, a good many accidents, but should be sorry—madam—or rather glad of any accidents—that are so agreeably concluded. Hem!

HASTINGS. [*To him.*] You never spoke better in your whole life. Keep it up, and I'll insure you the victory.

MISS HARD. I'm afraid you flatter, sir. You that have seen so much of the finest company can find little entertainment in an obscure corner of the country.

MARLOW. [*Gathering courage.*] I have lived, indeed, in the world, madam; but I have kept very little company. I have been but an observer upon life, madam, while others were enjoying it.

MISS NEVILLE. But that, I am told, is the way to enjoy it at last.

HASTINGS [*To him.*] Cicero[16] never spoke better. Once more, and you are confirmed in assurance for ever.

MARLOW. [*To him.*] Hem! Stand by me, then, and when I'm down, throw in a word or two to set me up again.

MISS HARD. An observer, like you, upon life, were, I fear, disagreeably employed, since you must have had much more to censure than to approve.

MARLOW. Pardon me, madam. I was always willing to be amused. The folly of most people is rather an object of mirth than uneasiness.

HASTINGS. [*To him.*] Bravo, bravo. Never spoke so well in your whole life. Well, Miss Hardcastle, I see that you and Mr Marlow are going to be very good company. I believe our being here will but embarrass the interview.

MARLOW. Not in the least, Mr Hastings. We like your company of all things. [*To him.*] Zounds! George, sure you won't go? How can you leave us?

HASTINGS. Our presence will but spoil conversation, so we'll retire to the next room. [*To him.*] You don't consider, man, that we are to manage a little *tête-à-tête* of our own.

[*Exeunt.*]

MISS HARD. [*After a pause.*] But you have not been wholly an observer, I presume, sir: the ladies, I should hope, have employed some part of your addresses.

MARLOW. [*Relapsing into timidity.*] Pardon me, madam, I—I—I—as yet have studied—only—to—deserve them.

MISS HARD. And that some say is the very worst way to obtain them.

MARLOW. Perhaps so, madam. But I love to converse only with the more grave and sensible part of the sex. But I'm afraid I grow tiresome.

---

16. *Cicero:* Marcus Tullius Cicero (106–43 B.C.), Roman statesman and philosopher, who is especially remembered for his powerful orations.

MISS HARD. Not at all, sir; there is nothing I like so much as grave conversation myself: I could hear it for ever. Indeed, I have often been surprised how a man of sentiment[17] could ever admire those light airy pleasures, where nothing reaches the heart.

MARLOW. It's—a disease—of the mind, madam. In the variety of tastes there must be some who, wanting a relish for—um-a-um.

MISS HARD. I understand you, sir. There must be some, who, wanting a relish for refined pleasures, pretend to despise what they are incapable of tasting.

MARLOW. My meaning, madam, but infinitely better expressed. And I can't help observing—a—

MISS HARD. [*Aside.*] Who could ever suppose this fellow impudent upon some occasions. [*To him.*] You were going to observe, sir—

MARLOW. I was observing, madam—I protest, madam, I forget what I was going to observe.

MISS HARD. [*Aside.*] I vow and so do I. [*To him.*] You were observing, sir, that in this age of hypocrisy—something about hypocrisy, sir.

MARLOW. Yes, madam. In this age of hypocrisy, there are few who upon strict inquiry do not—a—a—a—

MISS HARD. I understand you perfectly, sir.

MARLOW. [*Aside.*] Egad! and that's more than I do myself!

MISS HARD. You mean that in this hypocritical age there are few that do not condemn in public what they practise in private, and think they pay every debt to virtue when they praise it.

MARLOW. True, madam; those who have most virtue in their mouths, have least of it in their bosoms. But I'm sure I tire you, madam.

MISS HARD. Not in the least, sir; there's something so agreeable and spirited in your manner, such life and force—pray, sir, go on.

MARLOW. Yes, madam. I was saying—that there are some occasions—when a total want of courage, madam, destroys all the—and puts us—upon a—a—a—

MISS HARD. I agree with you entirely, a want of courage upon some occasions assumes the appearance of ignorance, and betrays us when we most want to excel. I beg you'll proceed.

MARLOW. Yes, madam. Morally speaking, madam—but I see Miss Neville expecting us in the next room. I would not intrude for the world.

---

17. *a man of sentiment:* a slap at the sentimental comedy school. This entire scene between Miss Hardcastle and Marlow abounds with sly references to persons of elevated sentiments and weighty gravity.

MISS HARD. I protest, sir, I never was more agreeably entertained in all my life. Pray go on.

MARLOW. Yes, madam. I was—but she beckons us to join her. Madam, shall I do myself the honour to attend you?

MISS HARD. Well then, I'll follow.

MARLOW. [*Aside.*] This pretty smooth dialogue has done for me.

[*Exit.*]

MISS HARD. [*Alone.*] Ha! ha! ha! Was there ever such a sober sentimental interview? I'm certain he scarce looked in my face the whole time. Yet the fellow, but for his unaccountable bashfulness, is pretty well, too. He has good sense, but then so buried in his fears, that it fatigues one more than ignorance. If I could teach him a little confidence, it would be doing somebody that I know of a piece of service. But who is that somebody?—that, faith, is a question I can scarce answer.

[*Exit.*]

[*Enter* TONY *and* MISS NEVILLE, *followed by* MRS HARDCASTLE *and* HASTINGS.]

TONY. What do you follow me for, cousin Con? I wonder you're not ashamed to be so very engaging.

MISS NEVILLE. I hope, cousin, one may speak to one's own relations, and not be to blame.

TONY. Ay, but I know what sort of a relation you want to make me, though; but it won't do. I tell you, cousin Con, it won't do; so I beg you'll keep your distance, I want no nearer relationship.

[*She follows, coquetting him to the back scene.*]

MRS HARD. Well! I vow, Mr Hastings, you are very entertaining. There's nothing in the world I love to talk of so much as London, and the fashions, though I was never there myself.

HASTINGS. Never there! You amaze me! From your air and manner, I concluded you had been bred all your life either at Ranelagh, St James's, or Tower Wharf.[18]

---

18. *at Ranelagh . . . Wharf:* Hastings takes advantage of Mrs. Hardcastle's ignorance of London. Ranelagh Gardens in Chelsea, and St. James's Park, between the palaces of St. James's and Whitehall, were places frequented by fashionable persons. Tower Wharf, on the other hand, was definitely a vulgar part of town. Mrs. Hardcastle does not know enough about London to notice the joke played upon her.

MRS HARD. Oh! sir, you're only pleased to say so. We country persons can have no manner at all. I'm in love with the town, and that serves to raise me above some of our neighbouring rustics; but who can have a manner, that has never seen the Pantheon, the Grotto Gardens, the Borough, and such places where the nobility chiefly resort?[19] All I can do is to enjoy London at second-hand. I take care to know every *tête-à-tête* from the Scandalous Magazine,[20] and have all the fashions as they come out, in a letter from the two Miss Rickets of Crooked Lane. Pray how do you like this head, Mr Hastings?

HASTINGS. Extremely elegant and *dégagée*,[21] upon my word, madam. Your friseur[22] is a Frenchman, I suppose?

MRS HARD. I protest, I dressed it myself from a print in the Ladies' Memorandum-book[23] for the last year.

HASTINGS. Indeed. Such a head in a side-box, at the playhouse, would draw as many gazers as my Lady Mayoress at a city ball.

MRS HARD. I vow, since inoculation began,[24] there is no such thing to be seen as a plain woman; so one must dress a little particular, or one may escape in the crowd.

HASTINGS. But that can never be your case, madam, in any dress! [*Bowing.*]

MRS HARD. Yet, what signifies my dressing when I have such a piece of antiquity by my side as Mr Hardcastle: all I can say will never argue down a single button from his clothes. I have often wanted him to throw off his great flaxen wig, and where he was bald, to plaster it over like my Lord Pately, with powder.

HASTINGS. You are right, madam; for, as among the ladies there are none ugly, so among the men there are none old.

MRS HARD. But what do you think his answer was? Why, with his usual Gothic vivacity, he said I only wanted him to throw off his wig to convert it into a *tête* for my own wearing.

---

19. *the Pantheon ... chiefly resort:* Mrs. Hardcastle unwittingly couples the Pantheon, which was a haunt of the nobility, with the Grotto Gardens, an inferior imitation of the Ranelagh Gardens, and the Borough, once a fashionable quarter, but fallen from favor at the time of *She Stoops to Conquer.*
20. *tête-à-tête ... Magazine:* The *Town and Country Magazine* published monthly articles of scandal. Opposite each scandalous article appeared the portrait head (the Tête-à-Tête) of the subject and his mistress.
21. *dégagée:* unconstrained, offhand.  22. *friseur:* hairdresser.
23. *the Ladies' Memorandum-book:* one of the annual diaries or pocket journals for women.
24. *since inoculation began:* inoculation for smallpox was introduced in 1721.

HASTINGS. Intolerable! At your age you may wear what you please, and it must become you.

MRS HARD. Pray, Mr Hastings, what do you take to be the most fashionable age about town?

HASTINGS. Some time ago forty was all the mode; but I'm told the ladies intend to bring up fifty for the ensuing winter.

MRS HARD. Seriously? Then I shall be too young for the fashion!

HASTINGS. No lady begins now to put on jewels till she's past forty. For instance, Miss there, in a polite circle, would be considered as a child, as a mere maker of samplers.

MRS HARD. And yet Mrs Niece thinks herself as much a woman, and is as fond of jewels as the oldest of us all.

HASTINGS. Your niece, is she? And that young gentleman, a brother of yours, I should presume?

MRS HARD. My son, sir. They are contracted to each other. Observe their little sports. They fall in and out ten times a day, as if they were man and wife already. [*To them.*] Well, Tony child, what soft things are you saying to your cousin Constance this evening?

TONY. I have been saying no soft things; but that it's very hard to be followed about so! Ecod! I've not a place in the house now that's left to myself but the stable.

MRS HARD. Never mind him, Con, my dear. He's in another story behind your back.

MISS NEVILLE. There's something generous in my cousin's manner. He falls out before faces to be forgiven in private.

TONY. That's a damned confounded—crack.

MRS HARD. Ah! he's a sly one. Don't you think they're like each other about the mouth, Mr Hastings? The Blenkinsop mouth to a T. They're of a size, too. Back to back, my pretties, that Mr Hastings may see you. Come, Tony.

TONY. You had as good not make me, I tell you. [*Measuring.*]

MISS NEVILLE. Oh lud! he has almost cracked my head.

MRS HARD. Oh, the monster! For shame, Tony. You a man, and behave so!

TONY. If I'm a man, let me have my fortin.[25] Ecod! I'll not be made a fool of no longer.

MRS HARD. Is this, ungrateful boy, all that I'm to get for the pains I have taken in your education? I that have rocked you in your cradle,

25. *fortin:* fortune.

and fed that pretty mouth with a spoon! Did not I work that waistcoat to make you genteel? Did not I prescribe for you every day, and weep while the receipt[26] was operating?

TONY. Ecod! you had reason to weep, for you have been dosing me ever since I was born. I have gone through every receipt in the complete housewife[27] ten times over; and you have thoughts of coursing me through Quincy[28] next spring. But, ecod! I tell you, I'll not be made a fool of no longer.

MRS HARD. Wasn't it all for your good, viper? Wasn't it all for your good?

TONY. I wish you'd let me and my good alone, then. Snubbing this way when I'm in spirits. If I'm to have any good, let it come of itself; not to keep dinging it, dinging it into one so.

MRS HARD. That's false; I never see you when you're in spirits. No, Tony, you then go to the alehouse or kennel. I'm never to be delighted with your agreeable wild notes, unfeeling monster!

TONY. Ecod! Mamma, your own notes are the wildest of the two.

MRS HARD. Was ever the like? But I see he wants to break my heart, I see he does.

HASTINGS. Dear Madam, permit me to lecture the young gentleman a little. I'm certain I can persuade him to his duty.

MRS HARD. Well, I must retire. Come, Constance, my love. You see, Mr Hastings, the wretchedness of my situation. Was ever poor woman so plagued with a dear, sweet, pretty, provoking, undutiful boy.

[*Exeunt* MRS HARDCASTLE *and* MISS NEVILLE, HASTINGS, TONY.]

TONY. [*Singing.*] 'There was a young man riding by, and fain would have his will. Rang do didlo dee.'
Don't mind her. Let her cry. It's the comfort of her heart. I have seen her and sister cry over a book for an hour together, and they said they liked the book the better the more it made them cry.

HASTINGS. Then you're no friend to the ladies, I find, my pretty young gentleman?

TONY. That's as I find 'um.

---

26. *receipt:* recipe.
27. *the complete housewife:* a combination guide to cooking and home remedies.
28. *Quincy:* the *Complete English Dispensatory*, written by a Dr. John Quincy.

HASTINGS. Not to her of your mother's choosing, I dare answer! And yet she appears to me a pretty, well-tempered girl.

TONY. That's because you don't know her as well as I. Ecod! I know every inch about her; and there's not a more bitter cantankerous toad in all Christendom!

HASTINGS. [*Aside.*] Pretty encouragement this for a lover!

TONY. I have seen her since the height of that. She has as many tricks as a hare in a thicket, or a colt the first day's breaking.

HASTINGS. To me she appears sensible and silent.

TONY. Ay, before company. But when she's with her playmates, she's as loud as a hog in a gate.

HASTINGS. But there is a meek modesty about her that charms me.

TONY. Yes, but curb her never so little, she kicks up, and you're flung in a ditch.

HASTINGS. Well, but you must allow her a little beauty. Yes, you must allow her some beauty.

TONY. Bandbox! She's all a made-up thing, mun. Ah! could you but see Bet Bouncer of these parts, you might then talk of beauty. Ecod, she has two eyes as black as sloes,[29] and cheeks as broad and red as a pulpit cushion. She'd make two of she.

HASTINGS. Well, what say you of a friend that would take this bitter bargain off your hands?

TONY. Anon?

HASTINGS. Would you thank him that would take Miss Neville, and leave you to happiness and your dear Betsy?

TONY. Ay; but where is there such a friend, for who would take her?

HASTINGS. I am he. If you but assist me, I'll engage to whip her off to France, and you shall never hear more of her.

TONY. Assist you! Ecod, I will, to the last drop of my blood. I'll clap a pair of horses to your chaise that shall trundle you off in a twinkling, and may be get you a part of her fortin beside in jewels that you little dream of.

HASTINGS. My dear 'squire, this looks like a lad of spirit.

TONY. Come along then, and you shall see more of my spirit before you have done with me. [*Singing.*]

We are the boys

---

29. *sloes:* The sloe is the fruit of the blackthorn; it is dark purple or black in color.

**She Stoops to Conquer**

That fears no noise
Where the thundering cannons roar.

[*Exeunt.*]

# ACT III

[*Enter* HARDCASTLE *alone.*]

HARD. What could my old friend Sir Charles mean by recommending his son as the modestest young man in town? To me he appears the most impudent piece of brass that ever spoke with a tongue. He has taken possession of the easy chair by the fireside already. He took off his boots in the parlour, and desired me to see them taken care of. I'm desirous to know how his impudence affects my daughter. She will certainly be shocked at it.

[*Enter* MISS HARDCASTLE *plainly dressed.*]

HARD. Well, my Kate, I see you have changed your dress, as I bid you; and yet, I believe, there was no great occasion.
MISS HARD. I find such a pleasure, sir, in obeying your commands, that I take care to observe them without ever debating their propriety.
HARD. And yet, Kate, I sometimes give you some cause, particularly when I recommended my modest gentleman to you as a lover to-day.
MISS HARD. You taught me to expect something extraordinary, and I find the original exceeds the description!
HARD. I was never so surprised in my life! He has quite confounded all my faculties!
MISS HARD. I never saw anything like it: and a man of the world, too!
HARD. Ay, he learned it all abroad,—what a fool was I, to think a young man could learn modesty by travelling. He might as soon learn wit at a masquerade.
MISS HARD. It seems all natural to him.
HARD. A good deal assisted by bad company and a French dancing-master.
MISS HARD. Sure, you mistake, papa! A French dancing-master could

never have taught him that timid look—that awkward address—that bashful manner—

HARD. Whose look? whose manner, child?

MISS HARD. Mr. Marlow's: his *mauvaise honte*,[1] his timidity, struck me at the first sight.

HARD. Then your first sight deceived you; for I think him one of the most brazen first sights that ever astonished my senses!

MISS HARD. Sure, sir, you rally! I never saw anyone so modest.

HARD. And can you be serious! I never saw such a bouncing swaggering puppy since I was born. Bully Dawson[2] was but a fool to him.

MISS HARD. Surprising! He met me with a respectful bow, a stammering voice, and a look fixed on the ground.

HARD. He met me with a loud voice, a lordly air, and a familiarity that made my blood freeze again.

MISS HARD. He treated me with diffidence and respect; censured the manners of the age; admired the prudence of girls that never laughed; tired me with apologies for being tiresome; then left the room with a bow, and 'Madam, I would not for the world detain you.'

HARD. He spoke to me as if he knew me all his life before; asked twenty questions, and never waited for an answer; interrupted my best remarks with some silly pun, and when I was in my best story of the Duke of Marlborough and Prince Eugene, he asked if I had not a good hand at making punch. Yes, Kate, he asked your father if he was a maker of punch!

MISS HARD. One of us must certainly be mistaken.

HARD. If he be what he has shown himself, I'm determined he shall never have my consent.

MISS HARD. And if he be the sullen thing I take him, he shall never have mine.

HARD. In one thing then we are agreed—to reject him.

MISS HARD. Yes: but upon conditions. For if you should find him less impudent, and I more presuming; if you find him more respectful, and I more importunate—I don't know—the fellow is well enough for a man. Certainly we don't meet many such at a horse-race in the country.

---

1. *mauvaise honte:* painful shyness.
2. *Bully Dawson:* a well-known bully and coward in London. He appears frequently in the literature of the eighteenth century.

HARD. If we should find him so—but that's impossible. The first appearance has done my business. I'm seldom deceived in that.

MISS HARD. And yet there may be many good qualities under that first appearance.

HARD. Ay, when a girl finds a fellow's outside to her taste, she then sets about guessing the rest of his furniture. With her, a smooth face stands for good sense, and a genteel figure for every virtue.

MISS HARD. I hope, sir, a conversation begun with a compliment to my good sense won't end with a sneer at my understanding?

HARD. Pardon me, Kate. But if young Mr. Brazen can find the art of reconciling contradictions, he may please us both, perhaps.

MISS HARD. And as one of us must be mistaken, what if we go to make further discoveries?

HARD. Agreed. But depend on't I'm in the right.

MISS HARD. And depend on't I'm not much in the wrong.

[*Exeunt.*]

[*Enter* TONY, *running in with a casket.*]

TONY. Ecod! I have got them. Here they are. My cousin Con's necklaces, bobs and all. My mother shan't cheat the poor souls out of their fortin neither. Oh! my genius, is that you?

[*Enter* HASTINGS.]

HASTINGS. My dear friend, how have you managed with your mother? I hope you have amused her with pretending love for your cousin, and that you are willing to be reconciled at last? Our horses will be refreshed in a short time, and we shall soon be ready to set off.

TONY. And here's something to bear your charges by the way. [*Giving the casket.*] Your sweetheart's jewels. Keep them, and hang those, I say, that would rob you of one of them.

HASTINGS. But how have you procured them from your mother?

TONY. Ask me no questions, and I'll tell you no fibs. I procured them by the rule of thumb. If I had not a key to every drawer in mother's bureau, how could I go to the alehouse so often as I do? An honest man may rob himself of his own at any time.

HASTINGS. Thousands do it every day. But to be plain with you, Miss Neville is endeavouring to procure them from her aunt this very instant. If she succeeds, it will be the most delicate way at least of obtaining them.

TONY. Well, keep them, till you know how it will be. But I know how it will be well enough; she'd as soon part with the only sound tooth in her head!

HASTINGS. But I dread the effects of her resentment, when she finds she has lost them.

TONY. Never you mind her resentment, leave *me* to manage that. I don't value her resentment the bounce of a cracker. Zounds! here they are! Morrice! prance!

[*Exit* HASTINGS.]

[TONY, MRS HARDCASTLE, *and* MISS NEVILLE.]

MRS HARD. Indeed, Constance, you amaze me. Such a girl as you want jewels? It will be time enough for jewels, my dear, twenty years hence, when your beauty begins to want repairs.

MISS NEVILLE. But what will repair beauty at forty, will certainly improve it at twenty, madam.

MRS HARD. Yours, my dear, can admit of none. That natural blush is beyond a thousand ornaments. Besides, child, jewels are quite out at present. Don't you see half the ladies of our acquaintance, my Lady Kill-daylight, and Mrs Crump, and the rest of them, carry their jewels to town, and bring nothing but paste and marcasites[3] back?

MISS NEVILLE. But who knows, madam, but somebody that shall be nameless would like me best with all my little finery about me?

MRS HARD. Consult your glass, my dear, and then see, if with such a pair of eyes, you want any better sparklers. What do you think, Tony, my dear, does your cousin Con want any jewels, in your eyes, to set off her beauty?

TONY. That's as thereafter may be.

MISS NEVILLE. My dear aunt, if you knew how it would oblige me.

MRS HARD. A parcel of old-fashioned rose and table-cut[4] things. They would make you look like the court of King Solomon at a puppet-show. Besides, I believe I can't readily come at them. They may be missing, for aught I know to the contrary.

TONY. [*Apart to* MRS HARD.] Then why don't you tell her so at once, as

---

3. *paste and marcasites:* Paste is a brilliant glass used to make artificial gems. Marcasites were ornaments made from the crystallized forms of iron pyrites (fool's gold).    4. *table-cut:* cut with flat surfaces.

She Stoops to Conquer     121

she's so longing for them. Tell her they're lost. It's the only way to quiet her. Say they're lost, and call me to bear witness.

MRS HARD. [*Apart to* TONY.] You know, my dear, I'm only keeping them for you. So if I say they're gone, you'll bear me witness, will you? He! he! he!

TONY. Never fear me. Ecod! I'll say I saw them taken out with my own eyes.

MISS NEVILLE. I desire them but for a day, madam. Just to be permitted to shew them as relics, and then they may be locked up again.

MRS HARD. To be plain with you, my dear Constance, if I could find them, you should have them. They're missing, I assure you. Lost, for aught I know; but we must have patience wherever they are.

MISS NEVILLE. I'll not believe it; this is but a shallow pretence to deny me. I know they're too valuable to be so slightly kept, and as you are to answer for the loss—

MRS HARD. Don't be alarmed, Constance. If they be lost, I must restore an equivalent. But my son knows they are missing, and not to be found.

TONY. That I can bear witness to. They are missing, and not to be found, I'll take my oath on't.

MRS HARD. You must learn resignation, my dear; for though we lose our fortune, yet we should not lose our patience. See me, how calm I am.

MISS NEVILLE. Ay, people are generally calm at the misfortunes of others.

MRS HARD. Now, I wonder a girl of your good sense should waste a thought upon such trumpery. We shall soon find them; and, in the meantime, you shall make use of my garnets till your jewels be found.

MISS NEVILLE. I detest garnets.

MRS HARD. The most becoming things in the world to set off a clear complexion. You have often seen how well they look upon me. You shall have them.

[*Exit.*]

MISS NEVILLE. [*Trying to detain her.*] I dislike them of all things. You shan't stir. Was ever anything so provoking to mislay my own jewels, and force me to wear her trumpery.

TONY. Don't be a fool. If she gives you the garnets, take what you can get. The jewels are your own already. I have stolen them out of her bureau, and she does not know it. Fly to your spark, he'll tell you more of the matter. Leave me to manage her.

MISS NEVILLE. My dear cousin!

TONY. Vanish. She's here, and has missed them already. Zounds! how she fidgets and spits about like a catherine wheel!⁵

[*Enter* MRS HARDCASTLE.]

MRS HARD. Confusion! thieves! robbers! We are cheated, plundered, broke open, undone!

TONY. What's the matter, what's the matter, mamma? I hope nothing has happened to any of the good family!

MRS HARD. We are robbed. My bureau has been broke open, the jewels taken out, and I'm undone!

TONY. Oh! is that all? Ha! ha! ha! By the laws, I never saw it better acted in my life. Ecod, I thought you was ruined in earnest, ha, ha, ha!

MRS HARD. Why, boy, I am ruined in earnest. My bureau has been broke open, and all taken away.

TONY. Stick to that; ha, ha, ha! stick to that. I'll bear witness, you know, call me to bear witness.

MRS HARD. I tell you, Tony, by all that's precious, the jewels are gone, and I shall be ruined for ever.

TONY. Sure I know they're gone, and I am to say so.

MRS HARD. My dearest Tony, but hear me. They're gone, I say.

TONY. By the laws, mamma, you make me for to laugh, ha! ha! I know who took them well enough, ha! ha! ha!

MRS HARD. Was there ever such a blockhead, that can't tell the difference between jest and earnest. I tell you I'm not in jest, booby!

TONY. That's right, that's right: you must be in a bitter passion, and then nobody will suspect either of us. I'll bear witness that they are gone.

MRS HARD. Was there ever such a cross-grained brute, that won't hear me! Can you bear witness that you're no better than a fool? Was ever poor woman so beset with fools on one hand, and thieves on the other?

TONY. I can bear witness to that.

---

5. *a catherine wheel:* a fireworks pinwheel.

MRS HARD. Bear witness again, you blockhead you, and I'll turn you out of the room directly. My poor niece, what will become of her? Do you laugh, you unfeeling brute, as if you enjoyed my distress?
TONY. I can bear witness to that.
MRS HARD. Do you insult me, monster? I'll teach you to vex your mother, I will.
TONY. I can bear witness to that. [*He runs off, she follows him.*]

[*Enter* MISS HARDCASTLE *and* MAID.]

MISS HARD. What an unaccountable creature is that brother of mine, to send them to the house as an inn, ha! ha! I don't wonder at his impudence.
MAID. But what is more, madam, the young gentleman as you passed by in your present dress, asked me if you were the barmaid. He mistook you for the barmaid, madam!
MISS HARD. Did he? Then as I live I'm resolved to keep up the delusion. Tell me, Pimple, how do you like my present dress? Don't you think I look something like Cherry in the *Beaux' Stratagem*?[6]
MAID. It's the dress, madam, that every lady wears in the country, but when she visits or receives company.
MISS HARD. And are you sure he does not remember my face or person?
MAID. Certain of it.
MISS HARD. I vow, I thought so; for though we spoke for some time together, yet his fears were such, that he never once looked up during the interview. Indeed, if he had, my bonnet would have kept him from seeing me.
MAID. But what do you hope from keeping him in his mistake?
MISS HARD. In the first place, I shall be seen, and that is no small advantage to a girl who brings her face to market. Then I shall perhaps make an acquaintance, and that's no small victory gained over one who never addresses any but the wildest of her sex. But my chief aim is to take my gentleman off his guard, and like an invisible champion of romance, examine the giant's force before I offer to combat.
MAID. But you are sure you can act your part, and disguise your voice, so that he may mistake that, as he has already mistaken your person?

---

6. *Cherry in the Beaux' Stratagem:* Cherry was the innkeeper's daughter in Farquhar's eighteenth-century comedy.

MISS HARD. Never fear me. I think I have got the true bar cant. Did your honour call? Attend the Lion there. Pipes and tobacco for the Angel. The Lamb has been outrageous this half-hour.[7]

MAID. It will do, madam. But he's here.

[*Exit* MAID.]

[*Enter* MARLOW.]

MARLOW. What a bawling in every part of the house; I have scarce a moment's repose. If I go to the best room, there I find my host and his story. If I fly to the gallery, there we have my hostess with her curtsy down to the ground. I have at last got a moment to myself, and now for recollection. [*Walks and muses.*]

MISS HARD. Did you call, sir? Did your honour call?

MARLOW. [*Musing.*] As for Miss Hardcastle, she's too grave and sentimental for me. [*Paces to left.*]

MISS HARD. Did your honour call? [*She still places herself before him, he turning away.*]

MARLOW. No, child. [*Musing.*] Besides from the glimpse I had of her, I think she squints.

MISS HARD. I'm sure, sir, I heard the bell ring.

MARLOW. No, no. [*Musing.*] I have pleased my father, however, by coming down, and I'll to-morrow please myself by returning. [*Taking out his tablets, and perusing.*]

MISS HARD. Perhaps the other gentleman called, sir?

MARLOW. I tell you, no.

MISS HARD. I should be glad to know, sir. We have such a parcel of servants.

MARLOW. No, no, I tell you. [*Looks full in her face.*] Yes, child, I think I did call. I wanted—I wanted—I vow, child, you are vastly handsome.

MISS HARD. O la, sir, you'll make one ashamed.

MARLOW. Never saw a more sprightly malicious eye. Yes, yes, my dear, I did call. Have you got any of your—a—what d'ye call it in the house?

MISS HARD. No, sir, we have been out of that these ten days.

MARLOW. One may call in this house, I find, to very little purpose. Sup-

---

7. *Attend . . . half-hour:* Private rooms at inns had names like these.

pose I should call for a taste, just by way of trial, of the nectar of your lips; perhaps I might be disappointed in that, too.

MISS HARD. Nectar! nectar! that's a liquor there's no call for in these parts. French, I suppose. We keep no French wines here, sir.

MARLOW. Of true English growth, I assure you.

MISS HARD. Then it's odd I should not know it. We brew all sorts of wines in this house, and I have lived here these eighteen years.

MARLOW. Eighteen years! Why one would think, child, you kept the bar before you were born. How old are you?

MISS HARD. O! sir, I must not tell my age. They say women and music should never be dated.

MARLOW. To guess at this distance, you can't be much above forty. [*Approaching.*] Yet nearer I don't think so much. [*Approaching.*] By coming close to some women they look younger still; but when we come very close indeed [*Attempting to kiss her.*]

MISS HARD. Pray, sir, keep your distance. One would think you wanted to know one's age as they do horses, by mark of mouth.

MARLOW. I protest, child, you use me extremely ill. If you keep me at this distance, how is it possible you and I can ever be acquainted?

MISS HARD. And who wants to be acquainted with you? I want no such acquaintance, not I. I'm sure you did not treat Miss Hardcastle that was here awhile ago in this obstropalous[8] manner. I'll warrant me, before her you looked dashed, and kept bowing to the ground, and talked, for all the world, as if you was before a justice of peace.

MARLOW. [*Aside.*] Egad! she has hit it, sure enough. [*To her.*] In awe of her, child? Ha! ha! ha! A mere awkward, squinting thing, no, no. I find you don't know me. I laughed, and rallied her a little; but I was unwilling to be too severe. No, I could not be too severe, curse me!

MISS HARD. Oh! then, sir, you are a favourite, I find, among the ladies?

MARLOW. Yes, my dear, a great favourite. And yet, hang me, I don't see what they find in me to follow. At the ladies' club in town[9] I'm called their agreeable Rattle. Rattle, child, is not my real name, but one I'm known by. My name is Solomons. Mr Solomons, my dear, at your service. [*Offering to salute*[10] *her.*]

---

8. *obstropalous:* obstreperous.
9. *the ladies' club in town:* a reference to the so-called Female Coterie in Albemarle Street.
10. *salute:* kiss.

MISS HARD. Hold, sir; you are introducing me to your club, not to yourself. And you're so great a favourite there, you say?

MARLOW. Yes, my dear. There's Mrs Mantrap, Lady Betty Blackleg, the Countess of Sligo, Mrs Langhorns, old Miss Biddy Buckskin and your humble servant, keep up the spirit of the place.

MISS HARD. Then it's a very merry place, I suppose?

MARLOW. Yes, as merry as cards, suppers, wine, and old women can make us.

MISS HARD. And their agreeable Rattle, ha! ha! ha!

MARLOW. [*Aside.*] Egad! I don't quite like this chit. She looks knowing, methinks. You laugh, child!

MISS HARD. I can't but laugh to think what time they all have for minding their work or their family.

MARLOW. [*Aside.*] All's well, she don't laugh at me. [*To her.*] Do you ever work, child?

MISS HARD. Ay, sure. There's not a screen or a quilt in the whole house but what can bear witness to that.

MARLOW. Odso! Then you must show me your embroidery. I embroider and draw patterns myself a little. If you want a judge of your work you must apply to me. [*Seizing her hand.*]

MISS HARD. Ay, but the colours don't look well by candlelight. You shall see all in the morning. [*Struggling.*]

MARLOW. And why not now, my angel? Such beauty fires beyond the power of resistance. Pshaw! the father here! My old luck: I never nicked seven[11] that I did not throw ames-ace[12] three times following.

[*Exit* MARLOW.]

[*Enter* HARDCASTLE, *who stands in surprise.*]

HARD. So, madam. So I find this is your modest lover. This is your humble admirer that kept his eyes fixed on the ground, and only adored at humble distance. Kate, Kate, art thou not ashamed to deceive your father so?

MISS HARD. Never trust me, dear papa, but he's still the modest man I first took him for, you'll be convinced of it as well as I.

---

11. *nicked seven:* to nick seven was to throw seven on a pair of dice. It was considered very lucky.
12. *ames-ace:* double ace (snake eyes); considered a very unlucky throw.

**She Stoops to Conquer**

HARD. By the hand of my body. I believe his impudence is infectious! Didn't I see him seize your hand? Didn't I see him haul you about like a milkmaid? and now you talk of his respect and his modesty, forsooth!

MISS HARD. But if I shortly convince you of his modesty, that he has only the faults that will pass off with time, and the virtues that will improve with age, I hope you'll forgive him.

HARD. The girl would actually make one run mad! I tell you I'll not be convinced. I am convinced. He has scarcely been three hours in the house, and he has already encroached on all my prerogatives. You may like his impudence, and call it modesty. But my son-in-law, madam, must have very different qualifications.

MISS HARD. Sir, I ask but this night to convince you.

HARD. You shall not have half the time, for I have thoughts of turning him out this very hour.

MISS HARD. Give me that hour then, and I hope to satisfy you.

HARD. Well, an hour let it be then. But I'll have no trifling with your father. All fair and open, do you mind me?

MISS HARD. I hope, sir, you have ever found that I considered your commands as my pride; for your kindness is such, that my duty as yet has been inclination.

# ACT IV

[*Enter* HASTINGS *and* MISS NEVILLE.]

HASTINGS. You surprise me! Sir Charles Marlow expected here this night? Where have you had your information?

MISS NEVILLE. You may depend upon it. I just saw his letter to Mr Hardcastle, in which he tells him he intends setting out a few hours after his son.

HASTINGS. Then, my Constance, all must be completed before he arrives. He knows me; and should he find me here, would discover my name, and perhaps my designs, to the rest of the family.

MISS NEVILLE. The jewels, I hope, are safe.

HASTINGS. Yes, yes. I have sent them to Marlow, who keeps the keys of our baggage. In the meantime, I'll go to prepare matters for our elopement. I have had the 'squire's promise of a fresh pair of horses; and, if I should not see him again, will write him further directions.

[*Exit.*]

MISS NEVILLE. Well! success attend you. In the meantime, I'll go amuse my aunt with the old pretence of a violent passion for my cousin.

[*Exit.*]

[*Enter* MARLOW *followed by* SERVANT.]

MARLOW. I wonder what Hastings could mean by sending me so valuable a thing as a casket to keep for him, when he knows the only place I have is the seat of a post-coach at an inn-door. Have you deposited the casket with the landlady, as I ordered you? Have you put it into her own hands?
SERVANT. Yes, your honour.
MARLOW. She said she'd keep it safe, did she?
SERVANT. Yes, she said she'd keep it safe enough; she asked me how I came by it, and she said she had a great mind to make me give an account of myself.

[*Exit* SERVANT.]

MARLOW. Ha! ha! ha! They're safe, however. What an unaccountable set of beings have we got amongst! This little barmaid, though, runs in my head most strangely, and drives out the absurdities of all the rest of the family. She's mine, she must be mine, or I'm greatly mistaken.

[*Enter* HASTINGS.]

HASTINGS. Bless me! I quite forgot to tell her that I intended to prepare at the bottom of the garden. Marlow here, and in spirits too!
MARLOW. Give me joy, George! Crown me, shadow me with laurels! Well, George, after all, we modest fellows don't want for success among the women.
HASTINGS. Some women, you mean. But what success has your honour's modesty been crowned with now, that it grows so insolent upon us?
MARLOW. Didn't you see the tempting, brisk, lovely little thing that runs about the house with a bunch of keys to its girdle?
HASTINGS. Well! and what then?

She Stoops to Conquer

MARLOW. She's mine, you rogue you. Such fire, such motions, such eyes, such lips—but, egad! she would not let me kiss them though.
HASTINGS. But are you so sure, so very sure of her?
MARLOW. Why man, she talked of showing me her work above stairs and I am to improve the pattern.
HASTINGS. But how can you, Charles, go about to rob a woman of her honour?
MARLOW. Pshaw! pshaw! We all know the honour of a barmaid of an inn. I don't intend to rob her, take my word for it, there's nothing in this house I shan't honestly pay for.
HASTINGS. I believe the girl has virtue.
MARLOW. And if she has, I should be the last man in the world that would attempt to corrupt it.
HASTINGS. You have taken care, I hope, of the casket I sent you to lock up? It's in safety?
MARLOW. Yes, yes. It's safe enough. I have taken care of it. But how could you think the seat of a post-coach at an inn-door a place of safety? Ah! numbskull! I have taken better precautions for you than you did for yourself. I have—
HASTINGS. What?
MARLOW. I have sent it to the landlady to keep for you.
HASTINGS. To the landlady!
MARLOW. The landlady.
HASTINGS. You did?
MARLOW. I did. She's to be answerable for its forthcoming, you know.
HASTINGS. Yes, she'll bring it forth with a witness.
MARLOW. Wasn't I right? I believe you'll allow that I acted prudently upon this occasion?
HASTINGS. [*Aside.*] He must not see my uneasiness.
MARLOW. You seem a little disconcerted, though, methinks. Sure nothing has happened?
HASTINGS. No, nothing. Never was in better spirits in all my life. And so you left it with the landlady, who, no doubt, very readily undertook the charge?
MARLOW. Rather too readily. For she not only kept the casket, but, through her great precautions, was going to keep the messenger too. Ha! ha! ha!
HASTINGS. He! he! he! They're safe, however.
MARLOW. As a guinea in a miser's purse.

HASTINGS. [*Aside.*] So now all hopes of fortune are at an end, and we must set off without it. [*To him.*] Well, Charles, I'll leave you to your meditations on the pretty barmaid, and, he! he! he! may you be as successful for yourself as you have been for me.

[*Exit.*]

MARLOW. Thank ye, George! I ask no more. Ha! ha! ha!

[*Enter* HARDCASTLE.]

HARD. I no longer know my own house. It's turned all topsy-turvy. His servants have got drunk already. I'll bear it no longer, and yet, from my respect for his father, I'll be calm. [*To him.*] Mr Marlow, your servant. I'm your very humble servant. [*Bowing low.*]

MARLOW. Sir, your humble servant. [*Aside.*] What's to be the wonder now?

HARD. I believe, sir, you must be sensible, sir, that no man alive ought to be more welcome than your father's son, sir. I hope you think so?

MARLOW. I do, from my soul, sir. I don't want much entreaty. I generally make my father's son welcome wherever he goes.

HARD. I believe you do, from my soul, sir. But though I say nothing to your own conduct, that of your servants is insufferable. Their manner of drinking is setting a very bad example in this house, I assure you.

MARLOW. I protest, my very good sir, that's no fault of mine. If they don't drink as they ought they are to blame. I ordered them not to spare the cellar. I did, I assure you. [*To the side scene.*] Here, let one of my servants come up. [*To him.*] My positive directions were, that as I did not drink myself, they should make up for my deficiencies below.

HARD. Then they had your orders for what they do! I'm satisfied!

MARLOW. They had, I assure you. You shall hear from one of themselves.

[*Enter* SERVANT, *drunk.*]

MARLOW. You, Jeremy! Come forward, sirrah! What were my orders? Were you not told to drink freely, and call for what you thought fit, for the good of the house?

HARD. [*Aside.*] I begin to lose my patience.

She Stoops to Conquer    131

JEREMY. [*Staggering forward.*] Please your honour, liberty and Fleet Street for ever![1] Though I'm but a servant, I'm as good as another man. I'll drink for no man before supper, sir, dammy! Good liquor will sit upon a good supper, but a good supper will not sit upon— hiccup—upon my conscience, sir.

MARLOW. You see, my old friend, the fellow is as drunk as he can possibly be. I don't know what you'd have more, unless you'd have the poor devil soused in a beer-barrel.

HARD. Zounds! He'll drive me distracted if I contain myself any longer. Mr Marlow, Sir; I have submitted to your insolence for more than four hours, and I see no likelihood of its coming to an end. I'm now resolved to be master here, sir, and I desire that you and your drunken pack may leave my house directly.

MARLOW. Leave your house! Sure, you jest, my good friend! What, when I'm doing what I can to please you!

HARD. I tell you, sir, you don't please me; so I desire you'll leave my house.

MARLOW. Sure, you cannot be serious! At this time o' night, and such a night! You only mean to banter me!

HARD. I tell you, sir, I'm serious; and, now that my passions are aroused, I say this house is mine, sir; this house is mine, and I command you to leave it directly.

MARLOW. Ha! ha! ha! A puddle in a storm. I shan't stir a step, I assure you. [*In a serious tone.*] This is your house, fellow! It's my house. This is my house. Mine, while I choose to stay. What right have you to bid me leave this house, sir? I never met with such impudence, curse me, never in my whole life before.

HARD. Nor I, confound me if ever I did! To come to my house, to call for what he likes, to turn me out of my own chair, to insult the family, to order his servants to get drunk, and then to tell me *This house is mine, sir.* By all that's impudent, it makes me laugh. Ha! ha! ha! Pray sir, [*Bantering.*] as you take the house, what think you of taking the rest of the furniture? There's a pair of silver candlesticks, and there's a firescreen, and here's a pair of brazen-nosed bellows, perhaps you may take a fancy to them?

MARLOW. Bring me your bill, sir, bring me your bill, and let's make no more words about it.

1. *liberty and Fleet Street for ever!* A parody of the political slogan *Wilkes and Liberty* then popular in England. Fleet Street is the headquarters of British journalism.

HARD. There are a set of prints, too. What think you of the Rake's Progress[2] for your own apartment?

MARLOW. Bring me your bill, I say; and I'll leave you and your infernal house directly.

HARD. Then there's a mahogany table, that you may see your own face in.

MARLOW. My bill, I say.

HARD. I had forgot the great chair, for your own particular slumbers, after a hearty meal.

MARLOW. Zounds! bring me my bill, I say, and let's hear no more on't.

HARD. Young man, young man, from your father's letter to me, I was taught to expect a well-bred modest man, as a visitor here, but now I find him no better than a coxcomb[3] and a bully; but he will be down here presently, and shall hear more of it.

[*Exit.*]

MARLOW. How's this! Sure I have not mistaken the house! Everything looks like an inn. The servants cry 'coming.' The attendance is awkward; the barmaid, too, to attend us. But she's here, and will further inform me. Whither so fast, child? A word with you.

[*Enter* MISS HARDCASTLE.]

MISS HARD. Let it be short, then. I'm in a hurry. [*Aside.*] I believe he begins to find out his mistake, but it's too soon quite to undeceive him.

MARLOW. Pray, child, answer me one question. What are you, and what may your business in this house be?

MISS HARD. A relation of the family, sir.

MARLOW. What, a poor relation?

MISS HARD. Yes, sir. A poor relation appointed to keep the keys, and to see that the guests want nothing in my power to give them.

MARLOW. That is, you act as the barmaid of this inn.

MISS HARD. Inn. O law! What brought that in your head? One of the best families in the country keep an inn! Ha, ha, ha, old Mr Hardcastle's house an inn!

MARLOW. Mr Hardcastle's house! Is this house Mr Hardcastle's house, child?

MISS HARD. Ay, sure. Whose else should it be?

MARLOW. So then all's out, and I have been damnably imposed on. O,

2. *the Rake's Progress:* a famous set of engravings by William Hogarth.
3. *a coxcomb:* a foolish, foppish, conceited showoff.

**She Stoops to Conquer**    133

confound my stupid head, I shall be laughed at over the whole town. I shall be stuck up in caricatura[4] in all the print-shops. The Dullissimo Maccaroni.[5] To mistake this house of all others for an inn, and my father's old friend for an innkeeper. What a swaggering puppy must he take me for. What a silly puppy do I find myself. There again, may I be hanged, my dear, but I mistook you for the barmaid.

MISS HARD. Dear me! dear me! I'm sure there's nothing in my behaviour to put me upon a level with one of that stamp.

MARLOW. Nothing, my dear, nothing. But I was in for a list of blunders, and could not help making you a subscriber. My stupidity saw everything the wrong way. I mistook your assiduity for assurance, and your simplicity for allurement. But it's over. This house I no more show my face in!

MISS HARD. I hope, sir, I have done nothing to disoblige you. I'm sure I should be sorry to affront any gentleman who has been so polite, and said so many civil things to me. I'm sure I should be sorry [*Pretending to cry.*] if he left the family upon my account. I'm sure I should be sorry people said anything amiss, since I have no fortune but my character.

MARLOW. [*Aside.*] By heaven, she weeps. This is the first mark of tenderness I ever had from a modest woman, and it touches me. [*To her.*] Excuse me, my lovely girl, you are the only part of the family I leave with reluctance. But to be plain with you, the difference of our birth, fortune, and education, make an honourable connexion impossible.

MISS HARD. [*Aside.*] Generous man! I now begin to admire him. [*To him.*] But I'm sure my family is as good as Miss Hardcastle's, and though I'm poor, that's no great misfortune to a contented mind, and, until this moment, I never thought that it was bad to want fortune.

MARLOW. And why now, my pretty simplicity?

MISS HARD. Because it puts me at a distance from one, that if I had a thousand pound I would give it all to.

MARLOW. [*Aside.*] This simplicity bewitches me, so that if I stay I'm undone. I must make one bold effort, and leave her. [*To her.*] Your partiality in my favour, my dear, touches me most sensibly,

---

4. *stuck up in caricatura*: At the time *She Stoops to Conquer* was first given, well-known persons were being satirized in a series of prints which appeared in various London shops.     5. *Maccaroni*: a fop or dandy; a term of ridicule.

and were I to live for myself alone, I could easily fix my choice. But I owe too much to the opinion of the world, too much to the authority of a father, so that—I can scarcely speak it—it affects me. Farewell.

[*Exit.*]

MISS HARD. I never knew half his merit till now. He shall not go, if I have power or art to detain him. I'll still preserve the character in which I stooped to conquer, but will undeceive my papa, who, perhaps, may laugh him out of his resolution.

[*Exit.*]

[*Enter* TONY, MISS NEVILLE.]

TONY. Ay, you may steal for yourselves the next time. I have done my duty. She has got the jewels again, that's a sure thing; but she believes it was all a mistake of the servants.

MISS NEVILLE. But, my dear cousin, sure, you won't forsake us in this distress. If she in the least suspects that I am going off, I shall certainly be locked up, or sent to my Aunt Pedigree's which is ten times worse.

TONY. To be sure, aunts of all kinds are damned bad things. But what can I do? I have got you a pair of horses that will fly like Whistlejacket,[6] and I'm sure you can't say but I have courted you nicely before her face. Here she comes, we must court a bit or two more, for fear she should suspect us.

[*They retire, and seem to fondle.*]

[*Enter* MRS HARDCASTLE.]

MRS HARD. Well, I was greatly fluttered, to be sure. But my son tells me it was all a mistake of the servants. I shan't be easy, however, till they are fairly married, and then let her keep her own fortune. But what do I see? Fondling together, as I'm alive! I never saw Tony so sprightly before. Ah! have I caught you, my pretty doves! What, billing, exchanging stolen glances, and broken murmurs! Ah!

TONY. As for murmurs, mother, we grumble a little now and then, to be sure. But there's no love lost between us.

MRS HARD. A mere sprinkling, Tony, upon the flame, only to make it burn brighter.

---

6. *Whistlejacket:* a famous racehorse.

MISS NEVILLE. Cousin Tony promises to give us more of his company at home. Indeed, he shan't leave us any more. It won't leave us, cousin Tony, will it?

TONY. O! it's a pretty creature. No, I'd sooner leave my horse in a pound, then leave you when you smile upon one so. Your laugh makes you so becoming.

MISS NEVILLE. Agreeable cousin! Who can help admiring that natural humour, that pleasant, broad, red, thoughtless [*Patting his cheek.*] ah! it's a bold face.

MRS HARD. Pretty innocence!

TONY. I'm sure I always loved cousin Con's hazel eyes, and her pretty long fingers, that she twists this way and that, over the haspicholls,[7] like a parcel of bobbins.

MRS HARD. Ah, he would charm the bird from the tree. I was never so happy before. My boy takes after his father, poor Mr Lumpkin, exactly. The jewels, my dear Con, shall be yours incontinently. You shall have them. Isn't he a sweet boy, my dear? You shall be married to-morrow, and we'll put off the rest of his education, like Dr Drowsy's sermons, to a fitter opportunity.

[*Enter* DIGGORY.]

DIGGORY. Where's the 'Squire? I have got a letter for your worship.

TONY. Give it to my mamma. She reads all my letters first.

DIGGORY. I had orders to deliver it into your own hands.

TONY. Who does it come from?

DIGGORY. Your worship mun ask that o' the letter itself.

TONY. I could wish to know, though. [*Turning the letter, and gazing on it.*]

MISS NEVILLE. [*Aside.*] Undone, undone. A letter to him from Hastings. I know the hand. If my aunt sees it we are ruined for ever. I'll keep her employed a little if I can. [*To* MRS HARDCASTLE.] But I have not told you, madam, of my cousin's smart answer just now to Mr Marlow. We so laughed. You must know, madam—This way a little, for he must not hear us. [*They confer.*]

TONY. [*Still gazing.*] A damned cramp piece of penmanship, as ever I saw in my life. I can read your print-hand very well. But here there are such handles, and shakes, and dashes, that one can scarce

---

7. *haspicholls*: harpsichord; a musical instrument resembling a piano. It is played by plucking wire strings with a quill or leather points.

tell the head from the tail. 'To Anthony Lumpkin, Esquire.' It's very odd, I can read the outside of my letters, where my own name is, well enough. But when I come to open it, it's all—buzz. That's hard, very hard; for the inside of the letter is always the cream of the correspondence.

MRS HARD. Ha! ha! ha! Very well, very well. And so my son was too hard for the philosopher.

MISS NEVILLE. Yes, madam; but you must hear the rest, madam. A little more this way, or he may hear us. You'll hear how he puzzled him again.

MRS HARD. He seems strangely puzzled now himself, methinks.

TONY. [*Still gazing.*] A damned up and down hand, as if it was disguised in liquor. [*Reading.*] Dear Sir. Ay, that's that. Then there's an M, and a T, and an S, but whether the next be an izzard[8] or an R, confound me, I cannot tell.

MRS HARD. What's that, my dear? Can I give you any assistance?

MISS NEVILLE. Pray, aunt, let me read it. Nobody reads a cramp hand better than I. [*Twitching the letter from her.*] Do you know who it is from?

TONY. Can't tell, except from Dick Ginger the feeder.[9]

MISS NEVILLE. Ay, so it is. [*Pretending to read.*] Dear 'Squire, Hoping that you're in health, as I am at this present. The gentlemen of the Shakebag[10] club has cut the gentlemen of Goose-green quite out of feather. The odds—um—odd battle—um—long fighting—um, here, here, it's all about cocks, and fighting; it's of no consequence, here, put it up, put it up. [*Thrusting the crumpled letter upon him.*]

TONY. But I tell you, miss, it's of all the consequence in the world. I would not lose the rest of it for a guinea. Here, mother, do you make it out? Of no consequence! [*Giving* MRS HARDCASTLE *the letter.*]

MRS HARD. How's this! [*Reads.*] 'Dear 'Squire, I'm now waiting for Miss Neville, with a post-chaise and pair, at the bottom of the garden but I find my horses yet unable to perform the journey. I expect you'll assist us with a pair of fresh horses, as you promised. Dispatch is necessary, as the hag'—ay, the hag—'your mother, will otherwise suspect us. Yours, Hastings.' Grant me patience. I shall run distracted. My rage chokes me.

---

8. *an izzard:* the letter z.   9. *the feeder:* the cock-feeder.
10. *Shakebag:* a large fighting cock.

MISS NEVILLE. I hope, madam, you'll suspend your resentment for a few moments, and not impute to me any impertinence, or sinister design, that belongs to another.

MRS HARD. [*Curtsying very low.*] Fine spoken, madam, you are most miraculously polite and engaging, and quite the very pink of courtesy and circumspection, madam. [*Changing her tone.*] And you, you great ill-fashioned oaf, with scarce sense enough to keep your mouth shut. Were you, too, joined against me? But I'll defeat all your plots in a moment. As for you, madam, since you have got a pair of fresh horses ready, it would be cruel to disappoint them. So, if you please, instead of running away with your spark, prepare, this very moment, to run off with me. Your old Aunt Pedigree will keep you secure, I'll warrant me. You too, sir, may mount your horse, and guard us upon the way. Here, Thomas, Roger, Diggory, I'll show you that I wish you better than you do yourselves.

[*Exit.*]

MISS NEVILLE. So now I'm completely ruined.

TONY. Ay, that's a sure thing.

MISS NEVILLE. What better could be expected from being connected with such a stupid fool, and after all the nods and signs I made him.

TONY. By the laws, miss, it was your own cleverness, and not my stupidity, that did your business. You were so nice and so busy with your Shakebags and Goose-greens, that I thought you could never be making believe.

[*Enter* HASTINGS.]

HASTINGS. So, sir, I find by my servant, that you have shown my letter, and betrayed us. Was this well done, young gentleman?

TONY. Here's another. Ask Miss there who betrayed you. Ecod, it was her doing, not mine.

[*Enter* MARLOW.]

MARLOW. So I have been finely used here among you. Rendered contemptible, driven into ill manners, despised, insulted, laughed at.

TONY. Here's another. We shall have old Bedlam broke loose presently.

MISS NEVILLE. And there, sir, is the gentleman to whom we all owe every obligation.

MARLOW. What can I say to him, a mere boy, an idiot, whose ignorance and age are a protection.

HASTINGS. A poor contemptible booby, that would but disgrace correction.
MISS NEVILLE. Yet with cunning and malice enough to make himself merry with all our embarrassments.
HASTINGS. An insensible cub.
MARLOW. Replete with tricks and mischief.
TONY. Baw! damme, but I'll fight you both one after the other—with baskets.[11]
MARLOW. As for him, he's below resentment. But your conduct, Mr Hastings, requires an explanation. You knew of my mistakes, yet would not undeceive me.
HASTINGS. Tortured as I am with my own disappointments, is this a time for explanations? It is not friendly, Mr Marlow.
MARLOW. But, sir—
MISS NEVILLE. Mr. Marlow, we never kept on your mistake, till it was too late to undeceive you. Be pacified.

[*Enter* SERVANT.]

SERVANT. My mistress desires you'll get ready immediately, madam. The horses are putting to. Your hat and things are in the next room. We are to go thirty miles before morning.

[*Exit* SERVANT.]

MISS NEVILLE. Well, well; I'll come presently.
MARLOW. [*To* HASTINGS.] Was it well done, sir, to assist in rendering me ridiculous? To hang me out for the scorn of all my acquaintance? Depend upon it, sir, I shall expect an explanation.
HASTINGS. Was it well done, sir, if you're upon that subject, to deliver what I entrusted to yourself, to the care of another, sir?
MISS NEVILLE. Mr Hastings, Mr Marlow. Why will you increase my distress by this groundless dispute? I implore, I entreat you—

[*Enter* SERVANT.]

SERVANT. Your cloak, madam. My mistress is impatient.

[*Exit* SERVANT.]

MISS NEVILLE. I come. Pray be pacified. If I leave you thus, I shall die with apprehension!

11. *baskets:* possibly swords with basket hilts.

[*Enter* SERVANT.]

SERVANT. Your fan, muff, and gloves, madam. The horses are waiting.

MISS NEVILLE. O, Mr Marlow! if you knew what a scene of constraint and ill-nature lies before me, I'm sure it would convert your resentment into pity.

MARLOW. I'm so distracted with a variety of passions, that I don't know what I do. Forgive me, madam. George, forgive me. You know my hasty temper, and should not exasperate it.

HASTINGS. The torture of my situation is my only excuse.

MISS NEVILLE. Well, my dear Hastings, if you have that esteem for me that I think, that I am sure you have, your constancy for three years will but increase the happiness of our future connexion. If—

MRS HARD. [*Within.*] Miss Neville. Constance, why, Constance, I say.

MISS NEVILLE. I'm coming. Well, constancy. Remember, constancy is the word.

[*Exit.*]

HASTINGS. My heart! How can I support this? To be so near happiness, and such happiness!

MARLOW. [*To* TONY.] You see now, young gentleman, the effects of your folly. What might be amusement to you, is here disappointment, and even distress.

TONY. [*From a reverie.*] Ecod, I have hit it. It's here. Your hands. Yours and yours, my poor Sulky. My boots there, ho! Meet me two hours hence at the bottom of the garden; and if you don't find Tony Lumpkin a more good-natur'd fellow than you thought for, I'll give you leave to take my best horse, and Bet Bouncer into the bargain. Come along. My boots, ho!

[*Exeunt.*]

# ACT V

Scene continues.

[*Enter* HASTINGS *and* SERVANT.]

HASTINGS. You saw the old lady and Miss Neville drive off, you say?

SERVANT. Yes, your honour. They went off in a post coach, and the

young 'squire went on horseback. They're thirty miles off by this time.
HASTINGS. Then all my hopes are over.
SERVANT. Yes, sir. Old Sir Charles is arrived. He and the old gentleman of the house have been laughing at Mr Marlow's mistake this half-hour. They are coming this way.
HASTINGS. Then I must not be seen. So now to my fruitless appointment at the bottom of the garden. This is about the time.

[*Exit.*]

[*Enter* SIR CHARLES *and* HARDCASTLE.]

HARD. Ha! ha! ha! The peremptory tone in which he sent forth his sublime commands.
SIR CHARLES. And the reserve with which I suppose he treated all your advances.
HARD. And yet he might have seen something in me above a common innkeeper, too.
SIR CHARLES. Yes, Dick, but he mistook you for an uncommon innkeeper, ha! ha! ha!
HARD. Well, I'm in too good spirits to think of anything but joy. Yes, my dear friend, this union of our families will make our personal friendships hereditary: and though my daughter's fortune is but small—
SIR CHARLES. Why, Dick, will you talk of fortune to me? My son is possessed of more than a competence already, and can want nothing but a good and virtuous girl to share his happiness and increase it. If they like each other, as you say they do—
HARD. If, man! I tell you they do like each other. My daughter as good as told me so.
SIR CHARLES. But girls are apt to flatter themselves, you know.
HARD. I saw him grasp her hand in the warmest manner myself; and here he comes to put you out of your ifs, I warrant him.

[*Enter* MARLOW.]

MARLOW. I come, sir, once more, to ask pardon for my strange conduct. I can scarce reflect on my insolence without confusion.
HARD. Tut, boy, a trifle. You take it too gravely. An hour or two's laughing with my daughter will set all to rights again. She'll never like you the worse for it.
MARLOW. Sir, I shall be always proud of her approbation.

HARD. Approbation is but a cold word, Mr Marlow; if I am not deceived, you have something more than approbation thereabouts. You take me.

MARLOW. Really, sir, I have not that happiness.

HARD. Come, boy, I'm an old fellow, and know what's what, as well as you that are younger. I know what has past between you; but mum.

MARLOW. Sure, sir, nothing has passed between us but the most profound respect on my side, and the most distant reserve on hers. You don't think, sir, that my impudence has been passed upon all the rest of the family.

HARD. Impudence! No, I don't say that—not quite impudence—though girls like to be played with, and rumpled a little too, sometimes. But she has told no tales, I assure you.

MARLOW. I never gave her the slightest cause.

HARD. Well, well, I like modesty in its place well enough. But this is over-acting, young gentleman. You may be open. Your father and I will like you the better for it.

MARLOW. May I die, sir, if I ever—

HARD. I tell you, she don't dislike you; and as I'm sure you like her—

MARLOW. Dear sir—I protest, sir—

HARD. I see no reason why you should not be joined as fast as the parson can tie you.

MARLOW. But hear me, sir—

HARD. Your father approves the match, I admire it, every moment's delay will be doing mischief, so—

MARLOW. But why won't you hear me? By all that's just and true, I never gave Miss Hardcastle the slightest mark of my attachment, or even the most distant hint to suspect me of affection. We had but one interview, and that was formal, modest, and uninteresting.

HARD. [*Aside.*] This fellow's formal modest impudence is beyond bearing.

SIR CHARLES. And you never grasped her hand, or made any protestations!

MARLOW. As heaven is my witness, I came down in obedience to your commands. I saw the lady without emotion, and parted without reluctance. I hope you'll exact no further proofs of my duty, nor prevent me from leaving a house in which I suffer so many mortifications.

[*Exit.*]

SIR CHARLES. I'm astonished at the air of sincerity with which he parted.
HARD. And I'm astonished at the deliberate intrepidity of his assurance.
SIR CHARLES. I dare pledge my life and honour upon his truth.
HARD. [*Looking out to right.*] Here comes my daughter, and I would stake my happiness upon her veracity.

[*Enter* MISS HARDCASTLE.]

HARD. Kate, come hither, child. Answer us sincerely, and without reserve; has Mr Marlow made you any professions of love and affection?
MISS HARD. The question is very abrupt, sir! But since you require unreserved sincerity, I think he has.
HARD. [*To* SIR CHARLES.] You see.
SIR CHARLES. And pray, madam, have you and my son had more than one interview?
MISS HARD. Yes, sir, several.
HARD. [*To* SIR CHARLES.] You see.
SIR CHARLES. But did he profess any attachment?
MISS HARD. A lasting one.
SIR CHARLES. Did he talk of love?
MISS HARD. Much, sir.
SIR CHARLES. Amazing! And all this formally?
MISS HARD. Formally.
HARD. Now, my friend, I hope you are satisfied.
SIR CHARLES. And how did he behave, madam?
MISS HARD. As most professed admirers do. Said some civil things of my face, talked much of his want of merit, and the greatness of mine; mentioned his heart, gave a short tragedy speech, and ended with pretended rapture.
SIR CHARLES. Now I'm perfectly convinced, indeed. I know his conversation among women to be modest and submissive. This forward, canting, ranting manner by no means describes him, and I am confident he never sat for the picture.
MISS HARD. Then what, sir, if I should convince you to your face of my sincerity? If you and my papa, in about half an hour, will place yourselves behind that screen, you shall hear him declare his passion to me in person.
SIR CHARLES. Agreed. And if I find him what you describe, all my happiness in him must have an end.

[*Exit.*]

MISS HARD. And if you don't find him what I describe—I fear my happiness must never have a beginning.

[*Exeunt.*]

Scene changes to the back of the garden.

[*Enter* HASTINGS.]

HASTINGS. What an idiot am I, to wait here for a fellow, who probably takes a delight in mortifying me. He never intended to be punctual, and I'll wait no longer. What do I see? It is he, and perhaps with news of my Constance.

[*Enter* TONY, *booted and spattered.*]

HASTINGS. My honest 'Squire! I now find you a man of your word. This looks like friendship.
TONY. Ay, I'm your friend, and the best friend you have in the world, if you knew but all. This riding by night, by the by, is cursedly tiresome. It has shook me worse than the basket of a stage-coach.
HASTINGS. But how? Where did you leave your fellow-travellers? Are they in safety? Are they housed?
TONY. Five and twenty miles in two hours and a half is no such bad driving. The poor beasts have smoked for it: rabbet me,[1] but I'd rather ride forty miles after a fox, than ten with such varmint.
HASTINGS. Well, but where have you left the ladies? I die with impatience.
TONY. Left them? Why, where should I leave them, but where I found them?
HASTINGS. This is a riddle.
TONY. Riddle me this, then. What's that goes round the house, and round the house, and never touches the house?
HASTINGS. I'm still astray.
TONY. Why, that's it, mon. I have led them astray. By jingo, there's not a pond or slough within five miles of the place but they can tell the taste of.

1. *rabbet me:* an oath.

HASTINGS. Ha, ha, ha, I understand; you took them in a round, while they supposed themselves going forward. And so you have at last brought them home again.

TONY. You shall hear. I first took them down Feather-Bed Lane, where we stuck fast in the mud. I then rattled them crack over the stones of Up-and-Down Hill—I then introduced them to the gibbet on Heavy-Tree Heath, and from that, with a circumbendibus,[2] I fairly lodged them in the horsepond at the bottom of the garden.

HASTINGS. But no accident, I hope.

TONY. No, no. Only mother is confoundedly frightened. She thinks herself forty miles off. She's sick of the journey, and the cattle can scarce crawl. So, if your own horses be ready, you may whip off with cousin, and I'll be bound that no soul here can budge a foot to follow you.

HASTINGS. My dear friend, how can I be grateful?

TONY. Ay, now it's dear friend, noble 'Squire. Just now, it was all idiot, cub, and run me through the guts. Damn your way of fighting, I say. After we take a knock in this part of the country, we kiss and be friends. But if you had run me through the guts, then I should be dead, and you might go kiss the hangman.

HASTINGS. The rebuke is just. But I must hasten to relieve Miss Neville; if you keep the old lady employed, I promise to take care of the young one.

[*Exit* HASTINGS.]

TONY. Never fear me. Here she comes. Vanish. She's got from the pond, and draggled up to the waist like a mermaid.

[*Enter* MRS HARDCASTLE.]

MRS HARD. Oh, Tony, I'm killed. Shook. Battered to death. I shall never survive it. That last jolt that laid us against the quickset hedge[3] has done my business.

TONY. Alack, mamma, it was all your own fault. You would be for running away by night, without knowing one inch of the way.

MRS HARD. I wish we were at home again. I never met so many accidents in so short a journey. Drenched in the mud, overturned in a ditch, stuck fast in a slough, jolted to a jelly, and at last to lose our way. Whereabouts do you think we are, Tony?

2. *circumbendibus*: a roundabout process.
3. *the quickset hedge*: a hedge made up of living plants.

**She Stoops to Conquer**

TONY. By my guess we should be upon Crackskull Common, about forty miles from home.

MRS HARD. O lud! O lud! the most notorious spot in all the country. We only want a robbery to make a complete night on't.

TONY. Don't be afraid, mamma, don't be afraid. Two of the five that kept here are hanged, and the other three may not find us. Don't be afraid. Is that a man that's galloping behind us? No; it's only a tree. Don't be afraid.

MRS HARD. The fright will certainly kill me.

TONY. Do you see any thing like a black hat moving behind the thicket?

MRS HARD. O death!

TONY. No, it's only a cow. Don't be afraid, mamma, don't be afraid.

MRS HARD. As I'm alive, Tony, I see a man coming towards us. Ah! I'm sure on't. If he perceives us, we are undone.

TONY. [*Aside.*] Father-in-law, by all that's unlucky, come to take one of his night walks. [*To her.*] Ah, it's a highwayman, with pistols as long as my arm. A damned ill-looking fellow.

MRS HARD. Good Heaven defend us! He approaches.

TONY. Do you hide yourself in that thicket and leave me to manage him. If there be any danger I'll cough and cry hem. When I cough be sure to keep close.

[MRS HARDCASTLE *hides behind a tree in the back scene.*]

[*Enter* HARDCASTLE.]

HARD. I'm mistaken, or I heard voices of people in want of help. Oh, Tony, is that you? I did not expect you so soon back. Are your mother and her charge in safety?

TONY. Very safe, sir, at my Aunt Pedigree's. Hem.

MRS HARD. [*From behind.*] Ah! I find there's danger.

HARD. Forty miles in three hours; sure, that's too much, my youngster.

TONY. Stout horses and willing minds make short journeys, as they say. Hem.

MRS HARD. [*From behind.*] Sure he'll do the dear boy no harm.

HARD. But I heard a voice here; I should be glad to know from whence it came?

TONY. It was I, sir, talking to myself, sir. I was saying that forty miles in four hours was very good going. Hem. As to be sure it was. Hem. I have got a sort of cold by being out in the air. We'll go in if you please. Hem.

HARD. But if you talked to yourself, you did not answer yourself. I am certain I heard two voices, and am resolved [*Raising his voice.*] to find the other out.

MRS HARD. [*From behind.*] Oh! he's coming to find me out. Oh!

TONY. What need you go, sir, if I tell you? Hem. I'll lay down my life for the truth—hem—I'll tell you all, sir. [*Detaining him.*]

HARD. I tell you I will not be detained. I insist on seeing. It's in vain to expect I'll believe you.

MRS HARD. [*Running forward from behind.*] O lud, he'll murder my poor boy, my darling. Here, good gentleman, whet your rage upon me. Take my money, my life, but spare that young gentleman, spare my child, if you have any mercy.

HARD. My wife! as I'm a Christian. From whence can she come, or what does she mean?

MRS HARD. [*Kneeling.*] Take compassion on us, good Mr Highwayman. Take our money, our watches, all we have, but spare our lives. We will never bring you to justice, indeed we won't, good Mr Highwayman.

HARD. I believe the woman's out of her senses. What, Dorothy, don't you know me?

MRS HARD. Mr Hardcastle, as I'm alive! My fears blinded me. But who, my dear, could have expected to meet you here, in this frightful place, so far from home. What has brought you to follow us?

HARD. Sure, Dorothy, you have not lost your wits. So far from home, when you are within forty yards of your own door! [*To him.*] This is one of your old tricks, you graceless rogue, you! [*To her.*] Don't you know the gate, and the mulberry-tree; and don't you remember the horsepond, my dear?

MRS HARD. Yes, I shall remember the horsepond as long as I live; I have caught my death in it. [*To* TONY.] And it is to you, you graceless varlet,[4] I owe all this? I'll teach you to abuse your mother, I will.

TONY. Ecod, mother, all the parish says you have spoiled me, and so you may take the fruits on't.

MRS HARD. I'll spoil you, I will. [*Follows him off the stage.*]

[*Exit.*]

HARD. There's morality, however, in his reply.

[*Enter* HASTINGS *and* MISS NEVILLE.]

---

4. *varlet:* knave, rascal.

She Stoops to Conquer    147

HASTINGS. My dear Constance, why will you deliberate thus? If we delay a moment, all is lost for ever. Pluck up a little resolution, and we shall soon be out of the reach of her malignity.

MISS NEVILLE. I find it impossible. My spirits are so sunk with the agitations I have suffered, that I am unable to face any new danger. Two or three years' patience will at last crown us with happiness.

HASTINGS. Such a tedious delay is worse than inconstancy. Let us fly, my charmer. Let us date our happiness from this very moment. Perish fortune. Love and content will increase what we possess beyond a monarch's revenue. Let me prevail.

MISS NEVILLE. No, Mr Hastings; no. Prudence once more comes to my relief, and I will obey its dictates. In the moment of passion, fortune may be despised, but it ever produces a lasting repentance. I'm resolved to apply to Mr Hardcastle's compassion and justice for redress.

HASTINGS. But though he had the will, he has not the power to relieve you.

MISS NEVILLE. But he has influence, and upon that I am resolved to rely.

HASTINGS. I have no hopes. But since you persist, I must reluctantly obey you.

[*Exeunt.*]

Scene changes.

[*Enter* SIR CHARLES *and* MISS HARDCASTLE.]

SIR CHARLES. What a situation am I in. If what you say appears, I shall then find a guilty son. If what he says be true, I shall then lose one that, of all others, I most wished for a daughter.

MISS HARD. I am proud of your approbation, and, to show I merit it, if you place yourselves as I directed, you shall hear his explicit declaration. But he comes.

SIR CHARLES. I'll to your father, and keep him to the appointment.

[*Exit.*]

[*Enter* MARLOW.]

MARLOW. Though prepared for setting out, I come once more to take leave, nor did I, till this moment, know the pain I feel in the separation.

MISS HARD. [*In her own natural manner.*] I believe sufferings cannot be very great, sir, which you can so easily remove. A day or two longer, perhaps, might lessen your uneasiness, by showing the little value of what you think proper to regret.

MARLOW. [*Aside.*] This girl every moment improves upon me. [*To her.*] It must not be, madam. I have already trifled too long with my heart. My very pride begins to submit to my passion. The disparity of education and fortune, the anger of a parent, and the contempt of my equals, begin to lose their weight; and nothing can restore me to myself but this painful effort of resolution.

MISS HARD. Then go, sir. I'll urge nothing more to detain you. Though my family be as good as hers you came down to visit, and my education, I hope, not inferior, what are these advantages without equal affluence? I must remain contented with the slight approbation of imputed merit; I must have only the mockery of your addresses, while all your serious aims are fixed on fortune.

[*Enter* HARDCASTLE *and* SIR CHARLES *from behind.*]

SIR CHARLES. Here, behind this screen.

HARD. Ay, ay, make no noise. I'll engage my Kate covers him with confusion at last.

MARLOW. By heavens, madam, fortune was ever my smallest consideration. Your beauty at first caught my eye; for who could see that without emotion? But every moment that I converse with you, steals in some new grace, heightens the picture, and gives it stronger expression. What at first seemed rustic plainness, now appears refined simplicity. What seemed forward assurance, now strikes me as the result of courageous innocence, and conscious virtue.

SIR CHARLES. What can it mean! He amazes me!

HARD. I told you how it would be. Hush!

MARLOW. I am now determined to stay, madam, and I have too good an opinion of my father's discernment, when he sees you, to doubt his approbation.

MISS HARD. No, Mr Marlow, I will not, cannot detain you. Do you think I could suffer a connexion, in which there is the smallest room for repentance? Do you think I would take the mean advantage of a transient passion, to load you with confusion? Do you think I could ever relish that happiness, which was acquired by lessening yours!

MARLOW. By all that's good, I can have no happiness but what's in your power to grant me. Nor shall I ever feel repentance, but in not having seen your merits before. I will stay, even contrary to your wishes; and though you should persist to shun me, I will make my respectful assiduities atone for the levity of my past conduct.

MISS HARD. Sir, I must entreat you'll desist. As our acquaintance began, so let it end, in indifference. I might have given an hour or two to levity; but, seriously, Mr Marlow, do you think I could ever submit to a connexion, where I must appear mercenary, and you imprudent? Do you think, I could ever catch at the confident addresses of a secure admirer?

MARLOW. [*Kneeling.*] Does this look like security? Does this look like confidence? No, madam, every moment that shows me your merit, only serves to increase my diffidence and confusion. Here let me continue—

SIR CHARLES. I can hold it no longer. Charles, Charles, how hast thou deceived me! Is this your indifference, your uninteresting conversation!

HARD. Your cold contempt; your formal interview. What have you to say now?

MARLOW. That I'm all amazement! What can it mean!

HARD. It means that you can say and unsay things at pleasure. That you can address a lady in private, and deny it in public; that you have one story for us, and another for my daughter!

MARLOW. Daughter! this lady your daughter!

HARD. Yes, sir, my only daughter. My Kate, whose else should she be?

MARLOW. Oh, the devil!

MISS HARD. Yes, sir, that very identical tall squinting lady you were pleased to take me for. [*Curtsying.*] She that you addressed as the mild, modest, sentimental man of gravity, and the bold, forward, agreeable Rattle of the Ladies' Club: ha, ha, ha.

MARLOW. Zounds, there's no bearing this; it's worse than death.

MISS HARD. In which of your characters, sir, will you give us leave to address you? As the faltering gentleman, with looks on the ground, that speaks just to be heard, and hates hypocrisy: or the loud confident creature, that keeps it up with Mrs Mantrap, and old Miss Biddy Buckskin, till three in the morning; ha, ha, ha!

MARLOW. Oh, curse on my noisy head. I never attempted to be impudent yet, that I was not taken down. I must be gone. [*Going.*]

HARD. By the hand of my body, but you shall not. I see it was all a mistake, and I am rejoiced to find it. You shall not, sir, I tell you. I know she'll forgive you. Won't you forgive him, Kate? We'll all forgive you. Take courage, man.

[*They retire, she tormenting him, to the back scene.*]

[*Enter* MRS HARDCASTLE, TONY.]

MRS HARD. So, so, they're gone off. Let them go, I care not.

HARD. Who gone?

MRS HARD. My dutiful niece and her gentleman, Mr Hastings, from town. He who came down with our modest visitor here.

SIR CHARLES. Who, my honest George Hastings? As worthy a fellow as lives, and the girl could not have made a more prudent choice.

HARD. Then, by the hand of my body, I'm proud of the connexion.

MRS HARD. Well, if he has taken away the lady, he has not taken her fortune, that remains in this family to console us for her loss.

HARD. Sure, Dorothy, you would not be so mercenary?

MRS HARD. Ay, that's my affair, not yours.

HARD. But you know, if your son, when of age, refuses to marry his cousin, her whole fortune is then at her own disposal.

MRS HARD. Ah, but he's not of age, and she has not thought proper to wait for his refusal.

[*Enter* HASTINGS *and* MISS NEVILLE.]

MRS HARD. [*Aside.*] What, returned so soon! I begin not to like it.

HASTINGS. [*To* HARDCASTLE.] For my late attempt to fly off with your niece, let my present confusion be my punishment. We are now come back, to appeal from your justice to your humanity. By her father's consent, I first paid her my addresses, and our passions were first founded in duty.

MISS NEVILLE. Since his death, I have been obliged to stoop to dissimulation to avoid oppression. In an hour of levity, I was ready even to give up my fortune to secure my choice. But I'm now recovered from the delusion, and hope from your tenderness what is denied me from a nearer connexion.

MRS HARD. Pshaw, pshaw, this is all but the whining end of a modern novel.

HARD. Be it what it will, I'm glad they're come back to reclaim their due. Come hither, Tony boy. Do you refuse this lady's hand whom I now offer you?

TONY. What signifies my refusing? You know I can't refuse her till I'm of age, father.

HARD. While I thought concealing your age, boy, was likely to conduce to your improvement, I concurred with your mother's desire to keep

it secret. But since I find she turns it to a wrong use, I must now declare, you have been of age these three months.
TONY. Of age! Am I of age, father?
HARD. Above three months.
TONY. Then you'll see the first use I'll make of my liberty. [*Taking* MISS NEVILLE's *hand.*] Witness all men by these presents, that I, Anthony Lumpkin, Esquire, of *blank* place, refuse you, Constantia Neville, spinster, of no place at all, for my true and lawful wife. So Constance Neville may marry whom she pleases and Tony Lumpkin is his own man again!
SIR CHARLES. O brave 'squire!
HASTINGS. My worthy friend!
MRS HARD. My undutiful offspring!
MARLOW. Joy, my dear George, I give you joy, sincerely. And could I prevail upon my little tyrant here to be less arbitrary, I should be the happiest man alive, if you would return me the favour.
HASTINGS. [*To* MISS HARDCASTLE.] Come, madam, you are now driven to the very last scene of all your contrivances. I know you like him, I'm sure he loves you, and you must and shall have him.
HARD. [*Joining their hands.*] And I say so, too. And Mr Marlow, if she makes as good a wife as she has a daughter, I don't believe you'll ever repent your bargain. So now to supper. To-morrow we shall gather all the poor of the parish about us, and the mistakes of the night shall be crowned with a merry morning; so boy, take her; and as you have been mistaken in the mistress, my wish is, that you may never be mistaken in the wife.

# Epilogue [1]

## By Dr Goldsmith

Well, having stooped to conquer with success,
    And gained a husband without aid from dress,
Still as a barmaid, I could wish it too,
    As I have conquered him to conquer you:
And let me say, for all your resolution,      5

---

1. The Epilogue was spoken by Mrs. Bulkley as Miss Hardcastle.

That pretty barmaids have done execution.
Our life is all a play, composed to please,
   'We have our exits and our entrances.'[2]
The first act shows the simple country maid,
   Harmless and young, of everything afraid;         10
Blushes when hired, and with unmeaning action,
   'I hopes as how to give you satisfaction.'
Her second act displays a livelier scene,
   Th' unblushing barmaid of a country inn,
Who whisks about the house, at market caters,       15
   Talks loud, coquets the guests, and scolds the waiters.
Next the scene shifts to town, and there she soars,
   The chop-house toast of ogling connoisseurs.
On 'squires and cits[3] she there displays her arts,
   And on the gridiron broils her lovers' hearts—     20
And as she smiles, her triumphs to complete,
   Even common councilmen forget to eat.
The fourth act shows her wedded to the 'squire,
   And madam now begins to hold it higher;
Pretends to taste, at Operas cries caro,[4]          25
   And quits her Nancy Dawson,[5] for Che Faro.[6]
Doats upon dancing, and in all her pride,
   Swims round the room, the Heinel[7] of Cheapside:
Ogles and leers with artificial skill,
   Till having lost in age the power to kill,       30
She sits all night at cards, and ogles at spadille.[8]
   Such, through our lives, the eventful history—
The fifth and last act still remains for me.
   The barmaid now for your protection prays,
Turns female Barrister,[9] and pleads for Bayes.[10]    35

2. 'We . . . entrances': *As You Like It*, II, 7.   3. *cits*: ordinary citizens.
4. *caro*: dear.   5. *Nancy Dawson*: a song about a famous hornpipe dancer.
6. *Che Faro*: the first words of a line from the opera *Orfeo* (1764).
7. *Heinel*: a celebrated Flemish dancer who appeared at the Haymarket.
8. *spadille*: the ace of spades.
9. *Barrister*: a lawyer who is admitted to plead at the bar in the superior courts of law.
10. *Bayes*: the dramatist; in this case, Goldsmith. The name was originally used in the farcical comedy *The Researsal* (1671).

# The Importance of Being Earnest

# OSCAR WILDE

## Introduction

The subtitle, *a trivial comedy for serious people,* sums up the tongue-in-cheek tone of this play almost as well as the title itself describes the superficial social behavior Oscar Wilde sought to attack in the most popular English comedy of the late nineteenth century. Although Wilde wrote his plays in the 1890's, he effectively bridges the gap between the comedy of manners of the seventeenth and eighteenth centuries and the barbed satire of Bernard Shaw. Shaw's *Candida* was produced in the same year as *The Importance of Being Earnest,* 1895, but Shaw is considered one of the great comic dramatists of the twentieth century.

In *The Importance of Being Earnest,* one finds the farce of a completely absurd situation balanced by a light and witty dialogue presented in a mock-earnest manner. The play dances along lightly but does not fail to step on a few toes, for, as the laughter subsides, the reader discovers that Wilde has effectively satirized Victorian customs and institutions: the theater, literature, church, politics, matrimony, and manners. The overall tone of the play reflects the ease of living enjoyed by the wealthy and the flow of clever language which comes from intelligent people who have little else to do but formulate aphorisms. *The Importance of Being Earnest,* then, is a nineteenth-century version of the comedy of manners.

The ever-vacillating Lady Bracknell embodies the kind of superficial society Wilde delights in attacking: petty, hypocritical, and contradictory. Such a fickle social order has a Science of Life built upon cucumber sandwiches, German lessons, and diaries. Jack and Algernon would sell each other out with few scruples if either felt he had anything to gain. Regarding this play, which is a flippant attack on Victorian moral earnestness, sentimental comedies, and Scribe's "well-made play," Wilde is said to have commented that "the first Act is ingenious, the second, beautiful, the third, abominably clever."

Beneath the ingenuity, beauty, and cleverness is a serious statement about the nature of pretense and earnestness. Much of the wit is simply an extended pun on the words *Ernest* and *earnest*. In order that he might go to town, Jack Worthing pretends that he has a wicked brother, Ernest, whom he must watch over in London. Nevertheless, when he is in town, Jack pretends that his name is Ernest Worthing. Algernon Moncrieff, on the other hand, in an excuse to get out of town, pretends to visit a sick friend, Bunbury, who lives in the country. Thus, Jack and Algy are both guilty of the great pretense of Bunburying—living dual lives for adventure and excitement.

A considerable amount of situational farce results from both Jack and Algy's adopting the name Ernest. Mistaken identities proliferate from this, complicating the plot and providing much witty repartee. Just as disaster seems imminent for all, the true identity of Jack Worthing is discovered, solving everyone's problems and uniting everyone happily. But it is an ironic ending, for, as Jack says, "it is a terrible thing for a man to find out suddenly that all his life he has been speaking nothing but the truth."

## Characters

JOHN WORTHING, *J.P.*
ALGERNON MONCRIEFF
REV. CANON CHASUBLE, *D.D.*
MERRIMAN, *butler*
LANE, *manservant*

LADY BRACKNELL
HON. GWENDOLEN FAIRFAX
CECILY CARDEW
MISS PRISM, *governess*

TIME: the 1890's; PLACE: London

## ACT I

Morning-room in ALGERNON's flat in Half-Moon Street. The room is luxuriously and artistically furnished. The sound of a piano is heard in the adjoining room.

[LANE *is arranging afternoon tea on the table, and after the music has ceased,* ALGERNON *enters.*]

ALGERNON. Did you hear what I was playing, Lane?

LANE. I didn't think it polite to listen, sir.

ALGERNON. I'm sorry for that, for your sake. I don't play accurately—anyone can play accurately—but I play with wonderful expression. As far as the piano is concerned, sentiment is my forte. I keep science for Life.

LANE. Yes, sir.

ALGERNON. And, speaking of the science of Life, have you got the cucumber sandwiches cut for Lady Bracknell?

LANE. Yes, sir. [*Hands them on a salver.*]

ALGERNON. [*Inspects them, takes two, and sits down on the sofa.*] Oh! . . . by the way, Lane, I see from your book that on Thursday night, when Lord Shoreman and Mr. Worthing were dining with me, eight bottles of champagne are entered as having been consumed.

LANE. Yes, sir; eight bottles and a pint.

ALGERNON. Why is it that at a bachelor's establishment the servants invariably drink the champagne? I ask merely for information.

LANE. I attribute it to the superior quality of the wine, sir. I have often observed that in married households the champagne is rarely of a first-rate brand.

ALGERNON. Good Heavens! Is marriage so demoralizing as that?

LANE. I believe it *is* a very pleasant state, sir. I have had very little experience of it myself up to the present. I have only been married once. That was in consequence of a misunderstanding between myself and a young woman.

ALGERNON. [*Languidly.*] I don't know that I am much interested in your family life, Lane.

LANE. No, sir; it is not a very interesting subject. I never think of it myself.

ALGERNON. Very natural, I am sure. That will do, Lane, thank you.

LANE. Thank you, sir.

[LANE *goes out.*]

ALGERNON. Lane's views on marriage seem somewhat lax. Really, if the lower orders don't set us a good example, what on earth is the use of them? They seem, as a class, to have absolutely no sense of moral responsibility.

[*Enter* LANE.]

LANE. Mr. Ernest Worthing.

[*Enter* JACK. LANE *goes out.*]

ALGERNON. How are you, my dear Ernest? What brings you up to town?

JACK. Oh, pleasure, pleasure! What else should bring one anywhere? Eating as usual, I see, Algy!

ALGERNON. [*Stiffly.*] I believe it is customary in good society to take some slight refreshment at five o'clock. Where have you been since last Thursday?

JACK. [*Sitting down on the sofa.*] In the country.

ALGERNON. What on earth do you do there?

JACK. [*Pulling off his gloves.*] When one is in town, one amuses oneself. When one is in the country, one amuses other people. It is excessively boring.

ALGERNON. And who are the people you amuse?

JACK [*Airily.*] Oh, neighbors, neighbors.

ALGERNON. Got nice neighbors in your part of Shropshire?

JACK. Perfectly horrid! Never speak to one of them.

ALGERNON. How immensely you must amuse them! [*Goes over and takes sandwich.*] By the way, Shropshire is your county, is it not?

JACK. Eh? Shropshire? Yes, of course. Hallo! Why all these cups? Why cucumber sandwiches? Why such reckless extravagance in one so young? Who is coming to tea?

ALGERNON. Oh! merely Aunt Augusta and Gwendolen.

JACK. How perfectly delightful!

ALGERNON. Yes, that is all very well; but I am afraid Aunt Augusta won't quite approve of your being here.

JACK. May I ask why?

ALGERNON. My dear fellow, the way you flirt with Gwendolen is perfectly disgraceful. It is almost as bad as the way Gwendolen flirts with you.

JACK. I am in love with Gwendolen. I have come up to town expressly to propose to her.

ALGERNON. I thought you had come up for pleasure? . . . I call that business.

JACK. How utterly unromantic you are!

ALGERNON. I really don't see anything romantic in proposing. It is very romantic to be in love. But there is nothing romantic about a definite proposal. Why, one may be accepted. One usually is, I believe. Then the excitement is all over. The very essence of romance is uncertainty. If ever I get married, I'll certainly try to forget the fact.

JACK. I have no doubt about that, dear Algy. The Divorce Court was specially invented for people whose memories are so curiously constituted.

ALGERNON. Oh! there is no use speculating on the subject. Divorces are made in Heaven— [JACK *puts out his hand to take a sandwich.* ALGERNON *at once interferes.*] Please don't touch the cucumber sandwiches. They are ordered specially for Aunt Augusta. [*Takes one and eats it.*]

JACK. Well, you have been eating them all the time.

ALGERNON. That is quite a different matter. She is my aunt. [*Takes plate from below.*] Have some bread and butter. The bread and butter is for Gwendolen. Gwendolen is devoted to bread and butter.

JACK. [*Advancing to table and helping himself.*] And very good bread and butter it is, too.

ALGERNON. Well, my dear fellow, you need not eat as if you were going to eat it all. You behave as if you were married to her already. You are not married to her already, and I don't think you ever will be.

JACK. Why on earth do you say that?

ALGERNON. Well, in the first place girls never marry the men they flirt with. Girls don't think it right.

JACK. Oh, that is nonsense!

ALGERNON. It isn't. It is a great truth. It accounts for the extraordinary number of bachelors that one sees all over the place. In the second place, I don't give my consent.

JACK. Your consent!

ALGERNON. My dear fellow, Gwendolen is my first cousin. And before I allow you to marry her, you will have to clear up the whole question of Cecily. [*Rings bell.*]

JACK. Cecily! What on earth do you mean? What do you mean, Algy, by Cecily? I don't know anyone of the name of Cecily.

[*Enter* LANE.]

ALGERNON. Bring me that cigarette case Mr. Worthing left in the smoking-room the last time he dined here.

LANE. Yes, sir.

[LANE *goes out.*]

JACK. Do you mean to say you have had my cigarette case all this time? I wish to goodness you had let me know. I have been writing frantic letters to Scotland Yard about it. I was very nearly offering a large reward.

ALGERNON. Well, I wish you would offer one. I happen to be more than usually hard up.

JACK. There is no good offering a large reward now that the thing is found.

[*Enter* LANE *with the cigarette case on a salver.* ALGERNON *takes it at once.* LANE *goes out.*]

ALGERNON. I think that is rather mean of you, Ernest, I must say. [*Opens case and examines it.*] However, it makes no matter, for, now that I look at the inscription, I find that the thing isn't yours after all.

JACK. Of course it's mine. [*Moving to him.*] You have seen me with it a hundred times, and you have no right whatsoever to read what is written inside. It is a very ungentlemanly thing to read a private cigarette case.

ALGERNON. Oh! it is absurd to have a hard-and-fast rule about what one should read and what one shouldn't. More than half of modern culture depends on what one shouldn't read.

JACK. I am quite aware of the fact, and I don't propose to discuss modern culture. It isn't the sort of thing one should talk of in private. I simply want my cigarette case back.

ALGERNON. Yes; but this isn't your cigarette case. This cigarette case is a present from someone of the name of Cecily, and you said you didn't know anyone of that name.

JACK. Well, if you want to know, Cecily happens to be my aunt.

ALGERNON. Your aunt!

JACK. Yes. Charming old lady she is, too. Lives at Tunbridge Wells. Just give it back to me, Algy.

ALGERNON. [*Retreating to back of sofa.*] But why does she call herself little Cecily if she is your aunt and lives at Tunbridge Wells? [*Reading.*] "From little Cecily with her fondest love."

JACK. [*Moving to sofa and kneeling upon it.*] My dear fellow, what on earth is there in that? Some aunts are tall, some aunts are not tall. That is a matter that surely an aunt may be allowed to decide for herself. You seem to think that every aunt should be exactly like your aunt! That is absurd! For Heaven's sake give me back my cigarette case. [*Follows* ALGERNON *round the room.*]

ALGERNON. Yes. But why does your aunt call you her uncle? "From little Cecily, with her fondest love to her dear Uncle Jack." There is no objection, I admit, to an aunt being a small aunt, but why an aunt, no matter what her size may be, should call her own nephew her uncle, I can't quite make out. Besides, your name isn't Jack at all! it is Ernest.

JACK. It isn't Ernest; it's Jack.

ALGERNON. You have always told me it was Ernest. I have introduced you to everyone as Ernest. You answer to the name of Ernest. You look as if your name was Ernest. You are the most earnest looking person I ever saw in my life. It is perfectly absurd your saying that your name isn't Ernest. It's on your cards. Here is one of them. [*Taking it from case.*] "Mr. Ernest Worthing, B 4, The Albany." I'll keep this as a proof your name is Ernest if ever you attempt to deny it to me, or to Gwendolen, or to anyone else. [*Puts the card in his pocket.*]

JACK. Well, my name is Ernest in town and Jack in the country, and the cigarette case was given to me in the country.

ALGERNON. Yes, but that does not account for the fact that your small Aunt Cecily, who lives at Tunbridge Wells, calls you her dear uncle. Come, old boy, you had much better have the thing out at once.

JACK. My dear Algy, you talk exactly as if you were a dentist. It is very vulgar to talk like a dentist when one isn't a dentist. It produces a false impression.

ALGERNON. Well, that is exactly what dentists always do. Now, go on! Tell me the whole thing. I may mention that I have always suspected you of being a confirmed and secret Bunburyist; and I am quite sure of it now.

JACK. Bunburyist? What on earth do you mean by a Bunburyist?

ALGERNON. I'll reveal to you the meaning of that incomparable expression as soon as you are kind enough to inform me why you are Ernest in town and Jack in the country.

JACK. Well, produce my cigarette case first.

ALGERNON. Here it is. [*Hands cigarette case.*] Now produce your explanation, and pray make it improbable. [*Sits on sofa.*]

JACK. My dear fellow, there is nothing improbable about my explanation at all. In fact it's perfectly ordinary. Old Mr. Thomas Cardew, who adopted me when I was a little boy, made me in his will guardian to his grand-daughter, Miss Cecily Cardew. Cecily, who addresses me as her uncle from motives of respect that you could not possibly appreciate, lives at my place in the country under the charge of her admirable governess, Miss Prism.

ALGERNON. Where is that place in the country, by the way?

JACK. That is nothing to you, dear boy. You are not going to be invited. ... I may tell you candidly that the place is not in Shropshire.

ALGERNON. I suspected that, my dear fellow! I have Bunburyed all over Shropshire on two separate occasions. Now, go on. Why are you Ernest in town and Jack in the country?

JACK. My dear Algy, I don't know whether you will be able to understand my real motives. You are hardly serious enough. When one is placed in the position of guardian, one has to adopt a very high moral tone on all subjects. It's one's duty to do so. And as a high moral tone can hardly be said to conduce very much to either one's health or one's happiness, in order to get up to town I have always pretended to have a younger brother of the name of Ernest, who lives in the Albany, and gets into the most dreadful scrapes. That, my dear Algy, is the whole truth pure and simple.

ALGERNON. The truth is rarely pure and never simple. Modern life would be very tedious if it were either, and modern literature a complete impossibility!

JACK. That wouldn't be at all a bad thing.

ALGERNON. Literary criticism is not your forte, my dear fellow. Don't try it. You should leave that to people who haven't been at a University. They do it so well in the daily papers. What you really are is a Bunburyist. I was quite right in saying you were a Bunburyist. You are one of the most advanced Bunburyists I know.

JACK. What on earth do you mean?

ALGERNON. You have invented a very useful younger brother called Ernest, in order that you may be able to come up to town as often as you like. I have invented an invaluable permanent invalid called Bunbury, in order that I may be able to go down into the country whenever I choose. Bunbury is perfectly invaluable. If it wasn't for Bunbury's extraordinary bad health, for instance, I wouldn't be able to dine with you at Willis's tonight, for I have been really engaged to Aunt Augusta for more than a week.

JACK. I haven't asked you to dine with me anywhere tonight.

ALGERNON. I know. You are absolutely careless about sending out invitations. It is very foolish of you. Nothing annoys people so much as not receiving invitations.

JACK. You had much better dine with your Aunt Augusta.

ALGERNON. I haven't the smallest intention of doing anything of the kind. To begin with, I dined there on Monday, and once a week is quite enough to dine with one's own relatives. In the second place, whenever I do dine there I am always treated as a member of the family, and sent down with either no woman at all, or two. In the third place, I know perfectly well whom she will place me next to, tonight. She will place me next Mary Farquhar, who always flirts with her own husband across the dinner-table. That is not very pleasant. Indeed, it is not even decent... and that sort of thing is enormously on the increase. The amount of women in London who flirt with their own husbands is perfectly scandalous. It looks so bad. It is simply washing one's clean linen in public. Besides, now that I know you to be a confirmed Bunburyist I naturally want to talk to you about Bunburying. I want to tell you the rules.

JACK. I'm not a Bunburyist at all. If Gwendolen accepts me, I am going to kill my brother, indeed I think I'll kill him in any case. Cecily is a little too much interested in him. It is rather a bore. So I am going to get rid of Ernest. And I strongly advise you to do the same with Mr.... with your invalid friend who has the absurd name.

ALGERNON. Nothing will induce me to part with Bunbury, and if you ever get married, which seems to me extremely problematic, you will be very glad to know Bunbury. A man who marries without knowing Bunbury has a very tedious time of it.

JACK. That is nonsense. If I marry a charming girl like Gwendolen, and she is the only girl I ever saw in my life that I would marry, I certainly don't want to know Bunbury.

ALGERNON. Then your wife will. You don't seem to realize, that in married life three is company and two is none.

JACK. [*Sententiously.*] That, my dear young friend, is the theory that the corrupt French drama has been propounding for the last fifty years.

ALGERNON. Yes; and that the happy English home has proved in half the time.

JACK. For heaven's sake, don't try to be cynical. It's perfectly easy to be cynical.

ALGERNON. My dear fellow, it isn't easy to be anything now-a-days. There's such a lot of beastly competition about.

[*The sound of an electric bell is heard.*]

Ah! that must be Aunt Augusta. Only relatives, or creditors, ever ring in that Wagnerian manner. Now, if I get her out of the way for ten minutes, so that you can have an opportunity for proposing to Gwendolen, may I dine with you tonight at Willis's?

JACK. I suppose so, if you want to.

ALGERNON. Yes, but you must be serious about it. I hate people who are not serious about meals. It is so shallow of them.

[*Enter* LANE.]

LANE. Lady Bracknell and Miss Fairfax.

[ALGERNON *goes forward to meet them. Enter* LADY BRACKNELL *and* GWENDOLEN.]

LADY BRACKNELL. Good afternoon, dear Algernon, I hope you are behaving very well.

ALGERNON. I'm feeling very well, Aunt Augusta.

LADY BRACKNELL. That's not quite the same thing. In fact the two things rarely go together. [*Sees* JACK *and bows to him with icy coldness.*]

ALGERNON. [*To* GWENDOLEN.] Dear me, you are smart!

GWENDOLEN. [*In her habitual tone of aristocratic and worldly superiority accompanied by a faint trace of boredom.*] I am always smart! Aren't I, Mr. Worthing?

JACK. You're quite perfect, Miss Fairfax.

GWENDOLEN. Oh! I hope I am not that. It would leave no room for developments, and I intend to develop in many directions.

[GWENDOLEN *and* JACK *sit down together in the corner.*]

LADY BRACKNELL. I'm sorry if we are a little late, Algernon, but I was obliged to call on dear Lady Harbury. I hadn't been there since her poor husband's death. I never saw a woman so altered; she looks quite twenty years younger. And now I'll have a cup of tea, and one of those nice cucumber sandwiches you promised me.

ALGERNON. Certainly, Aunt Augusta. [*Goes over to tea-table.*]
LADY BRACKNELL. [*Arranging herself on the sofa.*] Won't you come and sit here, Gwendolen?
GWENDOLEN. Thanks, mamma, I'm quite comfortable where I am.
ALGERNON. [*Picking up an empty plate in horror.*] Good heavens! Lane! Why are there no cucumber sandwiches? I ordered them specially.
LANE. [*Gravely.*] There were no cucumbers in the market this morning, sir. I went down twice.
ALGERNON. No cucumbers!
LANE. No, sir. Not even for ready money.
ALGERNON. That will do, Lane, thank you.
LANE. Thank you, sir.

[*He goes out.*]

ALGERNON. I am greatly distressed, Aunt Augusta, about there being no cucumbers, not even for ready money.
LADY BRACKNELL. It really makes no matter, Algernon. I had some crumpets with Lady Harbury, who seems to me to be living entirely for pleasure now.
ALGERNON. I hear her hair has turned quite gold from grief.
LADY BRACKNELL. It certainly had changed its color. From what cause I, of course, cannot say. [ALGERNON *crosses and hands tea.*] Thank you. I've quite a treat for you tonight, Algernon. I am going to send you down with Mary Farquhar. She is such a nice woman, and so attentive to her husband. It's delightful to watch them.
ALGERNON. I am afraid, Aunt Augusta, I shall have to give up the pleasure of dining with you tonight after all.
LADY BRACKNELL. [*Frowning.*] I hope not, Algernon. It would put my table completely out. Your uncle would have to dine upstairs. Fortunately he is accustomed to that.
ALGERNON. It is a great bore, and, I need hardly say, a terrible disappointment to me, but the fact is I have just had a telegram to say that my poor friend Bunbury is very ill again. [*Exchanges glances with* JACK.] They seem to think I should be with him.
LADY BRACKNELL. It is very strange. This Mr. Bunbury seems to suffer from curiously bad health.
ALGERNON. Yes; poor Bunbury is a dreadful invalid.
LADY BRACKNELL. Well, I must say, Algernon, that I think it is high time

that Mr. Bunbury made up his mind whether he was going to live or to die. [*In a tone of indignant impatience.*] This shilly-shallying with the question is absurd. Nor do I in any way approve of the modern sympathy with invalids. I consider it morbid. Illness of any kind is hardly a thing to be encouraged in others. Health is the primary duty of life. I am always telling that to your poor uncle, but he never seems to take much notice . . . as far as any improvements in his ailments goes. I should be much obliged if you would ask Mr. Bunbury, from me, to be kind enough not to have a relapse on Saturday, for I rely on you to arrange my music for me. It is my last reception and one wants something that will encourage conversation, particularly at the end of the season when everyone has practically said whatever they had to say, which, in most cases, was probably not much.

ALGERNON. I'll speak to Bunbury, Aunt Augusta, if he is still conscious, and I think I can promise you he'll be all right by Saturday. You see, if one plays good music, people don't listen, and if one plays bad music, people don't talk. But I'll run over the program I've drawn out, if you will kindly come into the next room for a moment.

LADY BRACKNELL. Thank you, Algernon. It is very thoughtful of you. [*Rising, and following* ALGERNON.] I'm sure the program will be delightful, after a few expurgations. French songs I cannot possibly allow. People always seem to think that they are improper, and either look shocked, which is vulgar, or laugh, which is worse. But German sounds a thoroughly respectable language, and indeed, I believe it is so. Gwendolen, you will accompany me.

GWENDOLEN. Certainly, mamma.

[LACY BRACKNELL *and* ALGERNON *go into the music-room,* GWENDOLEN *remains behind.*]

JACK. Charming day it has been, Miss Fairfax.

GWENDOLEN. Pray don't talk to me about the weather, Mr. Worthing. Whenever people talk to me about the weather, I always feel quite certain that they mean something else. And that makes me nervous.

JACK. I do mean something else.

GWENDOLEN. I thought so. In fact, I am never wrong.

JACK. And I would like to be allowed to take advantage of Lady Bracknell's temporary absence . . .

GWENDOLEN. I would certainly advise you to do so. Mamma has a way of coming back suddenly into a room that I have often had to speak to her about.

JACK. [*Nervously.*] Miss Fairfax, ever since I met you I have admired you more than any girl . . . I have ever met since . . . I met you.

GWENDOLEN. Yes, I am quite aware of the fact. And I often wish that in public, at any rate, you had been more demonstrative. For me you have always had an irresistible fascination. Even before I met you I was far from indifferent to you. [JACK *looks at her in amazement.*] We live, as I hope you know, Mr. Worthing, in an age of ideals. The fact is constantly mentioned in the more expensive monthly magazines, and has reached the provincial pulpits I am told: and my ideal has always been to love some one of the name of Ernest. There is something in that name that inspires absolute confidence. The moment Algernon first mentioned to me that he had a friend called Ernest, I knew I was destined to love you.

JACK. You really love me, Gwendolen?

GWENDOLEN. Passionately!

JACK. Darling! You don't know how happy you've made me.

GWENDOLEN. My own Ernest!

JACK. But you don't really mean to say that you couldn't love me if my name wasn't Ernest?

GWENDOLEN. But your name is Ernest.

JACK. Yes, I know it is. But supposing it was something else? Do you mean to say you couldn't love me then?

GWENDOLEN. [*Glibly.*] Ah! that is clearly a metaphysical speculation, and like most metaphysical speculations has very little reference at all to the actual facts of real life, as we know them.

JACK. Personally, darling, to speak quite candidly, I don't much care about the name of Ernest . . . I don't think that name suits me at all.

GWENDOLEN. It suits you perfectly. It is a divine name. It has a music of its own. It produces vibrations.

JACK. Well, really, Gwendolen, I must say that I think there are lots of other much nicer names. I think, Jack, for instance, a charming name.

GWENDOLEN. Jack? . . . No, there is very little music in the name Jack, if any at all, indeed. It does not thrill. It produces absolutely no vibrations. . . . I have known several Jacks, and they all, without exception, were more than usually plain. Besides, Jack is a notorious domesticity for John! And I pity any woman who is married to a man called John. She would probably never be allowed to know the entrancing pleasure of a single moment's solitude. The only really safe name is Ernest.

JACK. Gwendolen, I must get christened at once—I mean we must get married at once. There is no time to be lost.

GWENDOLEN. Married, Mr. Worthing?

JACK. [*Astounded.*] Well . . . surely. You know that I love you, and you led me to believe, Miss Fairfax, that you were not absolutely indifferent to me.

GWENDOLEN. I adore you. But you haven't proposed to me yet. Nothing has been said at all about marriage. The subject has not even been touched on.

JACK. Well . . . may I propose to you now?

GWENDOLEN. I think it would be an admirable opportunity. And to spare you any possible disappointment, Mr. Worthing, I think it only fair to tell you quite frankly beforehand that I am fully determined to accept you.

JACK. Gwendolen!

GWENDOLEN. Yes, Mr. Worthing, what have you got to say to me?

JACK. You know what I have got to say to you.

GWENDOLEN. Yes, but you don't say it.

JACK. Gwendolen, will you marry me? [*Goes to his knees.*]

GWENDOLEN. Of course I will, darling. How long you have been about it! I am afraid you have had very little experience in how to propose.

JACK. My own one, I have never loved anyone in the world but you.

GWENDOLEN. Yes, but men often propose for practice. I know my brother Gerald does. All my girl-friends tell me so. What wonderfully blue eyes you have, Ernest! They are quite, quite blue. I hope you will always look at me just like that, especially when there are other people present.

[*Enter* LADY BRACKNELL.]

LADY BRACKNELL. Mr. Worthing! Rise, sir, from this semi-recumbent posture. It is most indecorous.

GWENDOLEN. Mamma! [*He tries to rise; she restrains him.*] I must beg you to retire. This is no place for you. Besides, Mr. Worthing has not quite finished yet.

LADY BRACKNELL. Finished what, may I ask?

GWENDOLEN. I am engaged to Mr. Worthing, mamma. [*They rise together.*]
LADY BRACKNELL. Pardon me, you are not engaged to anyone. When you do become engaged to someone, I, or your father, should his health permit him, will inform you of the fact. An engagement should come on a young girl as a surprise, pleasant or unpleasant, as the case may be. It is hardly a matter that she could be allowed to arrange for herself. . . . And now I have a few questions to put to you, Mr. Worthing. While I am making these inquiries, you, Gwendolen, will wait for me below in the carriage.
GWENDOLEN. [*Reproachfully.*] Mamma!
LADY BRACKNELL. In the carriage, Gwendolen!

[GWENDOLEN *goes to the door. She and* JACK *blow kisses to each other behind* LADY BRACKNELL'S *back.* LADY BRACKNELL *looks vaguely about as if she could not understand what the noise was. Finally turns round.*]

Gwendolen, the carriage!
GWENDOLEN. Yes, mamma. [*Goes out, looking back at* JACK.]
LADY BRACKNELL. [*Sitting down.*] You can take a seat, Mr. Worthing. [*Looks in her pocket for notebook and pencil.*]
JACK. Thank you, Lady Bracknell, I prefer standing.
LADY BRACKNELL. [*Pencil and notebook in hand.*] I feel bound to tell you that you are not down on my list of eligible young men, although I have the same list as the dear Duchess of Bolton has. We work together, in fact. However, I am quite ready to enter your name, should your answers be what a really affectionate mother requires. Do you smoke?
JACK. Well, yes, I must admit I smoke.
LADY BRACKNELL. I am glad to hear it. A man should always have an occupation of some kind. There are far too many idle men in London as it is. How old are you?
JACK. Twenty-nine.
LADY BRACKNELL. A very good age to be married at. I have always been of opinion that a man who desires to get married should know either everything or nothing. Which do you know?
JACK. [*After some hesitation.*] I know nothing, Lady Bracknell.
LADY BRACKNELL. I am pleased to hear it. I do not approve of anything that tampers with natural ignorance. Ignorance is like a delicate exotic fruit; touch it and the bloom is gone. The whole theory of

modern education is radically unsound. Fortunately in England, at any rate, education produces no effect whatsoever. If it did, it would prove a serious danger to the upper classes, and probably lead to acts of violence in Grosvenor Square. What is your income?

JACK. Between seven and eight thousand[1] a year.

LADY BRACKNELL. [*Makes a note in her book.*] In land, or in investments?

JACK. In investments, chiefly.

LADY BRACKNELL. That is satisfactory. What between the duties expected of one during one's lifetime, and the duties exacted from one after one's death,[2] land has ceased to be either a profit or a pleasure. It gives one position, and prevents one from keeping it up. That's all that can be said about land.

JACK. I have a country house with some land, of course, attached to it, about fifteen hundred acres, I believe; but I don't depend on that for my real income. In fact, as far as I can make out, the poachers are the only people who make anything out of it.

LADY BRACKNELL. A country house! How many bedrooms? Well, that point can be cleared up afterwards. You have a town house, I hope? A girl with a simple, unspoiled nature, like Gwendolen, could hardly be expected to reside in the country.

JACK. Well, I own a house in Belgrave Square, but it is let by the year to Lady Bloxham. Of course, I can get it back whenever I like, at six months' notice.

LADY BRACKNELL. Lady Bloxham? I don't know her.

JACK. Oh, she goes about very little. She is a lady considerably advanced in years.

LADY BRACKNELL. Ah, now-a-days that is no guarantee of respectability of character. What number in Belgrave Square?

JACK. 149.

LADY BRACKNELL. [*Shaking her head.*] The unfashionable side. I thought there was something. However, that could easily be altered.

JACK. Do you mean the fashion, or the side?

LADY BRACKNELL. [*Sternly.*] Both, if necessary, I presume. What are your politics?

JACK. Well, I am afraid I really have none. I am a Liberal Unionist.

LADY BRACKNELL. Oh, they count as Tories. They dine with us. Or

---

1. *between seven and eight thousand:* about $34,000.
2. *duties exacted . . . death:* death duties (inheritance taxes).

come in the evening, at any rate. Now to minor matters. Are your parents living?

JACK. I have lost both my parents.

LADY BRACKNELL. Both? . . . That seems like carelessness. Who was your father? He was evidently a man of some wealth. Was he born in what the Radical papers call the purple of commerce, or did he rise from the ranks of the aristocracy?

JACK. I am afraid I really don't know. The fact is, Lady Bracknell, I said I had lost my parents. It would be nearer the truth to say that my parents seem to have lost me . . . I don't actually know who I am by birth. It was . . . well, I was found.

LADY BRACKNELL. Found!

JACK. The late Mr. Thomas Cardew, an old gentleman of a very charitable and kindly disposition, found me, and gave me the name of Worthing, because he happened to have a first-class ticket for Worthing in his pocket at the time. Worthing is a place in Sussex. It is a seaside resort.

LADY BRACKNELL. Where did the charitable gentleman who had a first-class ticket for this seaside resort find you?

JACK. [*Gravely.*] In a hand-bag.

LADY BRACKNELL. A hand-bag?

JACK. [*Very seriously.*] Yes, Lady Bracknell. I was in a hand-bag—a somewhat large, black leather hand-bag, with handles to it—an ordinary hand-bag in fact.

LADY BRACKNELL. In what locality did this Mr. James, or Thomas, Cardew come across this ordinary hand-bag?

JACK. In the cloak-room at Victoria Station. It was given to him in mistake for his own.

LADY BRACKNELL. The cloak-room at Victoria Station?

JACK. Yes. The Brighton line.

LADY BRACKNELL. The line is immaterial. Mr. Worthing, I confess I feel somewhat bewildered by what you have just told me. To be born, or at any rate bred, in a hand-bag, whether it had handles or not, seems to me to display a contempt for the ordinary decencies of family life that remind one of the worst excesses of the French Revolution. And I presume you know what that unfortunate movement led to? As for the particular locality in which the hand-bag was found, a cloak-room at a railway station might serve to conceal a social indiscretion—has probably, indeed, been used for that purpose before now—but it could hardly be regarded as an assured basis for a recognized position in good society.

JACK. May I ask you then what you would advise me to do? I need hardly say I would do anything in the world to ensure Gwendolen's happiness.

LADY BRACKNELL. I would strongly advise you, Mr. Worthing, to try and acquire some relations as soon as possible, and to make a definite effort to produce at any rate one parent, of either sex, before the season is quite over.

JACK. Well, I don't see how I could possibly manage to do that. I can produce the hand-bag at any moment. It is in my dressing-room at home. I really think that should satisfy you, Lady Bracknell.

LADY BRACKNELL. Me, sir! What has it to do with me? You can hardly imagine that I and Lord Bracknell would dream of allowing our only daughter—a girl brought up with the utmost care—to marry into a cloak-room, and form an alliance with a parcel? Good morning, Mr. Worthing!

[LADY BRACKNELL *sweeps out in majestic indignation.*]

JACK. Good morning!

[ALGERNON, *from the other room, strikes up the Wedding March.* JACK *looks perfectly furious, and goes to the door.*]

For goodness' sake don't play that ghastly tune, Algy! How idiotic you are!

[*The music stops, and* ALGERNON *enters cheerily.*]

ALGERNON. Didn't it go off all right, old boy? You don't mean to say Gwendolen refused you? I know it is a way she has. She is always refusing people. I think it is most ill-natured of her.

JACK. Oh, Gwendolen is as right as a trivet. As far as she is concerned, we are engaged. Her mother is perfectly unbearable. Never met such a Gorgon[3] . . . I don't really know what a Gorgon is like, but I am quite sure that Lady Bracknell is one. In any case, she is a monster, without being a myth, which is rather unfair. . . . I beg your pardon, Algy, I suppose I shouldn't talk about your own aunt in that way before you.

---

3. *Gorgon:* a terrifying woman. In Greek mythology the Gorgons were monstrous females with huge teeth and claws, and snaky hair.

ALGERNON. My dear boy, I love hearing my relations abused. It is the only thing that makes me put up with them at all. Relations are simply a tedious pack of people, who haven't got the remotest knowledge of how to live, nor the smallest instinct about when to die.

JACK. Oh, that is nonsense!

ALGERNON. It isn't!

JACK. Well, I won't argue about the matter. You always want to argue about things.

ALGERNON. That is exactly what things were originally made for.

JACK. Upon my word, if I thought that, I'd shoot myself . . . [*A pause.*] You don't think there is any chance of Gwendolen becoming like her mother in about a hundred and fifty years, do you, Algy?

ALGERNON. All women become like their mothers. That is their tragedy. No man does. That's his.

JACK. Is that clever?

ALGERNON. It is perfectly phrased! and quite as true as any observation in civilized life should be.

JACK. I am sick to death of cleverness. Everybody is clever now-a-days. You can't go anywhere without meeting clever people. The thing has become an absolute public nuisance. I wish to goodness we had a few fools left.

ALGERNON. We have.

JACK. I should extremely like to meet them. What do they talk about?

ALGERNON. The fools? Oh! about the clever people, of course.

JACK. What fools!

ALGERNON. By the way, did you tell Gwendolen the truth about your being Ernest in town, and Jack in the country?

JACK. [*In a very patronizing manner.*] My dear fellow, the truth isn't quite the sort of thing one tells to a nice, sweet, refined girl. What extraordinary ideas you have about the way to behave to a woman!

ALGERNON. The only way to behave to a woman is to make love to her, if she is pretty, and to someone else if she is plain.

JACK. Oh, that is nonsense.

ALGERNON. What about your brother? What about the profligate Ernest?

JACK. Oh, before the end of the week I shall have got rid of him. I'll say he died in Paris of apoplexy. Lots of people die of apoplexy, quite suddenly, don't they?

ALGERNON. Yes, but it's hereditary, my dear fellow. It's a sort of thing that runs in families. You had much better say a severe chill.

JACK. You are sure a severe chill isn't hereditary, or anything of that kind?

ALGERNON. Of course it isn't!

JACK. Very well, then. My poor brother Ernest is carried off suddenly in Paris, by a severe chill. That gets rid of him.

ALGERNON. But I thought you said that . . . Miss Cardew was a little too much interested in your poor brother Ernest? Won't she feel his loss a good deal?

JACK. Oh, that is all right. Cecily is not a silly, romantic girl, I am glad to say. She has got a capital appetite, goes for long walks, and pays no attention at all to her lessons.

ALGERNON. I would rather like to see Cecily.

JACK. I will take very good care you never do. She is excessively pretty, and she is only just eighteen.

ALGERNON. Have you told Gwendolen yet that you have an excessively pretty ward who is only just eighteen?

JACK. Oh! one doesn't blurt these things out to people. Cecily and Gwendolen are perfectly certain to be extremely great friends. I'll bet you anything you like that half an hour after they have met, they will be calling each other sister.

ALGERNON. Women only do that when they have called each other a lot of other things first. Now, my dear boy, if we want to get a good table at Willis's, we really must go and dress. Do you know it is nearly seven?

JACK. [*Irritably.*] Oh! it always is nearly seven.

ALGERNON. Well, I'm hungry.

JACK. I never knew you when you weren't. . . .

ALGERNON. What shall we do after dinner? Go to a theater?

JACK. Oh, no! I loathe listening.

ALGERNON. Well, let us go to the Club?

JACK. Oh, no! I hate talking.

ALGERNON. Well, we might trot round to the Empire[4] at ten?

JACK. Oh, no! I can't bear looking at things. It is so silly.

ALGERNON. Well, what shall we do?

JACK. Nothing!

ALGERNON. It is awfully hard work doing nothing. However, I don't mind hard work where there is no definite object of any kind.

---

4. *the Empire:* a popular amusement hall.

[*Enter* LANE.]

LANE. Miss Fairfax.

[*Enter* GWENDOLEN. LANE *goes out.*]

ALGERNON. Gwendolen, upon my word!
GWENDOLEN. Algy, kindly turn your back. I have something very particular to say to Mr. Worthing.
ALGERNON. Really, Gwendolen, I don't think I can allow this at all.
GWENDOLEN. Algy, you always adopt a strictly immoral attitude toward life. You are not quite old enough to do that.

[ALGERNON *retires to the fireplace.*]

JACK. My own darling!
GWENDOLEN. Ernest, we may never be married. From the expression on mamma's face I fear we never shall. Few parents now-a-days pay any regard to what their children say to them. The old-fashioned respect for the young is fast dying out. Whatever influence I ever had over mamma, I lost at the age of three. But although she may prevent us from becoming man and wife, and I may marry someone else, and marry often, nothing that she can possibly do can alter my eternal devotion to you.
JACK. Dear Gwendolen.
GWENDOLEN. The story of your romantic origin, as related to me by mamma, with unpleasing comments, has naturally stirred the deeper fibers of my nature. Your Christian name has an irresistible fascination. The simplicity of your character makes you exquisitely incomprehensible to me. Your town address at the Albany I have. What is your address in the country?
JACK. The Manor House, Woolton, Hertfordshire.

[ALGERNON, *who has been carefully listening, smiles to himself, and writes the address on his shirt-cuff. Then picks up the Railway Guide.*]

GWENDOLEN. There is a good postal service, I suppose? It may be necessary to do something desperate. That, of course, will require serious consideration. I will communicate with you daily.
JACK. My own one!
GWENDOLEN. How long do you remain in town?

JACK. Till Monday.
GWENDOLEN. Good! Algy, you may turn round now.
ALGERNON. Thanks, I've turned round already.
GWENDOLEN. You may also ring the bell.
JACK. You will let me see you to your carriage, my own darling?
GWENDOLEN. Certainly.
JACK. [*To* LANE, *who now enters.*] I will see Miss Fairfax out.
LANE. Yes, sir.

[JACK *and* GWENDOLEN *go off.* LANE *presents several letters on a salver to* ALGERNON. *It is to be surmised that they are bills, as* ALGERNON, *after looking at the envelopes, tears them up.*]

ALGERNON. A glassy of sherry, Lane.
LANE. Yes, sir.
ALGERNON. Tomorrow, Lane, I am going Bunburying.
LANE. Yes, sir.
ALGERNON. I shall probably not be back till Monday. You can put up my dress clothes, my smoking jacket, and all the Bunbury suits . . .
LANE. Yes, sir. [*Handing sherry.*]
ALGERNON. I hope tomorrow will be a fine day, Lane.
LANE. It never is, sir.
ALGERNON. Lane, you're a perfect pessimist.
LANE. I do my best to give satisfaction, sir.

[*Enter* JACK. LANE *goes off.*]

JACK. There's a sensible, intellectual girl! the only girl I ever cared for in my life. [ALGERNON *is laughing immoderately.*] What on earth are you so amused at?
ALGERNON. Oh, I'm a little anxious about poor Bunbury, that's all.
JACK. If you don't take care, your friend Bunbury will get you into a serious scrape some day.
ALGERNON. I love scrapes. They are the only things that are never serious.
JACK. Oh, that's nonsense, Algy. You never talk anything but nonsense.
ALGERNON. Nobody ever does.

[JACK *looks indignantly at him, and leaves the room.* ALGERNON *lights a cigarette, reads his shirt-cuff and smiles.*]

Act I

# ACT II

Garden at the Manor House. A flight of gray stone steps leads up to the house. The garden, an old-fashioned one, full of roses. Time of year, July. Basket chairs, and a table covered with books, are set under a large yew tree.

[MISS PRISM *discovered seated at the table.* CECILY *is at the back watering flowers.*]

MISS PRISM. [*Calling.*] Cecily, Cecily! Surely such a utilitarian occupation as the watering of flowers is rather Moulton's duty than yours? Especially at a moment when intellectual pleasures await you. Your German grammar is on the table. Pray open it at page fifteen. We will repeat yesterday's lesson.

CECILY. [*Coming over very slowly.*] But I don't like German. It isn't at all a becoming language. I know perfectly well that I look quite plain after my German lesson.

MISS PRISM. Child, you know how anxious your guardian is that you should improve yourself in every way. He laid particular stress on your German, as he was leaving for town yesterday. Indeed, he always lays stress on your German when he is leaving for town.

CECILY. Dear Uncle Jack is so very serious! Sometimes he is so serious that I think he cannot be quite well.

MISS PRISM. [*Drawing herself up.*] Your guardian enjoys the best of health, and his gravity of demeanor is especially to be commended in one so comparatively young as he is. I know no one who has a higher sense of duty and responsibility.

CECILY. I suppose that is why he often looks a little bored when we three are together.

MISS PRISM. Cecily! I am surprised at you. Mr. Worthing has many troubles in his life. Idle merriment and triviality would be out of place in his conversation. You must remember his constant anxiety about that unfortunate young man, his brother.

CECILY. I wish Uncle Jack would allow that unfortunate young man, his brother, to come down here sometimes. We might have a good influence over him, Miss Prism. I am sure you certainly would. You know German, and geology, and things of that kind influence a man very much.

[CECILY *begins to write in her diary.*]

MISS PRISM. [*Shaking her head.*] I do not think that even I could produce any effect on a character that, according to his own brother's admission, is irretrievably weak and vacillating. Indeed, I am not sure that I would desire to reclaim him. I am not in favor of this modern mania for turning bad people into good people at a moment's notice. As a man sows, so let him reap. You must put away your diary, Cecily. I really don't see why you should keep a diary at all.

CECILY. I keep a diary in order to enter the wonderful secrets of my life. If I didn't write them down I should probably forget all about them.

MISS PRISM. Memory, my dear Cecily, is the diary that we all carry about with us.

CECILY. Yes, but it usually chronicles the things that have never happened, and couldn't possibly have happened. I believe that Memory is responsible for nearly all the three-volume novels that Mudie[1] sends us.

MISS PRISM. Do not speak slightingly of the three-volume novel, Cecily. I wrote one myself in earlier days.

CECILY. Did you really, Miss Prism? How wonderfully clever you are! I hope it did not end happily? I don't like novels that end happily. They depress me so much.

MISS PRISM. The good ended happily, and the bad unhappily. That is what Fiction means.

CECILY. I suppose so. But it seems very unfair. And was your novel ever published?

MISS PRISM. Alas! no. The manuscript unfortunately was abandoned. I use the word in the sense of lost or mislaid. To your work, child, these speculations are profitless.

CECILY. [*Smiling.*] But I see dear Dr. Chasuble coming up through the garden.

MISS PRISM. [*Rising and advancing.*] Dr. Chasuble! This is indeed a pleasure.

[*Enter* CANON CHASUBLE.[2]]

---

1. *Mudie:* a London bookstore which maintained a circulating library.
2. *Canon Chasuble:* a canon is a clergyman who is a member of a cathedral chapter or one who is a member of a cathedral staff.

CHASUBLE. And how are we this morning? Miss Prism, you are, I trust, well?

CECILY. Miss Prism has just been complaining of a slight headache. I think it would do her so much good to have a short stroll with you in the park, Dr. Chasuble.

MISS PRISM. Cecily, I have not mentioned anything about a headache.

CECILY. No, dear Miss Prism, I know that, but I felt instinctively that you had a headache. Indeed I was thinking about that, and not about my German lesson, when the Rector came in.

CHASUBLE. I hope, Cecily, you are not inattentive.

CECILY. Oh, I am afraid I am.

CHASUBLE. That is strange. Were I fortunate enough to be Miss Prism's pupil, I would hang upon her lips. [MISS PRISM *glares.*] I spoke metaphorically.—My metaphor was drawn from bees. Ahem! Mr. Worthing, I suppose, has not returned from town yet?

MISS PRISM. We do not expect him till Monday afternoon.

CHASUBLE. Ah, yes, he usually likes to spend his Sunday in London. He is not one of those whose sole aim is enjoyment, as, by all accounts, that unfortunate young man, his brother, seems to be. But I must not disturb Egeria[3] and her pupil any longer.

MISS PRISM. Egeria? My name is Laetitia, Doctor.

CHASUBLE. [*Bowing.*] A classical allusion merely, drawn from the Pagan authors. I shall see you both no doubt at Evensong.

MISS PRISM. I think, dear Doctor, I will have a stroll with you. I find I have a headache, after all, and a walk might do it good.

CHASUBLE. With pleasure, Miss Prism, with pleasure. We might go as far as the schools and back.

MISS PRISM. That would be delightful. Cecily, you will read your Political Economy in my absence. The chapter on the Fall of the Rupee you may omit. It is somewhat too sensational. Even these metallic problems have their melodramatic side. [*Goes down the garden with* DR. CHASUBLE.]

CECILY. [*Picks up books and throws them back on table.*] Horrid Political Economy! Horrid Geography! Horrid, horrid German!

[*Enter* MERRIMAN *with a card on a salver.*]

---

3. *Egeria:* in Roman mythology, a fountain nymph who was said to have given secret interviews to Numa, the second king of Rome. During these interviews she taught him the principles of law and wisdom which he used in building his nation.

MERRIMAN. Mr. Ernest Worthing has just driven over from the station. He has brought his luggage with him.
CECILY. [*Takes the card and reads it.*] "Mr. Ernest Worthing, B 4 The Albany, W." Uncle Jack's brother! Did you tell him Mr. Worthing was in town?
MERRIMAN. Yes, Miss. He seemed very much disappointed. I mentioned that you and Miss Prism were in the garden. He said he was anxious to speak to you privately for a moment.
CECILY. Ask Mr. Ernest Worthing to come here. I suppose you had better talk to the housekeeper about a room for him.
MERRIMAN. Yes, Miss.

[MERRIMAN *goes off.*]

CECILY. I have never met any really wicked person before. I feel rather frightened. I am so afraid he will look just like everyone else.

[*Enter* ALGERNON, *very gay and debonair.*]

He does!
ALGERNON. [*Raising his hat.*] You are my little cousin Cecily, I'm sure.
CECILY. You are under some strange mistake. I am not little. In fact, I am more than usually tall for my age. [ALGERNON *is rather taken aback.*] But I am your cousin Cecily. You, I see from your card, are Uncle Jack's brother, my cousin Ernest, my wicked cousin Ernest.
ALGERNON. Oh! I am not really wicked at all, cousin Cecily. You musn't think that I am wicked.
CECILY. If you are not, then you have certainly been deceiving us all in a very inexcusable manner. I hope you have not been leading a double life, pretending to be wicked and being really good all the time. That would be hypocrisy.
ALGERNON. [*Looks at her in amazement.*] Oh! of course I have been rather reckless.
CECILY. I am glad to hear it.
ALGERNON. In fact, now you mention the subject, I have been very bad in my own small way.
CECILY. I don't think you should be so proud of that, though I am sure it must have been very pleasant.
ALGERNON. It is much pleasanter being here with you.

CECILY. I can't understand how you are here at all. Uncle Jack won't be back till Monday afternoon.
ALGERNON. That is a great disappointment. I am obliged to go up by the first train on Monday morning. I have a business appointment that I am anxious . . . to miss.
CECILY. Couldn't you miss it anywhere but in London?
ALGERNON. No; the appointment is in London.
CECILY. Well, I know, of course, how important it is not to keep a business engagement, if one wants to retain any sense of the beauty of life, but still I think you had better wait till Uncle Jack arrives. I know he wants to speak to you about your emigrating.
ALGERNON. About my what?
CECILY. Your emigrating. He has gone up to buy your outfit.
ALGERNON. I certainly wouldn't let Jack buy my outfit. He has no taste in neckties at all.
CECILY. I don't think you will require neckties. Uncle Jack is sending you to Australia.
ALGERNON. Australia! I'd sooner die.
CECILY. Well, he said at dinner on Wednesday night, that you would have to choose between this world, the next world, and Australia.
ALGERNON. Oh, well! The accounts I have received of Australia and the next world are not particularly encouraging. This world is good enough for me, cousin Cecily.
CECILY. Yes, but are you good enough for it?
ALGERNON. I'm afraid I'm not that. That is why I want you to reform me. You might make that your mission, if you don't mind, cousin Cecily.
CECILY. I'm afraid I've not time, this afternoon.
ALGERNON. Well, would you mind my reforming myself this afternoon?
CECILY. That is rather Quixotic of you. But I think you should try.
ALGERNON. I will. I feel better already.
CECILY. You are looking a little worse.
ALGERNON. That is because I am hungry.
CECILY. How thoughtless of me. I should have remembered that when one is going to lead an entirely new life, one requires regular and wholesome meals. Won't you come in?
ALGERNON. Thank you. Might I have a button-hole first? I never have any appetite unless I have a button-hole first.

CECILY. A Maréchal Niel?[4] [*Picks up scissors.*]

ALGERNON. No, I'd sooner have a pink rose.

CECILY. Why? [*Cuts a flower.*]

ALGERNON. Because you are like a pink rose, cousin Cecily.

CECILY. I don't think it can be right for you to talk to me like that. Miss Prism never says such things to me.

ALGERNON. Then Miss Prism is a short-sighted old lady. [*Cecily puts the rose in his button-hole.*] You are the prettiest girl I ever saw.

CECILY. Miss Prism says that all good looks are a snare.

ALGERNON. They are a snare that every sensible man would like to be caught in.

CECILY. Oh! I don't think I would care to catch a sensible man. I shouldn't know what to talk to him about.

[*They pass into the house.* MISS PRISM *and* DR. CHASUBLE *return.*]

MISS PRISM. You are too much alone, dear Dr. Chasuble. You should get married. A misanthrope[5] I can understand—a woman-thrope, never!

CHASUBLE. [*With a scholar's shudder.*] Believe me, I do not deserve so neologistic a phrase.[6] The precept as well as the practice of the Primitive Church was distinctly against matrimony.

MISS PRISM. [*Sententiously.*] That is obviously the reason why the Primitive Church has not lasted up to the present day. And you do not seem to realize, dear Doctor, that by persistently remaining single, a man converts himself into a permanent public temptation. Men should be careful; this very celibacy leads weaker vessels astray.

CHASUBLE. But is a man not equally attractive when married?

MISS PRISM. No married man is ever attractive except to his wife.

CHASUBLE. And often, I've been told, not even to her.

MISS PRISM. That depends on the intellectual sympathies of the woman. Maturity can always be depended on. Ripeness can be trusted. Young women are green. [DR. CHASUBLE *starts.*] I spoke horticulturally. My metaphor was drawn from fruits. But where is Cecily?

CHASUBLE. Perhaps she followed us to the schools.

[*Enter* JACK *slowly from the back of the garden. He is dressed in the deepest mourning, with crape hatband and black gloves.*]

---

4. *A Maréchal Niel:* a beautiful yellow rose.
5. *misanthrope:* one who hates mankind.
6. *so . . . phrase:* a neologistic term is one which is newly invented. Chasuble refers, of course, to Miss Prism's invention, *womanthrope*.

MISS PRISM. Mr. Worthing!
CHASUBLE. Mr. Worthing?
MISS PRISM. This is indeed a surprise. We did not look for you till Monday afternoon.
JACK. [*Shakes* MISS PRISM'S *hand in a tragic manner.*] I have returned sooner than I expected. Dr. Chasuble, I hope you are well?
CHASUBLE. Dear Mr. Worthing, I trust this garb of woe does not betoken some terrible calamity?
JACK. My brother.
MISS PRISM. More shameful debts and extravagance?
CHASUBLE. Still leading his life of pleasure?
JACK. [*Shaking his head.*] Dead!
CHASUBLE. Your brother Ernest dead?
JACK. Quite dead.
MISS PRISM. What a lesson for him! I trust he will profit by it.
CHASUBLE. Mr. Worthing, I offer you my sincere condolence. You have at least the consolation of knowing that you were always the most generous and forgiving of brothers.
JACK. Poor Ernest! He had many faults, but it is a sad, sad blow.
CHASUBLE. Very sad indeed. Were you with him at the end?
JACK. No. He died abroad; in Paris, in fact. I had a telegram last night from the manager of the Grand Hotel.
CHASUBLE. Was the cause of death mentioned?
JACK. A severe chill, it seems.
MISS PRISM. As a man sows, so shall he reap.
CHASUBLE. [*Raising his hand.*] Charity, dear Miss Prism, charity! None of us are perfect. I myself am peculiarly susceptible to draughts. Will the interment take place here?
JACK. No. He seems to have expressed a desire to be buried in Paris.
CHASUBLE. In Paris! [*Shakes his head.*] I fear that hardly points to any very serious state of mind at the last. You would no doubt wish me to make some slight allusion to this tragic domestic affliction next Sunday. [JACK *presses his hand convulsively.*] My sermon on the meaning of the manna in the wilderness can be adapted to almost any occasion, joyful, or, as in the present case, distressing. [*All sigh.*] I have preached it at harvest celebrations, christenings, confirmations, on days of humiliation and festal days. The last time I delivered it was in the Cathedral, as a charity sermon on behalf of the Society for the Prevention of Discontentment among the Upper

Orders. The Bishop, who was present, was much struck by some of the analogies I drew.

JACK. Ah, that reminds me, you mentioned christenings I think, Dr. Chasuble? I suppose you know how to christen all right? [DR. CHASUBLE *looks astounded.*] I mean, of course, you are continually christening, aren't you?

MISS PRISM. It is, I regret to say, one of the Rector's most constant duties in this parish. I have often spoken to the poorer classes on the subject. But they don't seem to know what thrift is.

CHASUBLE. But is there any particular infant in whom you are interested, Mr. Worthing? Your brother was, I believe, unmarried, was he not?

JACK. Oh, yes.

MISS PRISM. [*Bitterly.*] People who live entirely for pleasure usually are.

JACK. But it is not for any child, dear Doctor. I am very fond of children. No! the fact is, I would like to be christened myself, this afternoon, if you have nothing better to do.

CHASUBLE. But surely, Mr. Worthing, you have been christened already?

JACK. I don't remember anything about it.

CHASUBLE. But have you any grave doubts on the subject?

JACK. I certainly intend to have. Of course, I don't know if the thing would bother you in any way, or if you think I am a little too old now.

CHASUBLE. Not at all. The sprinkling, and indeed, the immersion of adults is a perfectly canonical practice.

JACK. Immersion!

CHASUBLE. You need have no apprehensions. Sprinkling is all that is necessary, or indeed I think advisable. Our weather is so changeable. At what hour would you wish the ceremony performed?

JACK. Oh, I might trot around about five if that would suit you.

CHASUBLE. Perfectly, perfectly! In fact I have two similar ceremonies to perform at that time. A case of twins that occurred recently in one of the outlying cottages on your own estate. Poor Jenkins the carter, a most hard-working man.

JACK. Oh! I don't see much fun in being christened along with other babies. It would be childish. Would half-past five do?

CHASUBLE. Admirably! Admirably! [*Takes out watch.*] And now, dear Mr. Worthing, I will not intrude any longer into a house of sorrow. I would merely beg you not to be too much bowed down by grief. What seem to us bitter trials at the moment are often blessings in disguise.

MISS PRISM. This seems to me a blessing of an extremely obvious kind.

[*Enter* CECILY *from the house.*]

CECILY. Uncle Jack! Oh, I am so pleased to see you back. But what horrid clothes you have on! Do go and change them.
MISS PRISM. Cecily!
CHASUBLE. My child! my child!

[CECILY *goes toward* JACK; *he kisses her brow in a melancholy manner.*]

CECILY. What is the matter, Uncle Jack? Do look happy! You look as if you had a toothache, and I have such a surprise for you. Who do you think is in the dining-room? Your brother!
JACK. Who?
CECILY. Your brother Ernest. He arrived about half an hour ago.
JACK. What nonsense! I haven't got a brother.
CECILY. Oh, don't say that. However badly he may have behaved to you in the past, he is still your brother. You couldn't be so heartless as to disown him. I'll tell him to come out. And you will shake hands with him, won't you, Uncle Jack? [*Runs back into the house.*]
CHASUBLE. These are very joyful tidings.
MISS PRISM. After we had all been resigned to his loss, his sudden return seems to me peculiarly distressing.
JACK. My brother is in the dining-room? I don't know what it all means. I think it is perfectly absurd.

[*Enter* ALGERNON *and* CECILY *hand in hand. They come slowly up to* JACK.]

JACK. Good heavens! [*Motions* ALGERNON *away.*]
ALGERNON. Brother John, I have come down from town to tell you that I am very sorry for all the trouble I have given you, and that I intend to lead a better life in the future. [JACK *glares at him and does not take his hand.*]
CECILY. Uncle Jack, you are not going to refuse your own brother's hand?
JACK. Nothing will induce me to take his hand. I think his coming down here disgraceful. He knows perfectly well why.
CECILY. Uncle Jack, do be nice. There is some good in everyone. Ernest has just been telling me about his poor invalid friend, Mr. Bunbury, whom he goes to visit so often. And surely there must be much good in one who is kind to an invalid, and leaves the pleasures of London to sit by a bed of pain.

JACK. Oh, he has been talking about Bunbury, has he?
CECILY. Yes, he has told me all about poor Mr. Bunbury, and his terrible state of health.
JACK. Bunbury! Well, I won't have him talk to you about Bunbury or about anything else. It is enough to drive one perfectly frantic.
ALGERNON. Of course I admit that the faults were all on my side. But I must say that I think that Brother John's coldness to me is peculiarly painful. I expected a more enthusiastic welcome, especially considering it is the first time I have come here.
CECILY. Uncle Jack, if you don't shake hands with Ernest, I will never forgive you.
JACK. Never forgive me?
CECILY. Never, never, never!
JACK. Well, this is the last time I shall ever do it. [*Shakes hands with* ALGERNON *and glares.*]
CHASUBLE. It's pleasant, is it not, to see so perfect a reconciliation? I think we might leave the two brothers together.
MISS PRISM. Cecily, you will come with us.
CECILY. Certainly, Miss Prism. My little task of reconciliation is over.
CHASUBLE. You have done a beautiful action today, dear child.
MISS PRISM. We must not be premature in our judgments.
CECILY. I feel very happy. [*They all go off.*]
JACK. You young scoundrel, Algy, you must get out of this place as soon as possible. I don't allow any Bunburying here.

[*Enter* MERRIMAN.]

MERRIMAN. I have put Mr. Ernest's things in the room next to yours, sir. I suppose that is all right?
JACK. What?
MERRIMAN. Mr. Ernest's luggage, sir. I have unpacked it and put it in the room next to your own.
JACK. His luggage?
MERRIMAN. Yes, sir. Three portmanteaus, a dressing-case, two hat-boxes, and a large luncheon-basket.
ALGERNON. I am afraid I can't stay more than a week this time.
JACK. Merriman, order the dog-cart at once. Mr. Ernest has been suddenly called back to town.
MERRIMAN. Yes, sir. [*Goes back into the house.*]
ALGERNON. What a fearful liar you are, Jack. I have not been called back to town at all.

JACK. Yes, you have.
ALGERNON. I haven't heard anyone call me.
JACK. Your duty as a gentleman calls you back.
ALGERNON. My duty as a gentleman has never interfered with my pleasures in the smallest degree.
JACK. I can quite understand that.
ALGERNON. Well, Cecily is a darling.
JACK. You are not to talk of Miss Cardew like that. I don't like it.
ALGERNON. Well, I don't like your clothes. You look perfectly ridiculous in them. Why on earth don't you go up and change? It is perfectly childish to be in deep mourning for a man who is actually staying for a whole week with you in your house as a guest. I call it grotesque.
JACK. You are certainly not staying with me for a whole week as a guest or anything else. You have got to leave . . . by the four-five train.
ALGERNON. I certainly won't leave you so long as you are in mourning. It would be most unfriendly. If I were in mourning, you would stay with me, I suppose. I should think it very unkind if you didn't.
JACK. Well, will you go if I change my clothes?
ALGERNON. Yes, if you are not too long. I never saw anybody take so long to dress, and with such little result.
JACK. Well, at any rate, that is better than being always over-dressed as you are.
ALGERNON. If I am occasionally a little over-dressed, I make up for it by being always immensely over-educated.
JACK. Your vanity is ridiculous, your conduct an outrage, and your presence in my garden utterly absurd. However, you have got to catch the four-five, and I hope you will have a pleasant journey back to town. This Bunburying, as you call it, has not been a great success for you. [*Goes into the house.*]
ALGERNON. I think it has been a great success. I'm in love with Cecily, and that is everything.

[*Enter* CECILY *at the back of the garden. She picks up the can and begins to water the flowers.*]

But I must see her before I go, and make arrangements for another Bunbury. Ah, there she is.
CECILY. Oh, I merely came back to water the roses. I thought you were with Uncle Jack.
ALGERNON. He's gone to order the dog-cart for me.

CECILY. Oh, is he going to take you for a nice drive?
ALGERNON. He's going to send me away.
CECILY. Then have we got to part?
ALGERNON. I am afraid so. It's a very painful parting.
CECILY. It is always painful to part from people whom one has known for a very brief space of time. The absence of old friends one can endure with equanimity. But even a momentary separation from anyone to whom one has just been introduced is almost unbearable.
ALGERNON. Thank you.

[*Enter* MERRIMAN.]

MERRIMAN. The dog-cart is at the door sir.

[ALGERNON *looks appealingly at* CECILY.]

CECILY. It can wait, Merriman . . . for . . . five minutes.
MERRIMAN. Yes, miss.

[*Exit* MERRIMAN.]

ALGERNON. I hope, Cecily, I shall not offend you if I state quite frankly and openly that you seem to me to be in every way the visible personification of absolute perfection.
CECILY. I think your frankness does you great credit, Ernest. If you will allow me I will copy your remarks into my diary. [*Goes over to the table and begins writing in diary.*]
ALGERNON. Do you really keep a diary? I'd give anything to look at it. May I?
CECILY. Oh, no. [*Puts her hand over it.*] You see, it is simply a very young girl's record of her own thoughts and impressions, and consequently meant for publication. When it appears in volume form I hope you will order a copy. But pray, Ernest, don't stop. I delight in taking down from dictation. I have reached "absolute perfection." You can go on. I am quite ready for more.
ALGERNON. [*Somewhat taken aback.*] Ahem! Ahem!
CECILY. Oh, don't cough, Ernest. When one is dictating, one should speak fluently and not cough. Besides, I don't know how to spell a cough. [*Writes as* ALGERNON *speaks.*]
ALGERNON. [*Speaking very rapidly.*] Cecily, ever since I first looked upon your wonderful and incomparable beauty, I have dared to love you wildly, passionately, devotedly, hopelessly.

CECILY. I don't think that you should tell me that you love me wildly, passionately, devotedly, hopelessly. Hopelessly doesn't seem to make much sense, does it?

[*Enter* MERRIMAN.]

MERRIMAN. The dog-cart is waiting, sir.
ALGERNON. Tell it to come round next week, at the same hour.
MERRIMAN. [*Looks at* CECILY, *who makes no sign.*] Yes, sir.

[MERRIMAN *retires.*]

CECILY. Uncle Jack would be very much annoyed if he knew you were staying on till next week, at the same hour.
ALGERNON. Oh, I don't care about Jack. I don't care for anybody in the whole world but you. I love you, Cecily. You will marry me, won't you?
CECILY. You silly you! Of course. Why, we have been engaged for the last three months.
ALGERNON. For the last three months?
CECILY. Yes, it will be exactly three months on Thursday.
ALGERNON. But how did we become engaged?
CECILY. Well, ever since dear Uncle Jack first confessed to us that he had a younger brother who was very wicked and bad, you of course have formed the chief topic of conversation between myself and Miss Prism. And of course a man who is much talked about is always very attractive. One feels there must be something in him after all. I daresay it was foolish of me, but I fell in love with you, Ernest.
ALGERNON. Darling! And when was the engagement actually settled?
CECILY. On the 4th of February last. Worn out by your entire ignorance of my existence, I determined to end the matter one way or the other, and after a long struggle with myself I accepted you under this dear old tree here. The next day I bought this little ring in your name, and this is the little bangle with the true lover's knot I promised you always to wear.
ALGERNON. Did I give you this? It's very pretty, isn't it?
CECILY. Yes, you've wonderfully good taste, Ernest. It's the excuse I've always given for your leading such a bad life. And this is the box in which I keep all your dear letters. [*Kneels at table, opens box, and produces letters tied up with blue ribbon.*]

ALGERNON. My letters! But my own sweet Cecily, I have never written you any letters.

CECILY. You need hardly remind me of that, Ernest. I remember only too well that I was forced to write your letters for you. I wrote always three times a week, and sometimes oftener.

ALGERNON. Oh, do let me read them, Cecily?

CECILY. Oh, I couldn't possibly. They would make you far too conceited. [*Replaces box.*] The three you wrote me after I had broken off the engagement are so beautiful, and so badly spelled, that even now I can hardly read them without crying a little.

ALGERNON. But was our engagement ever broken off?

CECILY. Of course it was. On the 22nd of last March. You can see the entry if you like. [*Shows diary.*] "Today I broke off my engagement with Ernest. I feel it is better to do so. The weather still continues charming."

ALGERNON. But why on earth did you break it off? What had I done? I had done nothing at all. Cecily, I am very much hurt indeed to hear you broke it off. Particularly when the weather was so charming.

CECILY. It would hardly have been a really serious engagement if it hadn't been broken off at least once. But I forgave you before the week was out.

ALGERNON. [*Crossing to her, and kneeling.*] What a perfect angel you are, Cecily.

CECILY. You dear romantic boy. [*He kisses her; she puts her fingers through his hair.*] I hope your hair curls naturally, does it?

ALGERNON. Yes, darling, with a little help from others.

CECILY. I am so glad.

ALGERNON. You'll never break off our engagement again, Cecily?

CECILY. I don't think I could break it off now that I have actually met you. Besides, of course, there is the question of your name.

ALGERNON. Yes, of course. [*Nervously.*]

CECILY. You must not laugh at me, darling, but it had always been a girlish dream of mine to love someone whose name was Ernest. [ALGERNON *rises*, CECILY *also.*] There is something in that name that seems to inspire absolute confidence. I pity any poor married woman whose husband is not called Ernest.

ALGERNON. But, my dear child, do you mean to say you could not love me if I had some other name?

CECILY. But what name?

ALGERNON. Oh, any name you like—Algernon, for instance. . . .

CECILY. But I don't like the name of Algernon.

ALGERNON. Well, my own dear, sweet, loving little darling, I really can't see why you should object to the name of Algernon. It is not at all a bad name. In fact, it is rather an aristocratic name. Half of the chaps who get into the Bankruptcy Court are called Algernon. But seriously, Cecily . . . [*Moving to her.*] . . . if my name was Algy, couldn't you love me?

CECILY. [*Rising.*] I might respect you, Ernest, I might admire your character, but I fear that I should not be able to give you my undivided attention.

ALGERNON. Ahem! Cecily! [*Picking up hat.*] Your Rector here is, I suppose, thoroughly experienced in the practice of all the rites and ceremonials of the church?

CECILY. Oh, yes. Dr. Chasuble is a most learned man. He has never written a single book, so you can imagine how much he knows.

ALGERNON. I must see him at once on a most important christening—I mean on most important business.

CECILY. Oh!

ALGERNON. I shan't be away more than half an hour.

CECILY. Considering that we have been engaged since February the 14th, and that I only met you today for the first time, I think it is rather hard that you should leave me for so long a period as half an hour. Couldn't you make it twenty minutes?

ALGERNON. I'll be back. in no time. [*Kisses her and rushes down the garden.*]

CECILY. What an impetuous boy he is. I like his hair so much. I must enter his proposal in my diary.

[*Enter* MERRIMAN.]

MERRIMAN. A Miss Fairfax has just called to see Mr. Worthing. On very important business, Miss Fairfax states.

CECILY. Isn't Mr. Worthing in his library?

MERRIMAN. Mr. Worthing went over in the direction of the Rectory some time ago.

CECILY. Pray ask the lady to come out here; Mr. Worthing is sure to be back soon. And you can bring tea.

MERRIMAN. Yes, miss.

[*Goes out.*]

CECILY. Miss Fairfax! I suppose one of the many good elderly women who are associated with Uncle Jack in some of his philanthropic work in London. I don't quite like women who are interested in philanthropic work. I think it is so forward of them.

[*Enter* MERRIMAN.]

MERRIMAN. Miss Fairfax.

[*Enter* GWENDOLEN. *Exit* MERRIMAN.]

CECILY. [*Advancing to meet her.*] Pray let me introduce myself to you. My name is Cecily Cardew.

GWENDOLEN. Cecily Cardew? [*Moving to her and shaking hands.*] What a very sweet name! Something tells me that we are going to be great friends. I like you already more than I can say. My first impressions of people are never wrong.

CECILY. How nice of you to like me so much after we have known each other such a comparatively short time. Pray sit down.

GWENDOLEN. [*Still standing up.*] I may call you Cecily, may I not?

CECILY. With pleasure!

GWENDOLEN. And you will always call me Gwendolen, won't you?

CECILY. If you wish.

GWENDOLEN. Then that is all quite settled, is it not?

CECILY. I hope so.

[*A pause. They both sit down together.*]

GWENDOLEN. Perhaps this might be a favorable opportunity for my mentioning who I am. My father is Lord Bracknell. You have never heard of papa, I suppose?

CECILY. I don't think so.

GWENDOLEN. Outside the family circle, papa, I am glad to say, is entirely unknown. I think that is quite as it should be. The home seems to me to be the proper sphere for the man. And certainly once a man begins to neglect his domestic duties he becomes painfully effeminate, does he not? And I don't like that. It makes men so very attractive. Cecily, mamma, whose views on education are remarkably strict, has brought me up to be extremely short-sighted; it is part of her system; so do you mind my looking at you through my glasses?

CECILY. Oh, not at all, Gwendolen. I am very fond of being looked at.

GWENDOLEN. [*After examining* CECILY *carefully through a lorgnette.*] You are here on a short visit, I suppose.

CECILY. Oh, no, I live here.

GWENDOLEN. [*Severely.*] Really? Your mother, no doubt, or some female relative of advanced years, resides here also?

CECILY. Oh, no. I have no mother, nor, in fact, any relations.

GWENDOLEN. Indeed?

CECILY. My dear guardian, with the assistance of Miss Prism, has the arduous task of looking after me.

GWENDOLEN. Your guardian?

CECILY. Yes, I am Mr. Worthing's ward.

GWENDOLEN. Oh! It is strange he never mentioned to me that he had a ward. How secretive of him! He grows more interesting hourly. I am not sure, however, that the news inspires me with feelings of unmixed delight. [*Rising and going to her.*] I am very fond of you Cecily; I have liked you ever since I met you. But I am bound to state that now that I know that you are Mr. Worthing's ward, I cannot help expressing a wish you were—well, just a little older than you seem to be—and not quite so very alluring in appearance. In fact, if I may speak candidly———

CECILY. Pray do! I think that whenever one has anything unpleasant to say, one should always be quite candid.

GWENDOLEN. Well, to speak with perfect candor, Cecily. I wish that you were fully forty-two, and more than usually plain for your age. Ernest has a strong upright nature. He is the very soul of truth and honor. Disloyalty would be as impossible to him as deception. But even men of the noblest possible moral character are extremely susceptible to the influence of the physical charms of others. Modern, no less than Ancient History, supplies us with many most painful examples of what I refer to. If it were not so, indeed, History would be quite unreadable.

CECILY. I beg your pardon, Gwendolen, did you say Ernest?

GWENDOLEN. Yes.

CECILY. Oh, but it is not Mr. Ernest Worthing who is my guardian. It is his brother—his elder brother.

GWENDOLEN. [*Sitting down again.*] Ernest never mentioned to me that he had a brother.

CECILY. I am sorry to say they have not been on good terms for a long time.

GWENDOLEN. Ah! that accounts for it. And now that I think of it, I have never heard any man mention his brother. The subject seems distasteful to most men. Cecily, you have lifted a load from my mind.

I was growing almost anxious. It would have been terrible if any cloud had come across a friendship like ours, would it not? Of course you are quite, quite sure that it is not Mr. Ernest Worthing who is your guardian?

CECILY. Quite sure. [*A pause.*] In fact, I am going to be his.

GWENDOLEN. [*Inquiringly.*] I beg your pardon?

CECILY. [*Rather shy and confidingly.*] Dearest Gwendolen, there is no reason why I should make a secret of it to you. Our little county newspaper is sure to chronicle the fact next week. Mr. Ernest Worthing and I are engaged to be married.

GWENDOLEN. [*Quite politely, rising.*] My darling Cecily, I think there must be some slight error. Mr. Ernest Worthing is engaged to me. The announcement will appear in the *Morning Post*[7] on Saturday at the latest.

CECILY. [*Very politely, rising.*] I am afraid you must be under some misconception. Ernest proposed to me exactly ten minutes ago. [*Shows diary.*]

GWENDOLEN. [*Examines diary through her lorgnette carefully.*] It is certainly very curious, for he asked me to be his wife yesterday afternoon at 5:30. If you would care to verify the incident, pray do so. [*Produces diary of her own.*] I never travel without my diary. One should always have something sensational to read in the train. I am so sorry, dear Cecily, if it is any disappointment to you, but I am afraid *I* have the prior claim.

CECILY. It would distress me more than I can tell you, dear Gwendolen, if it caused you any mental or physical anguish, but I feel bound to point out that since Ernest proposed to you he clearly has changed his mind.

GWENDOLEN. [*Meditatively.*] If the poor fellow has been entrapped into any foolish promise I shall consider it my duty to rescue him at once, and with a firm hand.

CECILY. [*Thoughtfully and sadly.*] Whatever unfortunate entanglement my dear boy may have got into, I will never reproach him with it after we are married.

GWENDOLEN. Do you allude to me, Miss Cardew, as an entanglement? You are presumptuous. On an occasion of this kind it becomes more than a moral duty to speak one's mind. It becomes a pleasure.

CECILY. Do you suggest, Miss Fairfax, that I entrapped Ernest into an

---

7. *Morning Post:* a London daily newspaper.

engagement? How dare you? This is no time for wearing the shallow mask of manners. When I see a spade I call it a spade.

GWENDOLEN. [*Satirically.*] I am glad to say that I have never seen a spade. It is obvious that our social spheres have been widely different.

[*Enter* MERRIMAN, *followed by the footman. He carries a salver, tablecloth, and plate-stand.* CECILY *is about to retort. The presence of the servants exercises a restraining influence, under which both girls chafe.*]

MERRIMAN. Shall I lay tea here as usual miss?

CECILY. [*Sternly, in a calm voice.*] Yes, as usual.

[MERRIMAN *begins to clear and lay cloth. A long pause.* CECILY *and* GWENDOLEN *glare at each other.*]

GWENDOLEN. Are there many interesting walks in the vicinity, Miss Cardew?

CECILY. Oh, yes, a great many. From the top of one of the hills quite close one can see five counties.

GWENDOLEN. Five counties! I don't think I should like that. I hate crowds.

CECILY. [*Sweetly.*] I suppose that is why you live in town? [GWENDOLEN *bites her lip, and beats her foot nervously with her parasol.*]

GWENDOLEN. [*Looking round.*] Quite a well-kept garden this is, Miss Cardew.

CECILY. So glad you like it, Miss Fairfax.

GWENDOLEN. I had no idea there were any flowers in the country.

CECILY. Oh, flowers are as common here, Miss Fairfax, as people are in London.

GWENDOLEN. Personally I cannot understand how anybody manages to exist in the country, if anybody who is anybody does. The country always bores me to death.

CECILY. Ah! This is what the newspapers call agricultural depression, is it not? I believe the aristocracy are suffering very much from it just at present. It is almost an epidemic amongst them, I have been told. May I offer you some tea, Miss Fairfax?

GWENDOLEN. [*With elaborate politeness.*] Thank you. [*Aside.*] Detestable girl! But I require tea!

CECILY. [*Sweetly.*] Sugar?

GWENDOLEN. [*Superciliously.*] No, thank you. Sugar is not fashionable any more.

[CECILY *looks angrily at her, takes up the tongs and puts four lumps of sugar into the cup.*]

CECILY. [*Severely.*] Cake or bread and butter?

GWENDOLEN. [*In a bored manner.*] Bread and butter, please. Cake is rarely seen at the best houses nowadays.

CECILY. [*Cuts a very large slice of cake, and puts it on the tray.*] Hand that to Miss Fairfax.

[MERRIMAN *does so, and goes out with footman.* GWENDOLEN *drinks the tea and makes a grimace. Puts down cup at once, reaches out her hand to the bread and butter, looks at it, and finds it is cake. Rises in indignation.*]

GWENDOLEN. You have filled my tea with lumps of sugar, and though I asked most distinctly for bread and butter, you have given me cake. I am known for the gentleness of my disposition, and the extraordinary sweetness of my nature, but I warn you, Miss Cardew, you may go too far.

CECILY. [*Rising.*] To save my poor, innocent, trusting boy from the machinations of any other girl, there are no lengths to which I would not go.

GWENDOLEN. From the moment I saw you I distrusted you. I felt that you were false and deceitful. I am never deceived in such matters. My first impressions of people are invariably right.

CECILY. It seems to me, Miss Fairfax, that I am trespassing on your valuable time. No doubt you have many other calls of a similar character to make in the neighborhood.

[*Enter* JACK.]

GWENDOLEN. [*Catching sight of him.*] Ernest! My own Ernest!

JACK. Gwendolen! Darling! [*Offers to kiss her.*]

GWENDOLEN. [*Drawing back.*] A moment! May I ask if you are engaged to be married to this young lady? [*Points to* CECILY.]

JACK. [*Laughing.*] To dear little Cecily! Of course not! What could have put such an idea into your pretty little head?

GWENDOLEN. Thank you. You may. [*Offers her cheek.*]

CECILY. [*Very sweetly.*] I knew there must be some misunderstanding, Miss Fairfax. The gentleman whose arm is at present around your waist is my dear guardian, Mr. John Worthing.

GWENDOLEN. I beg your pardon?

CECILY. This is Uncle Jack.

GWENDOLEN. [*Receding.*] Jack! Oh!

[*Enter* ALGERNON.]

CECILY. Here is Ernest.

ALGERNON. [*Goes straight over to* CECILY *without noticing anyone else.*] My own love! [*Offers to kiss her.*]

CECILY. [*Drawing back.*] A moment, Ernest! May I ask you—are you engaged to be married to this young lady?

ALGERNON. [*Looking round.*] To what young lady? Good heavens! Gwendolen!

CECILY. Yes, to good heavens, Gwendolen, I mean to Gwendolen.

ALGERNON. [*Laughing.*] Of course not! What could have put such an idea into your pretty little head?

CECILY. Thank you. [*Presenting her cheek to be kissed.*] You may.

[ALGERNON *kisses her.*]

GWENDOLEN. I felt there was some slight error, Miss Cardew. The gentleman who is now embracing you is my cousin, Mr. Algernon Moncrieff.

CECILY. [*Breaking away from* ALGERNON.] Algernon Moncrieff! Oh!

[*The two girls move toward each other and put their arms round each other's waists as if for protection.*]

CECILY. Are you called Algernon?

ALGERNON. I cannot deny it.

CECILY. Oh!

GWENDOLEN. Is your name really John?

JACK. [*Standing rather proudly.*] I could deny it if I liked. I could deny anything if I liked. But my name certainly is John. It has been John for years.

CECILY. [*To* GWENDOLEN.] A gross deception has been practiced on both of us.

GWENDOLEN. My poor wounded Cecily!

CECILY. My sweet, wronged Gwendolen!

GWENDOLEN. [*Slowly and seriously.*] You will call me sister, will you not? [*They embrace.* JACK *and* ALGERNON *groan and walk up and down.*]

CECILY. [*Rather brightly.*] There is just one question I would like to be allowed to ask my guardian.

GWENDOLEN. An admirable idea! Mr. Worthing, there is just one question I would like to be permitted to put to you. Where is your brother Ernest? We are both engaged to be married to your brother Ernest, so it is a matter of some importance to us to know where your brother Ernest is at present.

JACK. [*Slowly and hesitatingly.*] Gwendolen—Cecily—it is very painful for me to be forced to speak the truth. It is the first time in my life that I have ever been reduced to such a painful position, and I am really quite inexperienced in doing anything of the kind. However, I will tell you quite frankly that I have no brother Ernest. I have no brother at all. I never had a brother in my life, and I certainly have not the smallest intention of ever having one in the future.

CECILY. [*Surprised.*] No brother at all?

JACK. [*Cheerily.*] None!

GWENDOLEN. [*Severely.*] Had you never a brother of any kind?

JACK. [*Pleasantly.*] Never. Not even of any kind.

GWENDOLEN. I am afraid it is quite clear, Cecily, that neither of us is engaged to be married to anyone.

CECILY. It is not a very pleasant position for a young girl suddenly to find herself in. Is it?

GWENDOLEN. Let us go into the house. They will hardly venture to come after us there.

CECILY. No, men are so cowardly, aren't they? [*They retire into the house with scornful looks.*]

JACK. This ghastly state of things is what you call Bunburying, I suppose?

ALGERNON. Yes, and a perfectly wonderful Bunbury it is. The most wonderful Bunbury I have ever had in my life.

JACK. Well, you've no right whatsoever to Bunbury here.

ALGERNON. That is absurd. One has a right to Bunbury anywhere one chooses. Every serious Bunburyist knows that.

JACK. Serious Bunburyist! Good heavens!

ALGERNON. Well, one must be serious about something, if one wants to have any amusement in life. I happen to be serious about Bunburying. What on earth you are serious about I haven't got the remotest idea. About everything, I should fancy. You have such an absolutely trivial nature.

JACK. Well, the only small satisfaction I have in the whole of this wretched business is that your friend Bunbury is quite exploded. You won't be able to run down to the country quite so often as you used to do, dear Algy. And a very good thing, too.

ALGERNON. Your brother is a little off color, isn't he, dear Jack? You won't be able to disappear to London quite so frequently as your wicked custom was. And not a bad thing, either.

JACK. As for your conduct toward Miss Cardew, I must say that your taking in a sweet, simple, innocent girl like that is quite inexcusable. To say nothing of the fact that she is my ward.

ALGERNON. I can see no possible defense at all for your deceiving a brilliant, clever, thoroughly experienced young lady like Miss Fairfax. To say nothing of the fact that she is my cousin.

JACK. I wanted to be engaged to Gwendolen, that is all. I love her.

ALGERNON. Well, I simply wanted to be engaged to Cecily. I adore her.

JACK. There is certainly no chance of your marrying Miss Cardew.

ALGERNON. I don't think there is much likelihood, Jack, of you and Miss Fairfax being united.

JACK. Well, that is no business of yours.

ALGERNON. If it was my business, I wouldn't talk about it. [*Begins to eat muffins.*] It is very vulgar to talk about one's business. Only people like stock-brokers do that, and then merely at dinner parties.

JACK. How you can sit there, calmly eating muffins, when we are in this horrible trouble, I can't make out. You seem to me to be perfectly heartless.

ALGERNON. Well, I can't eat muffins in an agitated manner. The butter would probably get on my cuffs. One should always eat muffins quite calmly. It is the only way to eat them.

JACK. I say it's perfectly heartless your eating muffins at all, under the circumstances.

ALGERNON. When I am in trouble, eating is the only thing that consoles me. Indeed, when I am in really great trouble, as anyone who knows me intimately will tell you, I refuse everything except food and drink. At the present moment I am eating muffins because I am unhappy. Besides, I am particularly fond of muffins. [*Rising.*]

JACK. [*Rising.*] Well, that is no reason why you should eat them all in that greedy way. [*Takes muffins from* ALGERNON.]

ALGERNON. [*Offering tea-cake.*] I wish you would have tea-cake instead. I don't like tea-cake.

JACK. Good heavens! I suppose a man may eat his own muffins in his own garden.

ALGERNON. But you have just said it was perfectly heartless to eat muffins.

JACK. I said it was perfectly heartless of you, under the circumstances. That is a very different thing.

ALGERNON. That may be. But the muffins are the same. [*He seizes the muffin-dish from* JACK.]

JACK. Algy, I wish to goodness you would go.

ALGERNON. You can't possibly ask me to go without having some dinner. It's absurd. I never go without my dinner. No one ever does, except vegetarians and people like that. Besides I have just made arrangements with Dr. Chasuble to be christened at a quarter to six under the name of Ernest.

JACK. My dear fellow, the sooner you give up that nonsense the better. I made arrangements this morning with Dr. Chasuble to be christened myself at 5:30, and I naturally will take the name of Ernest. Gwendolen would wish it. We can't both be christened Ernest. It's absurd. Besides, I have a perfect right to be christened if I like. There is no evidence at all that I ever have been christened by anybody. I should think it extremely probable I never was, and so does Dr. Chasuble. It is entirely different in your case. You have been christened already.

ALGERNON. Yes, but I have not been christened for years.

JACK. Yes, but you have been christened. That is the important thing.

ALGERNON. Quite so. So I know my constitution can stand it. If you are not quite sure about you ever having been christened, I must say I think it rather dangerous your venturing on it now. It might make you very unwell. You can hardly have forgotten that someone very closely connected with you was very nearly carried off this week in Paris by a severe chill.

JACK. Yes, but you said yourself that a severe chill was not hereditary.

ALGERNON. It usedn't to be, I know—but I daresay it is now. Science is always making wonderful improvements in things.

JACK. [*Picking up the muffin-dish.*] Oh, that is nonsense; you are always talking nonsense.

ALGERNON. Jack, you are at the muffins again! I wish you wouldn't. There are only two left. [*Takes them.*] I told you I was particularly fond of muffins.

JACK. But I hate tea-cake.

ALGERNON. Why on earth then do you allow tea-cake to be served up for your guests? What ideas you have of hospitality!

JACK. Algernon! I have already told you to go. I don't want you here. Why don't you go?

ALGERNON. I haven't quite finished my tea yet, and there is still one muffin left.

[JACK *groans, and sinks into a chair.* ALGERNON *still continues eating.*]

## ACT III

Morning-room at the Manor House. GWENDOLEN and CECILY are at the window, looking out into the garden.

GWENDOLEN. That fact that they did not follow us at once into the house, as anyone else would have done, seems to me to show that they have some sense of shame left.
CECILY. They have been eating muffins. That looks like repentance.
GWENDOLEN. [*After a pause.*] They don't seem to notice us at all. Couldn't you cough?
GWENDOLEN. They're looking at us. What effrontery!
CECILY. They're approaching. That's very forward of them.
GWENDOLEN. Let us preserve a dignified silence.
CECILY. Certainly. It's the only thing to do now.

[*Enter* JACK, *followed by* ALGERNON. *They whistle some dreadful popular air from a British opera.*]

GWENDOLEN. This dignified silence seems to produce an unpleasant effect.
CECILY. A most distasteful one.
GWENDOLEN. But we will not be the first to speak.
CECILY. Certainly not.
GWENDOLEN. Mr. Worthing, I have something very particular to ask you. Much depends on your reply.
CECILY. Gwendolen, your common sense is invaluable. Mr. Moncrieff, kindly answer me the following question. Why did you pretend to be my guardian's brother?
ALGERNON. In order that I might have an opportunity of meeting you.
CECILY. [*To* GWENDOLEN.] That certainly seems a satisfactory explanation, does it not?
GWENDOLEN. Yes, dear, if you can believe him.
CECILY. I don't. But that does not affect the wonderful beauty of his answer.
GWENDOLEN. True. In matters of grave importance, style, not sincerity,

The Importance of Being Earnest

is the vital thing. Mr. Worthing, what explanation can you offer me for pretending to have a brother? Was it in order that you might have an opportunity of coming up to town to see me as often as possible?

JACK. Can you doubt it, Miss Fairfax?

GWENDOLEN. I have the gravest doubts upon the subject. But I intend to crush them. This is not the moment for German skepticism. [*Moving to* CECILY.] Their explanations appear to be quite satisfactory, especially Mr. Worthing's. That seems to me to have the stamp of truth upon it.

CECILY. I am more than content with what Mr. Moncrieff said. His voice alone inspires one with absolute credulity.

GWENDOLEN. Then you think we should forgive them?

CECILY. Yes. I mean no.

GWENDOLEN. True! I had forgotten. There are principles at stake that one cannot surrender. Which of us should tell them? The task is not a pleasant one.

CECILY. Could we not both speak at the same time?

GWENDOLEN. An excellent idea! I nearly always speak at the same time as other people. Will you take the time from me?

CECILY. Certainly.

[GWENDOLEN *beats time with uplifted finger.*]

GWENDOLEN AND CECILY. [*Speaking together.*] Your Christian names are still an insuperable barrier. That is all!

JACK AND ALGERNON. [*Speaking together.*] Our Christian names! Is that all? But we are going to be christened this afternoon.

GWENDOLEN. [*To* JACK.] For my sake you are prepared to do this terrible thing?

JACK. I am.

CECILY. [*To* ALGERNON.] To please me you are ready to face this fearful ordeal?

ALGERNON. I am!

GWENDOLEN. How absurd to talk of the equality of the sexes! Where questions of self-sacrifice are concerned, men are infinitely beyond us.

JACK. We are. [*Clasps hands with* ALGERNON.]

CECILY. They have moments of physical courage of which we women know absolutely nothing.

GWENDOLEN. [*To* JACK.] Darling!

ALGERNON. [*To* CECILY.] Darling! [*They fall into each other's arms.*]

[*Enter* MERRIMAN. *When he enters, he coughs loudly, seeing the situation.*]

MERRIMAN. Ahem! Ahem! Lady Bracknell!
JACK. Good heavens!

[*Enter* LADY BRACKNELL. *The couples separate in alarm. Exit* MERRIMAN.]

LADY BRACKNELL. Gwendolen! What does this mean?
GWENDOLEN. Merely that I am engaged to be married to Mr. Worthing, Mamma.
LADY BRACKNELL. Come here. Sit down. Sit down immediately. Hesitation of any kind is a sign of mental decay in the young, of physical weakness in the old. [*Turns to* JACK.] Apprised, sir, of my daughter's sudden flight by her trusty maid, whose confidence I purchased by means of a small coin, I followed her at once by a luggage train. Her unhappy father is, I am glad to say, under the impression that she is attending a more than usually lengthy lecture by the University Extension Scheme on the Influence of a Permanent Income on Thought. I do not propose to undeceive him. Indeed, I have never undeceived him on any question. I would consider it wrong. But of course, you will clearly understand that all communication between yourself and my daughter must cease immediately from this moment. On this point, as indeed on all points, I am firm.
JACK. I am engaged to be married to Gwendolen, Lady Bracknell!
LADY BRACKNELL. You are nothing of the kind, sir. And now, as regards Algernon! . . . Algernon!
ALGERNON. Yes, Aunt Augusta.
LADY BRACKNELL. May I ask if it is in this house that your invalid friend Mr. Bunbury resides?
ALGERNON. [*Stammering.*] Oh, no! Bunbury doesn't live here. Bunbury is somewhere else at present. In fact, Bunbury is dead.
LADY BRACKNELL. Dead! When did Mr. Bunbury die? His death must have been extremely sudden.
ALGERNON. [*Airily.*] Oh, I killed Bunbury this afternoon. I mean poor Bunbury died this afternoon.
LADY BRACKNELL. What did he die of?
ALGERNON. Bunbury? Oh, he was quite exploded.
LADY BRACKNELL. Exploded! Was he the victim of a revolutionary outrage? I was not aware that Mr. Bunbury was interested in social legislation. If so, he is well punished for his morbidity.

ALGERNON. My dear Aunt Augusta, I mean he was found out! The doctors found out that Bunbury could not live, that is what I mean—so Bunbury died.

LADY BRACKNELL. He seems to have had great confidence in the opinion of his physicians. I am glad, however, that he made up his mind at the last to some definite course of action, and acted under proper medical advice. And now that we have finally got rid of this Mr. Bunbury, may I ask, Mr. Worthing, who is that young person whose hand my nephew Algernon is now holding in what seems to me a peculiarly unnecessary manner?

JACK. That lady is Miss Cecily Cardew, my ward.

[LADY BRACKNELL *bows coldly to* CECILY.]

ALGERNON. I am engaged to be married to Cecily, Aunt Augusta.

LADY BRACKNELL. I beg your pardon?

CECILY. Mr. Moncrieff and I are engaged to be married, Lady Bracknell.

LADY BRACKNELL. [*With a shiver, crossing to the sofa and sitting down.*] I do not know whether there is anything peculiarly exciting in the air of this particular part of Hertfordshire, but the number of engagements that go on seems to me considerably above the proper average that statistics have laid down for our guidance. I think some preliminary enquiry on my part would not be out of place. Mr. Worthing, is Miss Cardew at all connected with any of the larger railway stations in London? I merely desire information. Until yesterday I had no idea that there were any families or persons whose origin was a Terminus.

[JACK *looks perfectly furious, but restrains himself.*]

JACK. [*In a clear, cold voice.*] Miss Cardew is the granddaughter of the late Mr. Thomas Cardew of 149, Belgrave Square, S.W.; Gervase Park, Dorking, Surrey; and the Sporran, Fifeshire, N.B.

LADY BRACKNELL. That sounds not unsatisfactory. Three addresses always inspire confidence, even in tradesmen. But what proof have I of their authenticity?

JACK. I have carefully preserved the Court Guide of the period. They are open to your inspection, Lady Bracknell.

LADY BRACKNELL. [*Grimly.*] I have known strange errors in that publication.

JACK. Miss Cardew's family solicitors are Messrs. Markby, Markby, and Markby.

LADY BRACKNELL. Markby, Markby, and Markby? A firm of the very highest position in their profession. Indeed I am told that one of the Mr. Markbys is occasionally to be seen at dinner parties. So far I am satisfied.

JACK. [*Very irritably.*] How extremely kind of you, Lady Bracknell! I have also in my possession, you will be pleased to hear, certificates of Miss Cardew's birth, baptism, whooping cough, registration, vaccination, confirmation, and the measles; both the German and the English variety.

LADY BRACKNELL. Ah! A life crowded with incident, I see; though perhaps somewhat too exciting for a young girl. I am not myself in favor of premature experiences. [*Rises, looks at her watch.*] Gwendolen! the time approaches for our departure. We have not a moment to lose. As a matter of form, Mr. Worthing, I had better ask you if Miss Cardew has any little fortune?

JACK. Oh, about a hundred and thirty thousand pounds in the Funds.[1] That is all. Goodby, Lady Bracknell. So pleased to have seen you.

LADY BRACKNELL. [*Sitting down again.*] A moment, Mr. Worthing. A hundred and thirty thousand pounds! And in the Funds! Miss Cardew seems to me a most attractive young lady, now that I look at her. Few girls of the present day have any really solid qualities, any of the qualities that last, and improve with time. We live, I regret to say, in an age of surfaces. [*To* CECILY.] Come over here, dear. [CECILY *goes across.*] Pretty child! your dress is sadly simple, and your hair seems almost as Nature might have left it. But we can soon alter all that. A thoroughly experienced French maid produces a really marvelous result in a very brief space of time. I remember recommending one to young Lady Lancing, and after three months her own husband did not know her.

JACK. [*Aside.*] And after six months nobody knew her.

LADY BRACKNELL. [*Glares at* JACK *for a few moments. Then bends, with a practiced smile, to* CECILY.] Kindly turn round, sweet child. [CECILY *turns completely round.*] No, the side view is what I want. [CECILY *presents her profile.*] Yes, quite as I expected. There are distinct social possibilities in your profile. The two weak points in our age are its want of principle and its want of profile. The chin a little higher, dear. Style largely depends on the way the chin is worn. They are worn very high, just at present. Algernon!

---

1. *the Funds:* government bonds.

ALGERNON. Yes, Aunt Augusta!

LADY BRACKNELL. There are distinct social possibilities in Miss Cardew's profile.

ALGERNON. Cecily is the sweetest, dearest, prettiest girl in the whole world. And I don't care twopence about social possibilities.

LADY BRACKNELL. Never speak disrespectfully of society, Algernon. Only people who can't get into it do that. [*To* CECILY.] Dear child, of course you know that Algernon has nothing but his debts to depend upon. But I do not approve of mercenary marriages. When I married Lord Bracknell, I had no fortune of any kind. But I never dreamed for a moment of allowing that to stand in my way. Well, I suppose I must give my consent.

ALGERNON. Thank you, Aunt Augusta.

LADY BRACKNELL. Cecily, you may kiss me!

CECILY. [*Kisses her.*] Thank you, Lady Bracknell.

LADY BRACKNELL. You may also address me as Aunt Augusta for the future.

CECILY. Thank you, Aunt Augusta.

LADY BRACKNELL. The marriage, I think, had better take place quite soon.

ALGERNON. Thank you, Aunt Augusta.

CECILY. Thank you, Aunt Augusta.

LADY BRACKNELL. To speak frankly, I am not in favor of long engagements. They give people the opportunity of finding out each other's character before marriage, which I think is never advisable.

JACK. I beg your pardon for interrupting you, Lady Bracknell, but this engagement is quite out of the question. I am Miss Cardew's guardian, and she cannot marry without my consent until she comes of age. That consent I absolutely decline to give.

LADY BRACKNELL. Upon what grounds, may I ask? Algernon is an extremely, I may almost say an ostentatiously, eligible young man. He has nothing, but he looks everything. What more can one desire?

JACK. It pains me very much to have to speak frankly to you, Lady Bracknell, about your nephew, but the fact is that I do not approve at all of his moral character. I suspect him of being untruthful.

[ALGERNON *and* CECILY *look at him in indignant amazement.*]

LADY BRACKNELL. Untruthful! My nephew Algernon? Impossible! He is an Oxonian.[2]

---

2. *an Oxonian:* an alumnus of Oxford University.

JACK. I fear there can be no possible doubt about the matter. This afternoon, during my temporary absence in London on an important question of romance, he obtained admission to my house by means of the false pretense of being my brother. Under an assumed name he drank, I've just been informed by my butler, an entire pint bottle of my Perrier-Jouet, Brut, '89; a wine I was specially reserving for myself. Continuing his disgraceful deception, he succeeded in the course of the afternoon in alienating the affections of my only ward. He subsequently stayed to tea, and devoured every single muffin. And what makes his conduct all the more heartless is that he was perfectly well aware from the first that I have no brother, that I never had a brother, and that I don't intend to have a brother, not even of any kind. I distinctly told him so myself yesterday afternoon.

LADY BRACKNELL. Ahem! Mr. Worthing, after careful consideration I have decided entirely to overlook my nephew's conduct to you.

JACK. That is very generous of you, Lady Bracknell. My own decision, however, is unalterable. I decline to give my consent.

LADY BRACKNELL. [*To* CECILY.] Come here, sweet child. [CECILY *goes over.*] How old are you, dear?

CECILY. Well, I am really only eighteen, but I always admit to twenty when I go to evening parties.

LADY BRACKNELL. You are perfectly right in making some slight alteration. Indeed, no woman should ever be quite accurate about her age. It looks so calculating. . . . [*In meditative manner.*] Eighteen, but admitting to twenty at evening parties. Well, it will not be very long before you are of age and free from the restraints of tutelage. So I don't think your guardian's consent is, after all, a matter of any importance.

JACK. Pray excuse me, Lady Bracknell, for interrupting you again, but it is only fair to tell you that according to the terms of her grandfather's will Miss Cardew does not come legally of age till she is thirty-five.

LADY BRACKNELL. That does not seem to me to be a grave objection. Thirty-five is a very attractive age. London society is full of women of the very highest birth who have, of their own free choice, remained thirty-five for years. Lady Dumbleton is an instance in point. To my own knowledge she has been thirty-five ever since she arrived at the age of forty, which was many years ago now. I see no reason why our dear Cecily should not be even still more attractive at the age you mention that she is at present. There will be a large accumulation of property.

CECILY. Algy, could you wait for me till I was thirty-five?

ALGERNON. Of course I could, Cecily. You know I could.

CECILY. Yes, I felt it instinctively, but I couldn't wait all that time. I hate waiting even five minutes for anybody. It always makes me rather cross. I am not punctual myself, I know, but I do like punctuality in others, and waiting, even to be married, is quite out of the question.

ALGERNON. Then what is to be done, Cecily?

CECILY. I don't know, Mr. Moncrieff.

LADY BRACKNELL. My dear Mr. Worthing, as Miss Cardew states positively that she cannot wait till she is thirty-five—a remark which I am bound to say seems to me to show a somewhat impatient nature —I would beg of you to reconsider your decision.

JACK. But my dear Lady Bracknell, the matter is entirely in your own hands. The moment you consent to my marriage with Gwendolen I will most gladly allow your nephew to form an alliance with my ward.

LADY BRACKNELL. [*Rising and drawing herself up.*] You must be quite aware that what you propose is out of the question.

JACK. Then a passionate celibacy is all that any of us can look forward to.

LADY BRACKNELL. That is not the destiny I propose for Gwendolen. Algernon, of course, can choose for himself. [*Pulls out her watch.*] Come, dear. [GWENDOLEN *rises.*] We have already missed five, if not six, trains. To miss any more might expose us to comment on the platform.

[*Enter* DR. CHASUBLE.]

CHASUBLE. Everything is quite ready for the christenings.

LADY BRACKNELL. The christenings, sir! Is not that somewhat premature?

CHASUBLE. [*Looking rather puzzled, and pointing to* JACK *and* ALGERNON.] Both these gentlemen have expressed a desire for immediate baptism.

LADY BRACKNELL. At their age? The idea is grotesque and irreligious! Algernon, I forbid you to be baptized. I will not hear of such excesses. Lord Bracknell would be highly displeased if he learned that that was the way in which you wasted your time and money.

CHASUBLE. Am I to understand then that there are to be no christenings at all this afternoon?

JACK. I don't think that, as things are now, it would be of much practical value to either of us, Dr. Chasuble.

CHASUBLE. I am grieved to hear such sentiments from you, Mr. Worthing. They savor of the heretical views of the Anabaptists,[3] views that I have completely refuted in four of my unpublished sermons. However, as your present mood seems to be one peculiarly secular, I will return to the church at once. Indeed, I have just been informed by the pew-opener that for the last hour and a half Miss Prism has been waiting for me in the vestry.

LADY BRACKNELL. [*Starting.*] Miss Prism! Did I hear you mention a Miss Prism?

CHASUBLE. Yes, Lady Bracknell. I am on my way to join her.

LADY BRACKNELL. Pray allow me to detain you for a moment. This matter may prove to be one of vital importance to Lord Bracknell and myself. Is this Miss Prism a female of repellent aspect, remotely connected with education?

CHASUBLE. [*Somewhat indignantly.*] She is the most cultivated of ladies, and the very picture of respectability.

LADY BRACKNELL. It is obviously the same person. May I ask what position she holds in your household?

CHASUBLE. [*Severely.*] I am a celibate, madam.

JACK. [*Interposing.*] Miss Prism, Lady Bracknell, has been for the last three years Miss Cardew's esteemed governess and valued companion.

LADY BRACKNELL. In spite of what I hear of her, I must see her at once. Let her be sent for..

CHASUBLE. [*Looking off.*] She approaches; she is nigh.

[*Enter* MISS PRISM *hurriedly.*]

MISS PRISM. I was told you expected me in the vestry, dear Canon. I have been waiting for you there for an hour and three-quarters. [*Catches sight of* LADY BRACKNELL, *who has fixed her with a stony glare.* MISS PRISM *grows pale and quails. She looks anxiously round as if desirous to escape.*]

LADY BRACKNELL. [*In a severe, judicial voice.*] Prism! [MISS PRISM *bows her head in shame.*] Come here, Prism! [MISS PRISM *approaches in a humble manner.*] Prism! Where is that baby? [*General consterna-*

---

3. *the Anabaptists:* literally, those who baptize over again. The Anabaptists were a Protestant religious sect that arose in Germany in 1521. The term *Anabaptist* was commonly applied in an uncomplimentary way to the Baptists.

tion. *The Canon starts back in horror.* ALGERNON *and* JACK *pretend to be anxious to shield* CECILY *and* GWENDOLEN *from hearing the details of a terrible public scandal.*] Twenty-eight years ago, Prism, you left Lord Bracknell's house, Number 104, Upper Grosvenor Street, in charge of a perambulator that contained a baby, of the male sex. You never returned. A few weeks later, through the elaborate investigations of the Metropolitan police, the perambulator was discovered at midnight, standing by itself in a remote corner of Bayswater. It contained the manuscript of a three-volume novel of more than usually revolting sentimentality. [MISS PRISM *starts in involuntary indignation.*] But the baby was not there! [*Everyone looks at* MISS PRISM.] Prism, where is that baby? [*A pause.*]

MISS PRISM. Lady Bracknell, I admit with shame that I do not know. I only wish I did. The plain facts of the case are these. On the morning of the day you mention, a day that is forever branded on my memory, I prepared as usual to take the baby out in its perambulator. I had also with me a somewhat old but capacious handbag in which I had intended to place the manuscript of a work of fiction that I had written during my few unoccupied hours. In a moment of mental abstraction, for which I never can forgive myself, I deposited the manuscript in the bassinette, and placed the baby in the hand-bag.

JACK. [*Who has been listening attentively.*] But where did you deposit the hand-bag?

MISS PRISM. Do not ask me, Mr. Worthing.

JACK. Miss Prism, this is a matter of no small importance to me. I insist on knowing where you deposited the hand-bag that contained that infant.

MISS PRISM. I left it in the cloak-room of one of the larger railway stations in London.

JACK. What railway station?

MISS PRISM. [*Quite crushed.*] Victoria. The Brighton line. [*Sinks into a chair.*]

JACK. I must retire to my room for a moment. Gwendolen, wait here for me.

GWENDOLEN. If you are not too long, I will wait here for you all my life.

[*Exit* JACK *in great excitement.*]

CHASUBLE. What do you think this means, Lady Bracknell?
LADY BRACKNELL. I dare not even suspect, Dr. Chasuble. I need hardly

tell you that in families of high position strange coincidences are not supposed to occur. They are hardly considered the thing.

[*Noises heard overhead as if someone was throwing trunks about. Everybody looks up.*]

CECILY. Uncle Jack seems strangely agitated.

CHASUBLE. Your guardian has a very emotional nature.

LADY BRACKNELL. This noise is extremely unpleasant. It sounds as if he was having an argument. I dislike arguments of any kind. They are always vulgar, and often convincing.

CHASUBLE. [*Looking up.*] It has stopped now.

[*The noise is redoubled.*]

LADY BRACKNELL. I wish he would arrive at some conclusion.

GWENDOLEN. This suspense is terrible. I hope it will last.

[*Enter* JACK *with a hand-bag of black leather in his hand.*]

JACK. [*Rushing over to* MISS PRISM.] Is this the hand-bag, Miss Prism? Examine it carefully before you speak. The happiness of more than one life depends on your answer.

MISS PRISM. [*Calmly.*] It seems to be mine. Yes, here is the injury it received through the upsetting of a Gower Street omnibus in younger and happier days. Here is the stain on the lining caused by the explosion of a temperance beverage, an incident that occurred at Leamington. And here, on the lock, are my initials. I had forgotten that in an extravagant mood I had had them placed there. The bag is undoubtedly mine. I am delighted to have it so unexpectedly restored to me. It has been a great inconvenience being without it all these years.

JACK. [*In a pathetic voice.*] Miss Prism, more is restored to you than this hand-bag. I was the baby you placed in it.

MISS PRISM. [*Amazed.*] You?

JACK. [*Embracing her.*] Yes . . . mother!

MISS PRISM. [*Recoiling in indignant astonishment.*] Mr. Worthing! I am unmarried!

JACK. Unmarried! I do not deny that is a serious blow. But after all, who has the right to cast a stone against one who has suffered? Cannot repentance wipe out an act of folly? Why should there be one law for men and another for women? Mother, I forgive you. [*Tries to embrace her again.*]

MISS PRISM. [*Still more indignant.*] Mr. Worthing, there is some error. [*Pointing to* LADY BRACKNELL.] There is the lady who can tell you who you really are.

JACK. [*After a pause.*] Lady Bracknell, I hate to seem inquisitive, but would you kindly inform me who I am?

LADY BRACKNELL. I am afraid that the news I have to give you will not altogether please you. You are the son of my poor sister, Mrs. Moncrieff, and consequently Algernon's elder brother.

JACK. Algy's elder brother! Then I have a brother after all. I knew I had a brother! I always said I had a brother! Cecily—how could you have ever doubted that I had a brother? [*Seizes hold of* ALGERNON.] Dr. Chasuble, my unfortunate brother. Miss Prism, my unfortunate brother. Gwendolen, my unfortunate brother. Algy, you young scoundrel, you will have to treat me with more respect in the future. You have never behaved to me like a brother in all your life.

ALGERNON. Well, not till today, old boy, I admit. I did my best, however, though I was out of practice. [*Shakes hands.*]

GWENDOLEN. [*To* JACK.] My own! But what own are you? What is your Christian name, now that you have become someone else?

JACK. Good heavens! . . . I had quite forgotten that point. Your decision on the subject of my name is irrevocable, I suppose?

GWENDOLEN. I never change, except in my affections.

CECILY. What a noble nature you have, Gwendolen!

JACK. Then the question had better be cleared up at once. Aunt Augusta, a moment. At the time when Miss Prism left me in the handbag, had I been christened already?

LADY BRACKNELL. Every luxury that money could buy, including christening, had been lavished on you by your fond and doting parents.

JACK. Then I was christened! That is settled. Now, what name was I given? Let me know the worst.

LADY BRACKNELL. Being the eldest son you were naturally christened after your father.

JACK. [*Irritably.*] Yes, but what was my father's Christian name?

LADY BRACKNELL. [*Meditatively.*] I cannot at the present moment recall what the General's Christian name was. But I have no doubt he had one. He was eccentric, I admit. But only in later years. And that was the result of the Indian climate, and marriage, and indigestion, and other things of that kind.

JACK. Algy! Can't you recollect what our father's Christian name was?

ALGERNON. My dear boy, we were never even on speaking terms. He died before I was a year old.

JACK. His name would appear in the Army Lists of the period, I suppose, Aunt Augusta?

LADY BRACKNELL. The General was essentially a man of peace, except in his domestic life. But I have no doubt his name would appear in any military directory.

JACK. The Army Lists of the last forty years are here. These delightful records should have been my constant study. [*Rushes to bookcase and tears the books out.*] M. Generals . . . Mallam, Maxbohm, Magley, what ghastly names they have—Markby, Migsby, Mobbs, Moncrieff! Lieutenant 1840, Captain, Lieutenant-Colonel, Colonel, General 1869, Christian names, Ernest John. [*Puts book very quietly down and speaks quite calmly.*] I always told you, Gwendolen, my name was Ernest, didn't I? Well, it is Ernest after all. I mean it naturally is Ernest.

LADY BRACKNELL. Yes, I remember that the General was called Ernest. I knew I had some particular reason for disliking the name.

GWENDOLEN. Ernest! My own Ernest! I felt from the first that you could have no other name!

JACK. Gwendolen, it is a terrible thing for a man to find out suddenly that all his life he has been speaking nothing but the truth. Can you forgive me?

GWENDOLEN. I can. For I feel that you are sure to change.

JACK. My own one!

CHASUBLE. [*To* MISS PRISM.] Laetitia! [*Embraces her.*]

MISS PRISM. [*Enthusiastically.*] Frederick! At last!

ALGERNON. Cecily! [*Embraces her.*] At last!

JACK. Gwendolen! [*Embraces her.*] At last!

LADY BRACKNELL. My nephew, you seem to be displaying signs of triviality.

JACK. On the contrary, Aunt Augusta, I've now realized for the first time in my life the vital Importance of Being Earnest.

# Candida

# BERNARD SHAW

## Introduction

Bernard Shaw, the playwright who spoke out with abrasive comments about society and its conventions, is one of the greatest dramatic satirists of the twentieth century. *Candida,* however, is a quite pleasant look at what seems on the surface to be a personal problem, the love triangle of Candida, Morell, and Marchbanks. Like many of Shaw's plays, *Candida* is a comedy of ideas; it is a play that, rather than making one laugh out loud, makes one wince at the truths revealed through clever dialogue.

Candida herself is one of the most fascinating women to appear on the English stage since Shakespeare's heroines. She is married to the Reverend James Morell, a clergyman who appears strong, complacent, and politically influential. And, just as she would affect most men, Candida seems to have captivated the heart of the young poet, Eugene Marchbanks. The young man openly challenges Morell for Candida's love, calling her husband "a moralist and a windbag." The self-assured Morell is visibly shaken by the poet's words and nobly informs his wife that she may choose between them. Candida elects the "weaker" of the two.

Shaw was an ardent follower of Henrik Ibsen, the "father of modern drama," as well as the leading critic of the Norwegian playwright; therefore, it is interesting to compare Candida with Nora of Ibsen's *A Doll's House.* Ibsen shocked Victorian audiences by having his heroine walk out on her husband in the final scene because he continued to treat her like a doll rather than a real person, even after she had sacrificed herself to save him. Candida, on the other hand, even though she sees her husband as he is, accepts him and coddles him somewhat like a doll.

Candida's personal appeal rests partly in her "immoral morality." Her charisma leads men on far enough to suit her desires. She seems accountable to no one, including her husband and takes full command of the situation and of those around her. We probably like her most because she possesses a unique individuality. While she possesses none of the saccharine sweetness of most Victorian heroines, she avoids the worldliness of so many of her twentieth-century successors. She also introduces two Shavian theories which pervade his later works. The first of these concepts Shaw calls the Life Force—the hidden drive within man that causes him to struggle to improve his species. Shaw believed that the Life Force surges within the human female, who bears the posterity of *man* within her. Candida certainly exhibits the dynamism from which the Life Force moves.

The second concept is Shaw's Thinking Man Theory. Out of every thousand men, Shaw says, there are seven hundred philistines —people who merely drift along in life, never questioning, never changing; their heads remain buried in the sand. There are two hundred ninety-nine idealists—those with sufficient insight to see the Truth, but completely immersed in conventions, platitudes, dreams, and utopias; their heads are in the clouds. That one remaining individual is the realist, or thinking man; his head is in the clouds but his feet are on the ground. He sees things as they are and takes action accordingly. The target of Shaw's satiric attack is the idealist. He is the one to try to change, for if one can get him to think, then he, too, might become a realist.

The play is further strengthened by the fact that Candida is surrounded by well-conceived supporting characters. Morell, with all his moral trappings, is never portrayed as a fool, but only as a victim of idealism. He is admired by his curate, Lexy, but it is the love of his typist, Prossy, that is incomprehensible to Marchbanks. Marchbanks himself is weak, cowardly, and emotional, but the truth of his inner sensitivity is indicated by the effect his words have upon his older, more secure rival. Sharply contrasted with both the moralist and the poet is Candida's father, Burgess, with his peculiar cockney dialect, his overly-polite crudeness, and his opportunist motivation.

The final scene of the play brings several idealistic notions into the clear light of Shavian reality. Morell realizes that whatever value he might have has come from the loving care of his wife. Candida sees clearly the needs of both her husband and Marchbanks, and she makes the choice which is consonant with her own view of life.

## Characters

THE REVEREND
  JAMES MAVOR MORELL
CANDIDA MORELL, *his wife*
PROSERPINE GARNETT,
  *his typist*

THE REVEREND
  ALEXANDER (LEXY) MILL
MR. BURGESS, *Candida's father*
EUGENE MARCHBANKS

## ACT I

A fine October morning in the northeast suburbs of London, a vast district many miles away from the London of Mayfair and St. James's, much less known there than the Paris of the Rue de Rivoli and the Champs Elysées, and much less narrow, squalid, fetid and airless in its slums; strong in comfortable, prosperous middle class life; wide streeted; myriad-populated; well-served with ugly iron urinals, Radical clubs, tram lines, and a perpetual stream of yellow cars; enjoying in its main thoroughfares the luxury of grass-grown "front gardens," untrodden by the foot of man save as to the path from the gate to the hall door; but blighted by an intolerable monotony of miles and miles of graceless, characterless brick houses, black iron railings, stony pavements, slated roofs, and respectably ill dressed or disreputably poorly dressed people, quite accustomed to the place, and mostly plodding about somebody else's work, which they would not do if they themselves could help it. The little energy and eagerness that crop up shew themselves in cockney cupidity and business "push." Even the policemen and the chapels are not infrequent enough to break the monotony. The sun is shining cheerfully; there is no fog; and though the smoke effectually prevents anything, whether faces and hands or bricks and mortar, from looking fresh and clean, it is not hanging heavily enough to trouble a Londoner.

    This desert of unattractiveness has its oasis. Near the outer end of the Hackney Road is a park of 217 acres, fenced in, not by railings, but by a wooden paling, and containing plenty of greensward, trees, a lake for bathers, flower beds with the flowers arranged carefully in patterns by the admired cockney art of carpet gardening and a sandpit, imported from the seaside for the delight of the children, but speedily deserted on its becoming a natural vermin preserve for all the petty fauna of Kingsland, Hackney and Hoxton. A bandstand, an unfinished forum for religious, anti-religious and political orators, cricket pitches, a gymnasium, and an old fashioned stone kiosk are among its attractions. Whenever the prospect is bounded by trees or rising green grounds, it is a pleasant place. Where the ground stretches flat to the grey palings, with bricks and mortar, sky signs, crowded chimneys and smoke beyond, the prospect makes it desolate and sordid.

The best view of Victoria Park is from the front window of St. Dominic's Parsonage, from which not a single chimney is visible. The parsonage is a semi-detached villa with a front garden and a porch. Visitors go up the flight of steps to the porch: tradespeople and members of the family go down by a door under the steps to the basement, with a breakfast room, used for all meals, in front, and the kitchen at the back. Upstairs, on the level of the hall door, is the drawing-room, with its large plate glass window looking on the park. In this room, the only sitting-room that can be spared from the children and the family meals, the parson, the REVEREND JAMES MAVOR MORELL, does his work. He is sitting in a strong round-backed revolving chair at the right hand end of a long table, which stands across the window, so that he can cheer himself with the view of the park at his elbow. At the opposite end of the table, adjoining it, is a little table only half the width of the other, with a typewriter on it. His typist is sitting at this machine, with her back to the window. The large table is littered with pamphlets, journals, letters, nests of drawers, an office diary, postage scales and the like. A spare chair for visitors having business with the parson is in the middle, turned to his end. Within reach of his hand is a stationery case, and a cabinet photograph in a frame. Behind him the right hand wall, recessed above the fireplace, is fitted with bookshelves, on which an adept eye can measure the parson's divinity and casuistry by a complete set of Browning's poems and Maurice's Theological Essays, and guess at his politics from a yellow backed Progress and Poverty, Fabian Essays, a Dream of John Ball, Marx's Capital, and half a dozen other literary landmarks in Socialism. Opposite him on the left, near the typewriter, is the door. Farther down the room, opposite the fireplace, a bookcase stands on a cellaret,[1] with a sofa near it. There is a generous fire burning; and the hearth, with a comfortable armchair and a japanned[2] flower-painted coal scuttle at one side, a miniature chair for a boy or girl on the other, a nicely varnished wooden mantelpiece, with neatly molded shelves, tiny bits of mirror let into the panels, and a travelling clock in a leather case (the inevitable wedding present), and on the wall above a large autotype of the chief figure in Titian's Virgin of the Assumption, is very inviting. Altogether the room is the room of a good housekeeper, vanquished, as far as the table is concerned, by an untidy man, but elsewhere mistress of the situation. The furniture, in its ornamental aspect, betrays the style of the advertised "drawing-room suite" of the pushing suburban furniture dealer; but there is nothing useless or pretentious in the room. The paper and panelling are dark, throwing the big cheery window and the park outside into strong relief.

The REVEREND JAMES MAVOR MORELL is a Christian Socialist clergyman of the Church of England, and an active member of the Guild of St. Matthew and the Christian Social Union. A vigorous, genial, popular man of forty, robust and good-looking, full of energy, with pleasant, hearty, considerate manners, and a sound, unaffected voice, which he uses with the clean, athletic articulation of a practised orator, and with a wide range and perfect command of expression. He is a first-rate clergyman, able to say what he likes to whom he likes, to lecture people without setting himself up against them, to impose his authority on them without humiliating them, and to interfere in their business without impertinence. His well-spring of spiritual enthusiasm and sympathetic emotion has never run dry for a moment: he still eats and sleeps heartily enough to win the daily battle between exhaustion and recuperation triumphantly. Withal, a great baby, pardonably vain of his powers and unconsciously pleased with himself. He has a healthy complexion, a good forehead, with the brows somewhat blunt, and the eyes bright and eager, a mouth resolute, but not particularly well cut, and a substantial nose, with the mobile, spreading nostrils of the dramatic orator, but, like all his features, void of subtlety.

The typist, MISS PROSERPINE GARNETT, is a brisk little woman of about

---

1. *cellaret:* a sideboard containing compartments for wine bottles or other objects.
2. *japanned:* lacquered or varnished.

30, of the lower middle class, neatly but cheaply dressed in a black merino[3] skirt and a blouse, rather pert and quick of speech, and not very civil in her manner, but sensitive and affectionate. She is clattering away busily at her machine whilst MORELL opens the last of his morning's letters. He realizes its contents with a comic groan of despair.

PROSERPINE. Another lecture?
MORELL. Yes. The Hoxton Freedom Group want me to address them on Sunday morning [*Great emphasis on "Sunday," this being the unreasonable part of the business.*] What are they?
PROSERPINE. Communist Anarchists, I think.
MORELL. Just like Anarchists not to know that they can't have a parson on Sunday! Tell them to come to church if they want to hear me: it will do them good. Say I can only come on Mondays and Thursdays. Have you the diary there?
PROSERPINE. [*Taking up the diary.*] Yes.
MORELL. Have I any lecture on for next Monday?
PROSERPINE. [*Referring to diary.*] Tower Hamlets Radical Club.
MORELL. Well, Thursday then?
PROSERPINE. English Land Restoration League.
MORELL. What next?
PROSERPINE. Guild of St. Matthew on Monday. Independent Labor Party, Greenwich Branch, on Thursday. Monday, Social-Democratic Federation, Mile End Branch. Thursday, first Confirmation class— [*Impatiently.*] Oh, I'd better tell them you can't come. They're only half a dozen ignorant and conceited costermongers[4] without five shillings between them.
MORELL. [*Amused.*] Ah; but you see they're near relatives of mine, Miss Garnett.
PROSERPINE. [*Staring at him.*] Relatives of yours!
MORELL. Yes: we have the same father—in Heaven.
PROSERPINE. [*Relieved.*] Oh, is that all?
MORELL. [*With a sadness which is a luxury to a man whose voice expresses it so finely.*] Ah, you don't believe it. Everybody says it: nobody believes it—nobody. [*Briskly, getting back to business.*] Well,

---

3. *merino:* a soft wool like cashmere.
4. *costermongers:* a term of abuse; specifically, a person who sells food from a barrow in the street.

well! Come, Miss Proserpine, can't you find a date for the costers? What about the 25th: that was vacant the day before yesterday.

PROSERPINE. [*Referring to diary.*] Engaged—the Fabian Society.

MORELL. Bother the Fabian Society! Is the 28th gone, too?

PROSERPINE. City dinner. You're invited to dine with the Founder's Company.

MORELL. That'll do; I'll go to the Hoxton Group of Freedom instead. [*She enters the engagement in silence, with implacable disparagement of the Hoxton Anarchists in every line of her face.* MORELL *bursts open the cover of a copy of The Church Reformer, which has come by post, and glances through Mr. Stewart Hendlam's leader and the Guild of St. Matthew news. These proceedings are presently enlivened by the appearance of* MORELL'S *curate, the* REVEREND ALEXANDER MILL, *a young gentleman gathered by Morell from the nearest University settlement, whither he had come from Oxford to give the east end of London the benefit of his university training. He is a conceitedly well intentioned, enthusiastic, immature person, with nothing positively unbearable about him except a habit of speaking with his lips carefully closed for half an inch from each corner, a finicking articulation, and a set of horribly corrupt vowels, notably ow for o, this being his chief means of bringing Oxford refinement to bear on Hackney vulgarity.* MORELL, *whom he has won over by a doglike devotion, looks up indulgently from The Church Reformer as he enters, and remarks.*] Well, Lexy! Late again, as usual.

LEXY. I'm afraid so. I wish I could get up in the morning.

MORELL. [*Exulting in his own energy.*] Ha! ha! [*Whimsically.*] Watch and pray, Lexy: watch and pray.

LEXY. I know. [*Rising wittily to the occasion.*] But how can I watch and pray when I am asleep? Isn't that so, Miss Prossy?

PROSERPINE. [*Sharply.*] Miss Garnett, if you please.

LEXY. I beg your pardon—Miss Garnett.

PROSERPINE. You've got to do all the work to-day.

LEXY. Why?

PROSERPINE. Never mind why. It will do you good to earn your supper before you eat it, for once in a way, as I do. Come: don't dawdle. You should have been off on your rounds half an hour ago.

LEXY. [*Perplexed.*] Is she in earnest, Morell?

MORELL. [*In the highest spirits—his eyes dancing.*] Yes. *I* am going to dawdle to-day.

LEXY. You! You don't know how.

MORELL. [*Heartily.*] Ha! ha! Don't I? I'm going to have this day all to myself—or at least the afternoon. My wife's coming back: she's due here at 11:45.

LEXY. [*Surprised.*] Coming back already—with the children? I thought they were to stay to the end of the month.

MORELL. So they are: she's only coming up for two days, to get some flannel things for Jimmy, and to see how we're getting on without her.

LEXY. [*Anxiously.*] But, my dear Morell, if what Jimmy and Fluffy had was scarlatina, do you think it wise—

MORELL. Scarlatina!—rubbish, German measles. I brought it into the house myself from the Pycroft Street School. A parson is like a doctor, my boy: he must face infection as a soldier must face bullets. [*He rises and claps* LEXY *on the shoulder.*] Catch the measles if you can, Lexy: she'll nurse you; and what a piece of luck that will be for you!—eh?

LEXY. [*Smiling uneasily.*] It's so hard to understand you about Mrs. Morell—

MORELL. [*Tenderly.*] Ah, my boy, get married—get married to a good woman; and then you'll understand. That's a foretaste of what will be best in the Kingdom of Heaven we are trying to establish on earth. That will cure you of dawdling. An honest man feels that he must pay Heaven for every hour of happiness with a good spell of hard, unselfish work to make others happy. We have no more right to consume happiness without producing it than to consume wealth without producing it. Get a wife like my Candida; and you'll always be in arrear with your repayment.

[*He pats* LEXY *affectionately on the back, and is leaving the room when* LEXY *calls to him.*]

LEXY. Oh, wait a bit: I forgot. [MORELL *halts and turns with the door knob in his hand.*] Your father-in-law is coming round to see you. [MORELL *shuts the door again, with a complete change of manner.*]

MORELL. [*Surprised and not pleased.*] Mr. Burgess?

LEXY. Yes. I passed him in the park, arguing with somebody. He gave me good day and asked me to let you know that he was coming.

MORELL. [*Half incredulous.*] But he hasn't called here for—I may almost say for years. Are you sure, Lexy? You're not joking, are you?

LEXY. [*Earnestly.*] No, sir, really.

MORELL. [*Thoughtfully.*] Hm! Time for him to take another look at Candida before she grows out of his knowledge.

[*He resigns himself to the inevitable, and goes out.* LEXY *looks after him with beaming, foolish worship.*]

LEXY. What a good man! What a thorough, loving soul he is!

[*He takes Morell's place at the table, making himself very comfortable as he takes out a cigaret.*]

PROSERPINE. [*Impatiently, pulling the letter she has been working at off the typewriter and folding it.*] Oh, a man ought to be able to be fond of his wife without making a fool of himself about her.

LEXY. [*Shocked.*] Oh, Miss Prossy!

PROSERPINE. [*Rising busily and coming to the stationery case to get an envelope, in which she encloses the letter as she speaks.*] Candida here, and Candida there, and Candida everywhere! [*She licks the envelope.*] It's enough to drive anyone out of their senses [*Thumping the envelope to make it stick.*] to hear a perfectly commonplace woman raved about in that absurd manner merely because she's got good hair, and a tolerable figure.

LEXY. [*With reproachful gravity.*] I think her extremely beautiful, Miss Garnett. [*He takes the photograph up; looks at it; and adds, with even greater impressiveness.*] Extremely beautiful. How fine her eyes are!

PROSERPINE. Her eyes are not a bit better than mine—now! [*He puts down the photograph and stares austerely at her.*] And you know very well that you think me dowdy and second rate enough.

LEXY. [*Rising majestically.*] Heaven forbid that I should think of God's creatures in such a way! [*He moves stiffly away from her across the room to the neighborhood of the bookcase.*]

PROSERPINE. Thank you. That's very nice and comforting.

LEXY. [*Saddened by her depravity.*] I had no idea you had any feeling against Mrs. Morell.

PROSERPINE. [*Indignantly.*] I have no feeling against her. She's very nice, very good-hearted: I'm very fond of her and can appreciate her real qualities far better than any man can. [*He shakes his head sadly and turns to the bookcase, looking along the shelves for a volume. She follows him with intense pepperiness.*] You don't believe me? [*He *turns and faces her. She pounces at him with spitfire energy.*] You think I'm jealous. Oh, what a profound knowledge of the human heart you have, Mr. Lexy Mill! How well you know the weaknesses of Woman, don't you? It must be so nice to be a man and have a fine penetrating intellect instead of mere emotions like us, and to know that the reason we don't share your amorous delusions is that we're all jealous of one another!

[*She abandons him with a toss of her shoulders, and crosses to the fire to warm her hands.*]

LEXY. Ah, if you women only had the same clue to Man's strength that you have to his weakness, Miss Prossy, there would be no Woman Question.

PROSERPINE. [*Over her shoulder, as she stoops, holding her hands to the blaze.*] Where did you hear Morell say that? You didn't invent it yourself: you're not clever enough.

LEXY. That's quite true. I am not ashamed of owing him that, as I owe him so many other spiritual truths. He said it at the annual conference of the Women's Liberal Federation. Allow me to add that though they didn't appreciate it, I, a mere man, did.

[*He turns to the bookcase again, hoping that this may leave her crushed.*]

PROSERPINE. [*Putting her hair straight at the little panel of mirror in the mantelpiece.*] Well, when you talk to me, give me your own ideas, such as they are, and not his. You never cut a poorer figure than when you are trying to imitate him.

LEXY. [*Stung.*] I try to follow his example, not to imitate him.

PROSERPINE. [*Coming at him again on her way back to her work.*] Yes, you do: you imitate him. Why do you tuck your umbrella under your left arm instead of carrying it in your hand like anyone else? Why do you walk with your chin stuck out before you, hurrying along with that eager look in your eyes—you, who never get up before half past nine in the morning? Why do you say "knoaledge" in church, though you always say "knolledge" in private conversation! Bah! do you think I don't know? [*She goes back to the typewriter.*] Here, come and set about your work: we've wasted enough time for one morning. Here's a copy of the diary for to-day. [*She hands him a memorandum.*]

LEXY. [*Deeply offended.*] Thank you.

[*He takes it and stands at the table with his back to her, reading it. She begins to transcribe her shorthand notes on the typewriter without troubling herself about his feelings.* MR. BURGESS *enters unannounced. He is a man of sixty, made coarse and sordid by the compulsory selfishness of petty commerce, and later on softened into sluggish bumptiousness by overfeeding and commercial success. A vulgar, ignorant, guzzling man, offensive and contemptuous to people whose labor is cheap, respectful to wealth and rank, and quite sincere and without rancor or envy in both attitudes. Finding him without talent, the world has offered him no decently paid work except ignoble work, and he has become in consequence, somewhat hoggish. But he has no suspicion of this himself, and honestly regards his commercial prosperity as the inevitable and socially wholesome triumph of the ability, industry, shrewdness and experience in business of a man who in private is easygoing, affectionate and humorously convivial to a fault. Corporeally, he is a podgy man, with a square, clean shaven face and a square beard under his chin; dust colored, with a patch of grey in the centre, and small watery blue eyes with a plaintively sentimental expression, which he transfers easily to his voice by his habit of pompously intoning his sentences.*]

BURGESS. [*Stopping on the threshold, and looking round.*] They told me Mr. Morell was here.

PROSERPINE. [*Rising.*] He's upstairs. I'll fetch him for you.

BURGESS. [*Staring boorishly at her.*] You're not the same young lady as hused to typewrite for him?

PROSERPINE. No.

BURGESS. [*Assenting.*] No: she was young-er. [MISS GARNETT *stolidly stares at him; then goes out with great dignity. He receives this quite obtusely, and crosses to the hearth-rug, where he turns and spreads himself with his back to the fire.*] Startin' on your rounds, Mr. Mill?

LEXY. [*Folding his paper and pocketing it.*] Yes: I must be off presently.

BURGESS. [*Momentously.*] Don't let me detain you, Mr. Mill. What I come about is private between me and Mr. Morell.

LEXY. [*Huffily.*] I have no intention of intruding, I am sure, Mr. Burgess. Good morning.

BURGESS. [*Patronizingly.*] Oh, good morning to you.

[MORELL *returns as* LEXY *is making for the door.*]

MORELL. [*To* LEXY.] Off to work?

LEXY. Yes, sir.

*Candida*

MORELL. [*Patting him affectionately on the shoulder.*] Take my silk handkerchief and wrap your throat up. There's a cold wind. Away with you.

[LEXY *brightens up, and goes out.*]

BURGESS. Spoilin' your curates, as usu'l, James. Good mornin.' When I pay a man, an' 'is livin' depen's on me, I keep him in his place.

MORELL. [*Rather shortly.*] I always keep my curates in their places as my helpers and comrades. If you get as much work out of your clerks and warehousemen as I do out of my curates, you must be getting rich pretty fast. Will you take your old chair?

[*He points with curt authority to the arm chair beside the fireplace; then takes the spare chair from the table and sits down in front of* BURGESS.]

BURGESS. [*Without moving.*] Just the same as hever, James!

MORELL. When you last called—it was about three years ago, I think—you said the same thing a little more frankly. Your exact words then were: "Just as big a fool as ever, James?"

BURGESS. [*Soothingly.*] Well, perhaps I did; but [*With conciliatory cheerfulness.*] I meant no offence by it. A clorgyman is privileged to be a bit of a fool, you know; it's on'y becomin' in his profession that he should. Anyhow, I come here, not to rake up hold differences, but to let bygones be bygones. [*Suddenly becoming very solemn, and approaching* MORELL.] James: three year ago, you done me a hill turn. You done me hout of a contrac'; an' when I gev you 'arsh words in my nat'ral disappointment, you turned my daughter again me. Well, I've come to act the part of a Cherischin.[5] [*Offering his hand.*] I forgive you, James.

MORELL. [*Starting up.*] Confound your impudence!

BURGESS. [*Retreating, with almost lachrymose deprecation of this treatment.*] Is that becomin' language for a clorgyman, James?—and you so partic'lar, too?

MORELL. [*Hotly.*] No, sir, it is not becoming language for a clergyman. I used the wrong word. I should have said damn your impudence: that's what St. Paul, or any honest priest would have said to you. Do you think I have forgotten that tender of yours for the contract to supply clothing to the workhouse?

5. *a Cherischin:* a Christian.

BURGESS. [*In a paroxysm of public spirit.*] I acted in the interest of the ratepayers, James. It was the lowest tender: you can't deny that.

MORELL. Yes, the lowest, because you paid worse wages than any other employer—starvation wages—aye, worse than starvation wages—to the women who made the clothing. Your wages would have driven them to the streets to keep body and soul together. [*Getting angrier and angrier.*] Those women were my parishioners. I shamed the Guardians out of accepting your tender: I shamed the ratepayers out of letting them do it: I shamed everybody but you. [*Boiling over.*] How dare you, sir, come here and offer to forgive me, and talk about your daughter, and—

BURGESS. Easy, James, easy, easy. Don't git hinto a fluster about nothink. I've howned I was wrong.

MORELL. [*Fuming about.*] Have you? I didn't hear you.

BURGESS. Of course I did. I hown it now. Come: I harsk your pardon for the letter I wrote you. Is that enough?

MORELL. [*Snapping his fingers.*] That's nothing. Have you raised the wages?

BURGESS. [*Triumphantly.*] Yes.

MORELL. [*Stopping dead.*] What!

BURGESS. [*Unctuously.*] I've turned a moddle hemployer. I don't hemploy no women now: they're all sacked; and the work is done by machinery. Not a man 'as less than sixpence a *hour*; and the skilled 'ands gits the Trade Union rate. [*Proudly.*] What 'ave you to say to me now?

MORELL. [*Overwhelmed.*] Is it possible? Well, there's more joy in heaven over one sinner that repenteth—[*Going to Burgess with an explosion of apologetic cordiality.*] My dear Burgess, I most heartily beg your pardon for my hard thoughts of you. [*Grasps his hand.*] And now, don't you feel the better for the change? Come, confess, you're happier. You look happier.

BURGESS. [*Ruefully.*] Well, p'raps I do. I s'pose I must, since you notice it. At all events, I git my contrax asseppit[6] by the County Council. [*Savagely.*] They dussent 'ave nothink to do with me unless I paid fair wages—curse 'em for a parcel o' meddlin' fools!

MORELL. [*Dropping his hand, utterly discouraged.*] So that was why you raised the wages! [*He sits down moodily.*]

---

6. *asseppit:* accepted.

Candida     227

BURGESS. [*Severely, in spreading, mounting tones.*] Why else should I do it? What does it lead to but drink and huppishness in workin' men? [*He seats himself magisterially in the easy chair.*] It's hall very well for you, James: it gits you hinto the papers and makes a great man of you; but you never think of the 'arm you do, puttin' money into the pockets of workin' men that they don't know 'ow to spend, and takin' it from people that might be makin' a good huse on it.

MORELL. [*With a heavy sigh, speaking with cold politeness.*] What is your business with me this morning? I shall not pretend to believe that you are here merely out of family sentiment.

BURGESS. [*Obstinately.*] Yes, I ham—just family sentiment and nothink else.

MORELL. [*With weary calm.*] I don't believe you!

BURGESS. [*Rising threateningly.*] Don't say that to me again, James Mavor Morell.

MORELL. [*Unmoved.*] I'll say it just as often as may be necessary to convince you that it's true. I don't believe you.

BURGESS. [*Collapsing into an abyss of wounded feeling.*] Oh, well, if you're determined to be unfriendly, I s'pose I'd better go. [*He moves reluctantly towards the door.* MORELL *makes no sign. He lingers.*] I didn't hexpect to find a hun-forgivin' spirit in you, James. [MORELL *still not responding, he takes a few more reluctant steps doorwards. Then he comes back whining.*] We huseter git on well enough, spite of our different opinions. Why are you so changed to me? I give you my word I come here in pyorr[7] frenliness, not wishin' to be on bad terms with my hown daughrter's 'usban'. Come, James: be a Cherischin and shake 'ands. [*He puts his hand sentimentally on* MORELL'S *shoulder.*]

MORELL. [*Looking up at him thoughtfully.*] Look here, Burgess. Do you want to be as welcome here as you were before you lost that contract?

BURGESS. I do, James. I do—honest.

MORELL. Then why don't you behave as you did then?

BURGESS. [*Cautiously removing his hand.*] 'Ow d'y'mean?

MORELL. I'll tell you. You thought me a young fool then.

BURGESS. [*Coaxingly.*] No, I didn't, James. I—

MORELL. [*Cutting him short.*] Yes, you did. And I thought you an old scoundrel.

BURGESS. [*Most vehemently deprecating this gross self-accusation on*

---

7. *pyorr:* pure.

MORELL'S *part.*] No, you didn't, James. Now you do yourself a hinjustice.

MORELL. Yes, I did. Well, that did not prevent our getting on very well together. God made you what I call a scoundrel as he made me what you call a fool. [*The effect of his observation on* BURGESS *is to remove the keystone of his moral arch. He becomes bodily weak, and, with his eyes fixed on* MORELL *in a helpless stare, puts out his hand apprehensively to balance himself, as if the floor had suddenly sloped under him.* MORELL *proceeds in the same tone of quiet conviction.*] It was not for me to quarrel with his handiwork in the one case more than in the other. So long as you come here honestly as a self-respecting, thorough, convinced scoundrel, justifying your scoundrelism, and proud of it, you are welcome. But [*And now* MORELL'S *tone becomes formidable: and he rises and strikes the back of the chair for greater emphasis.*] I won't have you here snivelling about being a model employer and a converted man when you're only an apostate with your coat turned for the sake of a County Council contract. [*He nods at him to enforce the point; then goes to the hearth-rug, where he takes up a comfortably commanding position with his back to the fire, and continues.*] No: I like a man to be true to himself, even in wickedness. Come now: either take your hat and go; or else sit down and give me a good scoundrelly reason for wanting to be friends with me. [BURGESS, *whose emotions have subsided sufficiently to be expressed by a dazed grin, is relieved by this concrete proposition. He ponders it for a moment, and then, slowly and very modestly, sits down in the chair* MORELL *has just left.*] That's right. Now, out with it.

BURGESS. [*Chuckling in spite of himself.*] Well, you are a queer bird, James, and no mistake. But [*Almost enthusiastically.*] one carnt 'elp likin' you; besides, as I said afore, of course one don't take all a clorgyman says seriously, or the world couldn't go on. Could it now? [*He composes himself for graver discourse, and turning his eyes on* MORELL *proceeds with dull seriousness.*] Well, I don't mind tellin' you, since it's your wish we should be free with one another, that I did think you a bit of a fool once; but I'm beginnin' to think that p'r'aps I was be'ind the times a bit.

MORELL. [*Delighted.*] Aha! You're finding that out at last, are you?

BURGESS. [*Portentously.*] Yes, times 'as changed mor'n I could a believed. Five yorr[8] ago, no sensible man would a thought o' takin' up with

---

8. *yorr:* year.

your ideas. I hused to wonder you was let preach at all. Why, I know a clorgyman that 'as bin kep' hout of his job for yorrs by the Bishop of London, although the pore feller's not a bit more religious than you are. But to-day, if henyone was to offer to bet me a thousan' poun' that you'll end by bein' a bishop yourself, I shouldn't venture to take the bet. You and yore crew are gettin' hinfluential: I can see that. They'll 'ave to give you something someday, if it's only to stop yore mouth. You 'ad the right instinc' arter all, James: the line you took is the payin' line in the long run fur a man o' your sort.

MORELL. [*Decisively—offering his hand.*] Shake hands, Burgess. Now you're talking honestly. I don't think they'll make me a bishop; but if they do, I'll introduce you to the biggest jobbers I can get to come to my dinner parties.

BURGESS. [*Who has risen with a sheepish grin and accepted the bond of friendship.*] You will 'ave your joke, James. Our quarrel's made up now, isn't it?

A WOMAN'S VOICE. Say yes, James.

[*Startled, they turn quickly and find that* CANDIDA *has just come in, and is looking at them with an amused maternal indulgence which is her characteristic expression. She is a woman of 33, well built, well nourished, likely, one guesses, to become matronly later on, but now quite at her best, with the double charm of youth and motherhood. Her ways are those of a woman who has found that she can always manage people by engaging their affection, and who does so frankly and instinctively without the smallest scruple. So far, she is like any other pretty woman who is just clever enough to make the most of her sexual attractions for trivially selfish ends; but* CANDIDA's *serene brow, courageous eyes, and well-set mouth and chin signify largeness of mind and dignity of character to ennoble her cunning in the affections. A wisehearted observer, looking at her, would at once guess that whoever had placed the Virgin of the Assumption over her hearth did so because he fancied some spiritual resemblance between them, and yet would not suspect either her husband or herself of any such idea, or indeed of any concern with the art of Titian.*

*Just now she is in bonnet and mantle, laden with a strapped rug with her umbrella stuck through it, a handbag, and a supply of illustrated papers.*]

MORELL. [*Shocked at his remissness.*] Candida! Why—[*Looks at his watch, and is horrified to find it so late.*] My darling! [*Hurrying to her and seizing the rug strap, pouring forth his remorseful regrets all the time.*] I intended to meet you at the train. I let the time slip. [*Flinging the rug on the sofa.*] I was so engrossed by—[*Returning to her.*]—I forgot—oh! [*He embraces her with penitent emotion.*]

BURGESS. [*A little shamefaced and doubtful of his reception.*] How orr you, Candy? [*She, still in* MORELL'S *arms, offers him her cheek, which he kisses.*] James and me is come to a unnerstandin'—a *h*onorable unnerstandin'. Ain' we, James?

MORELL. [*Impetuously.*] Oh, bother your understanding! You've kept me late for Candida. [*With compassionate fervor.*] My poor love: how did you manage about the luggage?—how—

CANDIDA. [*Stopping him and disengaging herself.*] There, there, there. I wasn't alone. Eugene came down yesterday; and we traveled up together.

MORELL. [*Pleased.*] Eugene!

CANDIDA. Yes: he's struggling with my luggage, poor boy. Go out, dear, at once; or he will pay for the cab; and I don't want that. [MORELL *hurries out.* CANDIDA *puts down her handbag; then takes off her mantle and bonnet and puts them on the sofa with the rug, chatting meanwhile.*] Well, papa, how are you getting on at home?

BURGESS. The 'ouse ain't worth livin' in since you left it, Candy. I wish you'd come round and give the gurl a talkin' to. Who's this Eugene that's come with you?

CANDIDA. Oh, Eugene's one of James's discoveries. He found him sleeping on the Embankment last June. Haven't you noticed our new picture [*Pointing to the Virgin.*]? He gave us that.

BURGESS. [*Incredulously.*] Garn! D'you mean to tell me—your hown father!—that cab touts[9] or such like, orf the Embankment, buys pictur's like that? [*Severely.*] Don't deceive me, Candy: it's a 'Igh Church pictur; and James chose it hisself.

CANDIDA. Guess again. Eugene isn't a cab tout.

BURGESS. Then wot is he? [*Sarcastically.*] A nobleman, I 'spose.

CANDIDA. [*Delighted—nodding.*] Yes. His uncle's a peer[10]—a real live earl.

---

9. *touts:* those who solicit business.
10. *peer:* a member of one of the degrees of nobility in the United Kingdom.

BURGESS. [*Not daring to believe such good news.*] No!
CANDIDA. Yes. He had a seven day bill for £55 in his pocket when James found him on the Embankment. He thought he couldn't get any money for it until the seven days were up; and he was too shy to ask for credit. Oh, he's a dear boy! We are very fond of him.
BURGESS. [*Pretending to belittle the aristocracy, but with his eyes gleaming.*] Hm, I thort you wouldn't git a piorr's[11] nevvy[12] visitin' in Victoria Park unless he were a bit of a flat. [*Looking again at the picture.*] Of course I don't 'old with that pictur, Candy; but still it's a 'igh class, fust-rate work of art: I can see that. Be sure you hintroduce me to him, Candy. [*He looks at his watch anxiously.*] I can only stay about two minutes.

[MORELL *comes back with* EUGENE, *whom* BURGESS *contemplates moist-eyed with enthusiasm. He is a strange, shy youth of eighteen, slight, effeminate, with a delicate childish voice, and a hunted, tormented expression and shrinking manner that shew the painful sensitiveness that very swift and acute apprehensiveness produces in youth, before the character has grown to its full strength. Yet everything that his timidity and frailty suggests is contradicted by his face. He is miserably irresolute, does not know where to stand or what to do with his hands and feet, is afraid of* BURGESS, *and would run away into solitude if he dared; but the very intensity with which he feels a perfectly commonplace position shews great nervous force, and his nostrils and mouth shew a fiercely petulant wilfulness, as to the quality of which his great imaginative eyes and fine brow are reassuring. He is so entirely uncommon as to be almost unearthly; and to prosaic people there is something noxious in this unearthliness, just as to poetic people there is something angelic in it. His dress is anarchic. He wears an old blue serge jacket, unbuttoned over a woolen lawn tennis shirt, with a silk handkerchief for a cravat, trousers matching the jacket, and brown canvas shoes. In these garments he has apparently lain in the heather and waded through the waters; but there is no evidence of his having ever brushed them.*

*As he catches sight of a stranger on entering, he stops, and edges along the wall on the opposite side of the room.*]

MORELL. [*As he enters.*] Come along: you can spare us quarter of an hour, at all events. This is my father-in-law, Mr. Burgess—Mr. Marchbanks.

11. *piorr's:* peer's.   12. *nevvy:* nephew.

MARCHBANKS. [*Nervously backing against the bookcase.*] Glad to meet you, sir.

BURGESS. [*Crossing to him with great heartiness, whilst* MORELL *joins* CANDIDA *at the fire.*] Glad to meet you, I'm shore, Mr. Marchbanks. [*Forcing him to shake hands.*] 'Ow do you find yoreself this weather? 'Ope you ain't lettin' James put no foolish ideas into your 'ed?

MARCHBANKS. Foolish ideas! Oh, you mean Socialism. No.

BURGESS. That's right. [*Again looking at his watch.*] Well, I must go now: there's no 'elp for it. Yo're not comin' my way, are you, Mr. Morchbanks?

MARCHBANKS. Which way is that?

BURGESS. Victawriar Pork[13] Station. There's a city train at 12:25.

MORELL. Nonsense. Eugene will stay to lunch with us, I expect.

MARCHBANKS. [*Anxiously excusing himself.*] No—I—I—

BURGESS. Well, well, I shan't press you: I bet you'd rather lunch with Candy. Some night, I 'ope, you'll come and dine with me at my club, the Freeman Founders in Nortn Folgit. Come, say you will.

MARCHBANKS. Thank you, Mr. Burgess. Where is Norton Folgate—down in Surrey, isn't it?

[BURGESS, *inexpressibly tickled, begins to splutter with laughter.*]

CANDIDA. [*Coming to the rescue.*] You'll lose your train, papa, if you don't go at once. Come back in the afternoon and tell Mr. Marchbanks where to find the club.

BURGESS. [*Roaring with glee.*] Down in Surrey—har, har! that's not a bad one. Well, I never met a man as didn't know Nortn Folgit before. [*Abashed at his own noisiness.*] Goodbye, Mr. Morchbanks: I know yo're too 'ighbred to take my pleasantry in bad part. [*He again offers his hand.*]

MARCHBANKS. [*Taking it with a nervous jerk.*] Not at all.

BURGESS. Bye, bye, Candy. I'll look in again later on. So long, James.

MORELL. Must you go?

BURGESS. Don't stir. [*He goes out with unabated heartiness.*]

MORELL. Oh, I'll see you out.

[*He follows him out.* EUGENE *stares after them apprehensively, holding his breath until* BURGESS *disappears.*]

CANDIDA. [*Laughing.*] Well, Eugene. [*He turns with a start and comes*

---

13. *Victawriar Pork*: Victoria Park.

*eagerly towards her, but stops irresolutely as he meets her amused look.*] What do you think of my father?

MARCHBANKS. I—I hardly know him yet. He seems to be a very nice old gentleman.

CANDIDA. [*With gentle irony.*] And you'll go to the Freeman Founders to dine with him, won't you?

MARCHBANKS. [*Miserably, taking it quite seriously.*] Yes, if it will please you.

CANDIDA. [*Touched.*] Do you know, you are a very nice boy, Eugene, with all your queerness. If you had laughed at my father I shouldn't have minded; but I like you ever so much better for being nice to him.

MARCHBANKS. Ought I to have laughed? I noticed that he said something funny; but I am so ill at ease with strangers; and I never can see a joke! I'm very sorry. [*He sits down on the sofa, his elbows on his knees and his temples between his fists, with an expression of hopeless suffering.*]

CANDIDA. [*Bustling him goodnaturedly.*] Oh, come! You great baby, you! You are worse than usual this morning. Why were you so melancholy as we came along in the cab?

MARCHBANKS. Oh, that was nothing. I was wondering how much I ought to give the cabman. I know it's utterly silly; but you don't know how dreadful such things are to me—how I shrink from having to deal with strange people. [*Quickly and reassuringly.*] But it's all right. He beamed all over and touched his hat when Morell gave him two shillings. I was on the point of offering him ten.

[CANDIDA *laughs heartily.* MORELL *comes back with a few letters and newspapers which have come by the midday post.*]

CANDIDA. Oh, James, dear, he was going to give the cabman ten shillings —ten shillings for a three minutes' drive—oh, dear!

MORELL. [*At the table, glancing through the letters.*] Never mind her, Marchbanks. The overpaying instinct is a generous one: better than the underpaying instinct, and not so common.

MARCHBANKS. [*Relapsing into dejection.*] No: cowardice, incompetence. Mrs. Morell's quite right.

CANDIDA. Of course she is. [*She takes up her handbag.*] And now I must leave you to James for the present. I suppose you are too much of a poet to know the state a woman finds her house in when she's been away for three weeks. Give me my rug. [EUGENE *takes the strapped rug from the couch, and gives it to her. She takes it in her left hand, having the bag in her right.*] Now hang my cloak across my arm. [*He obeys.*] Now my hat. [*He puts it into the hand which has the bag.*] Now open the door for me. [*He hurries up before her and opens the door.*] Thanks. [*She goes out; and* MARCHBANKS *shuts the door.*]

MORELL. [*Still busy at the table.*] You'll stay to lunch, Marchbanks, of course.

MARCHBANKS. [*Scared.*] I mustn't. [*He glances quickly at* MORELL, *but at once avoids his frank look, and adds, with obvious disingenuousness.*] I can't.

MORELL. [*Over his shoulder.*] You mean you won't.

MARCHBANKS. [*Earnestly.*] No: I should like to, indeed. Thank you very much. But—but—

MORELL. [*Breezily, finishing with the letters and coming close to him.*] But—but—but—but—bosh! If you'd like to stay, stay. You don't mean to persuade me you have anything else to do. If you're shy, go and take a turn in the park and write poetry until half past one; and then come in and have a good feed.

MARCHBANKS. Thank you, I should like that very much. But I really mustn't. The truth is, Mrs. Morell told me not to. She said she didn't think you'd ask me to stay to lunch, but that I was to remember, if you did, that you didn't really want me to. [*Plaintively.*] She said I'd understand; but I don't. Please don't tell her I told you.

MORELL. [*Drolly.*] Oh, is that all? Won't my suggestion that you should take a turn in the park meet the difficulty?

MARCHBANKS. How?

MORELL. [*Exploding good-humoredly.*] Why, you duffer—[*But this boisterousness jars himself as well as* EUGENE. *He checks himself, and resumes, with affectionate seriousness.*] No: I won't put it in that way. My dear lad: in a happy marriage like ours, there is something very sacred in the return of the wife to her home. [MARCHBANKS *looks quickly at him, half anticipating his meaning.*] An old friend or a truly noble and sympathetic soul is not in the way on such occasions; but a chance visitor is. [*The hunted, horror-stricken expression comes out with sudden vividness in* EUGENE'S *face as he understands.* MORELL, *occupied with his own thought, goes on without noticing it.*] Candida thought I would rather not have you here; but she was wrong. I'm very fond of you, my boy, and I should like you to see for yourself what a happy thing it is to be married as I am.

MARCHBANKS. Happy!—your marriage! You think that! You believe that!

MORELL. [*Buoyantly.*] I know it, my lad. La Rochefoucauld said that there are convenient marriages, but no delightful ones. You don't know the comfort of seeing through and through a thundering liar and rotten cynic like that fellow. Ha, ha! Now off with you to the park, and write your poem. Half past one, sharp, mind: we never wait for anybody.

MARCHBANKS. [*Wildly.*] No: stop: you shan't. I'll force it into the light.

MORELL. [*Puzzled.*] Eh? Force what?

MARCHBANKS. I must speak to you. There is something that must be settled between us.

MORELL. [*With a whimsical glance at the clock.*] Now?

MARCHBANKS. [*Passionately.*] Now. Before you leave this room. [*He retreats a few steps, and stands as if to bar* MORELL's *way to the door.*]

MORELL. [*Without moving, and gravely, perceiving now that there is something serious the matter.*] I'm not going to leave it, my dear boy: I thought you were. [EUGENE, *baffled by his firm tone, turns his back on him, writhing with anger.* MORELL *goes to him and puts his hand on his shoulder strongly and kindly, disregarding his attempt to shake it off.*] Come: sit down quietly; and tell me what it is. And remember: we are friends, and need not fear that either of us will be anything but patient and kind to the other, whatever we may have to say.

MARCHBANKS. [*Twisting himself round on him.*] Oh, I am not forgetting myself: I am only [*Covering his face desperately with his hands.*] full of horror. [*Then, dropping his hands, and thrusting his face forward fiercely at* MORELL, *he goes on threateningly.*] You shall see whether this is a time for patience and kindness. [MORELL, *firm as a rock, looks indulgently at him.*] Don't look at me in that self-complacent way. You think yourself stronger than I am; but I shall stagger you if you have a heart in your breast.

MORELL. [*Powerfully confident.*] Stagger me, my boy. Out with it.

MARCHBANKS. First—

MORELL. First?

MARCHBANKS. I love your wife.

[MORELL *recoils, and, after staring at him for a moment in utter amazement, bursts into uncontrollable laughter.* EUGENE *is taken aback, but not disconcerted; and he soon becomes indignant and contemptuous.*]

MORELL. [*Sitting down to have his laugh out.*] Why, my dear child, of course you do. Everybody loves her: they can't help it. I like it. But [*Looking up whimsically at him.*] I say, Eugene: do you think yours is a case to be talked about? You're under twenty: she's over thirty. Doesn't it look rather too like a case of calf love?

MARCHBANKS. [*Vehemently.*] You dare say that of her! You think that way of the love she inspires! It is an insult to her!

MORELL. [*Rising quickly, in an altered tone.*] To her! Eugene: take care. I have been patient. I hope to remain patient. But there are some things I won't allow. Don't force me to shew you the indulgence I should shew to a child. Be a man.

MARCHBANKS. [*With a gesture as if sweeping something behind him.*] Oh, let us put aside all that cant. It horrifies me when I think of the doses of it she has had to endure in all the weary years during which you have selfishly and blindly sacrificed her to minister to your self-sufficiency—you [*Turning on him.*] who have not one thought—one sense—in common with her.

MORELL. [*Philosophically.*] She seems to bear it pretty well. [*Looking him straight in the face.*] Eugene, my boy: you are making a fool of yourself—a very great fool of yourself. There's a piece of wholesome plain speaking for you.

MARCHBANKS. Oh, do you think I don't know all that? Do you think that the things people make fools of themselves about are any less real and true than the things they behave sensibly about? [MORELL'S *gaze wavers for the first time. He instinctively averts his face and stands listening, startled and thoughtful.*] They are more true: they are the only things that are true. You are very calm and sensible and moderate with me because you can see that I am a fool about your wife; just as no doubt that old man who was here just now is very wise over your socialism, because he sees that you are a fool about it. [MORELL'S *perplexity deepens markedly.* EUGENE *follows up his advantage, plying him fiercely with questions.*] Does that prove you wrong? Does your complacent superiority to me prove that *I* am wrong?

Candida 237

MORELL. [*Turning on* EUGENE, *who stands his ground.*] Marchbanks: some devil is putting these words into your mouth. It is easy—terribly easy—to shake a man's faith in himself. To take advantage of that to break a man's spirit is devil's work. Take care of what you are doing. Take care.

MARCHBANKS. [*Ruthlessly.*] I know. I'm doing it on purpose. I told you I should stagger you.

[*They confront one another threateningly for a moment. Then* MORELL *recovers his dignity.*]

MORELL. [*With noble tenderness.*] Eugene: listen to me. Some day, I hope and trust, you will be a happy man like me. [EUGENE *chafes intolerantly, repudiating the worth of his happiness.* MORELL, *deeply insulted, controls himself with fine forbearance, and continues steadily, with great artistic beauty of delivery.*] You will be married; and you will be working with all your might and valor to make every spot on earth as happy as your own home. You will be one of the makers of the Kingdom of Heaven on earth; and—who knows?—you may be a pioneer and master builder where I am only a humble journeyman; for don't think, my boy, that I cannot see in you, young as you are, promise of higher powers than I can ever pretend to. I well know that it is in the poet that the holy spirit of man—the god within him—is most godlike. It should make you tremble to think of that—to think that the heavy burthen and great gift of a poet may be laid upon you.

MARCHBANKS. [*Unimpressed and remorseless, his boyish crudity of assertion telling sharply against* MORELL'S *oratory.*] It does not make me tremble. It is the want of it in others that makes me tremble.

MORELL. [*Redoubling his force of style under the stimulus of his genuine feeling and* EUGENE'S *obduracy.*] Then help to kindle it in them—in me—not to extinguish it. In the future—when you are as happy as I am—I will be your true brother in the faith. I will help you to believe that God has given us a world that nothing but our own folly keeps from being a paradise. I will help you to believe that every stroke of your work is sowing happiness for the great harvest that all —even the humblest—shall one day reap. And last, but trust me, not least, I will help you to believe that your wife loves you and is happy in her home. We need such help, Marchbanks: we need it greatly and always. There are so many things to make us doubt, if once we let our understanding be troubled. Even at home, we sit as if in camp, encompassed by a hostile army of doubts. Will you play the traitor and let them in on me?

MARCHBANKS. [*Looking round him.*] Is it like this for her here always? A woman, with a great soul, craving for reality, truth, freedom, and being fed on metaphors, sermons, stale perorations, mere rhetoric. Do you think a woman's soul can live on your talent for preaching?

MORELL. [*Stung.*] Marchbanks: you make it hard for me to control myself. My talent is like yours insofar as it has any real worth at all. It is the gift of finding words for divine truth.

MARCHBANKS. [*Impetuously.*] It's the gift of the gab, nothing more and nothing less. What has your knack of fine talking to do with the truth, any more than playing the organ has? I've never been in your church; but I've been to your political meetings; and I've seen you do what's called rousing the meeting to enthusiasm: that is, you excited them until they behaved exactly as if they were drunk. And their wives looked on and saw clearly enough what fools they were. Oh, it's an old story: you'll find it in the Bible. I imagine King David, in his fits of enthusiasm, was very like you. [*Stabbing him with the words.*] "But his wife despised him in her heart."

MORELL. [*Wrathfully.*] Leave my house. Do you hear? [*He advances on him threateningly.*]

MARCHBANKS. [*Shrinking back against the couch.*] Let me alone. Don't touch me. [MORELL *grasps him powerfully by the lapel of his coat: he cowers down on the sofa and screams passionately.*] Stop, Morell, if you strike me, I'll kill myself: I won't bear it. [*Almost in hysterics.*] Let me go. Take your hand away.

MORELL. [*With slow, emphatic scorn.*] You little snivelling, cowardly whelp. [*Releasing him.*] Go, before you frighten yourself into a fit.

MARCHBANKS. [*On the sofa, gasping, but relieved by the withdrawal of* MORELL's *hand.*] I'm not afraid of you: it's you who are afraid of me.

MORELL. [*Quietly, as he stands over him.*] It looks like it, doesn't it?

MARCHBANKS. [*With petulant vehemence.*] Yes, it does. [MORELL *turns away contemptuously.* EUGENE *scrambles to his feet and follows him.*] You think because I shrink from being brutally handled—because [*With tears in his voice.*] I can do nothing but cry with rage when I am met with violence—because I can't lift a heavy trunk down from the top of a cab like you—because I can't fight you for your wife as a navvy[14] would: all that makes you think that I'm afraid of you. But you're wrong. If I haven't got what you call British pluck, I haven't British cowardice either: I'm not afraid of a clergyman's ideas. I'll fight your ideas. I'll rescue her from her slavery to them: I'll pit my own ideas against them. You are driving me out of the house because you daren't let her choose between your ideas and mine. You are afraid to let me see her again. [MORELL, *angered, turns suddenly on him. He flies to the door in involuntary dread.*] Let me alone, I say. I'm going.

MORELL. [*With cold scorn.*] Wait a moment: I am not going to touch you: don't be afraid. When my wife comes back she will want to know why you have gone. And when she finds that you are never going to cross our threshold again, she will want to have that explained, too. Now I don't wish to distress her by telling her that you have behaved like a blackguard.

MARCHBANKS. [*Coming back with renewed vehemence.*] You shall—you must. If you give any explanation but the true one; you are a liar and a coward. Tell her what I said; and how you were strong and manly, and shook me as a terrier shakes a rat; and how I shrank and was terrified; and how you called me a snivelling little whelp and put me out of the house. If you don't tell her, I will: I'll write it to her.

MORELL. [*Taken aback.*] Why do you want her to know this?

MARCHBANKS. [*With lyric rapture.*] Because she will understand me, and know that I understand her. If you keep back one word of it from her—if you are not ready to lay the truth at her feet as I am—then you will know to the end of your days that she really belongs to me and not to you. Good-bye. [*Going.*]

MORELL. [*Terribly disquieted.*] Stop: I will not tell her.

MARCHBANKS. [*Turning near the door.*] Either the truth or a lie you must tell her, if I go.

MORELL. [*Temporizing.*] Marchbanks: it is sometimes justifiable.

MARCHBANKS. [*Cutting him short.*] I know—to lie. It will be useless. Good-bye, Mr. Clergyman.

[*As he turns finally to the door, it open and* CANDIDA *enters in housekeeping attire.*]

14. *a navvy:* a laborer employed in such earthworks as canals, drains, etc.

CANDIDA. Are you going, Eugene? [*Looking more observantly at him.*] Well, dear me, just look at you, going out into the street in that state! You are a poet, certainly. Look at him, James! [*She takes him by the coat, and brings him forward to show him to* MORELL.] Look at his collar! look at his tie! look at his hair! One would think somebody had been throttling you. [*The two men guard themselves against betraying their consciousness.*] Here! Stand still. [*She buttons his collar; ties his neckerchief in a bow; and arranges his hair.*] There! Now you look so nice that I think you'd better stay to lunch after all, though I told you you mustn't. It will be ready in half an hour. [*She puts a final touch to the bow. He kisses her hand.*] Don't be silly.

MARCHBANKS. I want to stay, of course—unless the reverend gentleman, your husband, has anything to advance to the contrary.

CANDIDA. Shall he stay, James, if he promises to be a good boy and to help me to lay the table?

[MARCHBANKS *turns his head and looks steadfastly at* MORELL *over his shoulder, challenging his answer.*]

MORELL. [*Shortly.*] Oh, yes, certainly: he had better. [*He goes to the table and pretends to busy himself with his papers there.*]

MARCHBANKS. [*Offering his arm to* CANDIDA.] Come and lay the table. [*She takes it and they go to the door together. As they go out he adds.*] I am the happiest of men.

MORELL. So was I—an hour ago.

## ACT II

The same day. The same room. Late in the afternoon. The spare chair for visitors has been replaced at the table, which is, if possible, more untidy than before. MARCHBANKS, alone and idle, is trying to find out how the typewriter works. Hearing someone at the door, he steals guiltily away to the window and pretends to be absorbed in the view. MISS GARNETT, carrying the notebook in which she takes down MORELL's letters in shorthand from his dictation, sits down at the typewriter and sets to work transcribing them, much too busy to notice EUGENE. Unfortunately the first key she strikes sticks.

PROSERPINE. Bother! You've been meddling with my typewriter, Mr. Marchbanks; and there's not the least use in your trying to look as if you hadn't.

MARCHBANKS. [*Timidly.*] I'm very sorry, Miss Garnett. I only tried to make it write.

PROSERPINE. Well, you've made this key stick.

MARCHBANKS. [*Earnestly.*] I assure you I didn't touch the keys. I didn't, indeed. I only turned a little wheel. [*He points irresolutely at the tension wheel.*]

PROSERPINE. Oh, now I understand. [*She sets the machine to rights, talking volubly all the time.*] I suppose you thought it was a sort of barrel-organ. Nothing to do but turn the handle, and it would write a beautiful love letter for you straight off, eh?

MARCHBANKS. [*Seriously.*] I suppose a machine could be made to write love letters. They're all the same, aren't they?

PROSERPINE. [*Somewhat indignantly: any such discussion, except by way of pleasantry, being outside her code of manners.*] How do I know? Why do you ask me?

MARCHBANKS. I beg your pardon. I thought clever people—people who can do business and write letters, and that sort of thing—always had love affairs.

PROSERPINE. [*Rising, outraged.*] Mr. Marchbanks! [*She looks severely at him, and marches with much dignity to the bookcase.*]

MARCHBANKS. [*Approaching her humbly.*] I hope I haven't offended you. Perhaps I shouldn't have alluded to your love affairs.

PROSERPINE. [*Plucking a blue book from the shelf and turning sharply on him.*] I haven't any love affairs. How dare you say such a thing?

MARCHBANKS. [*Simply.*] Really! Oh, then you are shy, like me. Isn't that so?

PROSERPINE. Certainly I am not shy. What do you mean?

MARCHBANKS. [*Secretly.*] You must be: that is the reason there are so few love affairs in the world. We all go about longing for love: it is the first need of our natures, the loudest cry of our hearts; but we dare not utter our longing: we are too shy. [*Very earnestly.*] Oh, Miss Garnett, what would you not give to be without fear, without shame—

PROSERPINE. [*Scandalized.*] Well, upon my word!

MARCHBANKS. [*With petulant impatience.*] Ah, don't say those stupid things to me: they don't deceive me: what use are they? Why are you afraid to be your real self with me? I am just like you.

PROSERPINE. Like me! Pray, are you flattering me or flattering yourself? I don't feel quite sure which. [*She turns to go back to the typewriter.*]

MARCHBANKS. [*Stopping her mysteriously.*] Hush! I go about in search of love; and I find it in unmeasured stores in the bosoms of others. But when I try to ask for it, this horrible shyness strangles me; and I stand dumb, or worse than dumb, saying meaningless things—foolish lies. And I see the affection I am longing for given to dogs and cats and pet birds, because they come and ask for it. [*Almost whispering.*] It must be asked for: it is like a ghost: it cannot speak unless it is first spoken to. [*At his normal pitch, but with deep melancholy.*] All the love in the world is longing to speak; only it dare not, because it is shy, shy, shy. That is the world's tragedy. [*With a deep sigh he sits in the spare chair and buries his face in his hands.*]

PROSERPINE. [*Amazed, but keeping her wits about her—her point of honor in encounters with strange young men.*] Wicked people get over that shyness occasionally, don't they?

MARCHBANKS. [*Scrambling up almost fiercely.*] Wicked people means people who have no love: therefore they have no shame. They have the power to ask love because they don't need it: they have the power to offer it because they have none to give. [*He collapses into his seat, and adds, mournfully.*] But we, who have love, and long to mingle it with the love of others: we cannot utter a word. [*Timidly.*] You find that, don't you?

PROSERPINE. Look here: if you don't stop talking like this, I'll leave the room, Mr. Marchbanks: I really will. It's not proper.

[*She resumes her seat at the typewriter, opening the blue book and preparing to copy a passage from it.*]

MARCHBANKS. [*Hopelessly.*] Nothing that's worth saying is proper. [*He rises, and wanders about the room in his lost way, saying.*] I can't understand you, Miss Garnett. What am I to talk about?

PROSERPINE. [*Snubbing him.*] Talk about indifferent things. Talk about the weather.

MARCHBANKS. Would you stand and talk about indifferent things if a child were by, crying bitterly with hunger?

PROSERPINE. I suppose not.

MARCHBANKS. Well: *I* can't talk about indifferent things with my heart crying out bitterly in its hunger.

PROSERPINE. Then hold your tongue.

MARCHBANKS. Yes: that is what it always comes to. We hold our tongues. Does that stop the cry of your heart?—for it does cry: doesn't it? It must, if you have a heart.

PROSERPINE. [*Suddenly rising with her hand pressed on her heart.*] Oh, it's no use trying to work while you talk like that. [*She leaves her little table and sits on the sofa. Her feelings are evidently strongly worked on.*] It's no business of yours, whether my heart cries or not; but I have a mind to tell you, for all that.

MARCHBANKS. You needn't. I know already that it must.

PROSERPINE. But mind: if you ever say I said so, I'll deny it.

MARCHBANKS. [*Compassionately.*] Yes, I know. And so you haven't the courage to tell him?

PROSERPINE. [*Bouncing up.*] Him! Who?

MARCHBANKS. Whoever he is. The man you love. It might be anybody. The curate, Mr. Mill, perhaps.

PROSERPINE. [*With disdain.*] Mr. Mill!!! A fine man to break my heart about, indeed! I'd rather have you than Mr. Mill.

MARCHBANKS. [*Recoiling.*] No, really—I'm very sorry; but you mustn't think of that. I—

PROSERPINE. [*Testily, crossing to the fire and standing at it with her back to him.*] Oh, don't be frightened: it's not you. It's not any one particular person.

MARCHBANKS. I know. You feel that you could love anybody that offered—

PROSERPINE. [*Exasperated.*] Anybody that offered! No, I do not. What do you take me for?

MARCHBANKS. [*Discouraged.*] No use. You won't make me real answers—only those things that everybody says. [*He strays to the sofa and sits down disconsolately.*]

PROSERPINE. [*Nettled at what she takes to be a disparagement of her manners by an aristocrat.*] Oh, well, if you want original conversation, you'd better go and talk to yourself.

MARCHBANKS. That is what all poets do: they talk to themselves out loud; and the world overhears them. But it's horribly lonely not to hear someone else talk sometimes.

PROSERPINE. Wait until Mr. Morell comes. He'll talk to you. [MARCHBANKS *shudders.*] Oh, you needn't make wry faces over him: he can talk better than you. [*With temper.*] He'd talk your little head off. [*She is going back angrily to her place, when, suddenly enlightened, he springs up and stops her.*]

MARCHBANKS. Ah, I understand now!

PROSERPINE. [*Reddening.*] What do you understand?

MARCHBANKS. Your secret. Tell me: is it really and truly possible for a woman to love him?

PROSERPINE. [*As if this were beyond all bounds.*] Well!!

MARCHBANKS. [*Passionately.*] No, answer me. I want to know: I must know. *I* can't understand it. I can see nothing in him but words, pious resolutions, what people call goodness. You can't love that.

PROSERPINE. [*Attempting to snub him by an air of cool propriety.*] I simply don't know what you're talking about. I don't understand you.

MARCHBANKS. [*Vehemently.*] You do. You lie—

PROSERPINE. Oh!

MARCHBANKS. You do understand; and you know. [*Determined to have an answer.*] Is it possible for a woman to love him?

PROSERPINE. [*Looking him straight in the face.*] Yes. [*He covers his face with his hands.*] Whatever is the matter with you! [*He takes down his hands and looks at her. Frightened at the tragic mask presented to her, she hurries past him at the utmost possible distance, keeping her eyes on his face until he turns from her and goes to the child's chair beside the hearth, where he sits in the deepest dejection. As she approaches the door, it opens and* BURGESS *enters. On seeing him, she ejaculates.*] Praise heaven, here's somebody! [*She sits down, reassured, at her table. She puts a fresh sheet of paper into the typewriter as* BURGESS *crosses to* EUGENE.]

BURGESS. [*Bent on taking care of the distinguished visitor.*] Well: so this is the way they leave you to yourself, Mr. Morchbanks. I've come to keep you company. [MARCHBANKS *looks up at him in consternation, which is quite lost on him.*] James is receivin' a deppitation in the dinin' room; and Candy is hupstairs educatin' of a young stitcher[1] gurl she's hinterusted in. She's settin' there learnin' her to read out of the " 'Ev'nly Twins." [*Condolingly.*] You must find it lonesome

---

1. *stitcher:* one who stitches or sews; a term of contempt.

Candida   245

here with no one but the typist to talk to. [*He pulls round the easy chair above fire, and sits down.*]

PROSERPINE. [*Highly incensed.*] He'll be all right now that he has the advantage of your polished conversation: that's one comfort anyhow. [*She begins to typewrite with clattering asperity.*]

BURGESS. [*Amazed at her audacity.*] Hi was not addressin' myself to you, young woman, that I'm awerr of.

PROSERPINE. [*Tartly, to* MARCHBANKS.] Did you ever see worse manners, Mr. Marchbanks?

BURGESS. [*With pompous severity.*] Mr. Morchbanks is a gentleman and knows his place, which is more than some people do.

PROSERPINE. [*Fretfully.*] It's well you and I are not ladies and gentlemen: I'd talk to you pretty straight if Mr. Marchbanks wasn't here. [*She pulls the letter out of the machine so crossly that it tears.*] There, now I've spoiled this letter—have to be done all over again. Oh, I can't contain myself—silly old fathead!

BURGESS. [*Rising, breathless with indigation.*] Ho! I'm a silly ole fat'ead, am I? Ho, indeed [*Gasping.*] Hall right, my gurl! Hall right. You just wait till I tell that to your employer. You'll see. I'll teach you: see if I don't.

PROSERPINE. I——

BURGESS. [*Cutting her short.*] No, you've done it now. No huse a-talkin' to me. I'll let you know who I am. [PROSERPINE *shifts her paper carriage with a defiant bang, and disdainfully goes on with her work.*] Don't you take no notice of her, Mr. Morchbanks. She's beneath it. [*He sits down again loftily.*]

MARCHBANKS. [*Miserably nervous and disconcerted.*] Hadn't we better change the subject. I—I don't think Miss Garnett meant anything.

PROSERPINE. [*With intense conviction.*] Oh, didn't I though, just!

BURGESS. I wouldn't demean myself to take notice on her.

[*An electric bell rings twice.*]

PROSERPINE. [*Gathering up her note-book and papers.*] That's for me. [*She hurries out.*]

BURGESS. [*Calling after her.*] Oh, we can spare you. [*Somewhat relieved by the triumph of having the last word, and yet half inclined to try to improve on it, he looks after her for a moment; then subsides into his seat by* EUGENE, *and addresses him very confidentially.*] Now we're alone, Mr. Morchbanks, let me give you a friendly 'int that

I wouldn't give to everybody. 'Ow long 'ave you known my son-in-law James here?

MARCHBANKS. I don't know. I never can remember dates. A few months, perhaps.

BURGESS. Ever notice anything queer about him?

MARCHBANKS. I don't think so.

BURGESS. [*Impressively.*] No more you wouldn't. That's the danger in it. Well, he's mad.

MARCHBANKS. Mad!

BURGESS. Mad as a Morch 'are.[2] You take notice on him and you'll see.

MARCHBANKS. [*Beginning.*] But surely that is only because his opinions—

BURGESS. [*Touching him with his forefinger on his knee, and pressing it as if to hold his attention with it.*] That's wot I used ter think, Mr. Morchbanks. Hi thought long enough that it was honly 'is opinions; though, mind you, hopinions becomes vurry serious things when people takes to hactin' on 'em as 'e does. But that's not wot I go on. [*He looks round to make sure that they are alone, and bends over to* EUGENE'S *ear.*] Wot do you think he says to me this mornin' in this very room?

MARCHBANKS. What?

BURGESS. He sez to me—this is as sure as we're settin' here now—he sez: "I'm a fool," he sez; "and yore a scounderl"—as cool as possible. Me a scounderl, mind you! And then shook 'ands with me on it, as if it was to my credit! Do you mean to tell me that that man's sane?

MORELL. [*Outside, calling to* PROSERPINE, *holding the door open.*] Get all their names and addresses, Miss Garnett.

PROSERPINE. [*In the distance.*] Yes, Mr. Morell.

[MORELL *comes in, with the deputation's documents in his hands.*]

BURGESS. [*Aside to* MARCHBANKS.] Yorr he is. Just you keep your heye on him and see. [*Rising momentously.*] I'm sorry, James, to 'ave to make a complaint to you. I don't want to do it; but I feel I oughter, as a matter o' right and dooty.

MORELL. What's the matter?

BURGESS. Mr. Morchbanks will bear me out: he was a witness. [*Very solemnly.*] Your young woman so far forgot herself as to call me a silly ole fat'ead.

---

2. *a Morch 'are:* a March hare.

Candida 247

MORELL. [*Delighted—with tremendous heartiness.*] Oh, now, isn't that exactly like Prossy? She's so frank: she can't contain herself! Poor Prossy! Ha! Ha!

BURGESS. [*Trembling with rage.*] And do you hexpec me to put up with it from the like of 'er?

MORELL. Pooh, nonsense! you can't take any notice of it. Never mind. [*He goes to the cellaret and puts the papers into one of the drawers.*]

BURGESS. Oh, *I* don't mind. I'm above it. But is it right?—that's what I want to know. Is it right?

MORELL. That's a question for the Church, not for the laity. Has it done you any harm, that's the question for you, eh? Of course, it hasn't. Think no more of it. [*He dismisses the subject by going to his place at the table and setting to work at his correspondence.*]

BURGESS. [*Aside to* MARCHBANKS.] What did I tell you? Mad as a 'atter.[3] [*He goes to the table and asks, with the sickly civility of a hungry man.*] When's dinner, James?

MORELL. Not for half an hour yet.

BURGESS. [*With plaintive resignation.*] Gimme a nice book to read over the fire, will you, James: thur's a good chap.

MORELL. What sort of book? A good one?

BURGESS. [*With almost a yell of remonstrance.*] Nah-oo! Summat pleasant, just to pass the time. [MORELL *takes an illustrated paper from the table and offers it. He accepts it humbly.*] Thank yer, James. [*He goes back to his easy chair at the fire, and sits there at his ease, reading.*]

MORELL. [*As he writes.*] Candida will come to entertain you presently. She has got rid of her pupil. She is filling the lamps.

MARCHBANKS. [*Starting up in the wildest consternation.*] But that will soil her hands. I can't bear that, Morell: it's a shame. I'll go and fill them. [*He makes for the door.*]

MORELL. You'd better not. [MARCHBANKS *stops irresolutely.*] She'd only set you to clean my boots, to save me the trouble of doing it myself in the morning.

BURGESS. [*With grave disapproval.*] Don't you keep a servant now, James?

MORELL. Yes; but she isn't a slave; and the house looks as if I kept three. That means that everyone has to lend a hand. It's not a bad plan: Prossy and I can talk business after breakfast whilst we're washing up. Washing up's no trouble when there are two people to do it.

---

3. *a 'atter:* a hatter; a maker or dealer in hats.

MARCHBANKS. [*Tormentedly.*] Do you think every woman is as coarse-grained as Miss Garnett?

BURGESS. [*Emphatically.*] That's quite right, Mr. Morchbanks. That's quite right. She is coarse-grained.

MORELL. [*Quietly and significantly.*] Marchbanks!

MARCHBANKS. Yes.

MORELL. How many servants does your father keep?

MARCHBANKS. Oh, I don't know. [*He comes back uneasily to the sofa, as if to get as far as possible from* MORELL'*s questioning, and sits down in great agony of mind, thinking of the paraffin.*]

MORELL. [*Very gravely.*] So many that you don't know. [*More aggressively.*] Anyhow, when there's anything coarse-grained to be done, you ring the bell and throw it on to somebody else, eh? That's one of the great facts in your existence, isn't it?

MARCHBANKS. Oh, don't torture me. The one great fact now is that your wife's beautiful fingers are dabbling in paraffin oil, and that you are sitting here comfortably preaching about it—everlasting preaching, preaching, words, words, words.

BURGESS. [*Intensely appreciating this retort.*] Ha, ha! Devil a better. [*Radiantly.*] 'Ad you there, James, straight.

[CANDIDA *comes in, well aproned, with a reading lamp trimmed, filled, and ready for lighting. She places it on the table near* MORELL, *ready for use.*]

CANDIDA. [*Brushing her finger tips together with a slight twitch of her nose.*] If you stay with us, Eugene, I think I will hand over the lamps to you.

MARCHBANKS. I will stay on condition that you hand over all the rough work to me.

CANDIDA. That's very gallant; but I think I should like to see how you do it first. [*Turning to* MORELL.] James: you've not been looking after the house properly.

MORELL. What have I done—or not done—my love?

CANDIDA. [*With serious vexation.*] My own particular pet scrubbing brush has been used for blackleading. [*A heart-breaking wail bursts from* MARCHBANKS. BURGESS *looks round, amazed.* CANDIDA *hurries to the sofa.*] What's the matter? Are you ill, Eugene?

MARCHBANKS. No, not ill. Only horror, horror, horror! [*He bows his head on his hands.*]

Candida   249

BURGESS. [*Shocked.*] What! Got the 'orrors, Mr. Morchbanks! Oh, that's bad, at your age. You must leave it off grajally.

CANDIDA. [*Reassured.*] Nonsense, papa. It's only poetic horror, isn't it, Eugene? [*Petting him.*]

BURGESS. [*Abashed.*] Oh, poetic 'orror, is it? I beg your pordon, I'm shore. [*He turns to the fire again, deprecating his hasty conclusion.*]

CANDIDA. What is it, Eugene—the scrubbing brush? [*He shudders.*] Well, there! never mind. [*She sits down beside him.*] Wouldn't you like to present me with a nice new one, with an ivory back inlaid with mother-of-pearl?

MARCHBANKS. [*Softly and musically, but sadly and longingly.*] No not a scrubbing brush, but a boat—a tiny shallop to sail away in, far from the world, where the marble floors are washed by the rain and dried by the sun, where the south wind dusts the beautiful green and purple carpets. Or a chariot—to carry us up into the sky, where the lamps are stars, and don't need to be filled with paraffin oil every day.

MORELL. [*Harshly.*] And where there is nothing to do but to be idle, selfish and useless.

CANDIDA. [*Jarred.*] Oh, James, how could you spoil it all!

MARCHBANKS. [*Firing up.*] Yes, to be idle, selfish and useless: that is to be beautiful and free and happy: hasn't every man desired that with all his soul for the woman he loves? That's my ideal: what's yours, and that of all the dreadful people who live in these hideous rows of houses? Sermons and scrubbing brushes! With you to preach the sermon and your wife to scrub.

CANDIDA. [*Quaintly.*] He cleans the boots, Eugene. You will have to clean them to-morrow for saying that about him.

MARCHBANKS. Oh! don't talk about boots. Your feet should be beautiful on the mountains.

CANDIDA. My feet would not be beautiful on the Hackney Road without boots.

BURGESS. [*Scandalized.*] Come, Candy, don't be vulgar. Mr. Morchbanks ain't accustomed to it. You're givin' him the 'orrors again. I mean the poetic ones.

[MORELL *is silent. Apparently he is busy with his letters: really he is puzzling with misgiving over his new and alarming experience that the surer he is of his moral thrusts, the more swiftly and effectively* EUGENE *parries them. To find himself beginning to fear a man whom he does not respect afflicts him bitterly.* MISS GARNETT *comes in with a telegram.*]

PROSERPINE. [*Handing the telegram to* MORELL.] Reply paid. The boy's waiting. [*To* CANDIDA, *coming back to her machine and sitting down.*] Maria is ready for you now in the kitchen, Mrs. Morell. [CANDIDA *rises.*] The onions have come.

MARCHBANKS. [*Convulsively.*] Onions!

CANDIDA. Yes, onions. Not even Spanish ones—nasty little red onions. You shall help me to slice them. Come along.

[*She catches him by the wrist and runs out, pulling him after her.* BURGESS *rises in consternation, and stands aghast on the hearth-rug, staring after them.*]

BURGESS. Candy didn't oughter 'andle a peer's nevvy like that. It's goin' too fur with it. Lookee 'ere, James; do 'e often git taken queer like that?

MORELL. [*Shortly, writing a telegram.*] I don't know.

BURGESS. [*Sentimentally.*] He talks very pretty. I allus had a turn for a bit of poetry. Candy takes arter me that-a-way: huse ter make me tell her fairy stories when she was on'y a little kiddy not that 'igh [*Indicating a stature of two feet or thereabouts.*]

MORELL. [*Preoccupied.*] Ah, indeed. [*He blots the telegram, and goes out.*]

PROSERPINE. Used you to make the fairy stories up out of your own head?

[BURGESS, *not deigning to reply, strikes an attitude of the haughtiest disdain on the hearth-rug.*]

PROSERPINE. [*Calmly.*] I should never have supposed you had it in you. By the way, I'd better warn you, since you've taken such a fancy to Mr. Marchbanks. He's mad.

BURGESS. Mad! Wot! 'Im too!!

PROSERPINE. Mad as a March hare. He did frighten me, I can tell you just before you came in that time. Haven't you noticed the queer things he says?

BURGESS. So that's wot the poetic 'orrors means. Blame me if it didn't come into my head once or twyst that he must be off his chump! [*He crosses the room to the door, lifting up his voice as he goes.*] Well, this is a pretty sort of asylum for a man to be in, with no one but you to take care of him!

PROSERPINE. [*As he passes her.*] Yes, what a dreadful thing it would be if anything happened to you!

BURGESS. [*Loftily.*] Don't you address no remarks to me. Tell your hemployer that I've gone into the garden for a smoke.

PROSERPINE. [*Mocking.*] Oh!

[*Before* BURGESS *can retort,* MORELL *comes back.*]

BURGESS. [*Sentimentally.*] Goin' for a turn in the garden to smoke, James.

MORELL. [*Brusquely.*] Oh, all right, all right. [BURGESS *goes out pathetically in the character of the weary old man.* MORELL *stands at the table, turning over his papers, and adding, across to* PROSERPINE, *half humorously, half absently.*] Well, Miss Prossy, why have you been calling my father-in-law names?

PROSERPINE. [*Blushing fiery red, and looking quickly up at him, half scared, half reproachful.*] I— [*She bursts into tears.*]

MORELL. [*With tender gaiety, leaning across the table towards her, and consoling her.*] Oh, come, come, come! Never mind, Pross: he is a silly old fathead, isn't he?

[*With an explosive sob, she makes a dash at the door, and vanishes, banging it.* MORELL, *shaking his head resignedly, sighs, and goes wearily to his chair, where he sits down and sets to work, looking old and careworn.* CANDIDA *comes in. She has finished her household work and taken off the apron. She at once notices his dejected appearance, and posts herself quietly at the spare chair, looking down at him attentively; but she says nothing.*]

MORELL. [*Looking up, but with his pen raised ready to resume his work.*] Well? Where is Eugene?

CANDIDA. Washing his hands in the scullery—under the tap. He will make an excellent cook if he can only get over his dread of Maria.

MORELL. [*Shortly.*] Ha! No doubt. [*He begins writing again.*]

CANDIDA. [*Going nearer, and putting her hand down softly on his to stop him, as she says.*] Come here, dear. Let me look at you. [*He drops his pen and yields himself at her disposal. She makes him rise and brings him a little away from the table, looking at him critically all the time.*] Turn your face to the light. [*She places him facing the window.*] My boy is not looking well. Has he been overworking?

MORELL. Nothing more than usual.

CANDIDA. He looks very pale, and grey, and wrinkled, and old. [*His melancholy deepens; and she attacks it with willful gaiety.*] Here [*Pulling him towards the easy chair.*] you've done enough writing for to-day. Leave Prossy to finish it and come and talk to me.

MORELL. But—

CANDIDA. Yes, I must be talked to sometimes. [*She makes him sit down, and seats herself on the carpet beside his knee.*] Now [*Patting his hand.*] you're beginning to look better already. Why don't you give up all this tiresome overworking—going out every night lecturing and talking? Of course what you say is all very true and very right; but it does no good: they don't mind what you say to them one little bit. Of course they agree with you; but what's the use of people agreeing with you if they go and do just the opposite of what you tell them the moment your back is turned? Look at our congregation at St. Dominic's! Why do they come to hear you talking about Christianity every Sunday? Why, just because they've been so full of business and money-making for six days that they want to forget all about it and have a rest on the seventh, so that they can go back fresh and make money harder than ever! You positively help them at it instead of hindering them.

MORELL. [*With energetic seriousness.*] You know very well, Candida, that I often blow them up soundly for that. But if there is nothing in their church-going but rest and diversion, why don't they try something more amusing—more self-indulgent? There must be some good in the fact that they prefer St. Dominic's to worse places on Sundays.

CANDIDA. Oh, the worst places aren't open; and even if they were, they daren't be seen going to them. Besides, James, dear, you preach so splendidly that it's as good as a play for them. Why do you think the women are so enthusiastic?

MORELL. [*Shocked.*] Candida!

CANDIDA. Oh, *I* know. You silly boy: you think it's your Socialism and your religion; but if it was that, they'd do what you tell them instead of only coming to look at you. They all have Prossy's complaint.

MORELL. Prossy's complaint! What do you mean, Candida?

CANDIDA. Yes, Prossy, and all the other secretaries you ever had. Why does Prossy condescend to wash up the things, and to peel potatoes and abase herself in all manner of ways for six shillings a week less than she used to get in a city office? She's in love with you, James: that's the reason. They're all in love with you. And you are in love with preaching because you do it so beautifully. And you think it's all enthusiasm for the kingdom of Heaven on earth; and so do they. You dear silly!

MORELL. Candida: what dreadful, what soul-destroying cynicism! Are you jesting? Or—can it be?—are you jealous?

CANDIDA. [*With curious thoughtfulness.*] Yes, I feel a little jealous sometimes.

MORELL. [*Incredulously.*] What! Of Prossy!

CANDIDA. [*Laughing.*] No, no, no, no. Not jealous of anybody. Jealous for somebody else, who is not loved as he ought to be.

MORELL. Me!

CANDIDA. You! Why, you're spoiled with love and worship: you get far more than is good for you. No: I mean Eugene.

MORELL. [*Startled.*] Eugene!

CANDIDA. It seems unfair that all the love should go to you, and none to him, although he needs it so much more than you do. [*A convulsive movement shakes him in spite of himself.*] What's the matter? Am I worrying you?

MORELL. [*Hastily.*] Not at all. [*Looking at her with troubled intensity.*] You know that I have perfect confidence in you, Candida.

CANDIDA. You vain thing! Are you so sure of your irresistible attractions?

MORELL. Candida: you are shocking me. I never thought of my attractions. I thought of your goodness—your purity. That is what I confide in.

CANDIDA. What a nasty, uncomfortable thing to say to me! Oh, you are a clergyman, James—a thorough clergyman.

MORELL. [*Turning away from her, heart-stricken.*] So Eugene says.

CANDIDA. [*With lively interest, leaning over to him with her arms on his knee.*] Eugene's always right. He's a wonderful boy: I have grown fonder and fonder of him all the time I was away. Do you know, James, that though he has not the least suspicion of it himself, he is ready to fall madly in love with me?

MORELL. [*Grimly.*] Oh, he has no suspicion of it himself, hasn't he?

CANDIDA. Not a bit. [*She takes her arms from his knee, and turns thoughtfully, sinking into a more restful attitude with her hands in her lap.*] Some day he will know—when he is grown up and experienced, like you. And he will know that I must have known. I wonder what he will think of me then.

MORELL. No evil, Candida. I hope and trust, no evil.

CANDIDA. [*Dubiously.*] That will depend.

MORELL. [*Bewildered.*] Depend!

CANDIDA. [*Looking at him.*] Yes: it will depend on what happens to him. [*He looks vacantly at her.*] Don't you see? It will depend on how he comes to learn what love really is. I mean on the sort of woman who will teach it to him.

MORELL. [*Quite at a loss.*] Yes. No. I don't know what you mean.

CANDIDA. [*Explaining.*] If he learns it from a good woman, then it will be all right: he will forgive me.

MORELL. Forgive!

CANDIDA. But suppose he learns it from a bad woman, as so many men do, especially poetic men, who imagine all women are angels! Suppose he only discovers the value of love when he has thrown it away and degraded himself in his ignorance. Will he forgive me then, do you think?

MORELL. Forgive you for what?

CANDIDA. [*Realizing how stupid he is, and a little disappointed, though quite tenderly so.*] Don't you understand? [*He shakes his head. She turns to him again, so as to explain with the fondest intimacy.*] I mean, will he forgive me for not teaching him myself? For abandoning him to the bad women for the sake of my goodness—my purity, as you call it? Ah, James, how little you understand me, to talk of your confidence in my goodness and purity! I would give them both to poor Eugene as willingly as I would give my shawl to a beggar dying of cold, if there were nothing else to restrain me. Put your trust in my love for you, James, for if that went, I should care very little for your sermons—mere phrases that you cheat yourself and others with every day. [*She is about to rise.*]

MORELL. His words!

CANDIDA. [*Checking herself quickly in the act of getting up, so that she is on her knees, but upright.*] Whose words?

MORELL. Eugene's.

CANDIDA. [*Delighted.*] He is always right. He understands you; he understands me; he understands Prossy; and you, James—you understand nothing. [*She laughs, and kisses him to console him. He recoils as if stung, and springs up.*]

MORELL. How can you bear to do that when—oh, Candida [*With anguish in his voice.*] I had rather you had plunged a grappling iron into my heart than given me that kiss.

CANDIDA. [*Rising alarmed.*] My dear: what's the matter?
MORELL. [*Frantically waving her off.*] Don't touch me.
CANDIDA. [*Amazed.*] James!

[*They are interrupted by the entrance of* MARCHBANKS, *with* BURGESS, *who stops near the door, staring, whilst* EUGENE *hurries forward between them.*]

MARCHBANKS. Is anything the matter?
MORELL. [*Deadly white, putting an iron constraint on himself.*] Nothing but this: that either you were right this morning, or Candida is mad.
BURGESS. [*In loudest protest.*] Wot! Candy mad too! Oh, come, come come! [*He crosses the room to the fireplace, protesting as he goes, and knocks the ashes out of his pipe on the bars.* MORELL *sits down desperately, leaning forward to hide his face, and interlacing his fingers rigidly to keep them steady.*]
CANDIDA. [*To* MORELL, *relieved and laughing.*] Oh, you're only shocked! Is that all? How conventional all you unconventional people are!
BURGESS. Come: be'ave yourself, Candy. What'll Mr. Morchbanks think of you?
CANDIDA. This comes of James teaching me to think for myself, and never to hold back out of fear of what other people may think of me. It works beautifully as long as I think the same things as he does. But now, because I have just thought something different—look at him—just look! [*She points to* MORELL, *greatly amused.* EUGENE *looks, and instantly presses his hand on his heart, as if some deadly pain had shot through it, and sits down on the sofa like a man witnessing a tragedy.*]
BURGESS. [*On the hearth-rug.*] Well, James, you certainly ain't as himpressive lookin' as usu'l.
MORELL. [*With a laugh which is half a sob.*] I suppose not. I beg all your pardons: I was not conscious of making a fuss. [*Pulling himself together.*] Well, well, well, well, well! [*He goes back to his place at the table, setting to work at his papers again with resolute cheerfulness.*]
CANDIDA. [*Going to the sofa and sitting beside* MARCHBANKS, *still in a bantering humor.*] Well, Eugene, why are you so sad? Did the onions make you cry?

[MORELL *cannot prevent himself from watching them.*]

MARCHBANKS. [*Aside to her.*] It is your cruelty. I hate cruelty. It is a horrible thing to see one person make another suffer.

CANDIDA. [*Petting him ironically.*] Poor boy, have I been cruel? Did I make it slice nasty little red onions?

MARCHBANKS. [*Earnestly.*] Oh, stop, stop: I don't mean myself. You have made him suffer frightfully. I feel his pain in my own heart. I know that it is not your fault—it is something that must happen; but don't make light of it. I shudder when you torture him and laugh.

CANDIDA. [*Incredulously.*] I torture James! Nonsense, Eugene: how you exaggerate! Silly! [*She looks round at* MORELL, *who hastily resumes his writing. She goes to him and stands behind his chair, bending over him.*] Don't work any more, dear. Come and talk to us.

MORELL. [*Affectionately but bitterly.*] Ah no: I can't talk. I can only preach.

CANDIDA. [*Caressing him.*] Well, come and preach.

BURGESS. [*Strongly remonstrating.*] Aw, no, Candy, 'Ang it all!

[LEXY MILL *comes in, looking anxious and important.*]

LEXY. [*Hastening to shake hands with* CANDIDA.] How do you do, Mrs. Morell? So glad to see you back again.

CANDIDA. Thank you, Lexy. You know Eugene, don't you?

LEXY. Oh, yes. How do you do, Marchbanks?

MARCHBANKS. Quite well, thanks.

LEXY. [*To* MORELL.] I've just come from the Guild of St. Matthew. They are in the greatest consternation about your telegram. There's nothing wrong, is there?

CANDIDA. What did you telegraph about, James?

LEXY. [*To* CANDIDA.] He was to have spoken for them tonight. They've taken the large hall in Mare Street and spent a lot of money on posters. Morell's telegram was to say he couldn't come. It came on them like a thunderbolt.

CANDIDA. [*Surprized, and beginning to suspect something wrong.*] Given up an engagement to speak!

BURGESS. First time in his life, I'll bet. Ain't it, Candy?

LEXY. [*To* MORELL.] They decided to send an urgent telegram to you asking whether you could not change your mind. Have you received it?

MORELL. [*With restrained impatience.*] Yes, yes: I got it.

Candida

LEXY. It was reply paid.

MORELL. Yes, I know. I answered it. I can't go.

CANDIDA. But why, James?

MORELL. [*Almost fiercely.*] Because I don't choose. These people forget that I am a man: they think I am a talking machine to be turned on for their pleasure every evening of my life. May I not have one night at home, with my wife, and my friends?

[*They are all amazed at this outburst, except* EUGENE. *His expression remains unchanged.*]

CANDIDA. Oh, James, you know you'll have an attack of bad conscience to-morrow; and *I* shall have to suffer for that.

LEXY. [*Intimidated, but urgent.*] I know, of course, that they make the most unreasonable demands on you. But they have been telegraphing all over the place for another speaker: and they can get nobody but the President of the Agnostic League.

MORELL. [*Promptly.*] Well, an excellent man. What better do they want?

LEXY. But he always insists so powerfully on the divorce of Socialism from Christianity. He will undo all the good we have been doing. Of course you know best; but—[*He hesitates.*]

CANDIDA. [*Coaxingly.*] Oh, do go, James. We'll all go.

BURGESS. [*Grumbling.*] Look 'ere, Candy! I say! Let's stay at home by the fire, comfortable. He won't need to be more'n a couple-o'-hour away.

CANDIDA. You'll be just as comfortable at the meeting. We'll all sit on the platform and be great people.

MARCHBANKS. [*Terrified.*] Oh, please don't let us go on the platform. No—everyone will stare at us—I couldn't. I'll sit at the back of the room.

CANDIDA. Don't be afraid. They'll be too busy looking at James to notice you.

MORELL. [*Turning his head and looking meaningly at her over his shoulder.*] Prossy's complaint, Candida! Eh?

CANDIDA. [*Gaily.*] Yes.

BURGESS. [*Mystified.*] Prossy's complaint. Wot are you talking about, James?

MORELL. [*Not heeding him, rises; goes to the door; and holds it open, shouting in a commanding voice.*] Miss Garnett.

PROSERPINE. [*In the distance.*] Yes, Mr. Morell. Coming.

[*They all wait, except* BURGESS, *who goes stealthily to* LEXY *and draws him aside.*]

BURGESS. Listen here, Mr. Mill. Wot's Prossy's complaint? Wot's wrong with 'er?

LEXY. [*Confidentially.*] Well, I don't exactly know; but she spoke very strangely to me this morning. I'm afraid she's a little out of her mind sometimes.

BURGESS. [*Overwhelmed.*] Why, it must be catchin'! Four in the same 'ouse! [*He goes back to the hearth, quite lost before the instability of the human intellect in a clergyman's house.*]

PROSERPINE. [*Appearing on the threshold.*] What is it, Mr. Morell?

MORELL. Telegraph to the Guild of St. Matthew that I am coming.

PROSERPINE. [*Surprised.*] Don't they expect you?

MORELL. [*Peremptorily.*] Do as I tell you.

[PROSERPINE, *frightened, sits down at her typewriter, and obeys.* MORELL *goes across to* BURGESS, CANDIDA *watching his movements all the time with growing wonder and misgiving.*]

MORELL. Burgess: you don't want to come?

BURGESS. [*In deprecation.*] Oh, don't put it like that, James. It's only that it ain't Sunday, you know.

MORELL. I'm sorry. I thought you might like to be introduced to the chairman. He's on the Works Committee of the County Council and has some influence in the matter of contracts. [BURGESS *wakes up at once.* MORELL, *expecting as much, waits a moment, and says.*] Will you come?

BURGESS. [*With enthusiasm.*] Course I'll come, James. Ain't it always a pleasure to 'ear you?

MORELL. [*Turning from him.*] I shall want you to take some notes at the meeting, Miss Garnett, if you have no other engagement. [*She nods, afraid to speak.*] You are coming, Lexy, I suppose.

LEXY. Certainly.

CANDIDA. We are all coming, James.

MORELL. No: you are not coming; and Eugene is not coming. You will stay here and entertain him—to celebrate your return home. [EUGENE *rises, breathless.*]

Candida    259

CANDIDA. But, James—

MORELL. [*Authoritatively.*] I insist. You do not want to come; and he does not want to come. [CANDIDA *is about to protest.*] Oh, don't concern yourselves: I shall have plenty of people without you: your chairs will be wanted by unconverted people who have never heard me before.

CANDIDA. [*Troubled.*] Eugene: wouldn't you like to come?

MORELL. I should be afraid to let myself go before Eugene: he is so critical of sermons. [*Looking at him.*] He knows I am afraid of him: he told me as much this morning. Well, I shall shew[4] him how much afraid I am by leaving him here in your custody, Candida.

MARCHBANKS. [*To himself, with vivid feeling.*] That's brave. That's beautiful. [*He sits down again listening with parted lips.*]

CANDIDA. [*With anxious misgiving.*] But—but—Is anything the matter, James? [*Greatly troubled.*] I can't understand—

MORELL. Ah, I thought it was *I* who couldn't understand, dear.

[*He takes her tenderly in his arms and kisses her on the forehead; then looks round quietly at* MARCHBANKS.]

# ACT III

Late in the evening. Past ten. The curtains are drawn, and the lamps lighted. The typewriter is in its case; the large table has been cleared and tidied; everything indicates that the day's work is done.

CANDIDA and MARCHBANKS are seated at the fire. The reading lamp is on the mantelshelf above MARCHBANKS, who is sitting on the small chair reading aloud from a manuscript. A little pile of manuscripts and a couple of volumes of poetry are on the carpet beside him. CANDIDA is in the easy chair with the poker, a light brass one, upright in her hand. She is leaning back and looking at the point of it curiously, with her feet stretched towards the blaze and her heels resting on the fender, profoundly unconscious of her appearance and surroundings.

MARCHBANKS. [*Breaking off in his recitation.*] Every poet that ever lived has put that thought into a sonnet. He must: he can't help it. [*He*

---

4. *shew:* show.

*looks to her for assent, and notices her absorption in the poker.*] Haven't you been listening? [*No response.*] Mrs. Morell!

CANDIDA. [*Starting.*] Eh?

MARCHBANKS. Haven't you been listening?

CANDIDA. [*With a guilty excess of politeness.*] Oh, yes. It's very nice. Go on, Eugene. I'm longing to hear what happens to the angel.

MARCHBANKS. [*Crushed—the manuscript dropping from his hand to the floor.*] I beg your pardon for boring you.

CANDIDA. But you are not boring me, I assure you. Please go on. Do, Eugene.

MARCHBANKS. I finished the poem about the angel quarter of an hour ago. I've read you several things since.

CANDIDA. [*Remorsefully.*] I'm so sorry, Eugene. I think the poker must have fascinated me. [*She puts it down.*]

MARCHBANKS. I finished the poem about the angel quarter of an hour ago. I've read you several things since.

CANDIDA. [*Remorsefully.*] I'm so sorry, Eugene. I think the poker must have fascinated me. [*She puts it down.*]

MARCHBANKS. It made me horribly uneasy.

CANDIDA. Why didn't you tell me? I'd have put it down at once.

MARCHBANKS. I was afraid of making you uneasy, too. It looked as if it were a weapon. If I were a hero of old, I should have laid my drawn sword between us. If Morell had come in he would have thought you had taken up the poker because there was no sword between us.

CANDIDA. [*Wondering.*] What? [*With a puzzled glance at him.*] I can't quite follow that. Those sonnets of yours have perfectly addled me. Why should there be a sword between us?

MARCHBANKS. [*Evasively.*] Oh, never mind. [*He stoops to pick up the manuscript.*]

CANDIDA. Put that down again, Eugene. There are limits to my appetite for poetry—even your poetry. You've been reading to me for more than two hours—ever since James went out. I want to talk.

MARCHBANKS. [*Rising, scared.*] No: I mustn't talk. [*He looks round him in his lost way, and adds, suddenly.*] I think I'll go out and take a walk in the park. [*Making for the door.*]

CANDIDA. Nonsense: it's shut long ago. Come and sit down on the hearth-rug, and talk moonshine as you usually do. I want to be amused. Don't you want to?

MARCHBANKS. [*In half terror, half rapture.*] Yes.

CANDIDA. Then come along. [*She moves her chair back a little to make room. He hesitates; then timidly stretches himself on the hearth-rug, face upwards, and throws back his head across her knees, looking up at her.*]

MARCHBANKS. Oh, I've been so miserable all the evening, because I was doing right. Now I'm doing wrong; and I'm happy.

CANDIDA. [*Tenderly amused at him.*] Yes: I'm sure you feel a great grown up wicked deceiver—quite proud of yourself, aren't you?

MARCHBANKS. [*Raising his head quickly and turning a little to look round at her.*] Take care. I'm ever so much older than you, if you only knew. [*He turns quite over on his knees, with his hands clasped and his arms on her lap, and speaks with growing impulse, his blood beginning to stir.*] May I say some wicked things to you?

CANDIDA. [*Without the least fear of coldness, quite nobly, and with perfect respect for his passion, but with a touch of her wise-hearted maternal humor.*] No. But you may say anything you really and truly feel. Anything at all, no matter what it is. I am not afraid, so long as it is your real self that speaks, and not a mere attitude—a gallant attitude, or a wicked attitude, or even a poetic attitude. I put you on your honor and truth. Now say whatever you want to.

MARCHBANKS. [*The eager expression vanishing utterly from his lips and nostrils as his eyes light up with pathetic spirituality.*] Oh, now I can't say anything: all the words I know belong to some attitude or other—all except one.

CANDIDA. What one is that?

MARCHBANKS. [*Softly, losing himself in the music of the name.*] Candida, Candida, Candida, Candida, Candida. I must say that now, because you have put me on my honor and truth; and I never think or feel Mrs. Morell: it is always Candida.

CANDIDA. Of course. And what have you to say to Candida?

MARCHBANKS. Nothing, but to repeat your name a thousand times. Don't you feel that every time is a prayer to you?.

CANDIDA. Doesn't it make you happy to be able to pray?

MARCHBANKS. Yes, very happy.

CANDIDA. Well, that happiness is the answer to your prayer. Do you want anything more?

MARCHBANKS. [*In beatitude.*] No: I have come into heaven, where want is unknown.

[MORELL *comes in. He halts on the threshold, and takes in the scene at a glance.*]

MORELL. [*Grave and self-contained.*] I hope I don't disturb you.

[CANDIDA *starts up violently, but without the smallest embarrassment, laughing at herself.* EUGENE, *still kneeling, saves himself from falling by putting his hands on the seat of the chair, and remains there, staring open mouthed at* MORELL.]

CANDIDA. [*As she rises.*] Oh, James, how you startled me! I was so taken up with Eugene that I didn't hear your latchkey. How did the meeting go off? Did you speak well?

MORELL. I have never spoken better in my life.

CANDIDA. That was first rate? How much was the collection?

MORELL. I forgot to ask.

CANDIDA. [*To* EUGENE.] He must have spoken splendidly, or he would never have forgotten that. [*To* MORELL.] Where are all the others?

MORELL. They left long before I could get away: I thought I should never escape. I believe they are having supper somewhere.

CANDIDA. [*In her domestic business tone.*] Oh; in that case, Maria may go to bed. I'll tell her. [*She goes out to the kitchen.*]

MORELL. [*Looking sternly down at* MARCHBANKS.] Well?

MARCHBANKS. [*Squatting cross-legged on the hearth-rug, and actually at ease with* MORELL—*even impishly humorous.*] Well?

MORELL. Have you anything to tell me?

MARCHBANKS. Only that I have been making a fool of myself here in private whilst you have been making a fool of yourself in public.

MORELL. Hardly in the same way, I think.

MARCHBANKS. [*Scrambling up—eagerly.*] The very, very, very same way. I have been playing the good man just like you. When you began your heroics about leaving me here with Candida—

MORELL. [*Involuntarily.*] Candida?

MARCHBANKS. Oh, yes: I've got that far. Heroics are infectious: I caught the disease from you. I swore not to say a word in your absence that I would not have said a month ago in your presence.

MORELL. Did you keep your oath?

MARCHBANKS. [*Suddenly perching himself grotesquely on the easy chair.*] I was ass enough to keep it until about ten minutes ago. Up to that moment I went on desperately reading to her—reading my own poems—anybody's poems—to stave off a conversation. It was standing outside the gate of Heaven, and refusing to go in. Oh, you can't think how heroic it was, and how uncomfortable! Then—

MORELL. [*Steadily controlling his suspense.*] Then?—

MARCHBANKS. [*Prosaically slipping down into a quite ordinary attitude in the chair.*] Then she couldn't bear being read to any longer.

MORELL. And you approached the gate of Heaven at last?

MARCHBANKS. Yes.

MORELL. Well? [*Fiercely.*] Speak, man: have you no feeling for me?

MARCHBANKS. [*Softly and musically.*] Then she became an angel; and there was a flaming sword that turned every way, so that I couldn't go in; for I saw that that gate was really the gate of Hell.

MORELL. [*Triumphantly.*] She repulsed you!

MARCHBANKS. [*Rising in wild scorn.*] No, you fool: if she had done that I should never have seen that I was in Heaven already. Repulsed me! You think that would have saved me—virtuous indignation! Oh, you are not worthy to live in the same world with her. [*He turns away contemptuously to the other side of the room.*]

MORELL. [*Who has watched him quietly without changing his place.*] Do you think you make yourself more worthy by reviling me, Eugene?

MARCHBANKS. Here endeth the thousand and first lesson. Morell: I don't think much of your preaching after all: I believe I could do it better myself. The man I want to meet is the man that Candida married.

MORELL. The man that—? Do you mean me?

MARCHBANKS. I don't mean the Reverend James Mavor Morell, moralist and windbag. I mean the real man that the Reverend James must have hidden somewhere inside his black coat—the man that Candida loved. You can't make a woman like Candida love you by merely buttoning your collar at the back instead of in front.

MORELL. [*Boldly and steadily.*] When Candida promised to marry me, I was the same moralist and windbag that you now see. I wore my black coat; and my collar was buttoned behind instead of in front. Do you think she would have loved me any better for being insincere in my profession?

MARCHBANKS. [*On the sofa hugging his ankles.*] Oh, she forgave you, just as she forgives me for being a coward, and a weakling, and what you call a snivelling little whelp and all the rest of it. [*Dreamily.*] A woman like that has divine insight: she loves our souls, and not our follies and vanities and illusions, or our collars and coats, or any other of the rags and tatters we are rolled up in. [*He reflects on this for an instant; then turns intently to question* MORELL.] What I want to know is how you got past the flaming sword that stopped me.

MORELL. [*Meaningly.*] Perhaps because I was not interrupted at the end of ten minutes.

MARCHBANKS. [*Taken aback.*] What!

MORELL. Man can climb to the highest summits; but he cannot dwell there long.

MARCHBANKS. It's false: there can he dwell for ever and there only. It's in the other moments that he can find no rest, no sense of the silent glory of life. Where would you have me spend my moments, if not on the summits?

MORELL. In the scullery, slicing onions and filling lamps.

MARCHBANKS. Or in the pulpit, scrubbing cheap earthenware souls?

MORELL. Yes, that, too. It was there that I earned my golden moment, and the right, in that moment, to ask her to love me. *I* did not take the moment on credit; nor did I use it to steal another man's happiness.

MARCHBANKS. [*Rather disgustedly, trotting back towards the fireplace.*] I have no doubt you conducted the transaction as honestly as if you were buying a pound of cheese. [*He stops on the brink of the hearthrug and adds, thoughtfully, to himself, with his back turned to* MORELL.] *I* could only go to her as a beggar.

MORELL. [*Starting.*] A beggar dying of cold—asking for her shawl?

MARCHBANKS. [*Turning, surprised.*] Thank you for touching up my poetry. Yes, if you like, a beggar dying of cold asking for her shawl.

MORELL. [*Excitedly.*] And she refused. Shall I tell you why she refused? I can tell you, on her own authority. It was because of—

MARCHBANKS. She didn't refuse.

MORELL. Not!

MARCHBANKS. She offered me all I chose to ask for, her shawl, her wings, the wreath of stars on her head, the lilies in her hand, the crescent moon beneath her feet—

MORELL. [*Seizing him.*] Out with the truth, man: my wife is my wife: I want no more of your poetic fripperies. I know well that if I have lost her love and you have gained it, no law will bind her.

MARCHBANKS. [*Quaintly, without fear or resistance.*] Catch me by the

Candida     265

shirt collar, Morrell: she will arrange it for me afterwards as she did this morning. [*With quiet rapture.*] I shall feel her hands touch me.

MORELL. You young imp, do you know how dangerous it is to say that to me? Or [*With a sudden misgiving.*] has something made you brave?

MARCHBANKS. I'm not afraid now. I disliked you before: that was why I shrank from your touch. But I saw to-day—when she tortured you—that you love her. Since then I have been your friend: you may strangle me if you like.

MORELL. [*Releasing him.*] Eugene: if that is not a heartless lie—if you have a spark of human feeling left in you—will you tell me what has happened during my absence?

MARCHBANKS. What happened! Why, the flaming sword—[MORELL *stamps with impatience.*] Well, in plain prose, I loved her so exquisitely that I wanted nothing more than the happiness of being in such love. And before I had time to come down from the highest summits, you came in.

MORELL. [*Suffering deeply.*] So it is still unsettled—still the misery of doubt.

MARCHBANKS. Misery! I am the happiest of men. I desire nothing now but her happiness. [*With dreamy enthusiasm.*] Oh, Morell, let us both give her up. Why should she have to choose between a wretched little nervous disease like me, and a pig-headed parson like you? Let us go on a pilgrimage, you to the east and I to the west, in search of a worthy lover for her—some beautiful archangel with purple wings—

MORELL. Some fiddlestick. Oh, if she is mad enough to leave me for you, who will protect her? Who will help her? who will work for her? who will be a father to her children? [*He sits down distractedly on the sofa, with his elbows on his knees and his head propped on his clenched fists.*]

MARCHBANKS. [*Snapping his fingers wildly.*] She does not ask those silly questions. It is she who wants somebody to protect, to help, to work for—somebody to give her children to protect, to help and to work for. Some grown up man who has become as a little child again. Oh, you fool, you fool, you triple fool! I am the man, Morell: I am the man. [*He dances about excitedly, crying.*] You don't understand what a woman is. Send for her, Morell: send for her and let her choose between— [*The door opens and* CANDIDA *enters. He stops as if petrified.*]

CANDIDA. [*Amazed, on the threshold.*] What on earth are you at, Eugene?

MARCHBANKS. [*Oddly.*] James and I are having a preaching match; and he is getting the worst of it.

[CANDIDA *looks quickly round at* MORELL. *Seeing that he is distressed, she hurries down to him, greatly vexed, speaking with vigorous reproach to* MARCHBANKS.]

CANDIDA. You have been annoying him. Now I won't have it, Eugene: do you hear? [*Putting her hand on* MORELL'S *shoulder, and quite forgetting her wifely tact in her annoyance.*] My boy shall not be worried: I will protect him.

MORELL. [*Rising proudly.*] Protect!

CANDIDA. [*Not heeding him—to* EUGENE.] What have you been saying?

MARCHBANKS. [*Appalled.*] Nothing—I—

CANDIDA. Eugene! Nothing?

MARCHBANKS. [*Piteously.*] I mean—I—I'm very sorry. I won't do it again: indeed I won't. I'll let him alone.

MORELL. [*Indignantly, with an aggressive movement towards* EUGENE.] Let me alone! You young—

CANDIDA. [*Stopping him.*] Sh—no, let me deal with him, James.

MARCHBANKS. Oh, you're not angry with me, are you?

CANDIDA. [*Severely.*] Yes, I am—very angry. I have a great mind to pack you out of the house.

MORELL. [*Taken aback by* CANDIDA'S *vigor, and by no means relishing the sense of being rescued by her from another man.*] Gently, Candida, gently. I am able to take care of myself.

CANDIDA. [*Petting him.*] Yes, dear: of course you are. But you mustn't be annoyed and made miserable.

MARCHBANKS. [*Almost in tears, turning to the door.*] I'll go.

CANDIDA. Oh, you needn't go: I can't turn you out at this time of night. [*Vehemently.*] Shame on you! For shame!

MARCHBANKS. [*Desperately.*] But what have I done?

CANDIDA. I know what you have done—as well as if I had been here all the time. Oh, it was unworthy! You are like a child: you cannot hold your tongue.

MARCHBANKS. I would die ten times over sooner than give you a moment's pain.

CANDIDA. [*With infinite contempt for this puerility.*] Much good your dying would do me!

MORELL. Candida, my dear: this altercation is hardly quite seemly. It is a matter between two men; and I am the right person to settle it.

CANDIDA. Two men! Do you call that a man? [*To* EUGENE.] You bad boy!

MARCHBANKS. [*Gathering a whimsically affectionate courage from the scolding.*] If I am to be scolded like this, I must make a boy's excuse. He began it. And he's bigger than I am.

CANDIDA. [*Losing confidence a little as her concern for* MORELL'S *dignity takes the alarm.*] That can't be true. [*To* MORELL.] You didn't begin it, James, did you?

MORELL. [*Contemptuously.*] No.

MARCHBANKS. [*Indignant.*] Oh!

MORELL. [*To* EUGENE.] You began it—this morning. [CANDIDA, *instantly connecting this with his mysterious allusion in the afternoon to something told him by* EUGENE *in the morning, looks quickly at him, wrestling with the enigma.* MORELL *proceeds with the emphasis of offended superiority.*] But your other point is true. I am certainly the bigger of the two, and, I hope, the stronger, Candida. So you had better leave the matter in my hands.

CANDIDA. [*Again soothing him.*] Yes, dear; but—[*Troubled.*] I don't understand about this morning.

MORELL. [*Gently snubbing her.*] You need not understand, my dear.

CANDIDA. But, James, I— [*The street bell rings.*] Oh, bother! Here they all come. [*She goes out to let them in.*]

MARCHBANKS. [*Running to* MORELL.] Oh, Morell, isn't it dreadful? She's angry with us: she hates me. What shall I do?

MORELL. [*With quaint desperation, clutching himself by the hair.*] Eugene: my head is spinning round. I shall begin to laugh presently. [*He walks up and down the middle of the room.*]

MARCHBANKS. [*Following him anxiously.*] No, no: she'll think I've thrown you into hysterics. Don't laugh.

[*Boisterous voices and laughter are heard approaching.* LEXY MILL, *his eyes sparkling, and his bearing denoting unwonted elevation of spirit, enters with* BURGESS, *who is greasy and self-complacent, but has his wits about him.* MISS GARNETT, *with her smartest hat and jacket on, follows them; but though her eyes are brighter than before, she is evidently a prey to misgiving. She places herself with her back to her typewriting table, with one hand on it to rest herself, passes the other across her fore-*

*head as if she were a little tired and giddy.* MARCHBANKS *relapses into shyness and edges away into the corner near the window, where* MORELL'S *books are.*]

LEXY. [*Exhilaratedly.*] Morell: I must congratulate you. [*Grasping his hand.*] What a noble, splendid, inspired address you gave us! You surpassed yourself.

BURGESS. So you did, James. It fair kep' me awake to the last word. Didn't it, Miss Gornett?

PROSERPINE. [*Worriedly.*] Oh, I wasn't minding you: I was trying to make notes. [*She takes out her notebook, and looks at her stenography, which nearly makes her cry.*]

MORELL. Did I go too fast, Pross?

PROSERPINE. Much too fast. You know I can't do more than a hundred words a minute. [*She relieves her feelings by throwing her notebook angrily beside her machine, ready for use next morning.*]

MORELL. [*Soothingly.*] Oh, well, well, never mind, never mind, never mind. Have you all had supper?

LEXY. Mr. Burgess has been kind enough to give us a really splendid supper at the Belgrave.

BURGESS. [*With effusive magnanimity.*] Don't mention it, Mr. Mill. [*Modestly.*] You're 'arty welcome to my little treat.

PROSERPINE. We had champagne! I never tasted it before. I feel quite giddy.

MORELL. [*Surprised.*] A champagne supper! That was very handsome. Was it my eloquence that produced all this extravagance?

LEXY. [*Rhetorically.*] Your eloquence, and Mr. Burgess's goodness of heart. [*With a fresh burst of exhilaration.*] And what a very fine fellow the chairman is, Morell! He came to supper with us.

MORELL. [*With long drawn significance, looking at* BURGESS.] O-o-o-h, the chairman. Now I understand.

[BURGESS, *covering a lively satisfaction in his diplomatic cunning with a deprecatory cough, retires to the hearth.* LEXY *folds his arms and leans against the cellaret in a high-spirited attitude.* CANDIDA *comes in with glasses, lemons, and a jug of hot water on a tray.*]

CANDIDA. Who will have some lemonade? You know our rules: total abstinence. [*She puts the tray on the table, and takes up the lemon squeezers, looking enquiringly round at them.*]

MORELL. No use, dear. They've all had champagne. Pross has broken her pledge.

CANDIDA. [*To* PROSERPINE.] You don't mean to say you've been drinking champagne!

PROSERPINE. [*Stubbornly.*] Yes, I do. I'm only a beer teetotaller, not a champagne teetotaller. I don't like beer. Are there any letters for me to answer, Mr. Morell?

MORELL. No more to-night.

PROSERPINE. Very well. Good-night, everybody.

LEXY. [*Gallantly.*] Had I not better see you home, Miss Garnett?

PROSERPINE. No, thank you. I shan't trust myself with anybody to-night. I wish I hadn't taken any of that stuff. [*She walks straight out.*]

BURGESS. [*Indignantly.*] Stuff, indeed! That girl dunno wot champagne is! Pommery and Greeno at twelve and six a bottle. She took two glasses a'most straight hoff.

MORELL. [*A little anxious about her.*] Go and look after her, Lexy.

LEXY [*Alarmed.*] But if she should really be— Suppose she began to sing in the street, or anything of that sort.

MORELL. Just so: she may. That's why you'd better see her safely home.

CANDIDA. Do, Lexy: there's a good fellow. [*She shakes his hand and pushes him gently to the door.*]

LEXY. It's evidently my duty to go. I hope it may not be necessary. Good-night, Mrs. Morell. [*To the rest.*] Good-night. [*He goes.* CANDIDA *shuts the door.*]

BURGESS. He was gushin' with hextra piety hisself arter two sips. People can't drink like they huseter. [*Dismissing the subject and bustling away from the hearth.*] Well, James: it's time to lock up. Mr. Morchbanks: shall I 'ave the pleasure of your company for a bit of the way home?

MARCHBANKS. [*Affrightedly.*] Yes: I'd better go. [*He hurries across to the door; but* CANDIDA *places herself before it, barring his way.*]

CANDIDA. [*With quiet authority.*] You sit down. You're not going yet.

MARCHBANKS. [*Quailing.*] No: I—I didn't mean to. [*He comes back into the room and sits down abjectly on the sofa.*]

CANDIDA. Mr. Marchbanks will stay the night with us, papa.

BURGESS. Oh, well, I'll say good-night. So long, James. [*He shakes hands with* MORELL *and goes on to* EUGENE.] Make 'em give you a night light by your bed, Mr. Morchbanks: it'll comfort you if you wake up in the night with a touch of that complaint of yores. Good-night.

MARCHBANKS. Thank you: I will. Good-night, Mr. Burgess. [*They shake hands and* BURGESS *goes to the door.*]

CANDIDA. [*Intercepting* MORELL, *who is following* BURGESS.] Stay here, dear: I'll put on papa's coat for him. [*She goes out with* BURGESS.]

MARCHBANKS. Morell: there's going to be a terrible scene. Aren't you afraid?

MORELL. Not in the least.

MARCHBANKS. I never envied you your courage before. [*He rises timidly and puts his hand appealingly on* MORELL's *forearm.*] Stand by me, won't you?

MORELL. [*Casting him off gently, but resolutely.*] Each for himself, Eugene. She must choose between us now. [*He goes to the other side of the room as* CANDIDA *returns.* EUGENE *sits down again on the sofa like a guilty schoolboy on his best behavior.*]

CANDIDA. [*Between them, addressing* EUGENE.] Are you sorry?

MARCHBANKS. [*Earnestly.*] Yes, heartbroken.

CANDIDA. Well, then, you are forgiven. Now go off to bed like a good little boy: I want to talk to James about you.

MARCHBANKS. [*Rising in great consternation.*] Oh, I can't do that, Morell. I must be here. I'll not go away. Tell her.

CANDIDA. [*With quick suspicion.*] Tell me what? [*His eyes avoid hers furtively. She turns and mutely transfers the question to* MORELL.]

MORELL. [*Bracing himself for the catastrophe.*] I have nothing to tell her, except [*Here his voice deepens to a measured and mournful tenderness.*] that she is my greatest treasure on earth—if she is really mine.

CANDIDA. [*Coldly, offended by his yielding to his orator's instinct and treating her as if she were the audience at the Guild of St. Matthew.*] I am sure Eugene can say no less, if that is all.

MARCHBANKS. [*Discouraged.*] Morell: she's laughing at us.

MORELL. [*With a quick touch of temper.*] There is nothing to laugh at. Are you laughing at us, Candida?

CANDIDA. [*With quiet anger.*] Eugene is very quick-witted, James. I hope I am going to laugh; but I am not sure that I am not going to be very angry. [*She goes to the fireplace, and stands there leaning with her arm on the mantelpiece, and her foot on the fender, whilst* EUGENE *steals to* MORELL *and plucks him by the sleeve.*]

MARCHBANKS. [*Whispering.*] Stop, Morell. Don't let us say anything.

MORELL. [*Pushing* EUGENE *away without deigning to look at him.*] I hope you don't mean that as a threat, Candida.

CANDIDA. [*With emphatic warning.*] Take care, James. Eugene: I asked you to go. Are you going?

MORELL. [*Putting his foot down.*] He shall not go. I wish him to remain.

MARCHBANKS. I'll go. I'll do whatever you want. [*He turns to the door.*]

CANDIDA. Stop! [*He obeys.*] Didn't you hear James say he wished you to stay? James is master here. Don't you know that?

MARCHBANKS. [*Flushing with a young poet's rage against tyranny.*] By what right is he master?

CANDIDA. [*Quietly.*] Tell him, James.

MORELL. [*Taken aback.*] My dear: I don't know of any right that makes me master. I assert no such right.

CANDIDA. [*With infinite reproach.*] You don't know! Oh, James, James! [*To* EUGENE, *musingly.*] I wonder do you understand, Eugene! No: you're too young. Well, I give you leave to stay—to stay and learn. [*She comes away from the hearth and places herself between them.*] Now, James: what's the matter? Come: tell me.

MARCHBANKS. [*Whispering tremulously across to him.*] Don't.

CANDIDA. Come. Out with it!

MORELL. [*Slowly.*] I meant to prepare your mind carefully Candida, so as to prevent misunderstanding.

CANDIDA. Yes, dear: I am sure you did. But never mind: I shan't misunderstand.

MORELL. Well—er—[*He hesitates, unable to find the long explanation which he supposed to be available.*]

CANDIDA. Well?

MORELL. [*Badly.*] Eugene declares that you are in love with him.

MARCHBANKS. [*Frantically.*] No, no, no, no, never. I did not, Mrs. Morell: it's not true. I said I loved you, and that he didn't. I said that I understood you, and that he couldn't. And it was not after what passed there before the fire that I spoke: it was not, on my word. It was this morning.

CANDIDA. [*Enlightened.*] This morning!

MARCHBANKS. Yes. [*He looks at her, pleading for credence, and then adds, simply.*] That was what was the matter with my collar.

CANDIDA. [*After a pause; for she does not take in his meaning at once.*]

His collar! [*She turns to* MORELL, *shocked.*] Oh, James: did you—? [*She stops.*]

MORELL. [*Ashamed.*] You know, Candida, that I have a temper to struggle with. And he said [*Shuddering.*] that you despised me in your heart.

CANDIDA. [*Turning quickly on* EUGENE.] Did you say that?

MARCHBANKS. [*Terrified.*] No!

CANDIDA. [*Severely.*] Then James has just told me a falsehood. Is that what you mean?

MARCHBANKS. No, no: I—I—[*Blurting out the explanation desperately.*]—it was David's wife. And it wasn't at home: it was when she saw him dancing before all the people.

MORELL. [*Taking the cue with a debater's adroitness.*] Dancing before all the people, Candida; and thinking he was moving their hearts by his mission when they were only suffering from—Prossy's complaint. [*She is about to protest: he raises his hand to silence her, exclaiming.*] Don't try to look indignant, Candida:—

CANDIDA. [*Interjecting.*] Try!

MORELL. [*Continuing.*] Eugene was right. As you told me a few hours after, he is always right. He said nothing that you did not say far better yourself. He is the poet, who sees everything; and I am the poor parson, who understands nothing.

CANDIDA. [*Remorsefully.*] Do you mind what is said by a foolish boy, because I said something like it again in jest?

MORELL. That foolish boy can speak with the inspiration of a child and the cunning of a serpent. He has claimed that you belong to him and not to me; and, rightly or wrongly, I have come to fear that it may be true. I will not go about tortured with doubts and suspicions. I will not live with you and keep a secret from you. I will not suffer the intolerable degradation of jealousy. We have agreed—he and I—that you shall choose between us now. I await your decision.

CANDIDA. [*Slowly recoiling a step, her heart hardened by his rhetoric in spite of the sincere feeling behind it.*] Oh! I am to choose, am I? I suppose it is quite settled that I must belong to one or the other.

MORELL. [*Firmly.*] Quite. You must choose definitely.

MARCHBANKS. [*Anxiously.*] Morell: you don't understand. She means that she belongs to herself.

CANDIDA. [*Turning on him.*] I mean that and a good deal more, Master Eugene, as you will both find out presently. And pray, my lords and masters, what have you to offer for my choice? I am up for auction, it seems. What do you bid, James?

MORELL. [*Reproachfully*] Cand— [*He breaks down: his eyes and throat fill with tears: the orator becomes the wounded animal.*] I can't speak—

CANDIDA. [*Impulsively going to him.*] Ah, dearest—

MARCHBANKS. [*In wild alarm.*] Stop: it's not fair. You mustn't show her that you suffer, Morell. I am on the rack, too; but I am not crying.

MORELL. [*Rallying all his forces.*] Yes: you are right. It is not for pity that I am bidding. [*He disengages himself from* CANDIDA.]

CANDIDA. [*Retreating, chilled.*] I beg your pardon, James; I did not mean to touch you. I am waiting to hear your bid.

MORELL. [*With proud humility.*] I have nothing to offer you but my strength for your defence, my honesty of purpose for your surety, my ability and industry for your livelihood, and my authority and position for your dignity. That is all it becomes a man to offer to a woman.

CANDIDA. [*Quite quietly.*] And you, Eugene? What do you offer?

MARCHBANKS. My weakness! my desolation! my heart's need!

CANDIDA. [*Impressed.*] That's a good bid, Eugene. Now I know how to make my choice.

[*She pauses and looks curiously from one to the other, as if weighing them.* MORELL, *whose lofty confidence has changed into heartbreaking dread at* EUGENE's *bid, loses all power of concealing his anxiety.* EUGENE, *strung to the highest tension, does not move a muscle.*]

MORELL. [*In a suffocated voice—the appeal bursting from the depths of his anguish.*] Candida!

MARCHBANKS. [*Aside, in a flash of contempt.*] Coward!

CANDIDA. [*Significantly.*] I give myself to the weaker of the two.

[EUGENE *divines her meaning at once: his face whitens like steel in a furnace that cannot melt it.*]

MORELL. [*Bowing his head with the calm of collapse.*] I accept your sentence, Candida.

CANDIDA. Do you understand, Eugene?

MARCHBANKS. Oh, I feel I'm lost. He cannot bear the burden.

MORELL. [*Incredulously, raising his head with prosaic abruptness.*] Do you mean me, Candida?

CANDIDA. [*Smiling a little.*] Let us sit and talk comfortably over it like three friends. [*To* MORELL.] Sit down, dear. [MORELL *takes the chair from the fireside—the children's chair.*] Bring me that chair, Eugene. [*She indicates the easy chair. He fetches it silently, even with something like cold strength, and places it next to* MORELL, *a little behind him. She sits down. He goes to the sofa and sits there, still silent and inscrutable. When they are all settled she begins, throwing a spell of quietness on them by her calm, sane, tender tone.*] You remember what you told me about yourself, Eugene: how nobody has cared for you since your old nurse died: how those clever, fashionable sisters and successful brothers of yours were your mother's and father's pets: how miserable you were at Eton: how your father is trying to starve you into returning to Oxford: how you have had to live without comfort or welcome or refuge, always lonely, and nearly always disliked and misunderstood, poor boy!

MARCHBANKS. [*Faithful to the nobility of his lot.*] I had my books. I had Nature. And at last I met you.

CANDIDA. Never mind that just at present. Now I want you to look at this other boy here—my boy—spoiled from his cradle. We go once a fortnight to see his parents. You should come with us, Eugene, and see the pictures of the hero of that household. James as a baby! the most wonderful of all babies. James holding his first school prize, won at the ripe age of eight! James as the captain of his eleven! James in his first frock coat! James under all sorts of glorious circumstances! You know how strong he is (I hope he didn't hurt you)—how clever he is—how happy! [*With deepening gravity.*] Ask James's mother and his three sisters what it cost to save James the trouble of doing anything but be strong and clever and happy. Ask me what it costs to be James's mother and three sisters and wife and mother to his children all in one. Ask Prossy and Maria how troublesome the house is even when we have no visitors to help us to slice the onions. Ask the tradesmen who want to worry James and spoil his beautiful sermons who it is that puts them off. When there is money to give, he gives it: when there is money to refuse, I refuse it. I build a castle of comfort and indulgence and love for him, and stand sentinel always to keep little vulgar cares out. I make him master here, though he does not know it, and could not tell you a moment ago how it came to be so. [*With sweet irony.*] And when he thought I might go away with you, his only anxiety was what should become of me! And to tempt me to stay he offered me [*Leaning forward to stroke his hair caressingly at each phrase.*] his strength for my defence, his industry for my livelihood, his position for my dignity, his—[*Relenting.*] Ah, I am mixing up your beautiful sentences and spoiling them, am I not, darling? [*She lays her cheek fondly against his.*]

MORELL. [*Quite overcome, kneeling beside her chair and embracing her with boyish ingenuousness.*] It's all true, every word. What I am you have made me with the labor of your hands and the love of your heart! You are my wife, my mother, my sisters: you are the sum of all loving care to me.

CANDIDA. [*In his arms, smiling, to* EUGENE.] Am I your mother and sisters to you, Eugene?

MARCHBANKS. [*Rising with a fierce gesture of disgust.*] Ah, never. Out, then, into the night with me!

CANDIDA. [*Rising quickly and intercepting him.*] You are not going like that, Eugene?

MARCHBANKS. [*With the ring of a man's voice—no longer a boy's—in the words.*] I know the hour when it strikes. I am impatient to do what must be done.

MORELL. [*Rising from his knee, alarmed.*] Candida: don't let him do anything rash.

CANDIDA. [*Confident, smiling at* EUGENE.] Oh, there is no fear. He has learnt to live without happiness.

MARCHBANKS. I no longer desire happiness: life is nobler than that. Parson James: I give you my happiness with both hands: I love you because you have filled the heart of the woman I loved. Good-bye. [*He goes towards the door.*]

CANDIDA. One last word. [*He stops, but without turning to her.*] How old are you, Eugene?

MARCHBANKS. As old as the world now. This morning I was eighteen.

CANDIDA. [*Going to him, and standing behind him with one hand caressingly on his shoulder.*] Eighteen! Will you, for my sake, make a little poem out of the two sentences I am going to say to you? And will you promise to repeat it to yourself whenever you think of me?

MARCHBANKS. [*Without moving.*] Say the sentences.

CANDIDA. When I am thirty, she will be forty-five. When I am sixty, she will be seventy-five.

MARCHBANKS. [*Turning to her.*] In a hundred years, we shall be the same age. But I have a better secret than that in my heart. Let me go now. The night outside grows impatient.

CANDIDA. Good-bye. [*She takes his face in her hands; and as he divines her intention and bends his knee, she kisses his forehead. Then he flies out into the night. She turns to* MORELL, *holding out her arms to him.*] Ah, James! [*They embrace. But they do not know the secret in the poet's heart.*]

# Arsenic and Old Lace

# JOSEPH KESSELRING

## Introduction

Ever since its opening on Broadway in January of 1941, *Arsenic and Old Lace* has had audiences laughing. This fast-paced farce is built upon incongruous characters involved in incongruous situations. At first, insanity and murder may seem like strange topics for farce, but we will discover that the extremes of human behavior often provide some of the best subjects for laughter.

*Arsenic and Old Lace* is the story of the Brewsters of Brooklyn, a family whose minds seem to operate a little differently from those of the rest of the world. Martha and Abby Brewster are two of the sweetest old ladies imaginable. For example, one of their charities is relieving the miseries of lonely old men with a glass of elderberry wine containing a little arsenic and a pinch of strychnine. Brother Teddy Brewster is a loveable but harmless lunatic who thinks he is Teddy Roosevelt. He draws his imaginary sword at the foot of the staircase and charges up "San Juan Hill," blasts his bugle at all hours of the day or night, and buries the bodies of "yellow fever victims" in the locks of the Panama Canal he has been digging in the cellar. Jonathan Brewster is a homicidal maniac. In contrast to the pleasant madness of Martha, Abby, and Teddy, his is a dangerously violent type of insanity. He derives a macabre satisfaction from maiming his victims and inflicting cruelty for cruelty's sake. Mortimer Brewster is a drama critic who is supposedly a rational individual, although we wouldn't believe it if we judged by his wild actions onstage.

*Arsenic and Old Lace* is farce at its best. The incongruity of the homicides that the sweet old ladies

279

perpetrate and their complete lack of awareness that what they are doing is wrong provide the basis for much of the humor. Their innocence prevents us from reacting with horror. And the opening scenes show how the church, represented by Dr. Harper, and the law, represented by Officers Brophy and Klein, look innocently upon Martha and Abby as pillars of propriety. Nephew Mortimer also is an incongruous character. He dashes about the stage behaving as if he were a madman, yet we believe him to be the only sane Brewster. His aunts patiently accept his unnatural behavior, attributing it to his recent proposal to Elaine.

Farce contains a considerable amount of bodily action, and especially of physical contact. *Arsenic and Old Lace* has strong physical action, including such things as the lugging of the body to "Panama," the dumping of Mr. Spenalzo into the window seat, the frightening of Mr. Gibbs, the threatening of Elaine, the trussing up of Mortimer, and the knocking out of Jonathan.

Repetition and anticipation are also used effectively for laugh-getting. Count the number of times Teddy charges up "San Juan Hill" or blares his bugle. Particularly successful is the anticipation built around the bugle blast. We know that one more blast, and Teddy will be forced to go to a mental institution. The next time he starts to blow, Mortimer stops him at the last second. However, there is no one to silence him when he appears on the landing shortly thereafter to summon a cabinet meeting. Also, notice how the offering of elderberry wine is described, then illustrated, setting up the final repetition and anticipation with Mr. Witherspoon. The rapid pace of the farce may prevent us from thinking much about things as they happen, but there are moments when we look beneath the surface to see that Kesselring has something serious to say concerning "normal behavior" versus "insanity" and the deceptions of outward appearances.

## Characters

ABBY BREWSTER
THE REVEREND DR. HARPER
TEDDY BREWSTER
OFFICER BROPHY

MORTIMER BREWSTER
MR. GIBBS
JONATHAN BREWSTER
DR. EINSTEIN

OFFICER KLEIN  
MARTHA BREWSTER  
ELAINE HARPER

OFFICER O'HARA  
LIEUTENANT ROONEY  
MR. WITHERSPOON

The entire action of the play takes place in the living room of the Brewster home in Brooklyn. *Time:* the 1940's.

# ACT I

TIME: Late afternoon. September. Present. PLACE: The living-room of the old Brewster home in Brooklyn, N.Y. It is just as Victorian as the two sisters, Abby and Martha Brewster, who occupy the house with their nephew, Teddy.

There is a staircase U. R. leading to the upper floor, broken by a landing with a window looking out on the front porch. At the top of the stairs a balcony with a door leading to bedrooms, and an archway beyond which are stairs to the top floor. There is a large window D. L. below which is a long window-seat. There is a door U. C. that leads to the cellar, another to L. of it, that leads to the kitchen, and at R. the main door of the house, which opens onto the porch, D. R.

When the curtain rises, ABBY BREWSTER, a plump little darling in her late sixties, is presiding at the tea-table. The table is lighted by candles. Seated in armchair at her left is the REV. DR. HARPER and on her right, standing, her nephew, TEDDY, whose costume includes a frock coat and pince-nez attached to a black ribbon. TEDDY is in his forties and has a large black mustache, and his manner and makeup suggest Theodore Roosevelt.

ABBY. Yes, indeed, my sister Martha and I have been talking all week about your sermon last Sunday. It's really wonderful, Dr. Harper—in only two short years you've taken on the spirit of Brooklyn.
HARPER. That's very gratifying, Miss Brewster.
ABBY. You see, living here next to the church all our lives, we've seen so many ministers come and go. The spirit of Brooklyn we always say is friendliness—and your sermons are not so much sermons as friendly talks.
TEDDY. Personally, I've always enjoyed my talks with Cardinal Gibbons—or have I met him yet?

Arsenic and Old Lace

ABBY. No, dear, not yet. [*Changing the subject.*] Are the biscuits good?

TEDDY. [*He sits on sofa.*] Bully!

ABBY. Won't you have another biscuit, Dr. Harper?

HARPER. Oh, no, I'm afraid I'll have no appetite for dinner now. I always eat too many of your biscuits just to taste that lovely jam.

ABBY. But you haven't tried the quince. We always put a little apple in with it to take the tartness out.

HARPER. No, thank you.

ABBY. We'll send you over a jar.

HARPER. No, no. You keep it here so I can be sure of having your biscuits with it.

ABBY. I do hope they don't make us use that imitation flour again. I mean with this war trouble. It may not be very charitable of me, but I've almost come to the conclusion that this Mr. Hitler isn't a Christian.

HARPER. [*With a sigh.*] If only Europe were on another planet!

TEDDY. [*Sharply.*] Europe, sir?

HARPER. Yes, Teddy.

TEDDY. Point your gun the other way!

HARPER. Gun?

ABBY. [*Trying to calm him.*] Teddy.

TEDDY. To the West! There's your danger! There's your enemy! Japan!

HARPER. Why, yes—yes, of course.

ABBY. Teddy!

TEDDY. No, Aunt Abby! Not so much talk about Europe and more about the canal!

ABBY. Well, let's not talk about war. Will you have another cup of tea, dear?

TEDDY. No thank you, Aunt Abby.

ABBY. Dr. Harper?

HARPER. No, thank you. I must admit, Miss Abby, that war and violence seem far removed from these surroundings.

ABBY. It is peaceful here, isn't it?

HARPER. Yes—peaceful. The virtues of another day—they're all here in this house. The gentle virtues that went out with candlelight and good manners and low taxes.

ABBY. [*Glancing about her contentedly.*] It's one of the oldest houses in Brooklyn. It's just as it was when Grandfather Brewster built and furnished it—except for the electricity—and we use it as little as possible. It was Mortimer who persuaded us to put it in.

HARPER. [*Beginning to freeze.*] Yes, I can understand that. Your nephew Mortimer seems to live only by electric light.

ABBY. The poor boy has to work so late. I understand he's taking Elaine with him to the theatre again tonight. Teddy, your brother Mortimer will be here a little later.

TEDDY. [*Baring his teeth in a broad grin.*] Dee-lighted!

ABBY. [*To* HARPER.] We're so happy it's Elaine Mortimer takes to the theatre with him.

HARPER. Well, it's a new experience for me to wait up until three o'clock in the morning for my daughter to be brought home.

ABBY. Oh, Dr. Harper, I hope you don't disapprove of Mortimer.

HARPER. Well—

ABBY. We'd feel so guilty if you did—sister Martha and I. I mean since it was here in our home that your daughter met Mortimer.

HARPER. Of course, Miss Abby. And so I'll say immediately that I believe Mortimer himself to be quite a worthy gentleman. But I must also admit that I have watched the growing intimacy between him and my daughter with some trepidation. For one reason, Miss Abby.

ABBY. You mean his stomach, Dr. Harper?

HARPER. Stomach?

ABBY. His dyspepsia—he's bothered with it so, poor boy.

HARPER. No, Miss Abby, I'll be frank with you. I'm speaking of your nephew's unfortunate connection with the theatre.

ABBY. The theatre! Oh, no, Dr. Harper! Mortimer writes for a New York newspaper.

HARPER. I know, Miss Abby, I know. But a dramatic critic is constantly exposed to the theatre, and I don't doubt but what some of them do develop an interest in it.

ABBY. Well, not Mortimer. You need have no fear of that. Why, Mortimer hates the theatre.

HARPER. Really?

ABBY. Oh, yes! He writes awful things about the theatre. But you can't blame him, poor boy. He was so happy writing about real estate, which he really knew something about, and then they just made him take this terrible night position.

HARPER. My! My!

Arsenic and Old Lace

ABBY. But, as he says, the theatre can't last much longer anyway and in the meantime it's a living. [*Complacently.*] Yes, I think if we give the theatre another year or two, perhaps . . . [*A knock on* R. *door.*] Well, now, who do you suppose that is? [*They all rise as* ABBY *goes to door* R. TEDDY *starts for door at same time, but* ABBY *stops him.*] No, thank you, Teddy. I'll go. [*She opens door to admit two cops,* OFFICERS BROPHY *and* KLEIN.] Come in, Mr. Brophy.

BROPHY. Hello, Miss Brewster.

ABBY. How are you, Mr. Klein?

KLEIN. Very well, Miss Brewster.

[*The* COPS *cross to* TEDDY *who is standing near desk, and salute him.* TEDDY *returns salute.*]

TEDDY. What news have you brought me?

BROPHY. Colonel, we have nothing to report.

TEDDY. Splendid! Thank you, gentlemen! At ease!

[COPS *relax and drop* D. S. ABBY *has closed door, and turns to* COPS.]

ABBY. You know Dr. Harper.

KLEIN. Sure! Hello, Dr. Harper.

BROPHY. [*Turns to* ABBY, *doffing cap.*] We've come for the toys for the Christmas Fund.

ABBY. Oh, yes.

HARPER. [*Standing below table.*] That's a splendid work you men do—fixing up discarded toys to give poor children a happier Christmas.

KLEIN. It gives us something to do when we have to sit around the station. You get tired playing cards and then you start cleaning your gun, and the first thing you know you've shot yourself in the foot. [KLEIN *drifts* U. L. *around to window-seat.*]

ABBY. [*Crossing to* TEDDY.] Teddy, go upstairs and get that big box from your Aunt Martha's room. [TEDDY *crosses upstage toward stairs.* ABBY *speaks to* BROPHY.] How is Mrs. Brophy today? Mrs. Brophy has been quite ill, Dr. Harper.

BROPHY. [*To* HARPER.] Pneumonia!

HARPER. I'm sorry to hear that.

[TEDDY *has reached first landing on stairs where he stops and draws an imaginary sword.*]

TEDDY. [*Shouting.*] CHARGE! [*He charges up stairs and exits off balcony. The others pay no attention to this.*]

284                                                                                                    Act I

BROPHY. Oh, she's better now. A little weak still—
ABBY. [*Starting toward kitchen.*] I'm going to get some beef broth to take to her.
BROPHY. Don't bother, Miss Abby! You've done so much for her already.
ABBY. [*At kitchen door.*] We made it this morning. Sister Martha is taking some to poor Mr. Benitzky right now. I won't be a minute. Sit down and be comfortable, all of you. [*She exits into kitchen.*]

[HARPER *sits again.* BROPHY *crosses to table and addresses the other two.*]

BROPHY. She shouldn't go to all that trouble.
KLEIN. Listen, try to stop her or her sister from doing something nice—and for nothing! They don't even care how you vote. [*He sits on window-seat.*]
HARPER. When I received my call to Brooklyn and moved next door my wife wasn't well. When she died and for months before—well, if I know what pure kindness and absolute generosity are, it's because I've known the Brewster sisters.

[*At this moment* TEDDY *steps out on balcony and blows a bugle call. They all look.*]

BROPHY. [*Stepping* U. S. . . . *Remonstrating.*] Colonel, you promised not to do that.
TEDDY. But I have to call a Cabinet meeting to get the release of those supplies. [TEDDY *wheels and exits.*]
BROPHY. He used to do that in the middle of the night. The neighbors raised cain with us. They're a little afraid of him, anyway.
HARPER. Oh, he's quite harmless.
KLEIN. Suppose he does think he's Teddy Roosevelt. There's a lot worse people he could think he was.
BROPHY. Damn shame—a nice family like this hatching a cuckoo.
KLEIN. Well, his father—the old girls' brother, was some sort of a genius, wasn't he? And their father—Teddy's grandfather—seems to me I've heard he was a little crazy too.
BROPHY. Yeah—he was crazy like a fox. He made a million dollars.
HARPER. Really? Here in Brooklyn?
BROPHY. Yeah. Patent medicine. He was a kind of a quack of some sort. Old Sergeant Edwards remembers him. He used the house here as a sort of a clinic—tried 'em out on people.
KLEIN. Yeah, I hear he used to make mistakes occasionally, too.

Arsenic and Old Lace

BROPHY. The department never bothered him much because he was pretty useful on autopsies sometimes. Especially poison cases.
KLEIN. Well, whatever he did he left his daughters fixed for life. Thank God for that—
BROPHY. Not that they ever spend any of it on themselves.
HARPER. Yes, I'm well acquainted with their charities.
KLEIN. You don't know a tenth of it. When I was with the Missing Persons Bureau I was trying to trace an old man that we never did find [*Rises.*]—do you know there's a renting agency that's got this house down on its list for furnished rooms? They don't rent rooms— but you can bet that anybody who comes here lookin' for a room goes away with a good meal and probably a few dollars in their kick.
BROPHY. It's just their way of digging up people to do some good to.

[R. *door opens and* MARTHA BREWSTER *enters.* MARTHA *is also a sweet elderly woman with Victorian charm. She is dressed in the old-fashioned manner of* ABBY, *but with a high lace collar that covers her neck.* MEN *all on feet.*]

MARTHA. [*At door.*] Well, now, isn't this nice? [*Closes door.*]
BROPHY. [*Crosses to* MARTHA.] Good afternoon, Miss Brewster.
MARTHA. How do you do, Mr. Brophy? Dr. Harper. Mr. Klein.
KLEIN. How are you, Miss Brewster? We dropped in to get the Christmas toys.
MARTHA. Oh, yes, Teddy's Army and Navy. They wear out. They're all packed. [*She turns to stairs.* BROPHY *stops her.*]
BROPHY. The Colonel's upstairs after them—it seems the Cabinet has to O.K. it.
MARTHA. Yes, of course. I hope Mrs. Brophy's better?
BROPHY. She's doin' fine, ma'am. Your sister's getting some soup for me to take to her.
MARTHA. [*Crossing below* BROPHY *to* C.] Oh, yes, we made it this morning. I just took some to a poor man who broke ever so many bones.

[ABBY *enters from kitchen carrying a covered pail.*]

ABBY. Oh, you're back, Martha. How was Mr. Benitzky?
MARTHA. Well, dear, it's pretty serious, I'm afraid. The doctor was there. He's going to amputate in the morning.
ABBY. [*Hopefully.*] Can we be present?
MARTHA. [*Disappointment.*] No. I asked him but he says it's against the

rules of the hospital. [MARTHA *crosses to sideboard, puts pail down. Then puts cape and hat on small table* U. L.]

[TEDDY *enters on balcony with large cardboard box and comes downstairs to desk, putting box on stool.* KLEIN *crosses to toy box.* HARPER *speaks through this.*]

HARPER. You couldn't be of any service—and you must spare yourselves something.

ABBY. [*To* BROPHY.] Here's the broth, Mr. Brophy. Be sure it's good and hot.

BROPHY. Yes, ma'am. [*Drops* U. S.]

KLEIN. This is fine—it'll make a lot of kids happy. [*Lifts out toy soldier.*] That O'Malley boy is nuts about soldiers.

TEDDY. That's General Miles. I've retired him. [KLEIN *removes ship.*] What's this! The Oregon!

MARTHA. [*Crosses to* U. L.] Teddy, dear, put it back.

TEDDY. But the Oregon goes to Australia.

ABBY. Now, Teddy—

TEDDY. No, I've given my word to Fighting Bob Evans.

MARTHA. But, Teddy—

KLEIN. What's the difference what kid gets it—Bobby Evans, Izzy Cohen? [*Crosses to* R. *door with box, opens door.* BROPHY *follows.*] We'll run along, ma'am, and thank you very much.

ABBY. Not at all. [*The* COPS *stop in doorway, salute* TEDDY *and exit.* ABBY *crosses and shuts door as she speaks.* TEDDY *starts upstairs.*] Goodbye.

HARPER. [*Crosses to sofa, gets hat.*] I must be getting home.

ABBY. Before you go, Dr. Harper—

[TEDDY *has reached stair landing.*]

TEDDY. CHARGE! [*He dashes upstairs. At top he stops and with a sweeping gesture over the balcony rail, invites all to follow him as he speaks.*] Charge the blockhouse! [*He dashes through door, closing it after him.*]

[HARPER *looks after him.* MARTHA, *to* L. *of* HARPER, *is fooling with a pin on her dress.* ABBY R. *of* HARPER.]

HARPER. The blockhouse?
MARTHA. The stairs are always San Juan Hill.

Arsenic and Old Lace

HARPER. Have you ever tried to persuade him that he wasn't Teddy Roosevelt?

ABBY. Oh, no!

MARTHA. He's so happy being Teddy Roosevelt.

ABBY. Once, a long time ago—[*She crosses below to* MARTHA.] remember, Martha? We thought if he would be George Washington it might be a change for him—

MARTHA. But he stayed under his bed for days and just wouldn't be anybody.

ABBY. And we'd much rather he'd be Mr. Roosevelt than nobody.

HARPER. Well, if he's happy—and what's more important you're happy— [*He takes blue-backed legal paper from inside pocket.*] you'll see that he signs these.

MARTHA. What are they?

ABBY. Dr. Harper has made all arrangements for Teddy to go to Happy Dale Sanitarium after we pass on.

MARTHA. But why should Teddy sign any papers now?

HARPER. It's better to have it all settled. If the Lord should take you away suddenly perhaps we couldn't persuade Teddy to commit himself and that would mean an unpleasant legal procedure. Mr. Witherspoon understands they're to be filed away until the time comes to use them.

MARTHA. Mr. Witherspoon? Who's he?

HARPER. He's the Superintendent of Happy Dale.

ABBY. [*To* MARTHA.] Dr. Harper has arranged for him to drop in tomorrow or the next day to meet Teddy.

HARPER. [*Crossing to* R. *door and opening it.*] I'd better be running along or Elaine will be over here looking for me.

[ABBY *crosses to door and calls out after him.*]

ABBY. Give our love to Elaine—and Dr. Harper, please don't think harshly of Mortimer because he's a dramatic critic. Somebody has to do those things. [ABBY *closes door, comes back into room.*]

[MARTHA *crosses to sideboard, puts legal papers on it . . . notices tea things on table.*]

MARTHA. Did you just have tea? Isn't it rather late?

ABBY. [*As one who has a secret.*] Yes—and dinner's going to be late too.

[TEDDY *enters on balcony, starts downstairs to first landing.* MARTHA *steps to* ABBY.]

MARTHA. So? Why?

ABBY. Teddy! [TEDDY *stops on landing.*] Good news for you. You're going to Panama and dig another lock for the canal.

TEDDY. Dee-lighted! That's bully! Just bully! I shall prepare at once for the journey. [*He turns to go upstairs, stops as if puzzled, hurries back to landing, cries CHARGE!, and rushes up and off.*]

MARTHA. [*Elated.*] Abby! While I was out?

ABBY. [*Taking* MARTHA'S *hand.*] Yes, dear! I just couldn't wait for you. I didn't know when you'd be back and Dr. Harper was coming.

MARTHA. But all by yourself?

ABBY. Oh, I got along fine!

MARTHA. I'll run right downstairs and see. [*She starts happily for cellar door.*]

ABBY. Oh, no, there wasn't time, and I was all alone.

[MARTHA *looks around room toward kitchen.*]

MARTHA. Well—

ABBY. [*Coyly.*] Martha—just look in the window-seat. [MARTHA *almost skips to window-seat, and just as she gets there a knock is heard on* R. *door. She stops. They both look toward door.* ABBY *hurries to door and opens it.* ELAINE HARPER *enters.* ELAINE *is an attractive girl in her twenties; she looks surprisingly smart for a minister's daughter.*] Oh, it's Elaine. [*Opens door.*] Come in, dear.

[ELAINE *crosses to* C. ABBY *closes door, crosses to* C.]

ELAINE. Good afternoon, Miss Abby. Good afternoon, Miss Martha. I thought Father was here.

MARTHA. [*Stepping to* L. *of table.*] He just this minute left. Didn't you meet him?

ELAINE. [*Pointing to window in* L. *wall.*] No, I took the short cut through the cemetery. Mortimer hasn't come yet?

ABBY. No, dear.

ELAINE. Oh? He asked me to meet him here. Do you mind if I wait?

MARTHA. Not at all.

ABBY. Why don't you sit down, dear?

MARTHA. But we really must speak to Mortimer about doing this to you.

**Arsenic and Old Lace**

ELAINE. [*Sits chair* R. *of table.*] Doing what?

MARTHA. Well, he was brought up to know better. When a gentleman is taking a young lady out he should call for her at her house.

ELAINE. [*To both.*] Oh, there's something about calling for a girl at a parsonage that discourages any man who doesn't embroider.

ABBY. He's done this too often—we're going to speak to him.

ELAINE. Oh, please don't. After young men whose idea of night life was to take me to prayer meeting, it's wonderful to go to the theatre almost every night of my life.

MARTHA. It's comforting for us too, because if Mortimer has to see some of those plays he has to see—at least he's sitting next to a minister's daughter. [MARTHA *steps to back of table.*]

[ABBY *crosses to back of table, starts putting tea things on tray.* ELAINE *and* MARTHA *help.*]

ABBY. My goodness, Elaine, what must you think of us—not having tea cleared away by this time. [*She picks up tray and exits to kitchen.*]

[MARTHA *blows out one candle and takes it to sideboard.* ELAINE *blows out other, takes to sideboard.*]

MARTHA. [*As* ABBY *exits.*] Now don't bother with anything in the kitchen until Mortimer comes, and then I'll help you. [*To* ELAINE.] Mortimer should be here any minute now.

ELAINE. Yes. Father must have been surprised not to find me at home. I'd better run over and say good night to him. [*She crosses to* R. *door.*]

MARTHA. It's a shame you missed him, dear.

ELAINE. [*Opening door.*] If Mortimer comes you tell him I'll be right back. [*She has opened door, but sees* MORTIMER *just outside.*] Hello, Mort!

[MORTIMER BREWSTER *walks in. He is a dramatic critic.*]

MORTIMER. Hello, Elaine. [*As he passes her going toward* MARTHA, *thus placing himself between* ELAINE *and* MARTHA, *he reaches back and pats* ELAINE *on the fanny . . . then embraces* MARTHA.] Hello, Aunt Martha.

[MARTHA *exits to kitchen, calling as she goes.*]

MARTHA. Abby, Mortimer's here!

[ELAINE *slowly closes door.*]

MORTIMER. [*Turning* R.] Were you going somewhere?

ELAINE. I was just going over to tell Father not to wait up for me.

MORTIMER. I didn't know that was still being done, even in Brooklyn. [*He throws his hat on sofa.*]

[ABBY *enters from kitchen.* MARTHA *follows, stays in doorway* R.]

ABBY. [*Crosses to* MORTIMER *at* C.] Hello, Mortimer.

MORTIMER. [*Embraces and kisses her.*] Hello, Aunt Abby.

ABBY. How are you, dear?

MORTIMER. All right. And you look well. You haven't changed much since yesterday.

ABBY. Oh, my goodness, it was yesterday, wasn't it? We're seeing a great deal of you lately. [*She crosses and starts to sit in a chair above table.*] Well, come, sit down. Sit down.

[MARTHA *stops her from sitting.*]

MARTHA. Abby—haven't we something to do in the kitchen?

ABBY. Huh?

MARTHA. You know—the tea things.

ABBY. [*Suddenly seeing* MORTIMER *and* ELAINE, *and catching on.*] Oh, yes! Yes! The tea things—[*She backs toward kitchen.*] Well—you two just make yourselves at home. Just—

MARTHA. —make yourselves at home.

[*They exit kitchen door,* ABBY *closing door.*]

ELAINE. [*Stepping to* MORTIMER, *ready to be kissed.*] Well, can't you take a hint?

MORTIMER. [*Complaining.*] No . . . that was pretty obvious. A lack of inventiveness, I should say.

ELAINE. [*Only slightly annoyed as she crosses to table, and puts handbag on it.*] Yes—that's exactly what you'd say.

MORTIMER. [*He is at desk, fishing various pieces of notepaper from his pockets, and separating dollar bills that are mixed in with papers.*] Where do you want to go for dinner?

ELAINE. [*Opening bag, looking in hand mirror.*] I don't care. I'm not very hungry.

MORTIMER. Well, I just had breakfast. Suppose we wait until after the show?

Arsenic and Old Lace

ELAINE. But that'll make it pretty late, won't it?
MORTIMER. Not with the little stinker we're seeing tonight. From what I've heard about it we'll be at Blake's by ten o'clock.
ELAINE. [*Crosses to* U. S. C.] You ought to be fair to these plays.
MORTIMER. Are these plays fair to me?
ELAINE. *I've* never seen you walk out on a musical.
MORTIMER. That musical isn't opening tonight.
ELAINE. [*Disappointed.*] No?
MORTIMER. Darling, you'll have to learn the rules. With a musical there are always four changes of title and three postponements. They liked it in New Haven but it needs a lot of work.
ELAINE. Oh, I was hoping it was a musical.
MORTIMER. You have such a light mind.
ELAINE. Not a bit. Musicals somehow have a humanizing effect on you. [*He gives her a look.*] After a serious play we join the proletariat in the subway and I listen to a lecture on the drama. After a musical you bring me home in a taxi, [*Turning away.*] and you make a few passes.
MORTIMER. [*Crossing* D. C.] Now wait a minute, darling, that's a very inaccurate piece of reporting.
ELAINE. [*Leaning against* D. S. *end of table.*] Oh, I will admit that after the Behrman play you told me I had authentic beauty—and that's a hell of a thing to say to a girl. It wasn't until after our first musical you told me I had nice legs. And I have too.

[MORTIMER *stares at her legs a moment, then walks over and kisses her.*]

MORTIMER. For a minister's daughter you know a lot about life. Where'd you learn it?
ELAINE. [*Casually.*] In the choir loft.
MORTIMER. I'll explain that to you some time, darling—the close connection between eroticism and religion.
ELAINE. Religion never gets as high as the choir loft. [*Crosses below table, gathers up bag.*] Which reminds me, I'd better tell Father please not to wait up for me tonight.
MORTIMER. [*Almost to himself.*] I've never been able to rationalize it.
ELAINE. What?
MORTIMER. My falling in love with a girl who lives in Brooklyn.
ELAINE. Falling in love? You're not stooping to the articulate, are you?

MORTIMER. [*Ignoring this.*] The only way I can regain my self respect is to keep you in New York.

ELAINE. [*Few steps toward him.*] Did you say keep?

MORTIMER. No, no. I've come to the conclusion that you're holding out for the legalities.

ELAINE. [*Crossing to him as he backs away.*] I can afford to be a good girl for quite a few years yet.

MORTIMER. [*Stops and embraces her.*] And I can't wait that long. Where could we be married in a hurry—say tonight?

ELAINE. I'm afraid Father will insist on officiating.

MORTIMER. [*Turning away R. from her.*] Oh, God! I'll bet your father could make even the marriage service sound pedestrian.

ELAINE. Are you by any chance writing a review of it?

MORTIMER. Forgive me, darling. It's an occupational disease. [*She smiles at him lovingly and walks toward him. He meets her halfway and they forget themselves for a moment in a sentimental embrace and kiss. When they come out of it, he turns away from her quickly... breaking U. S. near desk.*] I may give that play tonight a good notice.

ELAINE. Now, darling, don't pretend you love me that much.

MORTIMER. [*Looks at her with polite lechery, then starts toward her.*] Be sure to tell your father not to wait up tonight.

ELAINE. [*Aware that she can't trust either of them, and backing U. S.*] I think tonight I'd better tell him to wait up.

MORTIMER. [*Following her.*] I'll telephone Winchell to publish the banns.

ELAINE. [*Backing D. S.*] Nevertheless—

MORTIMER. All right, everything formal and legal. But not later than next month.

ELAINE. [*Runs into his arms.*] Darling! I'll talk it over with Father and set the date.

MORTIMER. No—we'll have to see what's in rehearsal. There'll be a lot of other first nights in October.

[TEDDY *enters from balcony and comes downstairs dressed in tropical clothes and a solar topee. At foot of stairs he sees* MORTIMER, *crosses to him and shakes hands.*]

TEDDY. Hello, Mortimer!

MORTIMER. [*Gravely.*] How are you, Mr. President?

TEDDY. Bully, thank you. Just bully! What news have you brought me?

MORTIMER. Just this, Mr. President—the country is squarely behind you.
TEDDY. [*Beaming.*] Yes, I know. Isn't it wonderful? [*He shakes* MORTIMER's *hand again.*] Well, good-bye. [*He crosses to* ELAINE *and shakes hands with her.*] Good-bye. [*He goes to cellar door.*]
ELAINE. Where are you off too, Teddy?
TEDDY. Panama. [*He exits through cellar door, shutting it.* ELAINE *looks at* MORTIMER *inquiringly.*]
MORTIMER. Panama's the cellar. He digs locks for the canal down there.

[ELAINE *takes his arm and they stroll* D. L. *to* R. *of table.*]

ELAINE. You're so sweet with him—and he's very fond of you.
MORTIMER. Well, Teddy was always my favorite brother.
ELAINE. [*Stopping and turning to him.*] Favorite? Were there more of you?
MORTIMER. There's another brother—Jonathan.
ELAINE. I never heard of him. Your aunts never mention him.
MORTIMER. No, we don't like to talk about Jonathan. He left Brooklyn very early—by request. Jonathan was the kind of boy who liked to cut worms in two—with his teeth.
ELAINE. What became of him?
MORTIMER. I don't know. He wanted to become a surgeon like Grandfather but he wouldn't go to medical school first and his practice got him into trouble.

[ABBY *enters from kitchen, crossing* D. L. *of table.*]

ABBY. Aren't you two going to be late for the theatre?

[MORTIMER's L. *arm around* ELAINE's *neck, he looks at his wristwatch.*]

MORTIMER. We're skipping dinner. We won't have to start for half an hour.
ABBY. [*Backing* U. L.] Well, then I'll leave you two alone together again.
ELAINE. Don't bother, darling. [*Breaking* R. *in front of* MORTIMER.] I'm going to run over to speak to Father. [*To* MORTIMER.] Before I go out with you he likes to pray over me a little. [*She runs to* R. *door and opens it, keeping her* L. *hand on outside doorknob.*] I'll be right back—I'll cut through the cemetery.
MORTIMER. [*Crosses to her, puts his hand on hers.*] If the prayer isn't too long, I'd have time to lead you beside distilled waters.

[ELAINE *laughs and exits.* MORTIMER *shuts door.*]

ABBY. [*Happily, as she crosses to* C.] Mortimer, that's the first time I've ever heard you quote the bible. We knew Elaine would be a good influence for you.

MORTIMER. [*Laughs, crosses* L., *then turns to* ABBY.] Oh, by the way—I'm going to marry her.

ABBY. What? Oh, darling! [*She runs and embraces him. Then she dashes toward kitchen door as* MORTIMER *crosses to window* L. *and looks out.*] Martha, Martha! [MARTHA *enters from kitchen.*] Come right in here. I've got the most wonderful news for you—Mortimer and Elaine are going to be married.

MARTHA. Married? Oh, Mortimer! [*She runs over to* R. *of* MORTIMER, *who is looking out window* L., *embraces and kisses him.* ABBY *comes down to his* L. *He has his arms around both of them.*]

ABBY. We hoped it would happen just like this.

MARTHA. Well, Elaine must be the happiest girl in the world.

MORTIMER. [*Pulls curtain back, looks out window.*] Happy! Just look at her leaping over those gravestones. [*As he looks out window* MORTIMER's *attention is suddenly drawn to something.*] Say! What's that?

MARTHA. [*Looking out on his* R. ABBY *is on his* L.] What's what, dear?

MORTIMER. See that statue there. That's a horundinida carnina.

MARTHA. Oh, no, dear—that's Emma B. Stout ascending to heaven.

MOTIMER. No, no,—standing on Mrs. Stout's left ear. That bird—that's a red-crested swallow. I've only seen one of those before in my life.

ABBY. [*Crosses around above table and pushes chair* R. *into table.*] I don't know how you can be thinking about a bird now—what with Elaine and the engagement and everything.

MORTIMER. It's a vanishing species. [*He turns away from window.*] Thoreau was very fond of them. [*As he crosses to desk to look through various drawers and papers.*] By the way, I left a large envelope around here last week. It was one of the chapters of my book on Thoreau. Have you seen it?

MARTHA. [*Pushing armchair into table.*] Well, if you left it here it must be here somewhere.

ABBY. [*Crossing to* D. L. *of* MORTIMER.] When are you going to be married? What are your plans? There must be something more you can tell us about Elaine.

MORTIMER. Elaine? Oh, yes, Elaine thought it was brilliant. [*He crosses to sideboard, looks through cupboards and drawers.*]

MARTHA. What was, dear?

MORTIMER. My chapter on Thoreau. [*He finds a bundle of paper (script) in* R. *drawer and takes them to table and looks through them.*]
ABBY. [*At* C.] Well, when Elaine comes back I think we ought to have a little celebration. We must drink to your happiness. Martha, isn't there some of that Lady Baltimore cake left?

[*During last few speeches* MARTHA *has picked up pail from sideboard and her cape, hat and gloves from table in* U. L. *corner.*]

MARTHA. [*Crossing* D. L.] Oh, yes!
ABBY. And I'll open a bottle of wine.
MARTHA. [*As she exits to kitchen.*] Oh, and to think it happened in this room!
MORTIMER. [*Has finished looking through papers, is gazing around room.*] Now where could I have put that?
ABBY. Well, with your fiancée sitting beside you tonight, I do hope the play will be something you can enjoy for once. It may be something romantic. What's the name of it?
MORTIMER. "Murder Will Out."
ABBY. Oh dear! [*She disappears into kitchen as* MORTIMER *goes on talking.*]
MORTIMER. When the curtain goes up the first thing you'll see will be a dead body. [*He lifts window-seat and sees one. Not believing it, he drops window-seat again and starts downstage. He suddenly stops with a "take," then goes back, throws window-seat open and stares in. He goes slightly mad for a moment. He backs away, then hears* ABBY *humming on her way into the room. He drops window-seat again and holds it down, staring around the room.* ABBY *enters carrying a silencer and tablecloth which she puts on armchair, then picks up bundle of papers and returns them to drawer in sideboard.* MORTIMER *speaks in a somewhat strained voice.*] Aunt Abby!
ABBY. [*At sideboard.*] Yes, dear?
MORTIMER. You were going to make plans for Teddy to go to that . . . sanitarium—Happy Dale—
ABBY. [*Bringing legal papers from sideboard to* MORTIMER.] Yes, dear, it's all arranged. Dr. Harper was here today and brought the papers for Teddy to sign. Here they are.

[*He takes them from her.*]

MORTIMER. He's got to sign them right away.

ABBY. [*Arranging silencer on table.* MARTHA *enters from kitchen door with table silver and plates on a tray. She sets tray on sideboard. Goes to table* R.] That's what Dr. Harper thinks. Then there won't be any legal difficulties after we pass on.

MORTIMER. He's got to sign them this minute! He's down in the cellar—get him up here right away.

MARTHA. [*Unfolding tablecloth. She's above table on* R.] There's no such hurry as that.

ABBY. No. When Teddy starts working on the canal you can't get his mind on anything else.

MORTIMER. Teddy's got to go to Happy Dale now—tonight.

MARTHA. Oh, no, dear, that's not until after we're gone.

MORTIMER. Right away, I tell you!—right away!

ABBY. [*Turning to* MORTIMER.] Why, Mortimer, how can you say such a thing? Why, as long as we live we'll never be separated from Teddy.

MORTIMER. [*Trying to be calm.*] Listen, darlings, I'm frightfully sorry, but I've got some shocking news for you. [*The* AUNTS *stop work and look at him with some interest.*] Now we've all got to try and keep our heads. You know we've sort of humored Teddy because we thought he was harmless.

MARTHA. Why he *is* harmless!

MORTIMER. He *was* harmless. That's why he has to go to Happy Dale. Why he has to be confined.

ABBY. [*Stepping to* MORTIMER.] Mortimer, why have you suddenly turned against Teddy?—your own brother?

MORTIMER. You've got to know sometime. It might as well be now, Teddy's—killed a man!

MARTHA. Nonsense, dear.

[MORTIMER *rises and points to window-seat.*]

MORTIMER. There's a body in the window-seat!

ABBY. Yes, dear, we know.

[MORTIMER *"takes" as* ABBY *and* MARTHA *busy themselves again at table.*]

MORTIMER. You *know*?

MARTHA. Of course, dear, but it has nothing to do with Teddy. [*Gets tray from sideboard—arranges silver and plates on table: 3 places,* U. L. *and* R.]

ABBY. Now, Mortimer, just forget about it—forget you ever saw the gentleman.

MORTIMER. *Forget?*

ABBY. We never dreamed you'd peek.

MORTIMER. But who is he?

ABBY. His name's Hoskins—Adam Hoskins. That's really all *I* know about him—except that he's a Methodist.

MORTIMER. That's all you know about him? Well, what's he doing here? What happened to him?

MARTHA. He died.

MORTIMER. Aunt Martha, men don't just get into window-seats and die.

ABBY. [*Silly boy.*] No, he died first.

MORTIMER. Well, how?

ABBY. Oh, Mortimer, don't be so inquisitive. The gentleman died because he drank some wine with poison in it.

MORTIMER. How did the poison get in the wine?

MARTHA. Well, we put it in wine because it's less noticeable—when it's in tea it has a distinct odor.

MORTIMER. *You* put it in the wine?

ABBY. Yes. And I put Mr. Hoskins in the window-seat because Dr. Harper was coming.

MORTIMER. So you knew what you'd done! You didn't want Dr. Harper to see the body!

ABBY. Well, not at tea—that wouldn't have been very nice. Now, Mortimer, you know the whole thing, just forget about it. I do think Martha and I have the right to our own little secrets. [*She crosses to sideboard to get two goblets from* L. *cupboard as* MARTHA *comes to table from sideboard with salt dish and pepper shaker.*]

MARTHA. And don't you tell Elaine! [*She gets 3d goblet from sideboard, then turns to* ABBY *who takes tray from sideboard.*] Oh, Abby, while I was out I dropped in on Mrs. Schultz. She's much better but she would like us to take Junior to the movies again.

ABBY. Well, we must do that tomorrow or next day.

MARTHA. Yes, but this time we'll go where we want to go. [*She starts for kitchen door.* ABBY *follows.*] Junior's not going to drag me into another one of those scary pictures. [*They exit into kitchen as* MORTIMER *wheels around and looks after them.* ABBY *shuts door.*]

MORTIMER. [*Dazed, looks around the room. His eyes come to rest on phone on desk; he crosses to it and dials a number. Into phone.*]

298                                                                                                Act I

City desk! [*There is a pause.*] Hello, Al. Do you know who this is? [*Pause.*] That's right. Say, Al, when I left the office I told you where I was going, remember?—Well, where did I say? [*Pause.*] Uh-huh. Well, it would take me about half an hour to get to Brooklyn. What time have you got? [*He looks at his watch.*] That's right. I must be here. [*He hangs up, sits for a moment, then suddenly leaps off stool toward kitchen.*] Aunt Abby! Aunt Martha! Come in here! [*He backs to* C. *stage as the two* AUNTS *bustle in.* MARTHA *has tray with plates, cups, saucers and soup cups.*] What are we going to do? What are we going to do?

MARTHA. [R. *of table.*] What are we going to do about what, dear?

MORTIMER. [*Pointing to window-seat.*] There's a body in there.

ABBY. [U. L. *of* MORTIMER.] Yes—Mr. Hoskins.

MORTIMER. Well, good heavens, I can't turn you over to the police! But what am I going to do?

MARTHA. Well, for one thing, dear, stop being so excited.

ABBY. And for pity's sake stop worrying. We told you to forget the whole thing.

MORTIMER. Forget! My dear Aunt Abby, can't I make you realize that something has to be done?

ABBY. [*A little sharply.*] Now, Mortimer, you behave yourself. You're too old to be flying off the handle like this.

MORTIMER. But Mr. Hotchkiss—

[ABBY, *on her way to sideboard, stops and turns to* MORTIMER.]

ABBY. Hoskins, dear. [*She continues on her way to sideboard and gets napkins and rings from* L. *drawer.* MARTHA *puts her try, with cups, plates, etc., on table.* MORTIMER *continues speaking through this.*]

MORTIMER. Well, whatever his name is, you can't leave him there.

MARTHA. We don't intend to, dear.

ABBY. [*Crossing to table* L. *with napkins and rings.*] No, Teddy's down in the cellar now digging the lock.

MORTIMER. You mean you're going to bury Mr. Hotchkiss in the cellar?

MARTHA. [*Stepping to him.*] Oh, yes, dear,—that's what we did with the others.

MORTIMER. [*Walking away to* R.] No! You can't bury Mr.—[*Double take. Turns back to them.*]—others?

ABBY. The other gentlemen.

MORTIMER. When you say others—do you mean—others? More than one others?
MARTHA. Oh, yes, dear. Let me see, this is eleven. [*To* ABBY U. L. *of table.*] Isn't it, Abby?
ABBY. No, dear, this makes twelve.

[MORTIMER *backs away from them, stunned, toward phone stool at desk.*]

MARTHA. Oh, I think you're wrong, Abby. This is only eleven.
ABBY. No, dear, because I remember when Mr. Hoskins first came in, it occurred to me that he would make just an even dozen.
MARTHA. Well, you really shouldn't count the first one.
ABBY. Oh, *I* was counting the first one. So that makes it twelve.

[*Phone rings.* MORTIMER, *in a daze, turns toward it and without picking up receiver, speaks.*]

MORTIMER. Hello! [*He comes to, picks up receiver.*] Hello. Oh, hello, Al. My, it's good to hear your voice.

[ABBY, *at table, is still holding out for a "twelve" count.*]

ABBY. Well, anyway, they're all down in the cellar—
MORTIMER. [*To* AUNTS.] Ssshhh—[*Into phone, as* AUNTS *cross to sideboard and put candelabras from top to bottom shelf.*] Oh, no, Al, I'm sober as a lark. I just called you because I was feeling a little Pirandello —Piran—you wouldn't know, Al. Look, I'm glad you called. Get hold of George right away. He's got to review the play tonight. I can't make it. No, Al, you're wrong. I'll tell you all about it tomorrow. Well, George has got to cover the play tonight! This is my department and I'm running it! You get ahold of George! [*He hangs up and sits a moment trying to collect himself.*] Now let's see, where were we? [*He suddenly leaps from stool.*] TWELVE!
MARTHA. Yes, Abby thinks we ought to count the first one and that makes twelve. [*She goes back to sideboard.*]

[MORTIMER *takes chair* R. *of table and faces it toward* R. *stage, then takes* MARTHA *by the hand, leads her to chair and sets her in it.*]

MORTIMER. All right—now—who was the first one?
ABBY. [*Crossing from above table to* MORTIMER.] Mr. Midgely. He was a Baptist.

MARTHA. Of course, I still think we can't claim full credit for him because he just died.
ABBY. Martha means without any help from us. You see, Mr. Midgely came here looking for a room—
MARTHA. It was right after you moved to New York.
ABBY. —And it didn't seem right for that lovely room to be going to waste when there were so many people who needed it—
MARTHA. —He was such a lonely old man. . . .
ABBY. All his kith and kin were dead and it left him so forlorn and unhappy—
MARTHA. —We felt so sorry for him.
ABBY. And then when his heart attack came—and he sat dead in that chair [*Pointing to armchair.*] looking so peaceful—remember, Martha —we made up our minds then and there that if we could help other lonely old men to that same peace—we would!
MORTIMER. [*All ears.*] He dropped dead right in that chair! How awful for you!
MARTHA. Oh, no, dear. Why, it was rather like old times. Your grandfather always used to have a cadaver or two around the house. You see, Teddy had been digging in Panama and he thought Mr. Midgely was a Yellow Fever victim.
ABBY. That meant he had to be buried immediately.
MARTHA. So we all took him down to Panama and put him in the lock. [*She rises, puts her arm around* ABBY.] Now that's why we told you not to worry about it because we know exactly what's to be done.
MORTIMER. And that's how all this started—that man walking in here and dropping dead.
ABBY. Of course, we realized we couldn't depend on that happening again. So—
MARTHA. [*Crosses to* MORTIMER.] You remember those jars of poison that have been up on the shelves in Grandfather's laboratory all these years—?
ABBY. You know your Aunt Martha's knack for mixing things. You've eaten enough of her piccalilli.
MARTHA. Well, dear, for a gallon of elderberry wine I take one teaspoonful of arsenic, then add a half teaspoonful of strychnine and then just a pinch of cyanide.
MORTIMER. [*Appraisingly.*] Should have quite a kick.

ABBY. Yes! As a matter of fact one of our gentlemen found time to say "How delicious!"

MARTHA. [*Stepping* U. S.] Well, I'll have to get things started in the kitchen.

ABBY. [*To* MORTIMER.] I wish you could stay for dinner.

MARTHA. I'm trying out a new recipe.

MORTIMER. I couldn't eat a thing.

[MARTHA *goes out to kitchen.*]

ABBY. [*Calling after* MARTHA.] I'll come and help you, dear. [*She pushes chair* R. *into table.*] Well, I feel so much better now. Oh, you have to wait for Elaine, don't you? [*She smiles.*] How happy you must be. [*She goes to kitchen doorway.*] Well, dear, I'll leave you alone with your thoughts. [*She exits, shutting door.*]

[*The shutting of the door wakes* MORTIMER *from his trance. He crosses to window-seat kneels down, raises cover, looks in. Not believing, he lowers cover, rubs his eyes, raises cover again. This time he really sees Mr. Hoskins. Closes window-seat hastily, rises, steps back. Runs over and closes drapes over window. Backs up to above table. Sees water glass on table, picks it up, raises it to lips, suddenly remembers that poisoned wine comes in glasses, puts it down quickly. Crosses to cellar door, opens it.* ELAINE *enters* R., *he closes cellar door with a bang. As* ELAINE *puts her bag on top of desk he looks at her, and it dawns on him that he knows her. He speaks with faint surprise.*]

MORTIMER. Oh, it's you. [*He drops* D. S. ELAINE *crosses to him, takes his hand.*]

ELAINE. Don't be cross, darling! Father could see that I was excited—so I told him about us and that made it hard for me to get away. But listen, darling—he's not going to wait up for me tonight.

MORTIMER. [*Looking at window-seat.*] You run along home, Elaine, and I'll call you up tomorrow.

ELAINE. Tomorrow!

MORTIMER. [*Irritated.*] You know I always call you up every day or two.

ELAINE. But we're going to the theatre tonight.

MORTIMER. No—no we're not!

ELAINE. Well, why not?

MORTIMER. [*Turning to her.*] Elaine, something's come up.

ELAINE. What, darling? Mortimer—you've lost your job!

MORTIMER. No—no—I haven't lost my job. I'm just not covering that play tonight. [*Pushing her* R.] Now you run along home, Elaine.

ELAINE. But I've got to know what's happened. Certainly you can tell me.

MORTIMER. No, dear, I can't.

ELAINE. But if we're going to be married—

MORTIMER. Married?

ELAINE. Have you forgotten that not fifteen minutes ago you proposed to me?

MORTIMER. [*Vaguely.*] I did? Oh—yes! Well, as far as I know that's still on. [*Urging her* R. *again.*] Now you run along home, Elaine. I've got to do something.

ELAINE. Listen, you can't propose to me one minute and throw me out of the house the next.

MORTIMER. [*Pleading.*] I'm not throwing you out of the house, darling. Will you get out of here?

ELAINE. No, I won't get out of here. [MORTIMER *crosses toward kitchen.* ELAINE *crosses below to window-seat.*] Not until I've had some kind of explanation. [ELAINE *is about to sit on window-seat.* MORTIMER *grabs her by the hand. Phone rings.*]

MORTIMER. Elaine! [*He goes to phone, dragging* ELAINE *with him.*] Hello! Oh, hello, Al. Hold on a minute, will you?—All right, it's important! But it can wait a minute, can't it? Hold on! [*He puts receiver on desk. Takes* ELAINE'S *bag from top of desk and hands it to her. Then takes her by hand and leads her to door* R. *and opens it.*] Look, Elaine, you're a sweet girl and I love you. But I have something on my mind now and I want you to go home and wait until I call you.

ELAINE. [*In doorway.*] Don't try to be masterful.

MORTIMER. [*Annoyed to the point of being literate.*] When we're married and I have problems to face I hope you're less tedious and uninspired!

ELAINE. And when we're married *if* we're married—I hope I find you adequate! [*She exits.* MORTIMER *does take, then runs out on porch after her, calling*—]

MORTIMER. Elaine! Elaine! [*He runs back in, shutting door, crosses and kneels on window-seat to open window. Suddenly remembers contents of window-seat and leaps off it. Dashes into kitchen but remembers Al is on phone, re-enters immediately and crosses to phone.*] Hello, Al? Hello . . . hello. . . . [*He pushes hook down and*

Arsenic and Old Lace 303

*starts to dial when doorbell rings. He thinks it's the phone.* ABBY *enters from kitchen.*] Hello. Hello, Al?

ABBY. [*Crossing to* R. *door and opening it.*] That's the doorbell, dear, not the telephone. [MORTIMER *pushes hook down . . . dials.* MR. GIBBS *steps in doorway* R.] How do you do? Come in.

GIBBS. I understand you have a room to rent.

[MARTHA *enters from kitchen. Puts "Lazy Susan" on sideboard, then gets to* R. *of table.*]

ABBY. Yes. Won't you step in?

GIBBS. [*Stepping into room.*] Are you the lady of the house?

ABBY. Yes, I'm Miss Brewster. And this is my sister, another Miss Brewster.

GIBBS. My name is Gibbs.

ABBY. [*Easing him to chair* R. *of table.*] Oh, won't you sit down? I'm sorry we were just setting the table for dinner.

MORTIMER. [*Into phone.*] Hello—let me talk to Al again. City desk. [*Loud.*] AL!! CITY DESK! WHAT? I'm sorry, wrong number. [*He hangs up and starts dialing again as* GIBBS *looks at him.* GIBBS *turns to* ABBY.]

GIBBS. May I see the room?

MARTHA. [D. L. *of table.*] Why don't you sit down a minute and let's get acquainted.

GIBBS. That won't do much good if I don't like the room.

ABBY. Is Brooklyn your home?

GIBBS. Haven't got a home. Live in a hotel. Don't like it.

MORTIMER. [*Into phone.*] Hello. City desk.

MARTHA. Are your family Brooklyn people?

GIBBS. Haven't got any family.

ABBY. [*Another victim.*] All alone in the world?

GIBBS. Yep.

ABBY. Well, Martha—[MARTHA *goes happily to sideboard, gets bottle of wine from* U. L. *cupboard, and a wine glass, and sets them on table,* U. S. *end.* ABBY *eases* GIBBS *into chair* R. *of table and continues speaking to him, then to above table.*] Well, you've come to just the right house. Do sit down.

MORTIMER. [*Into phone.*] Hello, Al? Mort. We got cut off. Al, I can't cover the play tonight—that's all there is to it, I can't!

MARTHA. [L. *of table.*] What church do you go to? There's an Episcopal church practically next door. [*Her gesture toward window brings her to window-seat and she sits.*]

GIBBS. I'm Presbyterian. Used to be.

MORTIMER. [*Into phone.*] What's George doing in Bermuda? [*Rises and gets loud.*] Certainly I told him he could go to Bermuda—it's my department, isn't it? Well, you've got to get somebody. Who else is there around the office? [*He sits on second chair.*]

GIBBS. [*Annoyed. Rises and crosses below table to* L. *of it.*] Is there always this much noise?

MARTHA. Oh, he doesn't live with us.

[ABBY *sits above table.*]

MORTIMER. [*Into phone.*] There must be somebody around the place. Look, Al, how about the office boy? You know the bright one—the one we don't like? Well, you look around the office, I'll hold on.

GIBBS. I'd really like to see the room.

ABBY. [*After seating* GIBBS R. *of table she has sat in chair above table.*] It's upstairs. Won't you try a glass of our wine before we start up?

GIBBS. Never touch it.

MARTHA. We make this ourselves. It's elderberry wine.

GIBBS. [*To* MARTHA.] Elderberry wine. Hmmph. Haven't tasted elderberry wine since I was a boy. Thank you. [*He pulls armchair around and sits as* ABBY *uncorks bottle and starts to pour wine.*]

MORTIMER. [*Into phone.*] Well, there must be some printers around. Look, Al, the fellow who sets my copy. He ought to know about what I'd write. His name is Joe. He's the third machine from the left. But, Al, he might turn out to be another Burns Mantle!

GIBBS. [*To* MARTHA.] Do you have your own elderberry bushes?

MARTHA. No, but the cemetery is full of them.

MORTIMER. [*Rising.*] No, I'm not drinking, but I'm going to start now.

GIBBS. Do you serve meals?

ABBY. We might, but first just see whether you like our wine.

[MORTIMER *hangs up, puts phone on top of desk and crosses* L. *He sees wine on table. Goes to sideboard, gets glass, brings it to table and pours drink.* GIBBS *has his glass in hand and is getting ready to drink.*]

MARTHA. [*Sees* MORTIMER *pouring wine.*] Mortimer! Eh eh eh eh! [GIBBS *stops and looks at* MARTHA. MORTIMER *pays no attention.*] Eh eh eh eh!

[As MORTIMER *raises glass to lips with* L. *hand,* ABBY *reaches up and pulls his arm down.*]

ABBY. Mortimer. Not that. [MORTIMER, *still dumb, puts his glass down on table. Then he suddenly sees* GIBBS *who has just got glass to his lips and is about to drink. He points across table at* GIBBS *and gives a wild cry.* GIBBS *looks at him, putting his glass down.* MORTIMER, *still pointing at* GIBBS, *goes around above table toward him.* GIBBS, *seeing a madman, rises slowly and backs toward* C., *then turns and runs for exit* R., MORTIMER *following him.* GIBBS *opens* R. *door and* MORTIMER *pushes him out, closing door after him. Then he turns and leans on door in exhausted relief. Meantime,* MARTHA *has risen and crossed to below armchair, while* ABBY *has risen and crossed to* D. C. (*If necessary to cover* GIBBS' *cross and exit,* MORTIMER *has the following lines . . . "Get out of here! Do you want to be poisoned? Do you want to be killed? Do you want to be murdered?"*) ABBY, *great disappointment.*] Now you've spoiled everything. [*She goes to sofa and sits.*]

[MARTHA *sits in armchair.* MORTIMER *crosses to* C. *and looks from one to the other . . . then speaks to* ABBY.]

MORTIMER. You can't do things like that. I don't know how to explain this to you, but it's not only against the law. It's wrong! [*To* MARTHA.] It's not a nice thing to do. [MARTHA *turns away from him as* ABBY *has done in his lines to her.*] People wouldn't understand. [*Points to door after* GIBBS.] He wouldn't understand.

MARTHA. Abby, we shouldn't have told Mortimer!

MORTIMER. What I mean is—well, this has developed into a very bad habit.

ABBY. [*Rises.*] Mortimer, we don't try to stop you from doing things you like to do. I don't see why you should interfere with us.

[*Phone rings.* MORTIMER *answers.* MARTHA *rises to below table.*]

MORTIMER. Hello? [*It's Al again.*] All right, I'll see the first act and I'll pan the hell out of it. But look, Al, you've got to do something for me. Get hold of O'Brien—our lawyer, the head of our legal department. Have him meet me at the theatre. Now, don't let me down. O.K. I'm starting now. [*He hangs up and turns to* AUNTS.] Look, I've got to go to the theatre. I can't get out of it. But before I go will you promise me something?

MARTHA. [*Crossing to* ABBY *at* C.] We'd have to know what it was first.

MORTIMER. I love you very much and I know you love me. You know I'd do anything in the world for you and I want you to do just this little thing for me.

ABBY. What do you want us to do?

MORTIMER. Don't *do* anything. I mean don't do *anything*. Don't let anyone in this house—and leave Mr. Hoskins right where he is.

MARTHA. Why?

MORTIMER. I want time to think—and I've got quite a little to think about. You know I wouldn't want anything to happen to you.

ABBY. Well, what on earth could happen to us?

MORTIMER. [*Beside himself.*] Anyway—you'll do this for me, won't you?

MARTHA. Well—we were planning on holding services before dinner.

MORTIMER. Services!

MARTHA. [*A little indignant.*] Certainly. You don't think we'd bury Mr. Hoskins without a full Methodist service, do you? Why he was a Methodist.

MORTIMER. But can't that wait until I get back?

ABBY. Oh, then you could join us.

MORTIMER. [*Going crazy himself.*] Yes! Yes!

ABBY. Oh, Mortimer, you'll enjoy the services—especially the hymns. [*To* MARTHA.] Remember how beautifully Mortimer used to sing in the choir before his voice changed?

MORTIMER. And remember, you're not going to let anyone in this house while I'm gone—it's a promise!

MARTHA. Well—

ABBY. Oh, Martha, we can do that now that Mortimer's cooperating with us. [*To* MORTIMER.] Well, all right, Mortimer.

[MORTIMER *heaves a sigh of relief. Crosses to sofa and gets his hat. Then on his way to opening* R. *door, he speaks.*]

MORTIMER. Have you got some paper? I'll get back as soon as I can. [*Taking legal papers from coat pocket as he crosses.*] There's a man I've got to see.

[ABBY *has gone to desk for stationery. She hands it to* MORTIMER.]

ABBY. Here's some stationery. Will this do?

MORTIMER. [*Taking stationery.*] That'll be fine. I can save time if I write my review on the way to the theatre. [*He exits* R.]

Arsenic and Old Lace

[*The* AUNTS *stare after him.* MARTHA *crosses and closes door.* ABBY *goes to sideboard and brings 2 candelabras to table. Then gets matches from sideboard—lights candles during lines.*]

MARTHA. Mortimer didn't seem quite himself today.
ABBY. [*Lighting candles.*] Well, that's only natural—I think I know why.
MARTHA. [*Lighting floor lamp.*] Why?
ABBY. He's just become engaged to be married. I suppose that always makes a man nervous.
MARTHA. [*During this speech she goes to 1st landing and closes drapes over window, then comes downstairs and turns off remote switch.*] Well, I'm so happy for Elaine—and their honeymoon ought to give Mortimer a real vacation. I don't think he got much rest this summer.
ABBY. Well, at least he didn't go kiting off to China or Spain.
MARTHA. I could never understand why he wanted to go to those places.
ABBY. Well, I think to Mortimer the theatre has always seemed pretty small potatoes. He needs something big to criticize—something like the human race. [*She sets one candelabra* D. L.*, the other* U. R. *on table.*]
MARTHA. [*At* C.] Oh, Abby, if Mortimer's coming back for the services for Mr. Hoskins, we'll need another hymnal. There's one in my room. [*She starts upstairs to 1st landing.*]
ABBY. You know, dear, it's really my turn to read the services, but since you weren't here when Mr. Hoskins came I want you to do it.
MARTHA. [*Pleased.*] That's very nice of you, dear—but, are you sure you want me to?
ABBY. It's only fair.
MARTHA. Well, I think I'll wear my black bombazine and Mother's old brooch. [*She starts up again when doorbell rings.*]
ABBY. [*Crossing as far as desk.*] I'll go, dear.
MARTHA. [*Hushed.*] We promised Mortimer we wouldn't let anyone in.
ABBY. [*Trying to peer through curtained window in door.*] Who do you suppose it is?
MARTHA. Wait a minute, I'll look. [*She turns to landing window and peeks out the curtains.*] It's two men—and I've never seen them before.
ABBY. Are you sure?
MARTHA. There's a car at the curb—they must have come in that.

ABBY. Let me look! [*She hurries up stairs. There is a knock on door.* ABBY *peeks out the curtains.*]

MARTHA. Do you recognize them?

ABBY. They're strangers to me.

MARTHA. We'll just have to pretend we're not at home. [*The two of them huddle back in corner of landing.*]

[*Another knock at the door* R., *the knob is turned, and door swings slowly open. A tall* MAN *walks to* C., *looking about the room. He walks in with assurance and ease as though the room were familiar to him—in every direction but that of the stairs. There is something sinister about the man—something that brings a slight chill in his presence. It is in his walk, his bearing, and his strange resemblance to Boris Karloff. From stair-landing* ABBY *and* MARTHA *watch him, almost afraid to speak. Having completed his survey of the room, the* MAN *turns and addresses someone outside the front door.*]

JONATHAN. Come in, Doctor. [DR. EINSTEIN *enters* R. *He is somewhat ratty in appearance. His face wears the benevolent smirk of a man who lives in a pleasant haze of alcohol. There is something about him that suggests the unfrocked priest. He stands just inside the door, timid but expectant.*] This is the home of my youth. As a boy I couldn't wait to escape from this place—now I'm glad to escape back into it.

EINSTEIN. [*Shutting door. His back to* AUNTS.] Yah, Chonny, it's a fine hideout.

JONATHAN. The family must still live here. There's something so unmistakably Brewster about the Brewsters. I hope there's a fatted calf awaiting the return of the prodigal.

EINSTEIN. Yah, I'm hungry. [*He suddenly sees the fatted calf in the form of the 2 glasses of wine on table.*] Look, Chonny, drinks! [*He runs over below to table.* JONATHAN *crosses to above side.*]

JONATHAN. As though we were expected. A good omen.

[*They raise glasses to their lips as* ABBY *steps down a couple of stairs and speaks.*]

ABBY. Who are you? What are you doing here?

[*They both put glasses down.* EINSTEIN *picks up his hat from armchair, ready to run for it.* JONATHAN *turns to* ABBY.]

Arsenic and Old Lace

JONATHAN. Why, Aunt Abby! Aunt Martha! It's Jonathan.
MARTHA. [*Frightened.*] You get out of here.
JONATHAN. [*Crossing to* AUNTS.] I'm Jonathan—your nephew, Jonathan.
ABBY. Oh, no, you're not. You're nothing like Jonathan, so don't pretend you are! You just get out of here!
JONATHAN. [*Crossing closer.*] But I am Jonathan. And this [*Indicating* EINSTEIN.] is Dr. Einstein.
ABBY. And he's not Dr. Einstein either.
JONATHAN. Not Dr. Albert Einstein—Dr. Herman Einstein.
ABBY. [*Down another step.*] Who are you? You're not our nephew, Jonathan.
JONATHAN. [*Peering at* ABBY's *outstretched hand.*] I see you're still wearing the lovely garnet ring that Grandma Brewster bought in England. [ABBY *gasps, looks at ring.*] And you, Aunt Martha, still the high collar—to hide the scar where Grandfather's acid burned you.

[MARTHA's *hand goes to her throat. The* AUNTS *look at* JONATHAN. MARTHA *comes down a few steps to behind* ABBY. EINSTEIN *gets to* C.]

MARTHA. His voice is like Jonathan's.
ABBY. [*Stepping down to stage floor.*] Have you been in an accident?
JONATHAN. [*His hand goes to side of his face.*] No—[*He clouds.*]—my face—Dr. Einstein is responsible for that. He's a plastic surgeon. He changes people's faces.
MARTHA. [*Comes down to* ABBY.] But I've seen that face before. [*To* ABBY.] Abby, remember when we took the little Schultz boy to the movies and I was so frightened? It was that face!

[JONATHAN *grows tense and looks toward* EINSTEIN. EINSTEIN *crosses to* C. *and addresses* AUNTS.]

EINSTEIN. Easy, Chonny—easy! [*To* AUNTS.] Don't worry, ladies. The last five years I give Chonny three new faces. I give him another one right away. This last face—well, I saw that picture too—just before I operate. And I was intoxicated.
JONATHAN. [*With a growing and dangerous intensity as he walks toward* EINSTEIN, *who backs* D. S.] You see, Doctor—you see what you've done to me. Even my own family—
EINSTEIN. [*To calm him, as he is forced around* R. *stage.*] Chonny—you're home—in this lovely house—[*To* AUNTS.] How often he tells me about Brooklyn—about this house—about his aunts that he lofes so

much. [*To* JONATHAN.] They know you, Chonny. [*To* ABBY *as he leads her toward* JONATHAN.] You know it's Jonathan. Speak to him. Tell him so. [*He drifts above table to* D. L. *of it.*]

ABBY. Well—Jonathan—it's been a long time—what have you been doing all these years?

MARTHA. [*Has come to far* D. R.] Yes, Jonathan, where have you been?

JONATHAN. [*Recovering his composure.*] Oh, England, South Africa, Australia,—the last five years Chicago. Dr. Einstein and I were in business there together.

ABBY. Oh, we were in Chicago for the World's Fair.

MARTHA. [*For want of something to say.*] Yes—we found Chicago awfully warm.

EINSTEIN. [*He has wandered above* U. L. *and down to below table.*] Yah—it got hot for us too.

JONATHAN. [*Turning on the charm as he crosses above* ABBY, *placing himself between the* AUNTS.] Well, it's wonderful to be in Brooklyn again. And you—Abby—Martha you don't look a day older. Just as I remember you—sweet—charming—hospitable. [*The* AUNTS *don't react too well to this charm.*] And dear Teddy—[*He indicates with his hand a lad of eight or ten.*]—did he get into politics? [*He turns to* EINSTEIN.] My little brother, Doctor, was determined to become President.

ABBY. Oh, Teddy's fine! Just fine! And Mortimer's well too.

JONATHAN. [*A bit of a sneer.*] I know about Mortimer. I've seen his picture at the head of his column. He's evidently fulfilled all the promise of his early nasty nature.

ABBY. [*Defensively.*] We're very fond of Mortimer.

[*There is a slight pause. Then* MARTHA *speaks uneasily as she gestures toward* R. *door.*]

MARTHA. Well, Jonathan, it's very nice to have seen you again.

JONATHAN. [*Expanding.*] Bless you, Aunt Martha. [*Crosses and sits chair* R. *of table.*] It's good to be home again.

[*The* AUNTS *look at each other with dismay.*]

ABBY. Well, Martha, we mustn't let what's on the stove boil over. [*She starts to kitchen, then sees* MARTHA *isn't following. She crosses back and tugs at* MARTHA, *then crosses toward kitchen again.* MARTHA *follows to* C., *then speaks to* JONATHAN.]

Arsenic and Old Lace

MARTHA. Yes. If you'll excuse us for a minute, Jonathan. Unless you're in a hurry to go somewhere.

[JONATHAN *looks at her balefully.* MARTHA *crosses around above table, takes bottle of wine and puts it back in sideboard, then exits with* ABBY. ABBY, *who has been waiting in kitchen doorway for* MARTHA, *closes door after them.* EINSTEIN *crosses* U. L. *around to behind* JONATHAN.]

EINSTEIN. Well, Chonny, where do we go from here? We got to think fast. The police. The police have got pictures of that face. I got to operate on you right away. We got to find some place for that—and we got to find a place for Mr. Spenalzo too.

JONATHAN. Don't waste any worry on that rat.

EINSTEIN. But, Chonny, we got a hot stiff on our hands.

JONATHAN. [*Flinging hat onto sofa.*] Forget Mr. Spenalzo.

EINSTEIN. But you can't leave a dead body in the rumble seat. You shouldn't have killed him, Chonny. He's a nice fellow—he gives us a lift—and what happens?

JONATHAN. [*Remembering bitterly.*] He said I looked like Boris Karloff! [*He starts for* EINSTEIN.] That's your work, Doctor. You did that to me!

EINSTEIN. [*He's backed away to* D. L. *of table.*] Now, Chonny—we find a place somewhere—I fix you up quick!

JONATHAN. Tonight!

EINSTEIN. Chonny—I got to eat first. I'm hungry—I'm weak.

[*The* AUNTS *enter from kitchen.* ABBY *comes to* JONATHAN *at* C. MARTHA *remains in kitchen doorway.*]

ABBY. Jonathan—we're glad that you remembered us and took the trouble to come in and say "Hello." But you were never happy in this house and we were never happy while you were in it—so, we've just come in to say good-bye.

JONATHAN. [*Takes a menacing step toward* ABBY. *Then decides to try the "charm" again.*] Aunt Abby, I can't say that your feeling toward me comes as a surprise. I've spent a great many hours regretting the many heartaches I must have given you as a boy.

ABBY. You were quite a trial to us, Jonathan.

JONATHAN. But my great disappointment is for Dr. Einstein. [EINSTEIN *is a little surprised.*] I promised him that no matter how rushed we were in passing through Brooklyn, I'd take the time to bring him here for one of Aunt Martha's home-cooked dinners.

[MARTHA *rises to this a bit, stepping* D. S.]

MARTHA. Oh...
ABBY. [*Backing* U. L.] I'm sorry. I'm afraid there wouldn't be enough.
MARTHA. Abby, it's a pretty good-sized pot roast.
JONATHAN. [*How wonderful.*] Pot roast!
MARTHA. I think the least we can do is to—
JONATHAN. Thank you, Aunt Martha! We'll stay to dinner.
ABBY. [*Backing to kitchen door and not at all pleased.*] Well, we'll hurry it along.
MARTHA. Yes! [*She exits into kitchen.*]
ABBY. [*Stopping in doorway.*] Oh, Jonathan, if you want to freshen up—why don't you use the washroom in Grandfather's old laboratory?
JONATHAN. [*Crossing to her.*] Is that still there?
ABBY. Oh, yes. Just as he left it. Well, I'll help Martha get things started—since we're all in a hurry. [*She exits into kitchen.*]
EINSTEIN. [*Stepping* U. S.] Well, we get a meal anyway.
JONATHAN. [*Above table.*] Grandfather's laboratory! [*Looks upstairs.*] And just as it was. Doctor, a perfect operating room.
EINSTEIN. Too bad we can't use it.
JONATHAN. After you've finished with me—Why, we could make a fortune here. The laboratory—that large ward in the attic—ten beds, Doctor—and Brooklyn is crying for your talents.
EINSTEIN. Vy vork yourself up, Chonny? Anyway, for Brooklyn I think we're a year too late.
JONATHAN. You don't know this town, Doctor. Practically everybody in Brooklyn needs a new face.
EINSTEIN. But so many of the old faces are locked up.
JONATHAN. A very small percentage—and the boys in Brooklyn are famous for paying generously to stay out of jail.
EINSTEIN. Take it easy, Chonny. Your aunts—they don't want us here.
JONATHAN. We're here for dinner, aren't we?
EINSTEIN. Yah—but after dinner?
JONATHAN. [*Crossing up to sofa.*] Leave it to me, Doctor. I'll handle it. Why, this house'll be our headquarters for years.
EINSTEIN. [*A pretty picture.*] Oh, that would be beautiful, Chonny! This

nice quiet house. Those aunts of yours—what sweet ladies. I love them already. I get the bags, yah?

JONATHAN. [*Stopping him.*] Doctor! We must wait until we're invited.

EINSTEIN. But you chust said that—

JONATHAN. We'll be invited.

EINSTEIN. And if they say no—?

JONATHAN. Doctor—two helpless old women—? [*He sits on sofa.*]

EINSTEIN. [*Takes bottle flask from hip pocket and unscrews cork as he crosses to window-seat.*] It's like comes true a beautiful dream—Only I hope you're not dreaming. [*He stretches out on window-seat, taking a swig from bottle.*] It's so peaceful.

JONATHAN. [*Stretched out on sofa.*] That's what makes this house so perfect for us—it's so peaceful.

[TEDDY *enters from cellar, blows a terrific blast on his bugle, as* JONATHAN *backs* R. TEDDY *marches to stairs and on up to 1st landing as the two* MEN *look at his tropical garb with some astonishment.*]

TEDDY. CHARGE! [*He rushes up the stairs and off.*]

[JONATHAN *watches him from foot of stairs.* EINSTEIN, *sitting on window-seat, takes a hasty swig from his flask as the curtain comes down on the word* CHARGE!]

# ACT II

SCENE: The same. Later that night.

JONATHAN, with an after-dinner cigar, is occupying armchair L. of table completely at his ease. ABBY and MARTHA, seated on window-seat, are giving him a nervous attention in the attitude of people who wish their guests would go home. EINSTEIN is relaxed and happy in chair R. of table. Dinner dishes have been cleared. There is a red cloth on table, with a saucer to serve as ash-tray for JONATHAN. The room is in order. All doors are closed, as are drapes over windows.

JONATHAN. Yes, Aunties, those five years in Chicago were amongst the busiest and happiest of my life.

EINSTEIN. And from Chicago we go to South Bend, Indiana. [*He shakes his head as though he wishes they hadn't.*]

[JONATHAN *gives him a look.*]

JONATHAN. They wouldn't be interested in our experience in Indiana.
ABBY. Well, Jonathan, you've led a very interesting life, I'm sure—but we really shouldn't have allowed you to talk so late. [*She starts to rise.* JONATHAN *seats her just by the tone of his voice.*]
JONATHAN. My meeting Dr. Einstein in London, I might say, changed the whole course of my life. You remember I had been in South Africa, in the diamond business—then Amsterdam, the diamond market. I wanted to go back to South Africa—and Dr. Einstein made it possible for me.
EINSTEIN. A good job, Chonny. [*To* AUNTS.] When we take off the bandages—his face look so different, the nurse had to introduce me.
JONATHAN. I loved that face. I still carry the picture with me. [*He produces snapshot-size picture from inside coat pocket, looks at it a moment, then hands it to* MARTHA. *She looks at it and hands it to* ABBY.]
ABBY. This looks more the way you used to look, but still I wouldn't know you.
JONATHAN. I think we'll go back to that face, Doctor.
EINSTEIN. Yah, it's safe now.
ABBY. [*Rising.*] Well, I know you both want to get to—where you're going.
JONATHAN. [*Relaxing even more.*] My dear aunts—I'm so full of that delicious dinner I'm unable to move a muscle.
EINSTEIN. [*Relaxing too.*] Yah, it's nice here.
MARTHA. [*Rises.*] After all—it's very late and—

[TEDDY *enters on balcony wearing his solar topee, carrying a book, open, and another topee.*]

TEDDY. [*Descending stairs.*] I found it! I found it!
JONATHAN. What did you find, Teddy?
TEDDY. The story of my life—my biography. [*He crosses above to* L. *of* EINSTEIN.] Here's the picture I was telling you about, General. [*He lays open book on table showing picture to* EINSTEIN.] Here we are, both of us. "President Roosevelt and General Goethals at Culebra Cut." That's me, General, and that's you.

[EINSTEIN *looks at picture.*]

Arsenic and Old Lace     315

EINSTEIN. My, how I've changed.

[TEDDY *looks at* EINSTEIN, *a little puzzled, but makes adjustment.*]

TEDDY. Well, you see that picture hasn't been taken yet. We haven't even started work on Culebra Cut. We're still digging locks. And now, General, we will both go to Panama and inspect the new lock.

[*Hands him topee.*]

ABBY. No, Teddy—not to Panama.
EINSTEIN. We go some other time. Panama's a long way off.
TEDDY. Nonsense, it's just down in the cellar.
JONATHAN. The cellar?
MARTHA. We let him dig the Panama Canal in the cellar.
TEDDY. [*Severely.*] General Goethals, as President of the United States, Commander-in-Chief of the Army and Navy and the man who gave you this job, I demand that you accompany me on the inspection of the new lock.
JONATHAN. Teddy! I think it's time you went to bed.
TEDDY. I beg your pardon! [*He crosses above to* L. *of* JONATHAN, *putting on his pince-nez as he crosses.*] Who are you?
JONATHAN. I'm Woodrow Wilson. Go to bed.
TEDDY. No—you're not Wilson. But your face is familiar. Let me see— You're not anyone I know now. Perhaps later— On my hunting trip to Africa—yes, you look like someone I might meet in the jungle.

[JONATHAN *stiffens.* ABBY *crosses in front of* TEDDY, *getting between him and* JONATHAN.]

ABBY. It's your brother, Jonathan, dear.
MARTHA. [*Rising.*] He's had his face changed.
TEDDY. So that's it—a nature faker!
ABBY. And perhaps you had better go to bed, Teddy—Jonathan and his friend have to go back to their hotel.
JONATHAN. [*Rising.*] General Goethals, [*To* EINSTEIN.] inspect the canal. [*He crosses to* U. C.]
EINSTEIN. [*Rising.*] All right, Mr. President. We go to Panama.
TEDDY. Bully! Bully! [*He crosses to cellar door, opens it.*] Follow me, General. [EINSTEIN *goes up to* L. *of* TEDDY. TEDDY *taps sola topee in* EINSTEIN's *hand, then taps his own head.*] It's down south you know. [*He exits downstairs.*]

[EINSTEIN *puts on topee, which is to large for him. Then turns in cellar doorway and speaks.*]

EINSTEIN. Well—bon voyage. [*He exits, closing door.*]
JONATHAN. Aunt Abby, I must correct your misapprehension. You spoke of our hotel. We have no hotel. We came directly here—
MARTHA. Well, there's a very nice little hotel just three blocks down the—
JONATHAN. [*Cutting her off.*] Aunt Martha, this is my home.
ABBY. But, Jonathan, you can't stay here. We need our rooms.
JONATHAN. You need them?
ABBY. Yes, for our lodgers.
JONATHAN. [*Alarmed.*] Are there lodgers in this house?
MARTHA. Well, not just now, but we plan to have some.
JONATHAN. [*Cutting her off again.*] Then my old room is still free.
ABBY. But, Jonathan, there's no place for Dr. Einstein.
JONATHAN. [*Crosses to below table, drops cigar ashes into saucer.*] He'll share the room with me.
ABBY. No, Jonathan, I'm afraid you can't stay here.

[JONATHAN *is below table. He grinds cigar out in saucer, then starts toward* AUNTS. *They back around above table to* C., MARTHA *first.* JONATHAN *turns back and crosses below table to* ABBY *at* C.]

JONATHAN. Dr. Einstein and I need a place to sleep. You remembered, this afternoon, that as a boy I could be disagreeable. It wouldn't be very pleasant for any of us if—
MARTHA. [R. C., *and frightened.*] Perhaps we'd better let them stay here tonight—
ABBY. Well, just overnight, Jonathan.
JONATHAN. That's settled. Now, if you'll get my room ready—
MARTHA. [*Starting upstairs,* ABBY *following.*] It only needs airing out.
ABBY. We keep it ready to show our lodgers. I think you and Dr. Einstein will find it comfortable.

[JONATHAN *follows them to 1st landing and leans on newel-post.* AUNTS *are on balcony.*]

JONATHAN. You have a most distinguished guest in Dr. Einstein. I'm afraid you don't appreciate his skill. But you will. In a few weeks you'll see me looking like a very different Jonathan.
MARTHA. He can't operate on you here.

Arsenic and Old Lace     317

JONATHAN. [*Ignoring.*] When Dr. Einstein and I get organized—when we resume practice—Oh, I forgot to tell you. We're turning Grandfather's laboratory into an operating room. We expect to be quite busy.

ABBY. Jonathan, we will not let you turn this house into a hospital.

JONATHAN. [*Laughing.*] A hospital—heavens no! It will be a beauty parlor.

[EINSTEIN *enters excitedly from cellar.*]

EINSTEIN. Hey, Chonny, down in the cellar—[*He sees* AUNTS *and stops.*]

JONATHAN. Dr. Einstein—my dear aunts have invited us to live with them.

EINSTEIN. Oh, you fixed it?

ABBY. Well, you're sleeping here tonight.

JONATHAN. Please get our room ready immediately.

MARTHA. Well—

ABBY. For tonight.

[*They exit through arch.* JONATHAN *comes to foot of stairs.*]

EINSTEIN. Chonny, when I go down in the cellar, what do you think I find?

JONATHAN. What?

EINSTEIN. The Panama Canal.

JONATHAN. [*Disgusted, crossing to* C.] The Panama Canal.

EINSTEIN. It just fits Mr. Spenalzo. It's a hole Teddy dug. Six feet long and four feet wide.

JONATHAN. [*Gets the idea. Opens cellar door and looks down.*] Down there!

EINSTEIN. You'd think they knew we were bringing Mr. Spenalzo along. That's hospitality.

JONATHAN. [*Closing cellar door.*] Rather a good joke on my aunts—their living in a house with a body buried in the cellar.

EINSTEIN. How do we get him in?

JONATHAN. [*Drops* D. S.] Yes. We can't just walk him through the door. [*He sees window in* L. *wall.*] We'll drive the car up between the house and the cemetery—then when they've gone to *bed*, we'll bring Mr. Spenalzo in through the window.

EINSTEIN. [*Taking out bottle flask.*] Bed! Just think, we've got a bed tonight! [*He starts swigging.*]

JONATHAN. [*Grabbing his arm.*] Easy, Doctor. Remember you're operating tomorrow. And this time you'd better be sober.

EINSTEIN. I fix you up beautiful.

JONATHAN. And if you don't—[*Gives* EINSTEIN *shove to door.*]

ABBY. [*She and* MARTHA *enter on balcony.*] Jonathan! Your room is ready.

JONATHAN. Then you can go to bed. We're moving the car up behind the house.

MARTHA. It's all right where it is—until morning.

JONATHAN. [EINSTEIN *has opened door.*] I don't want to leave it in the street—that might be against the law. [*He exits.*]

[EINSTEIN *follows him out, closing door.* ABBY *and* MARTHA *start downstairs and reach below table.*]

MARTHA. Abby, what are we going to do?

ABBY. Well, we're not going to let them stay more than one night in this house for one thing. What would the neighbors think? People coming in here with one face and going out with another.

[*She has reached table* D. S. MARTHA *is at her* R.]

MARTHA. What are we going to do about Mr. Hoskins?

ABBY. [*Crosses to window-seat.* MARTHA *follows.*] Oh, Mr. Hoskins. It can't be very comfortable for him in there. And he's been so patient, the poor dear. Well, I think Teddy had better get Mr. Hoskins downstairs right away.

MARTHA. [*Adamant.*] Abby—I will not invite Jonathan to the funeral services.

ABBY. Oh, no. We'll wait until they've gone to bed and then come down and hold the services.

[TEDDY *enters from cellar, gets book from table and starts* R. ABBY *stops him at* C.]

TEDDY. General Goethals was very pleased. He says the Canal is just the right size.

ABBY. [*Crosses to* C.] Teddy! Teddy, there's been another Yellow Fever victim.

TEDDY. [*Takes off pince-nez.*] Dear me—this will be a shock to the General.

MARTHA. [*Stepping* R.] Then we mustn't tell him about it.

Arsenic and Old Lace

TEDDY. [*Crosses below* ABBY *to* MARTHA.] But it's his department.
ABBY. No, we mustn't tell him, Teddy. It would just spoil his visit.
TEDDY. I'm sorry, Aunt Abby. It's out of my hands—he'll have to be told. Army regulations, you know.
ABBY. No, Teddy, we *must* keep it a secret.
MARTHA. Yes!
TEDDY. [*He loves them.*] A **state** secret?
ABBY. Yes, a state secret.
MARTHA. Promise?
TEDDY. [*What a silly request.*] You have the word of the President of the United States. [*Crosses his heart.*] Cross my heart and hope to die. [*He spits.*] Now let's see—[*Puts pince-nez on, then puts arms around both* AUNTS.] how are we going to keep it a secret?
ABBY. Well, Teddy, you go back down in the cellar and when I turn out the lights—when it's all dark—you come up and take the poor man down to the Canal. [*Urging him to cellar door, which he opens.*] Now go along, Teddy.
MARTHA. [*Following* U. S.] And we'll come down later and hold services.
TEDDY. [*In doorway.*] You may announce the President will say a few words. [*He starts, then turns back.*] Where is the poor devil?
MARTHA. He's in the window-seat.
TEDDY. It seems to be spreading. We've never had Yellow Fever there before. [*He exits, closing door.*]
ABBY. Martha, when Jonathan and Dr. Einstein come back, let's see if we can get them to go to bed right away.
MARTHA. Yes. Then by the time they're asleep, we'll be dressed for the funeral. [*Sudden thought.*] Abby; I've never even seen Mr. Hoskins.
ABBY. Oh, my goodness, that's right—you were out. Well, you just come right over and see him now. [*They go to window-seat,* ABBY *first.*] He's really very nice looking—considering he's a Methodist. [*As they go to lift window-seat,* JONATHAN *throws window open from outside with a bang.* AUNTS *scream and draw back.* JONATHAN *puts his head in through drapes.*]
JONATHAN. We're bringing—the luggage through here.
ABBY. [*Now at* C.] Jonathan, your room's waiting for you. You can go right up.

[*Two dusty bags and a large instrument case are passed through window by* EINSTEIN. JONATHAN *puts them on floor.*]

JONATHAN. I'm afraid we don't keep Brooklyn hours—but you two run along to bed.

ABBY. Now, you must be very tired, both of you—and we don't go to bed this early.

JONATHAN. Well, you should. It's time I came home to take care of you.

MARTHA. We weren't planning to go until—

JONATHAN. [*The master.*] Aunt Martha, did you hear me say go to bed! [AUNT MARTHA *starts upstairs as* EINSTEIN *comes in through window and picks up 2 bags.* JONATHAN *takes instrument case and puts it* U. S. *of window-seat.*] The instruments can go to the laboratory in the morning. [EINSTEIN *starts upstairs.* JONATHAN *closes window.* MARTHA *is partway upstairs as* EINSTEIN *passes her.* ABBY *is at* R. C.] Now, then, we're all going to bed. [*He crosses to* C. *as* ABBY *breaks* D. R. *to light-switch.*]

ABBY. I'll wait till you're up, then turn out the lights.

[JONATHAN, *going upstairs, sees* EINSTEIN *pausing at balcony door.* MARTHA *is almost up to balcony.*]

JONATHAN. Another flight, Doctor. [*To* MARTHA.] Run along, Aunt Martha. [MARTHA *hurries into doorway.* EINSTEIN *goes through arch to 3d floor.* JONATHAN *continues on to* L. *end of balcony.* ABBY *is at light-switch.*] All right, Aunt Abby.

ABBY. [*Stalling. Looks toward cellar door.*] I'll be right up.

JONATHAN. Now, Aunt Abby. [*Definite.*] Turn out the lights!

[ABBY *turns switch, plunging stage into darkness except for spot shining down stairway from arch.* ABBY *goes up stairs to her door where* MARTHA *is waiting. She takes a last frightened look at* JONATHAN *and exits.* MARTHA *closes door.* JONATHAN *goes off through arch, closing that door, blotting out the spot. A street light shines through main door* R. *on stage floor.* TEDDY *opens cellar door, then turns on cellar light, outlining him in doorway. He crosses to window-seat and opens it—the window-seat cover giving out its usual rusty squeak. He reaches in and pulls Mr. Hoskins (a live "dummy" light enough to carry and who can remain stiff as in rigor mortis). He gets Mr. Hoskins over his shoulder and, leaving window-seat open, crosses to cellar door and goes down into cellar with Mr. Hoskins. Closes door.* JONATHAN *and* EINSTEIN *come through arch. It is dark. They light matches and listen at the* AUNTS' *door for a moment.* EINSTEIN *speaks.*]

Arsenic and Old Lace

EINSTEIN. All right, Chonny.

[*The matches go out.* JONATHAN *lights another and they come down to foot of stairs.*]

JONATHAN. I'll get the window open. You go around and hand him through.
EINSTEIN. No, he's too heavy for me. You go outside and push—I stay here and pull. Then together we get him down to Panama.
JONATHAN. All right. [*He blows out match, crosses and opens door.* EINSTEIN *to his* L.] I'll take a look around outside the house. When I tap on the glass, you open the window.
EINSTEIN. All right. [JONATHAN *exits, closing door.* EINSTEIN *lights match and crosses* L. *He bumps into table and match goes out. He feels his way* L. *from there. We hear ejaculations and noise.* EINSTEIN *has fallen into window-seat. In window-seat he lights another match and slowly rises up to a sitting position and looks around. He blows out match and hauls himself out of window-seat, speaking.*] Who left dis open? Dummkopf! [*We hear the creak of the cover as he closes it. In the darkness we hear a tap on* L. *window.* EINSTEIN *opens it. Then in a hushed voice.*] Chonny? O.K. Allez Oop. Wait—wait a minute. You lost a leg somewhere.—Ach—now I got him. Come on —ugh—[*He falls on floor and there is a crash of a body and the sound of a "Sshhhh" from outside.*] That was me, Chonny. I schlipped.
JONATHAN. [*Voice.*] Be more careful.

[*Pause.*]

EINSTEIN. Well, his shoe came off. [*Pause.*] All right, Chonny. I got him! [*There is a knock at* R. *door.*] Chonny! Somebody at the door! Go quick. NO. I manage here—go quick!

[*A second knock at door. A moment's silence and we hear the creak of window-seat as* EINSTEIN *puts Mr. Spenalzo in Mr. Hoskins' place. A third knock, as* EINSTEIN *struggles with body. A fourth knock and then the creak of the window-seat as* EINSTEIN *closes it. He scurries around to beside desk, keeping low to avoid being seen through door.* ELAINE *enters* R., *calling softly.*]

ELAINE. Miss Abby! Miss Martha! [*In the dim path of light she comes toward* C., *calling toward balcony.*] Miss Abby! Miss Martha! [*Sud-*

*denly* JONATHAN *steps through door and closes it. The noise swings* ELAINE *around and she gasps.*] Uhhh! Who is it? Is that you, Teddy? [JONATHAN *comes toward her as she backs into chair* R. *of table.*] Who *are* you?

JONATHAN. Who are *you?*

ELAINE. I'm Elaine Harper—I live next door!

JONATHAN. Then what are you doing here?

ELAINE. I came over to see Miss Abby and Miss Martha.

JONATHAN. [*To* EINSTEIN, *without turning.* EINSTEIN *has crept to light-switch after* JONATHAN'S *cross.*] Turn on the lights, Doctor. [*The lights go on.* ELAINE *gasps as she sees* JONATHAN *and sits in chair.* JONATHAN *looks at her for a moment.*] You chose rather an untimely moment for a social call. [*He crosses toward window-seat, looking for Spenalzo, but doesn't see him. He looks up, behind table. Looks out window, then comes back into the room.*]

ELAINE. [*Trying to summon courage.*] I think you'd better explain what you're doing here.

JONATHAN. [D. L. *of table.*] We happen to live here.

ELAINE. You *don't* live here. I'm in this house every day and I've never seen you before. [*Frightened.*] Where are Miss Abby and Miss Martha? What have you done to them?

JONATHAN. [*A step to below table.*] Perhaps we'd better introduce ourselves. This—[*Indicating.*]—is Dr. Einstein.

ELAINE. [*Looks at* EINSTEIN.] Dr. Einstein? [*She turns back to* JONATHAN. EINSTEIN, *behind her back, is gesturing to* JONATHAN *the whereabouts of Spenalzo.*]

JONATHAN. A surgeon of great distinction—[*He looks under table for Spenalzo, and not finding him—*]—and something of a magician.

ELAINE. And I suppose you're going to tell me you're Boris Kar —

JONATHAN. I'm Jonathan Brewster.

ELAINE. [*Drawing back almost with fright.*] Oh—you're Jonathan!

JONATHAN. I see you've heard of me.

[EINSTEIN *drifts to front of sofa.*]

ELAINE. Yes—just this afternoon for the first time.

JONATHAN. [*Stepping toward her.*] And what did they say about me?

ELAINE. Only that there was another brother named Jonathan—that's all that was said. [*Calming.*] Well, that explains everything. Now that I know who you are—[*Running to* R. *door.*] I'll be running along back home. [*The door is locked. She turns to* JONATHAN.] If you'll kindly unlock the door.

[JONATHAN *crosses to her, then, before reaching her, he turns* D. S. *to* R. *door and unlocks it.* EINSTEIN *drifts down to chair* R. *of table. As* JONATHAN *opens door partway,* ELAINE *starts toward it. He turns and stops her with a gesture.*]

JONATHAN. "That explains everything"? Just what did you mean by that? Why did you come here at this time of night?
ELAINE. I thought I saw someone prowling around the house. I suppose it was you.

[JONATHAN *closes door and locks it, leaving key in lock.*]

JONATHAN. You thought you saw someone prowling around the house?
ELAINE. Yes—weren't you outside? Isn't that your car?
JONATHAN. You saw someone at the car?
ELAINE. Yes.
JONATHAN. [*Coming toward her as she backs* U. L.] What else did you see?
ELAINE. Just someone walking around the house to the car.
JONATHAN. What else did you see?
ELAINE. Just that—that's all. That's why I came over here. I wanted to tell Miss Abby to call the police. But if it was you, and that's your car, I don't need to bother Miss Abby. I'll be running along. [*She takes a step toward door above* JONATHAN. *He steps in her path.*]
JONATHAN. What was the man doing at the car?
ELAINE. [*Excited.*] I don't know. You see I was on my way over here.
JONATHAN. [*Forcing her as she backs* L.] I think you're lying.
EINSTEIN. [*Crosses to* U. R. C.] I think she tells the truth, Chonny. We let her go now, huh?
JONATHAN. [*Still forcing her* L.] I think she's lying. Breaking into a house this time of night. I think she's dangerous. She shouldn't be allowed around loose. [*He seizes* ELAINE's *arm. She screams.*]
ELAINE. Take your hands off me—
JONATHAN. Doctor—

[*As* EINSTEIN *starts* L., TEDDY *enters from cellar, shutting door. He looks at* JONATHAN L., *then speaks to* EINSTEIN R.]

TEDDY. [*Simply.*] It's going to be a private funeral. [*He goes up stairs to 1st landing.* ELAINE *crosses to desk, dragging* JONATHAN *with her.*]

ELAINE. Teddy! Teddy! Tell these men who I am.

[TEDDY *turns and looks at her.*]

TEDDY. That's my daughter—Alice. [*He cries "CHARGE!" Dashes up stairs and exits.*]

ELAINE. [*Struggling to get away from* JONATHAN *and dragging him to* R. C.] No! No! Teddy!

[JONATHAN *has* ELAINE's *arm twisted in back of her, his other hand is over her mouth.*]

JONATHAN. Doctor! Your handkerchief! [*As* EINSTEIN *hands him a handkerchief,* JONATHAN *releases his hand from* ELAINE's *mouth to take it. She screams. He puts his hand over her mouth again. Spies the cellar door and speaks to* EINSTEIN.] The cellar!

[EINSTEIN *runs and opens cellar door. (Cellar light is on.) Then he runs back and turns off light-switch, putting stage in darkness.* JONATHAN *pushes* ELAINE *through cellar doorway.* EINSTEIN *runs back and down cellar stairs with* ELAINE. JONATHAN *shuts door, remaining on stage as the* AUNTS *enter on balcony above in their mourning clothes. Everything is in complete darkness except for street lamp.*]

ABBY. What's the matter?

MARTHA. What's happening down there? [MARTHA *shuts her door and* ABBY *puts on lights from switch on balcony. They look down at the room a moment, then come downstairs, speaking as they come.*]

ABBY. What's the matter? [*Reaching foot of stairs as she sees* JONATHAN.] What are you doing?

JONATHAN. We caught a burglar—a sneak thief. Go back to your room.

ABBY. We'll call the police.

JONATHAN. We've called the police. We'll handle this. Go back to your room. Do you hear me?

[*The doorbell rings, followed by several knocks.* ABBY *runs and opens* R. *door.* MORTIMER *enters with suitcase. At the same time,* ELAINE *runs out of cellar and into* MORTIMER's *arms.* JONATHAN *makes a grab for* ELAINE *but misses. This leaves him* D. S. C. EINSTEIN *sneaks* D. S. *behind* JONATHAN.]

ELAINE. Mortimer! [*He drops suitcase.*] Where have you been?

MORTIMER. To the Nora Bayes Theatre and I should have known better. [*He sees* JONATHAN.] My God!—I'm still there.

Arsenic and Old Lace

[ABBY *is at* R. *of* MORTIMER.]

ABBY. This is your brother Jonathan—and this is Dr. Einstein.

[MORTIMER *surveys his* AUNTS *all dressed in black.*]

MORTIMER. I know this isn't a nightmare, but what is it?
JONATHAN. I've come back home, Mortimer.
MORTIMER. [*Looking at him, and then to* ABBY.] Who did you say this was?
ABBY. It's your brother Jonathan. He's had his face changed. Dr. Einstein performed the operation.
MORTIMER. [*Taking a closer look at* JONATHAN.] Jonathan! Jonathan, you always were a horror, but do you have to look like one?

[JONATHAN *takes a step toward him.* EINSTEIN *pulls on his sleeve.* ELAINE *and* MARTHA *draw back to desk.*]

EINSTEIN. Easy, Chonny! Easy.
JONATHAN. Mortimer, have you forgotten the things I used to do to you when we were boys? Remember the time you were tied to the bedpost—the needles under your fingernails—?
MORTIMER. By God, it is Jonathan.—Yes, I remember. I remember you as the most detestable, vicious, venomous form of animal life I ever knew.

[JONATHAN *grows tense.* ABBY *steps between them.*]

ABBY. Now don't you two boys start quarrelling again the minute you've seen each other.
MORTIMER. [*Crosses to door, opens it.*] There won't be any fight, Aunt Abby. Jonathan, you're not wanted here—get out!
JONATHAN. Dr. Einstein and I have been invited to stay.
MORTIMER. Not in this house.
ABBY. Just for tonight.
MORTIMER. I don't want him anywhere near me.
ABBY. But we did invite them for tonight, and it wouldn't be very nice to go back on our word.
MORTIMER. [*Unwillingly.*] All right, tonight. But the first thing in the morning—out! [*He picks up his suitcase.*] Where are they sleeping?
ABBY. We put them in Jonathan's old room.
MORTIMER. That's my old room. [*Starts upstairs.*] I'm sleeping in that room. I'm here to stay.
MARTHA. Oh, Mortimer, I'm so glad.

EINSTEIN. Chonny, we sleep down here.
MORTIMER. You bet your life you sleep down here.
EINSTEIN. [*To* JONATHAN.] You sleep on the sofa and I sleep on the window-seat.

[*At the mention of window-seat,* MORTIMER *has reached the landing; after hanging his hat on hall tree, he turns and comes slowly downstairs, speaking as he reaches the floor and crossing over to window-seat. He drops back at* U. S. *end of window-seat.*]

MORTIMER. The window-seat! Oh, well, let's not argue about it. That window-seat's good enough for me for tonight. I'll sleep on the window-seat. [*As* MORTIMER *crosses above table,* EINSTEIN *makes a gesture as though to stop him from going to window-seat, but he's too late. He turns to* JONATHAN *as* MORTIMER *sits on window-seat.*]
EINSTEIN. You know, Chonny—all this argument—it makes me think of Mr. Spenalzo.
JONATHAN. Spenalzo! [*He steps* U. S. *looking around for Spenalzo again. Realizing it would be best for them to remain downstairs, he speaks to* MORTIMER.] Well, now, Mortimer—It really isn't necessary to inconvenience you like this—we'll sleep down here.
MORTIMER. [*Rising.*] Jonathan, your sudden consideration for me is very unconvincing.
EINSTEIN. [*Goes upstairs to landing.*] Come along, Chonny. We get our things out of the room, eh?
MORTIMER. Don't bother, Doctor!
JONATHAN. By the way, Doctor, I've completely lost track of Mr. Spenalzo.
MORTIMER. Who's this Mr. Spenalzo?
EINSTEIN. [*From landing.*] Just a friend of ours Chonny's been looking for.
MORTIMER. Well, don't bring anyone else in here!
EINSTEIN. It's all right, Chonny. While we pack I tell you all about it. [*He goes on up and through arch.* JONATHAN *starts upstairs.*]
ABBY. [*Dropping* D. S.] Mortimer, you don't have to sleep down here. I can go in with Martha and you can take my room.
JONATHAN. [*He has reached the balcony.*] No trouble at all, Aunt Abby. We'll be packed in a few minutes. And then you can have the room, Mortimer. [*He exits through arch.*]

[MORTIMER *crosses up to sofa.* MARTHA *crosses to above armchair at* L. *of table and as* MORTIMER *speaks she picks up sport shoe belonging to*

Arsenic and Old Lace 327

*Spenalzo, that* EINSTEIN *puts there in blackout scene, unnoticed by anyone. She pretends to dust hem of her dress.*]

MORTIMER. You're just wasting your time—I told you I'm sleeping down here.

[ELAINE *leaps up from stool into* MORTIMER'S *arms.*]

ELAINE. Mortimer!
MORTIMER. What's the matter with you, dear?
ELAINE. [*Semi-hysterical.*] I've almost been killed.
MORTIMER. You've almost been—[*He looks quickly at the* AUNTS.] Abby! Martha!
MARTHA. No! It was Jonathan.
ABBY. He mistook her for a sneak-thief.
ELAINE. No, it was more than that. He's some kind of maniac. Mortimer, I'm afraid of him.
MORTIMER. Why, darling, you're trembling. [*Seats her on sofa. To* AUNTS.] Have you got any smelling salts?
MARTHA. No, but do you think some hot tea, or coffee—?
MORTIMER. Coffee. Make some for me, too—and some sandwiches. I haven't had any dinner.
MARTHA. We'll make something for both of you.

[MORTIMER *starts to question* ELAINE *as* ABBY *takes off her hat and gloves and puts them on sideboard. Talking to* MARTHA *at the same time.*]

ABBY. Martha, we can leave our hats downstairs here, now.

[MORTIMER *turns and sees her. Steps* L.]

MORTIMER. You weren't going out somewhere, were you? Do you know what time it is? It's after twelve. [*The word twelve rings a bell.*] TWELVE! [*He turns to* ELAINE.] Elaine, you've got to go home!
ELAINE. Whaa-t?
ABBY. Why, you wanted some sandwiches for you both. It won't take a minute. [*She exits into kitchen.*]

[MORTIMER *is looking at* ELAINE *with his back to* MARTHA. MARTHA *crosses to him with shoe in hand by her* U. S. *side.*]

MARTHA. Why, don't you remember—we wanted to celebrate your engagement? [*She punctuates the word "engagement" by pointing the shoe at* MORTIMER'S *back. She looks at the shoe in wonderment.*

*Wondering how that shoe ever got in her hand. She stares at it a moment (the other two do not see it, of course), then puts it on top of the table. Finally dismissing it she turns to* MORTIMER *again.*] That's what we'll do dear. We'll make a nice supper for both of you. [*She starts out kitchen door, then turns back.*] And we'll open a bottle of wine! [*She exits kitchen door.*]

MORTIMER. [*Vaguely.*] All right. [*Suddenly changes his mind and runs to kitchen door.*] No WINE! [*He closes the door and comes back to* C. *as* ELAINE *rises from the sofa to him. She is still very upset.*]

ELAINE. Mortimer! What's going on in this house?

MORTIMER. [*Suspicious.*] What do you mean—what's going on in this house?

ELAINE. You were supposed to take me to dinner and the theatre tonight—you called it off. You asked me to marry you—I said I would—and five minutes later you threw me out of the house. Tonight, just after your brother tries to strangle me, you want to chase me home. Now, listen, Mr. Brewster—before I go home, I want to know where I stand. Do you love me?

MORTIMER. [*Taking her hands.*] I love you very much, Elaine. In fact I love you so much I can't marry you.

ELAINE. Have you suddenly gone crazy?

MORTIMER. I don't think so but it's just a matter of time. [*They both sit on sofa as* MORTIMER *begins to explain.*] You see, insanity runs in my family. [*He looks upstairs and toward kitchen.*] It practically gallops. That's why I can't marry you, dear.

ELAINE. Now wait a minute, you've got to do better than that.

MORTIMER. No, dear—there's a strange taint in the Brewster blood. If you really knew my family it's—well—it's what you'd expect if Strindberg had written *Hellzapoppin*.

ELAINE. Now just because Teddy is a little—

MORTIMER. No, it goes way back. The first Brewster—the one who came over on the Mayflower. You know in those days the Indians used to scalp the settlers—he used to scalp the Indians.

ELAINE. Mortimer, that's ancient history.

MORTIMER. No, the whole family . . . [*He rises and points to a picture of Grandfather over the sideboard.*] Take my grandfather—he tried his patent medicines out on dead people to be sure he wouldn't kill them.

ELAINE. He wasn't so crazy. He made a million dollars.

MORTIMER. And then there's Jonathan. You just said he was a maniac—he tried to kill you.

Arsenic and Old Lace

ELAINE. [*Rises, crosses to him.*] But he's your brother, not you. I'm in love with you.

MORTIMER. And there's Teddy, too. You *know* Teddy. He thinks he's Roosevelt. No, dear, no Brewster should marry. I realize now that if I'd met my father in time I'd have stopped him.

ELAINE. Now, darling, all this doesn't prove *you're* crazy. Look at your aunts—they're Brewsters, aren't they?—and the sanest, sweetest people I've ever known.

[MORTIMER *crosses above table to window-seat, speaking as he goes.*]

MORTIMER. Well, even they have their peculiarities.

ELAINE. [*Turning and drifting* R.] Yes, but what lovely peculiarities!— Kindness, generosity—human sympathy—

[MORTIMER *sees* ELAINE'S *back is to him. He lifts window-seat to take a peek, and sees Mr. Spenalzo instead of Mr. Hoskins. He puts window-seat down again and staggers to table, and leans on it.*]

MORTIMER. [*To himself.*] There's another one!

ELAINE. [*Turning to* MORTIMER.] Oh, Mortimer, there are plenty of others. You can't tell me anything about your aunts.

MORTIMER. I'm not going to. [*Crossing to her.*] Look, Elaine, you've got to go home. Something very important has just come up.

ELAINE. Up, from where? We're here alone together.

MORTIMER. I know I'm acting irrationally, but just put it down to the fact that I'm a mad Brewster.

ELAINE. If you think you're going to get out of this by pretending you're insane—you're crazy. Maybe you're not going to marry me, but I'm going to marry you. I love you, you dope.

MORTIMER. [*Urging her to* R. *door.*] Well, if you love me will you get the hell out of here!

ELAINE. Well, at least take me home, won't you? I'm afraid.

MORTIMER. Afraid! A little walk through the cemetery?

[ELAINE *crosses to door, then changing tactics, turns to* MORTIMER.]

ELAINE. Mortimer, will you kiss me good night?

MORTIMER. [*Holding out arms.*] Of course, dear. [*What* MORTIMER *plans to be a desultory peck,* ELAINE *turns into a production number. He comes out of it with no less of poise.*] Good night, dear. I'll call you up in a day or two.

ELAINE. [*She walks to* R. *door in a cold fury, opens it and turns to* MORTIMER.] You—you critic! [*She slams door after her.*]

[MORTIMER *looks at the door helplessly then turns and stalks to the kitchen door.*]

MORTIMER. [*In doorway.*] Aunt Abby! Aunt Martha! Come in here!
ABBY. [*Offstage.*] We'll be in in a minute, dear.
MORTIMER. Come in here now! [*He stands down by* U. S. *end of window-seat.*]

[ABBY *enters from kitchen.*]

ABBY. Yes, dear, what is it? Where's Elaine?
MORTIMER. I thought you promised me not to let anyone in this house while I was gone!

[*The following speeches overlap.*]

ABBY. Well, Jonathan just walked in—
MORTIMER. I don't mean Jonathan—
ABBY. And Dr. Einstein was with him—
MORTIMER. I don't mean Dr. Einstein. Who's that in the window-seat?
ABBY. We told you—Mr. Hoskins.

[MORTIMER *throws open the window-seat and steps back* U. L.]

MORTIMER. It is *not* Mr. Hoskins.

[ABBY, *a little puzzled, walks to window-seat and looks in at* D. S. *end then speaks very simply.*]

ABBY. Who can that be?
MORTIMER. [R. *of* ABBY.] Are you trying to tell me you've never seen this man before?
ABBY. I certainly am. Why, this is a fine how do you do! It's getting so anybody thinks he can walk into this house.
MORTIMER. Now Aunt Abby, don't you try to get out of this. That's another one of your gentlemen!
ABBY. Mortimer, how can you say such a thing! That man's an impostor! And if he came here to be buried in our cellar he's mistaken.
MORTIMER. Oh, Aunt Abby, you admitted to me that you put Mr. Hoskins in the window-seat.
ABBY. Yes, I did.

MORTIMER. Well, this man couldn't have just got the idea from Mr. Hoskins. By the way—where is Mr. Hoskins? [*He looks toward cellar door.*]

[ABBY *crosses above table to* U. C.]

ABBY. He must have gone to Panama.

MORTIMER. Oh, you buried him?

ABBY. No, not yet. He's just down there waiting for the services, poor dear. We haven't had a minute what with Jonathan in the house. [*At the mention of* JONATHAN's *name,* MORTIMER *closes the window-seat.*] Oh, dear. We've always wanted to hold a double funeral, [*Crossing to kitchen door.*] but I will not read services over a total stranger.

MORTIMER. [*Going up to her.*] A stranger! Aunt Abby, how can I believe you? There are twelve men in the cellar and you admit you poisoned them.

ABBY. Yes, I did. But you don't think I'd stoop to telling a fib. Martha! [*She exits into kitchen.*]

[*At the same time* JONATHAN *enters thorough the arch onto balcony and comes down quickly to foot of stairs.* MORTIMER *crosses to* D. R. C. JONATHAN *sees him and crosses to him.*]

JONATHAN. Oh, Mortimer—I'd like to have a word with you.

MORTIMER. [*Standing up to him.*] A word's about all you'll have time for, Jonathan, because I've decided you and your Doctor friend are going to have to get out of this house just as quickly as possible.

JONATHAN. [*Smoothly.*] I'm glad you recognize the fact that you and I can't live under the same roof—but you've arrived at the wrong solution. Take your suitcase and get out! [*He starts to cross above* MORTIMER, *anxious to get to the window-seat, but* MORTIMER *makes big sweep around above table and comes back to him at* D. S. C.]

MORTIMER. Jonathan!—You're beginning to bore me. You've played your one night stand in Brooklyn—move on!

JONATHAN. My dear Mortimer, just because you've graduated from the back fence to the typewriter, don't think you've grown up. . . . [*He takes a sudden step* U. S. *around* MORTIMER *and gets to the window-seat and sits.*] I'm staying, and you're leaving—and I mean now!

MORTIMER. [*Crossing to him.*] If you think I can be frightened—if you think there's anything I fear—

JONATHAN. [*He rises, they stand facing each other.*] I've lived a strange life, Mortimer. But it's taught me one thing—to be afraid of nothing! [*They glare at each other with equal courage when* ABBY *marches in from kitchen, followed by* MARTHA.]

ABBY. Martha, just look and see what's in that window-seat.

[*Both* MEN *throw themselves on the window-seat simultaneously.* JONATHAN D. S. *end.*]

MORTIMER *and* JONATHAN. Now, Aunt Abby!

[MORTIMER *turns his head slowly to* JONATHAN, *light dawning on his face. He rises with smiling assurance.*]

MORTIMER. Jonathan, let Aunt Martha see what's in the window-seat. [JONATHAN *freezes dangerously.* MORTIMER *crosses below table up to* ABBY.] Aunt Abby, I owe you an apology. [*He kisses her on forehead.*] I have very good news for you. Jonathan is leaving. He's taking Dr. Einstein and their cold companion with him. [JONATHAN *rises but holds his ground.*] Jonathan, you're my brother. You're a Brewster. I'm going to give you a chance to get away and take the evidence with you—you can't ask for more than that. [JONATHAN *doesn't move.*] Very well,—in that case I'll have to call the police. [MORTIMER *crosses to phone and picks it up.*]

JONATHAN. Don't reach for that telephone. [*He crosses to* L. *of* MORTIMER.] Are you still giving me orders after seeing what's happened to Mr. Spenalzo?

MARTHA. [*She's above table.*] Spenalzo?

ABBY. [U. C.] I knew he was a foreigner.

JONATHAN. Remember what happened to Mr. Spenalzo can happen to you too.

[*There is a knock on* R. *door.* ABBY *crosses and opens it and* OFFICER O'HARA *sticks his head in.*]

O'HARA. Hello, Miss Abby.

ABBY. Oh, Officer O'Hara. Is there something we can do for you?

[MORTIMER *puts phone down and drifts down close to* O'HARA. JONATHAN *turns* L.]

O'HARA. I saw your lights on and thought there might be sickness in the house. [*He sees* MORTIMER.] Oh, you got company—I'm sorry I disturbed you.

Arsenic and Old Lace 333

MORTIMER. [*Taking* O'HARA *by the arm.*] No, no, come in.
ABBY. Yes, come in.
MARTHA. [*Crossing to door.*] Come right in, Officer O'Hara. [MORTIMER *leads* O'HARA *in a couple of steps and shuts door.* ABBY *crosses back to* U. S. C. MARTHA *is near desk.* JONATHAN *is in front of sofa* R. *of* ABBY. MARTHA, *to* O'HARA.] This is our nephew, Mortimer.
O'HARA. Pleased to meet you.

[JONATHAN *starts toward kitchen.*]

ABBY. [*Stopping* JONATHAN.] And this is another nephew, Jonathan.
O'HARA. [*Crosses below* MORTIMER *and gestures to* JONATHAN *with his night stick.*] Pleased to make your acquaintance. [JONATHAN *ignores him.* O'HARA *sepaks to* AUNTS.] Well, it must be nice havin' your nephews visitin' you. Are they going to stay with you for a bit?
MORTIMER. I'm staying. My brother Jonathan is just leaving.

[JONATHAN *starts for stairs.* O'HARA *stops him.*]

O'HARA. I've met you here before, haven't I?
ABBY. I'm afraid not. Jonathan hasn't been home for years.
O'HARA. Your face looks familiar to me. Maybe I seen a picture of you somewheres.
JONATHAN. I don't think so. [*He hurries upstairs.*]
MORTIMER. Yes, Jonathan, I'd hurry if I were you. Your things are all packed anyway, aren't they?
O'HARA. Well, you'll be wanting to say your good-byes. I'll be running along.
MORTIMER. What's the rush? I'd like to have you stick around until my brother goes.

[JONATHAN *exits through arch.*]

O'HARA. I just dropped in to make sure everything was all right.
MORTIMER. We're going to have some coffee in a minute. Won't you join us?
ABBY. Oh, I forgot the coffee. [*She goes out to kitchen.*]
MARTHA. [*Crossing to kitchen door.*] Well, I'd better make some more sandwiches. I ought to know your appetite by this time, Officer O'Hara. [*She goes out to kitchen as* O'HARA *follows as far as* C.]
O'HARA. Don't bother. I'm due to ring in in a few minutes.

MORTIMER. You can have a cup of coffee with us. My brother will be gone soon. [*He leads* O'HARA *below table to armchair.*] Sit down.
O'HARA. Say—ain't I seen a photograph of your brother around here some place?
MORTIMER. I don't think so. [*He sits* R. *of table.*]
O'HARA. He certainly reminds me of somebody.
MORTIMER. He looks like somebody you've probably seen in the movies.
O'HARA. I never go to the movies. I hate 'em! My mother says the movies is a bastard art.
MORTIMER. Yes, it's full of them.—Your, er, mother said that?
O'HARA. Yeah. My mother was an actress—a stage actress. Perhaps you heard of her—Peaches Latour.
MORTIMER. It sounds like a name I've seen on a program. What did she play?
O'HARA. Well, her big hit was "Mutt and Jeff." Played it for three years. I was born on tour—the third season.
MORTIMER. You were?
O'HARA. Yep. Sioux City, Iowa. I was born in the dressing room at the end of the second act, and Mother made the finale.
MORTIMER. What a trouper! There must be a good story in your mother —you know, I write about the theatre.
O'HARA. You do? Saay!—you're not Mortimer Brewster, the dramatic critic!
MORTIMER. Yes.
O'HARA. Well, I certainly am glad to meet you. [*He moves his hat and stick preparatory to shaking hands with* MORTIMER. *He also picks up the sport shoe which* MARTHA *has left on the table. He looks at it just for a split second and puts it on the* D. S. *end of table.* MORTIMER *sees it and stares at it.*] Say, Mr. Brewster—we're in the same line of business.
MORTIMER. [*Still intent on shoe.*] We are?
O'HARA. Yeah. I'm a playwright. Oh, this being on the police force is just temporary.
MORTIMER. How long have you been on the force?
O'HARA. Twelve years. I'm collecting material for a play.
MORTIMER. I'll bet it's a honey.
O'HARA. Well, it ought to be. With all the drama I see being a cop. Mr. Brewster—you got no idea what goes on in Brooklyn.

Arsenic and Old Lace

MORTIMER. I think I have. [*He puts the shoe under his chair, then looks at his watch, then looks toward balcony.*]

O'HARA. Say, what time you got?

MORTIMER. Ten after one.

O'HARA. Gee, I gotta ring in. [*He starts for* R. *door but* MORTIMER *stops him at* C.]

MORTIMER. Wait a minute, O'Hara. On that play of yours—I may be able to help you. [*Sits him in chair* R.]

O'HARA. [*Ecstasy.*] You would! [*Rises.*] Say, it was fate my walking in here tonight. Look—I'll tell you the plot!

[*At this point* JONATHAN *enters on the balcony followed by* DR. EINSTEIN. *They each have a bag. At the same moment* ABBY *enters from the kitchen. Helpful as the cop has been,* MORTIMER *does not want to listen to his plot. As he backs away from him he speaks to* JONATHAN *as they come down stairs.*]

MORTIMER. Oh, you're on your way, eh? Good! You haven't got much time, you know.

ABBY. [U. L.] Well, everything's just about ready. [*Sees* JONATHAN *and* EINSTEIN *at foot of stairs.*] Oh, you leaving now, Jonathan? Good-bye. Good-bye, Dr. Einstein. [*She sees instrument case above window-seat.*] Oh, doesn't this case belong to you?

[*This reminds* MORTIMER *of Mr. Spenalzo, also.*]

MORTIMER. Yes, Jonathan—you can't go without *all* of your things. [*Now to get rid of* O'HARA. *He turns to him.*] Well, O'Hara, it was nice meeting you. I'll see you again and we'll talk about your play.

O'HARA. [*Refusing to leave.*] Oh, I'm not leaving now, Mr. Brewster.

MORTIMER. Why not?

O'HARA. Well, you just offered to help me with my play, didn't you? You and me are going to write my play together.

MORTIMER. I can't do that, O'Hara—I'm not a creative writer.

O'HARA. I'll do the creating. You just put the words to it.

MORTIMER. But, O'Hara—

O'HARA. No, sir, Mr. Brewster. I ain't leaving this house till I tell you the plot. [*He crosses and sits on window-seat.*]

JONATHAN. [*Starting for* R. *door.*] In that case, Mortimer . . . we'll be running along.

MORTIMER. Don't try that. You can't go yet. You've got to take *every-*

*thing* with you, you know. [*He turns and sees* O'HARA *on window-seat and runs to him.*] Look, O'Hara, you run along now, eh? My brother's just going—

O'HARA. I can wait. I've been waiting twelve years.

[MARTHA *enters from kitchen with a tray of coffee and sandwiches.*]

MARTHA. I'm sorry I was so long.

MORTIMER. Don't bring that in here. O'Hara, would you join us for a bite in the kitchen?

MARTHA. The kitchen?

ABBY. [*To* MARTHA.] Jonathan's leaving.

MARTHA. Oh. Well, that's nice. Come along, Officer O'Hara. [*She exits to kitchen.*]

[O'HARA *gets to kitchen doorway as* ABBY *speaks.*]

ABBY. Sure you don't mind eating in the kitchen, Mr. O'Hara?

O'HARA. And where else would you eat?

ABBY. Good-bye, Jonathan, nice to have seen you again.

[O'HARA *exits to kitchen, followed by* ABBY. MORTIMER *crosses to kitchen doorway and shuts door, then turns to* JONATHAN.]

MORTIMER. I'm glad you came back to Brooklyn, Jonathan, because it gives me a chance to throw you out—and the first one out is your boy friend, Mr. Spenalzo.

[*He lifts up window-seat. As he does so,* O'HARA, *sandwich in hand, enters from kitchen.* MORTIMER *drops window-seat.*]

O'HARA. Look, Mr. Brewster, we can talk in here.

MORTIMER. [*Pushing him into kitchen.*] Coming right out.

JONATHAN. I might have known you'd grow up to write a play with a policeman.

MORTIMER. [*From kitchen doorway.*] Get going now—all three of you. [*He exits, shutting door.*]

[JONATHAN *puts bag down and crosses to window-seat.*]

JONATHAN. Doctor, this affair between my brother and me has got to be settled.

EINSTEIN. [*Crossing to window-seat for instrument case and bringing it back to foot of stairs.*] Now, Chonny, we got trouble enough. Your brother gives us a chance to get away—what more could you ask?

Arsenic and Old Lace

JONATHAN. You don't understand. [*He lifts window-seat.*] This goes back a good many years.

EINSTEIN. [*Foot of stairs.*] Now, Chonny, let's get going.

JONATHAN. [*Harshly.*] We're not going. We're going to sleep right here tonight.

EINSTEIN. With a cop in the kitchen and Mr. Spenalzo in the window-seat.

JONATHAN. That's all he's got on us. [*Puts window-seat down.*] We'll take Mr. Spenalzo down and dump him in the bay, and come right back here.—Then if he tries to interfere—[*He crosses to* C. EINSTEIN *crosses to* L. *of him and faces him.*]

EINSTEIN. Now, Chonny.

JONATHAN. Doctor, you know when I make up my mind—

EINSTEIN. Yeah—when you make up your mind, you lose your head. Brooklyn ain't a good place for you.

JONATHAN. [*Peremptorily.*] Doctor!

EINSTEIN. O.K. We got to stick together. [*He crosses to bags.*] Some day we get stuck together. If we're coming back here do we got to take these with us?

JONATHAN. No. leave them here. Hide them in the cellar. Move fast! [*He moves to bags to* L. *end of sofa as* EINSTEIN *goes down cellar with instrument case.*] Spenalzo can go out the same way he came in! [*He kneels on window-seat and looks out. Then as he starts to lift window-seat,* EINSTEIN *comes in from the cellar with some excitement.*]

EINSTEIN. Hey, Chonny, come quick!

JONATHAN. [*Crossing to him.*] What's the matter?

EINSTEIN. You know that hole in the cellar?

JONATHAN. Yes.

EINSTEIN. We got an *ace* in the hole. Come on I show you. [*They both exit into cellar.* JONATHAN *shuts door.*]

[MORTIMER *enters from kitchen, sees their bags still there. He opens window-seat and sees Spenalzo. Then he puts his head out window and yells.*]

MORTIMER. Jonathan! Jonathan! [JONATHAN *comes through cellar door unnoticed by* MORTIMER *and crosses to back of him.* EINSTEIN *comes down into* C. *of room.*] Jonathan!

JONATHAN. [*Quietly.*] Yes, Mortimer.

MORTIMER. [*Leaping backwards to below table.*] Where have you two been? I thought I told you to get—
JONATHAN. We're not going.
MORTIMER. Oh, you're not? You think I'm not serious about this, eh? Do you want O'Hara to know what's in that window-seat?
JONATHAN. We're staying here.
MORTIMER. [*Crossing around above table to kitchen door.*] All right! You asked for it. This gets me rid of you and Officer O'Hara at the same time. [*Opens kitchen door, yells out.*] Officer O'Hara, come in here!
JONATHAN. If you tell O'Hara what's in the window-seat, I'll tell him what's down in the cellar.

[MORTIMER *closes kitchen door quickly.*]

MORTIMER. The cellar?
JONATHAN. There's an elderly gentleman down there who seems to be very dead.
MORTIMER. What were you doing down in the cellar?
EINSTEIN. What's *he* doing down in the cellar?

[O'HARA's *voice is heard offstage.*]

O'HARA. No, thanks, ma'am. They were fine. I've had plenty.
JONATHAN. Now what are you going to say to O'Hara?

[O'HARA *walks in kitchen door.*]

O'HARA. Say, Mr. Brewster, your aunts want to hear it too. Shall I get them in here?
MORTIMER. [*Pulling him* R.] No, O'Hara, you can't do that now. You've got to ring in.

[O'HARA *stops at* C. *as* MORTIMER *opens the door.*]

O'HARA. The hell with ringing in. I'll get your aunts in here and tell you the plot. [*He starts for kitchen door.*]
MORTIMER. [*Grabbing him.*] No, O'Hara, not in front of all these people. We'll get together alone, some place later.
O'HARA. How about the back room at Kelly's?
MORTIMER. [*Passing* O'HARA R. *in front of him.*] Fine! You go ring in, and I'll meet you at Kelly's.

Arsenic and Old Lace

JONATHAN. [*At window-seat.*] Why don't you two go down in the cellar?
O'HARA. That's all right with me. [*Starts for cellar door.*] Is this the cellar?
MORTIMER. [*Grabbing him again, pushing toward door.*] Nooo! We'll go to Kelly's. But you're going to ring in on the way.
O'HARA. [*As he exits* R.] All right, that'll only take a couple of minutes. [*He's gone.*]

[MORTIMER *takes his hat from hall tree and crosses to open* R. *door.*]

MORTIMER. I'll ditch this guy and be back in five minutes. I'll expect to find you gone. [*Changes his mind.*] Wait for me. [*He exits* R.]

[EINSTEIN *sits* R. *of table.*]

JONATHAN. We'll wait for him, Doctor. I've waited a great many years for a chance like this.
EINSTEIN. We got him right where we want him. Did he look guilty!
JONATHAN. [*Rising.*] Take the bags back up to our room, Doctor.

[EINSTEIN *gets bags and reaches foot of stairs with them.* ABBY *and* MARTHA *enter from kitchen.* ABBY *speaks as she enters.*]

ABBY. Have they gone? [*Sees* JONATHAN *and* EINSTEIN.] Oh—we thought we heard somebody leave.
JONATHAN. [*Crossing to* R. C.] Just Mortimer, and he'll be back in a few minutes. Is there any food left in the kitchen? I think Dr. Einstein and I would enjoy a bite.
MARTHA. [L. *of table.*] But you won't have time.
ABBY. [*At* C.] No, if you're still here when Mortimer gets back he won't like it.
EINSTEIN. [*Dropping* D. S. R.] He'll like it. He's gotta like it.
JONATHAN. Get something for us to eat while we bury Mr. Spenalzo in the cellar.
MARTHA. [*Crossing to below table.*] Oh no!
ABBY. He can't stay in our cellar. No, Jonathan, you've got to take him with you.
JONATHAN. There's a friend of Mortimer's downstairs waiting for him.
ABBY. A friend of Mortimer's?
JONATHAN. He and Mr. Spenalzo will get along fine together. They're both dead.
MARTHA. They must mean Mr. Hoskins.
EINSTEIN. Mr. Hoskins?

JONATHAN. You know about what's downstairs?
ABBY. Of course we do, and he's no friend of Mortimer's. He's one of our gentlemen.
EINSTEIN. Your chentlemen?
MARTHA. And we won't have any strangers buried in our cellar.
JONATHAN. [*Noncomprehending.*] But Mr. Hoskins—
MARTHA. Mr. Hoskins isn't a stranger.
ABBY. Besides, there's no room for Mr. Spenalzo. The cellar's crowded already.
JONATHAN. Crowded? With what?
ABBY. There are twelve graves down there now.

[*The two* MEN *draw back in amazement.*]

JONATHAN. Twelve graves!
ABBY. That leaves very little room and we're going to need it.
JONATHAN. You mean you and Aunt Martha have murdered—?
ABBY. Murdered! Certainly not. It's one of our charities.
MARTHA. [*Indignantly.*] Why, what we've been doing is a mercy.
ABBY. [*Gesturing outside.*] So you just take your Mr. Spenalzo out of here.
JONATHAN. [*Still unable to believe.*] You've done that—here in this house —[*Points to floor.*] and you've buried them down there!
EINSTEIN. Chonny—we've been chased all over the world—they stay right here in Brooklyn and do just as good as you do.
JONATHAN. [*Facing him.*] What?
EINSTEIN. You've got twelve and they've got twelve.
JONATHAN. [*Slowly.*] I've got thirteen.
EINSTEIN. No, Chonny, twelve.
JONATHAN. Thirteen! [*Counting on fingers.*] There's Mr. Spenalzo. Then the first one in London—two in Johannesburg—one in Sydney—one in Melbourne—two in San Francisco—one in Phoenix, Arizona—
EINSTEIN. Phoenix?
JONATHAN. The filling station. The three in Chicago and the one in South Bend. That makes thirteen!
EINSTEIN. But you can't count the one in South Bend. He died of pneumonia.
JONATHAN. He wouldn't have got pneumonia if I hadn't shot him.
EINSTEIN. [*Adamant.*] No, Chonny, he died of pneumonia. He don't count.

Arsenic and Old Lace 341

JONATHAN. He counts with me. I say thirteen.

EINSTEIN. No, Chonny. You got twelve and they got twelve. [*Crossing to* AUNTS.] The old ladies are just as good as you are.

[*The two* AUNTS *smile at each other happily.* JONATHAN *turns, facing the three of them and speaks menacingly.*]

JONATHAN. Oh, they are, are they? Well, that's easily taken care of. All I need is one more, that's all—just one more.

[MORTIMER *enters hastily* R., *closing door behind him, and turns to them with a nervous smile.*]

MORTIMER. Well, here I am!

[JONATHAN *turns and looks at him with the widening eyes of someone who has just solved a problem, as the curtain falls.*]

# ACT III

SCENE 1: The scene is the same. Still later that night. The curtain rises on an empty stage. The window-seat is open and we see that it's empty. The armchair has been shifted to R. of table. The drapes over the windows are closed. All doors except cellar are closed. ABBY's hymnal and black gloves are on sideboard. MARTHA's hymnal and gloves are on table. Otherwise the room is the same. As the curtain rises we hear a row from the cellar, through the open door. The speeches overlap in excitement and anger until the AUNTS appear on the stage, from cellar door.

MARTHA. You stop doing that!

ABBY. This is our house and this is our cellar and you can't do that.

EINSTEIN. Ladies! Please!—Go back upstairs where you belong.

JONATHAN. Abby! Martha! Go upstairs!

MARTHA. There's no use your doing what you're doing because it will just have to be undone.

ABBY. I tell you we won't have it and you'd better stop it right now.

MARTHA. [*Entering from cellar.*] All right! You'll find out. You'll find out whose house this is. [*She crosses to door* D. R., *opens it and looks out. Then closes it.*]

ABBY. [*Entering.*] I'm warning you! You'd better stop it! [D. S. C. *To* MARTHA.] Hasn't Mortimer come back yet?

MARTHA. No.

ABBY. It's a terrible thing to do—to bury a good Methodist with a foreigner. [*She crosses to window-seat.*]

MARTHA. [*Crossing to cellar door.*] I will not have our cellar desecrated!

ABBY. [*Drops window-seat.*] And we promised Mr. Hoskins a full Christian funeral. Where do you suppose Mortimer went?

MARTHA. [*Drops D. S.*] I don't know, but he must be doing something—because he said to Jonathan, "You just wait, I'll settle this."

ABBY. [*Crossing up to sideboard.*] Well, he can't very well settle it while he's out of the house. That's all we want settled—what's going on down there.

[MORTIMER *enters R., closes door.*]

MORTIMER. [*As one who has everything settled.*] All right. Now, where's Teddy?

[*The* AUNTS *are very much annoyed with* MORTIMER.]

ABBY. Mortimer, where have you been?

MORTIMER. I've been over to Dr. Gilchrist's. I've got his signature on Teddy's commitment papers.

MARTHA. Mortimer, what is the matter with you?

ABBY. [*To below table.*] Running around getting papers signed at a time like this!

MARTHA. Do you know what Jonathan's doing?

ABBY. He's putting Mr. Hoskins and Mr. Spenalzo in together.

MORTIMER. [*To cellar door.*] Oh, he is, is he? Well, let him. [*He shuts cellar door.*] Is Teddy in his room?

MARTHA. Teddy won't be any help.

MORTIMER. When he signs these commitment papers I can tackle Jonathan.

ABBY. What have they got to do with it?

MORTIMER. You had to go and tell Jonathan about those twelve graves. If I can make Teddy responsible for those I can protect you, don't you see?

ABBY. No, I don't see. And we pay taxes to have the police protect us.

MORTIMER. [*Going upstairs.*] I'll be back down in a minute.

ABBY. [*Takes gloves and hymnal from table.*] Come, Martha. We're going for the police.

[MARTHA *gets her gloves and hymnal from sideboard. They both start* R. *to door.*]

MORTIMER. [*On landing.*] All right. [*He turns and rushes downstairs to* R. *door before they can reach it.*] The police. You can't go for the police.

MARTHA. [D. R., *but* L. *of* ABBY.] Why can't we?

MORTIMER. [*Near* R. *door.*] Because if you tell the police about Mr. Spenalzo they'd find Mr. Hoskins too, [*Crosses to* MARTHA.] and that might make them curious, and they'd find out about the other twelve gentlemen.

ABBY. Mortimer, we know the police better than you do. I don't think they'd pry into our private affairs if we asked them not to.

MORTIMER. But if they found your twelve gentlemen they'd have to report to headquarters.

MARTHA. [*Pulling on her gloves.*] I'm not so sure they'd bother. They'd have to make out a very long report—and if there's one thing a policeman hates to do, it's to write.

MORTIMER. You can't depend on that. It might leak out!—and you couldn't expect a judge and jury to understand.

MARTHA. Oh, Judge Cullman would.

ABBY. [*Drawing on her gloves.*] We know him very well.

MARTHA. He always comes to church to pray—just before election.

ABBY. And he's coming here to tea some day. He promised.

MARTHA. Oh, Abby, we must speak to him again about that. [*To* MORTIMER.] His wife died a few years ago and it's left him very lonely.

ABBY. Well, come along, Martha. [*She starts toward door* R. MORTIMER *gets there first.*]

MORTIMER. No! You can't do this. I won't let you. You can't leave this house, and you can't have Judge Cullman to tea.

ABBY. Well, if you're not going to do something about Mr. Spenalzo, we are.

MORTIMER. I am going to do something. We may have to call the police in later, but if we do, I want to be ready for them.

MARTHA. You've got to get Jonathan out of this house!

ABBY. And Mr. Spenalzo, too!

MORTIMER. Will you please let me do this my own way? [*He starts upstairs.*] I've got to see Teddy.

ABBY. [*Facing* MORTIMER *on stairs.*] If they're not out of here by morning, Mortimer, we're going to call the police.

MORTIMER. [*On balcony.*] They'll be out, I promise you that! Go to bed, will you? And for God's sake get out of those clothes—you look like Judith Anderson. [*He exits into hall, closing door.*]

[*The* AUNTS *watch him off.* MARTHA *turns to* ABBY.]

MARTHA. Well, Abby, that's a relief, isn't it?

ABBY. Yes—if Mortimer's really going to do something at last, it just means Jonathan's going to a lot of unnecessary trouble. We'd better tell him. [ABBY *starts to cellar door as* JONATHAN *comes in. They meet* U. S. C. *front of sofa. His clothes are dirty.*] Oh, Jonathan—you might as well stop what you're doing.

JONATHAN. It's all done. Did I hear Mortimer?

ABBY. Well, it will just have to be undone. You're all going to be out of this house by morning. Mortimer's promised.

JONATHAN. Oh, are we? In that case, you and Aunt Martha can go to bed and have a pleasant night's sleep.

MARTHA. [*Always a little frightened by* JONATHAN, *starts upstairs.*] Yes. Come, Abby.

[ABBY *follows* MARTHA *upstairs.*]

JONATHAN. Good night, Aunties.

ABBY. Not good night, Jonathan. Good-bye. By the time we get up you'll be out of this house. Mortimer's promised.

MARTHA. [*On balcony.*] And he has a way of doing it too!

JONATHAN. Then Mortimer is back?

ABBY. Oh, yes, he's up here talking to Teddy.

MARTHA. Good-bye, Jonathan.

ABBY. Good-bye, Jonathan.

JONATHAN. Perhaps you'd better say good-bye to Mortimer.

ABBY. Oh, you'll see Mortimer.

JONATHAN. [*Sitting on stool.*] Yes—I'll see Mortimer.

[ABBY *and* MARTHA *exit.* JONATHAN *sits without moving. There is murder in his thought.* EINSTEIN *enters from cellar. He dusts off his trouser cuffs, lifting his leg, and we see he is wearing Spenalzo's sport shoes.*]

EINSTEIN. Whew! That's all fixed up. Smooth like a lake. Nobody'd ever know they were down there. [JONATHAN *still sits without*

Arsenic and Old Lace     345

*moving.*] That bed feels good already. Forty-eight hours we didn't sleep. [*Crossing to second stair.*] Come on, Chonny, let's go up, yes?

JONATHAN. You're forgetting, Doctor.

EINSTEIN. Vat?

JONATHAN. My brother Mortimer.

EINSTEIN. Chonny—tonight? We do that tomorrow or the next day.

JONATHAN. [*Just able to control himself.*] No, tonight! Now!

EINSTEIN. [*Down to floor.*] Chonny, please—I'm tired—and tomorrow I got to operate.

JONATHAN. Yes, you're operating tomorrow, Doctor. But tonight we take care of Mortimer.

EINSTEIN. [*Kneeling in front of* JONATHAN, *trying to pacify him.*] But, Chonny, not tonight—we go to bed, eh?

JONATHAN. [*Rising.* EINSTEIN *straightens up too.*] Doctor, look at me. You can see it's going to be done, can't you?

EINSTEIN. [*Retreating.*] Ach, Chonny—I can see. I know dat look!

JONATHAN. It's a little too late for us to dissolve our partnership.

EINSTEIN. O.K., we do it. But the quick way. The quick twist like in London. [*He gives that London neck another twist with his hands and makes a noise suggesting strangulation.*]

JONATHAN. No, Doctor, I think this calls for something special. [*He walks toward* EINSTEIN, *who breaks* U. S. JONATHAN *has the look of beginning to anticipate a rare pleasure.*] I think perhaps the Melbourne method.

EINSTEIN. Chonny—no—not that. Two hours! And when it was all over, what? The fellow in London was just as dead as the fellow in Melbourne.

JONATHAN. We had to work too fast in London. There was no esthetic satisfaction in it—but Melbourne, ah, there was something to remember.

EINSTEIN. [*Dropping* D. S. *as* JONATHAN *crosses him.*] Remember! [*He shivers.*] I vish I didn't. No, Chonny—not Melbourne—not me!

JONATHAN. Yes, Doctor. Where are the instruments?

EINSTEIN. I won't do it, Chonny.—I won't do it.

JONATHAN. [*Advancing on him as* EINSTEIN *backs* D. S.] Get your instruments!

EINSTEIN. No, Chonny!

JONATHAN. Where are they? Oh, yes—you hid them in the cellar. Where?

EINSTEIN. I won't tell you.
JONATHAN. [*Going to cellar door.*] I'll find them, Doctor. [*He exits to cellar, closing door.*]

[TEDDY *enters on balcony and lifts his bugle to blow.* MORTIMER *dashes out and grabs his arm.* EINSTEIN *has rushed to cellar door. He stands there as* MORTIMER *and* TEDDY *speak.*]

MORTIMER. Don't do that, Mr. President.
TEDDY. I cannot sign any proclamation without consulting my cabinet.
MORTIMER. But this must be a secret.
TEDDY. A secret proclamation? How unusual.
MORTIMER. Japan mustn't know until it's signed.
TEDDY. Japan! Those yellow devils. I'll sign it right away. [*Taking legal paper from* MORTIMER.] You have my word for it. I can let the cabinet know later.
MORTIMER. Yes, let's go and sign it.
TEDDY. You wait here. A secret proclamation has to be signed in secret.
MORTIMER. But at once, Mr. President.
TEDDY. I'll have to put on my signing clothes. [TEDDY *exits.*]

[MORTIMER *comes downstairs.* EINSTEIN *crosses and takes* MORTIMER'S *hat off of hall tree and hands it to him.*]

EINSTEIN. [*Anxious to get* MORTIMER *out of the house.*] Ah, you go now, eh?
MORTIMER. [*Takes hat and puts it on desk.*] No, Doctor, I'm waiting for something. Something important.
EINSTEIN. [L. *of* MORTIMER.] Please— you go now!
MORTIMER. Dr. Einstein, I have nothing against you personally. You seem to be a nice fellow. Take my advice and get out of this house and get just as far away as possible.
EINSTEIN. Trouble, yah! You get out.
MORTIMER. [*Crossing to* C.] All right, don't say I didn't warn you.
EINSTEIN. I'm warning you—get away quick.
MORTIMER. Things are going to start popping around here any minute.
EINSTEIN. [D. R.] Listen—Chonny's in a bad mood. When he's like dis, he's a madman—things happen—terrible things.
MORTIMER. Jonathan doesn't worry me now.
EINSTEIN. Ach, himmel—don't those plays you see teach you anything?
MORTIMER. About what?

EINSTEIN. Vell, at least people in plays act like they got sense—that's more than you do.
MORTIMER. [*Interested in this observation.*] Oh, you think so, do you? You think people in plays act intelligently. I wish you had to sit through some of the ones I have to sit through. Take the little opus I saw tonight for instance. In this play, there's a man—he's supposed to be bright . . . [JONATHAN *enters from cellar with instrument case, stands in doorway and listens to* MORTIMER.]—he knows he's in a house with murderers—he ought to know he's in danger—he's even been warned to get out of the house—but does he go? No, he stays there. Now I ask you, Doctor, is that what an intelligent person would do?
EINSTEIN. You're asking me?
MORTIMER. He didn't even have sense enough to be frightened, to be on guard. For instance, the murderer invites him to sit down.
EINSTEIN. [*He moves so as to keep* MORTIMER *from seeing* JONATHAN.] You mean—"Won't you sit down?"
MORTIMER. [*Reaches out and pulls armchair to him* R. *of table without turning his head from* EINSTEIN.] Believe it or not, that one was in there too.
EINSTEIN. And what did he do?
MORTIMER. [*Sitting in armchair.*] He sat down. Now mind you, this fellow's supposed to be bright. There he sits—just waiting to be trussed up. And what do you think they use to tie him with.
EINSTEIN. Vat?
MORTIMER. The curtain cord.

[JONATHAN *spies curtain cords on either side of window in* L. *wall. He crosses, stands on window-seat and cuts cords with penknife.*]

EINSTEIN. Vell, why not? A good idea. Very convenient.
MORTIMER. A little too convenient. When are playwrights going to use some imagination! The curtain cord!

[JONATHAN *has got the curtain cord and is moving in slowly behind* MORTIMER.]

EINSTEIN. He didn't see him get it?
MORTIMER. See him? He sat there with his back to him. That's the kind of stuff we have to suffer through night after night. And they say the critics are killing the theatre—it's the playwrights who are killing

the theatre. So there he sits—the big dope—this fellow who's supposed to be bright—just waiting to be trussed up and gagged.

[JONATHAN *drops loop of curtain cord over* MORTIMER's *shoulder and draws it taut. At the same time he throws other loop of cord on floor beside* EINSTEIN. *Simultaneously,* EINSTEIN *leaps to* MORTIMER *and gags him with handkerchief, then takes his curtain cord and ties* MORTIMER's *legs to chair.*]

EINSTEIN. [*Finishing up the tying.*] You're right about dat fella—he vasn't very bright.

JONATHAN. Now, Mortimer, if you don't mind—we'll finish the story. [*He goes to sideboard and brings two candelabras to table and speaks as he lights them.* EINSTEIN *remains kneeling beside* MORTIMER.] Mortimer, I've been away for twenty years, but never once in all that time —my dear brother—were you out of my mind. In Melbourne one night, I dreamed of you—when I landed in San Francisco I felt a strange satisfaction—once more I was in the same country with you. [JONATHAN *has finished lighting candles. He crosses* D. R. *and flips light-switch, darkening stage. As he crosses,* EINSTEIN *gets up and crosses to window-seat.* JONATHAN *picks up instrument case at cellar doorway and sets it on table between candelabras and opens it, revealing various surgical instruments both in the bottom of case and on the inside of the cover.*] Now, Doctor, we go to work! [*He removes an instrument from the case and fingers it lovingly, as* EINSTEIN *crosses and kneels on chair* L. *of table. He is not too happy about all this.*]

EINSTEIN. Please, Chonny, for me, the quick way!

JONATHAN. Doctor! This must really be an artistic achievement. After all, we're performing before a very distinguished critic.

EINSTEIN. Chonny!

JONATHAN. [*Flaring.*] Doctor!

EINSTEIN. [*Beaten.*] All right. Let's get it over. [*He closes drapes tightly and sits on window-seat.* JONATHAN *takes three or four more instruments out of the case and fingers them. At last, having the necessary equipment laid out on the towel (also in case) he begins to put on a pair of rubber gloves (also in case).*]

JONATHAN. All ready for you, Doctor!

EINSTEIN. I gotta have a drink. I can't do this without a drink.

[*He takes bottle from pocket. Drinks. Finds it's empty. Rises.*]

Arsenic and Old Lace

JONATHAN. Pull yourself together, Doctor.
EINSTEIN. I gotta have a drink. Ven ve valked in here this afternoon there was wine here—remember? Vere did she put that? [*He looks at sideboard and remembers. He goes to it, opens* L. *cupboard and brings bottle and two wine glasses to* D. S. *end of table top.*] Look, Chonny, we got a drink. [*He pours wine into the two glasses, emptying the bottle.* MORTIMER *watches him.*] Dat's all dere is. I split it with you. We both need a drink. [*He hands one glass to* JONATHAN, *then raises his own glass to his lips.* JONATHAN *stops him.*]
JONATHAN. One moment, Doctor—please. Where are you manners? [*He drops* D. S. *to* R. *of* MORTIMER *and looks at him.*] Yes, Mortimer, I realize now it was you who brought me back to Brooklyn. . . . [*He looks at wine, then draws it back and forth under his nose smelling it. He decides that it's all right apparently for he raises his glass—*] Doctor—to my dear dead brother—

[*As they get the glasses to their lips,* TEDDY *steps out on the balcony and blows a terrific call on his bugle.* EINSTEIN *and* JONATHAN *drop their glasses, spilling the wine.* TEDDY *turns and exits.*]

EINSTEIN. Ach Gott!
JONATHAN. Damn that idiot! [*He starts for stairs.* EINSTEIN *rushes over and intercepts him.*] He goes next! That's all—he goes next!
EINSTEIN. No, Chonny, not Teddy—that's where I shtop—not Teddy!
JONATHAN. We get to Teddy later!
EINSTEIN. We don't get to him at all.
JONATHAN. Now we've got to work fast! [*He crosses above to* L. *of* MORTIMER. EINSTEIN *in front of* MORTIMER.]
EINSTEIN. Yah, the quick way—eh, Chonny?
JONATHAN. Yes, Doctor, the quick way! [*He pulls a large silk handkerchief from his inside pocket and drops it around* MORTIMER'S *neck.*]

[*At this point the door bursts open and* OFFICER O'HARA *comes in to* C., *very excited.*]

O'HARA. Hey! The Colonel's gotta quit blowing that horn!
JONATHAN. [*He and* EINSTEIN *are standing in front of* MORTIMER, *hiding him from* O'HARA.] It's all right, Officer. We're taking the bugle away from him.
O'HARA. There's going to be hell to pay in the morning. We promised the neighbors he wouldn't do that any more.

JONATHAN. It won't happen again, Officer. Good night.
O'HARA. I'd better speak to him myself. Where are the lights? [O'HARA *puts on lights and goes upstairs to landing, when he sees* MORTIMER.] Hey! You stood me up. I waited an hour at Kelly's for you. [*He comes downstairs and over to* MORTIMER *and looks at him then speaks to* JONATHAN *and* EINSTEIN.] What happened to him?
EINSTEIN. [*Thinking fast.*] He was explaining the play he saw tonight—that's what happened to the fella in the play.
O'HARA. Did they have that in the play you saw tonight? [MORTIMER *nods his head—yes.*] Gee, they practically stole that from the second act of my play—[*He starts to explain.*] Why, in my second act, just before the—[*He turns back to* MORTIMER.] I'd better begin at the beginning. It opens in my mother's dressing room, where I was born—only I ain't born yet—[MORTIMER *rubs his shoes together to attract* O'HARA's *attention.*] Huh? Oh, yeah. [O'HARA *starts to remove the gag from* MORTIMER's *mouth and then decides not to.*] No! You've got to hear the plot. [*He gets stool and brings it to* R. *of* MORTIMER *and sits, continuing on with his "plot" as the curtain falls.*] Well, she's sitting there making up, see—when all of a sudden through the door—a man with a black mustache walks in—turns to my mother and says—"Miss Latour, will you marry me?" He doesn't know she's pregnant.

SCENE 2: Scene is the same. Early the next morning. When the curtain rises again, daylight is streaming through the windows. All doors closed. All drapes open. MORTIMER is still tied in his chair and seems to be in a semi-conscious state. JONATHAN is asleep on sofa. EINSTEIN, pleasantly intoxicated, is seated L. of table, his head resting on table top. O'HARA, *with his coat off and his collar loosened, is standing over the stool which is between him and* MORTIMER. He has progressed to the most exciting scene of his play. There is a bottle of whiskey and a water tumbler on the table along with a plate full of cigarette butts.

O'HARA. —there she is lying unconscious across the table in her lingerie—the chink is standing over her with a hatchet—[*He takes the pose.*] —I'm tied up in a chair just like you are—the place is an inferno of flames—it's on fire—when all of a sudden—through the window—in comes Mayor LaGuardia. [EINSTEIN *raises his head and looks out the window. Not seeing anyone he reaches for the bottle and pours himself another drink.* O'HARA *crosses above to him and takes the bottle.*] Hey, remember who paid for that—go easy on it.

EINSTEIN. Vell, I'm listening, ain't I? [*He crosses to* JONATHAN *on the sofa.*]

O'HARA. How do you like it so far?

EINSTEIN. Vell, it put Chonny to sleep.

[O'HARA *has just finished a swig from the bottle.*]

O'HARA. Let him alone. If he ain't got no more interest than that—he don't get a drink. [EINSTEIN *takes his glass and sits on bottom stair. At the same time* O'HARA *crosses, puts stool under desk and whiskey bottle on top of desk, then comes back to center and goes on with his play—*] All right. It's three days later—I been transferred and I'm under charges—that's because somebody stole my badge. [*He pantomimes through following lines.*] All right. I'm walking my beat on Staten Island—forty-sixth precinct—when a guy I'm following, it turns out—is really following me. [*There is a knock on door.* EINSTEIN *goes up and looks out landing window. Leaves glass behind* D. S. *drape.*] Don't let anybody in.—So I figure I'll outsmart him. There's a vacant house on the corner. I goes in.

EINSTEIN. It's cops!

O'HARA. I stands there in the dark and I see the door handle turn.

EINSTEIN. [*Rushing downstairs, shakes* JONATHAN *by the shoulder.*] Chonny! It's cops! Cops! [JONATHAN *doesn't move.* EINSTEIN *rushes upstairs and off through the arch.*]

[O'HARA *is going on with his story without a stop.*]

O'HARA. I pulls my guns—braces myself against the wall—and I says—"Come in." [OFFICERS BROPHY *and* KLEIN *walk in* R., *see* O'HARA *with gun pointed at them and raise their hands. Then, recognizing their fellow officer, lower them.*] Hello, boys.

BROPHY. What the hell is going on here?

O'HARA. [*Goes to* BROPHY.] Hey, Pat, whaddya know? This is Mortimer Brewster! He's going to write my play with me. I'm just tellin' him the story.

KLEIN. [*Crossing to* MORTIMER *and untying him.*] Did you have to tie him up to make him listen?

BROPHY. Joe, you better report in at the station. The whole force is out looking for ya.

O'HARA. Did they send you here for me?

KLEIN. We didn't know you was here.

BROPHY. We came to warn the old ladies that there's hell to pay. The Colonel blew that bugle again in the middle of the night.

KLEIN. From the way the neighbors have been calling in about it you'd think the Germans had dropped a bomb on Flatbush Avenue.

[*He has finished untying* MORTIMER. *Puts cords on sideboard.*]

BROPHY. The Lieutenant's on the warpath. He says the Colonel's got to be put away some place.

MORTIMER. [*Staggers to feet.*] Yes! Yes!

O'HARA. [*Going to* MORTIMER.] Gee, Mr. Brewster, I got to get away, so I'll just run through the third act quick.

MORTIMER. [*Staggering* R.] Get away from me.

[BROPHY *gives* KLEIN *a look, goes to phone and dials.*]

KLEIN. Say, do you know what time it is? It's after eight o'clock in the morning.

O'HARA. It is? [*He follows* MORTIMER *to stairs.*] Gee, Mr. Brewster, them first two acts run a little long, but I don't see anything we can leave out.

MORTIMER. [*Almost to landing.*] You can leave it *all* out.

[BROPHY *sees* JONATHAN *on sofa.*]

BROPHY. Who the hell is this guy?

MORTIMER. [*Hanging on railing, almost to balcony.*] That's my brother.

BROPHY. Oh, the one that ran away? So he came back.

MORTIMER. Yes, he came back!

[JONATHAN *stirs as if to get up.*]

BROPHY. [*Into phone.*] This is Brophy. Get me Mac. [*To* O'HARA, *sitting on bottom stair.*] I'd better let them know we found you, Joe. [*Into phone.*] Mac? Tell the Lieutenant he can call off the big manhunt—we got him. In the Brewster house. [JONATHAN *hears this and suddenly becomes very much awake, looking up to see* KLEIN *to* L. *of him and* BROPHY *to his* R.] Do you want us to bring him in? Oh—all right, we'll hold him right here. [*He hangs up.*] The Lieutenant's on his way over. JONATHAN. [*Rising.*] So I've been turned in, eh? [BROPHY *and* KLEIN *look at him with some interest.*] All right, you've

Arsenic and Old Lace 353

got me! [*Turning to* MORTIMER, *who is on balcony looking down.*] And I suppose you and that stool-pigeon brother of mine will split the reward?

KLEIN. Reward?

[*Instinctively* KLEIN *and* BROPHY *both grab* JONATHAN *by an arm.*]

JONATHAN. [*Dragging* COPS D. S. C.] Now I'll do some turning in! You think my aunts are sweet charming old ladies, don't you? Well, there are thirteen bodies buried in their cellar.

MORTIMER. [*As he rushes off to see* TEDDY.] Teddy! Teddy! Teddy!

KLEIN. What the hell are you talking about?

BROPHY. You'd better be careful what you're saying about your aunts—they happen to be friends of ours.

JONATHAN. [*Raving as he drags them toward cellar door.*] I'll show you! I'll prove it to you! You come to the cellar with me!

KLEIN. Wait a minute! Wait a minute!

JONATHAN. Thirteen bodies! I'll show you where they're buried.

KLEIN. [*Refusing to be kidded.*] Oh, yeah?

JONATHAN. You don't want to see what's down in the cellar?

BROPHY. [*Releases* JONATHAN'S *arm, then to* KLEIN.] Go on down in the cellar with him, Abe.

KLEIN. [*Drops* JONATHAN'S *arm, backs* D. S. *a step and looks at him.*] I'm not so sure I want to be down in the cellar with him. Look at that puss. He looks like Boris Karloff. [JONATHAN, *at mention of Karloff, grabs* KLEIN *by the throat, starts choking him.*] Hey—what the hell— Hey, Pat! Get him off me.

[BROPHY *takes out rubber blackjack.*]

BROPHY. Here, what do you think you're doing! [*He socks* JONATHAN *on head.* JONATHAN *falls unconscious, face down.*]

[KLEIN, *throwing* JONATHAN'S *weight to floor, backs away, rubbing his throat.*]

KLEIN. Well what do you know about that?

[*There is a knock on door* R.]

O'HARA. Come in.

[LIEUTENANT ROONEY *bursts in* R., *slamming door after him. He is a very tough, driving, dominating officer.*]

Act III, 2

ROONEY. What the hell are you men doing here? I told you *I* was going to handle this.
KLEIN. Well, sir, we was just about to—[KLEIN's *eyes go to* JONATHAN *and* ROONEY *sees him.*]
ROONEY. What happened? Did he put up a fight?
BROPHY. This ain't the guy that blows the bugle. This is his brother. He tried to kill Klein.
KLEIN. [*Feeling his throat.*] All I said was he looked like Boris Karloff.
ROONEY. [*His face lights up.*] Turn him over.

[*The two* COPS *turn* JONATHAN *over on his back.* KLEIN *steps back.* ROONEY *crosses front of* BROPHY *to take a look at* JONATHAN. BROPHY *drifts to* R. *of* ROONEY. O'HARA *is still at foot of stairs.*]

BROPHY. We kinda think he's wanted somewhere.
ROONEY. Oh, you kinda *think* he's wanted somewhere? If you guys don't look at the circulars we hang up in the station, at least you could read *True Detective.* [*Big.*] Certainly he's wanted. In Indiana! Escaped from the prison for the Criminal Insane! He's a lifer. For God's sake that's how he was described—he *looked* like Karloff!
KLEIN. Was there a reward mentioned?
ROONEY. Yeah—and *I'm* claiming it.
BROPHY. He was trying to get us down in the cellar.
KLEIN. He said there was thirteen bodies buried down there.
ROONEY. [*Suspicious.*] Thirteen bodies buried in the cellar? [*Deciding it's ridiculous.*] And that didn't tip you off he came out of a nut-house!
O'HARA. I thought all along he talked kinda crazy.

[ROONEY *sees* O'HARA *for the first time. Turns to him.*]

ROONEY. Oh, it's Shakespeare! [*Crossing to him.*] Where have you been all night? And you needn't bother to tell me.
O'HARA. I've been right here, sir. Writing a play with Mortimer Brewster.
ROONEY. [*Tough.*] Yeah? Well, you're gonna have plenty of time to write that play. You're suspended! Now get back and report in!

[O'HARA *takes his coat, night stick, and cap from top of desk. Goes to* R. *door and opens it. Then turns to* ROONEY.]

O'HARA. Can I come over some time and use the station typewriter?
ROONEY. No!—Get out of here. [O'HARA *runs out.* ROONEY *closes door and*

Arsenic and Old Lace     355

turns to the COPS. TEDDY *enters on balcony and comes downstairs unnoticed and stands at* ROONEY's *back to the* R. *of him.* ROONEY, *to* COPS.] Take that guy somewhere else and bring him to. [*The* COPS *bend down to pick up* JONATHAN.] See what you can find out about his accomplice. [*The* COPS *stand up again in a questioning attitude.* ROONEY *explains.*] The guy that helped him escape. He's wanted too. No wonder Brooklyn's in the shape it's in, with the police force full of flatheads like you—falling for that kind of a story—thirteen bodies in the cellar!

TEDDY. But there are thirteen bodies in the cellar.

ROONEY. [*Turning on him.*] Who are you?

TEDDY. I'm President Roosevelt.

[ROONEY *does a walk* U. S. *on this, then comes down again.*]

ROONEY. What the hell is this?

BROPHY. He's the fellow that blows the bugle.

KLEIN. Good morning, Colonel.

[*They salute* TEDDY, *who returns it.* ROONEY *finds himself saluting* TEDDY *also. He pulls his hand down in disgust.*]

ROONEY. Well, Colonel, you've blown your last bugle.

TEDDY. [*Seeing* JONATHAN *on floor.*] Dear me—another Yellow Fever victim?

ROONEY. Whaat?

TEDDY. All the bodies in the cellar are Yellow Fever victims.

[ROONEY *crosses exasperatedly to* R. *door on this.*]

BROPHY. No, Colonel, this is a spy we caught in the White House.

ROONEY. [*Pointing to* JONATHAN.] Will you get that guy out of here!

[COPS *pick up* JONATHAN *and drag him to kitchen.* TEDDY *follows them.* MORTIMER *enters, comes down stairs.*]

TEDDY. [*Turning back to* ROONEY.] If there's any questioning of spies, that's my department!

ROONEY. You keep out of this!

TEDDY. You're forgetting! As President, I am also head of the Secret Service.

[BROPHY *and* KLEIN *exit with* JONATHAN *into kitchen.* TEDDY *follows them briskly.* MORTIMER *has come to* C.]

MORTIMER. Captain—I'm Mortimer Brewster.

ROONEY. Are you sure?

MORTIMER. I'd like to talk to you about my brother Teddy—the one who blew the bugle.

ROONEY. Mr. Brewster, we ain't going to talk about that—he's got to be put away!

MORTIMER. I quite agree with you. In fact, it's all arranged for. I had these commitment papers signed by Dr. Gilchrist, our family physician. Teddy has signed them himself, you see—and I've signed them as next of kin.

ROONEY. Where's he going?

MORTIMER. Happy Dale.

ROONEY. All right, I don't care where he goes as long as he goes!

MORTIMER. Oh, he's going all right. But I want you to know that everything that's happened around here Teddy's responsible for. Now, those thirteen bodies in the cellar—

ROONEY. [*He's had enough of those thirteen.*] Yeah—yeah—those thirteen bodies in the cellar! It ain't enough that the neighbors are all afraid of him, and his disturbing the peace with that bugle—but can you imagine what would happen if that cock-eyed story about thirteen bodies in the cellar got around? And now he's starting a Yellow Fever scare. Cute, ain't it?

MORTIMER. [*Greatly relieved, with an embarrassed laugh.*] Thirteen bodies. Do you think anybody would believe that story?

ROONEY. Well, you can't tell. Some people are just dumb enough. You don't know what to believe sometimes. About a year ago a crazy guy starts a murder rumor over in Greenpoint, and I had to dig up a half acre lot, just to prove that—

[*There is a knock on* R. *door.*]

MORTIMER. Will you excuse me? [*He goes to door and admits* ELAINE *and* MR. WITHERSPOON, *an elderly, tight-lipped disciplinarian. He is carrying a brief case.*]

ELAINE. [*Briskly.*] Good morning, Mortimer.

MORTIMER. [*Not knowing what to expect.*] Good morning, dear.

ELAINE. This is Mr. Witherspoon. He's come to meet Teddy.

MORTIMER. To meet Teddy?

ELAINE. Mr. Witherspoon's the superintendent of Happy Dale.

MORTIMER. [*Eagerly.*] Oh, come right in. [*They shakes hands.* MORTIMER *indicates* ROONEY.] This is Captain—

Arsenic and Old Lace

ROONEY. *Lieutenant* Rooney. I'm glad you're here, Super, because you're taking him back with you today!

WITHERSPOON. Today? I didn't know that—

ELAINE. [*Cutting in.*] Not today!

MORTIMER. Look, Elaine, I've got a lot of business to attend to, so you run along home and I'll call you up.

ELAINE. Nuts! [*She crosses to window-seat and sits.*]

WITHERSPOON. I had no idea it was this immediate.

ROONEY. The papers are all signed, he goes today!

[TEDDY *backs into room from kitchen, speaking sharply in the direction whence he's come.*]

TEDDY. Complete insubordination! You men will find out I'm no mollycoddle. [*He slams door and comes down to below table.*] When the President of the United States is treated like that—what's this country coming to?

ROONEY. There's your man, Super.

MORTIMER. Just a minute! [*He crosses to* TEDDY *and speaks to him as to a child.*] Mr. President, I have very good news for you. Your term of office is over.

TEDDY. Is this March the Fourth?

MORTIMER. Practically.

TEDDY. [*Thinking.*] Let's see—OH!—Now I go on my hunting trip to Africa! Well, I must get started immediately. [*He starts across the room and almost bumps into* WITHERSPOON *at* C. *He looks at him then steps back to* MORTIMER.] Is he trying to move into the White House before I've moved out?

MORTIMER. Who, Teddy?

TEDDY. [*Indicating* WITHERSPOON.] Taft!

MORTIMER. This isn't Mr. Taft, Teddy. This is Mr. Witherspoon—he's to be your guide in Africa.

TEDDY. [*Shakes hands with* WITHERSPOON *enthusiastically.*] Bully! Bully! I'll bring down my equipment. [*He crosses to stairs.* MARTHA *and* ABBY *have entered on balcony during last speech and are coming downstairs.*] When the safari comes, tell them to wait. [*As he passes the* AUNTS *on his way to landing, he shakes hands with each, without stopping his walk.*] Good-bye, Aunt Abby. Good-bye, Aunt Martha. I'm on my way to Africa—isn't it wonderful? [*He has reached the landing.*] CHARGE! [*He charges up the stairs and off.*]

[*The* AUNTS *are at foot of stairs.*]

MORTIMER. [*Crossing to* AUNTS.] Good morning, darlings.

MARTHA. Oh, we have visitors.

MORTIMER. [*He indicates* ROONEY *at* C.] This is Lieutenant Rooney.

ABBY. [*Crossing, shakes hands with him.*] How do you do, Lieutenant? My, you don't look like the fussbudget the policemen say you are.

MORTIMER. Why the Lieutenant is here—You know, Teddy blew his bugle again last night.

MARTHA. Yes, we're going to speak to Teddy about that.

ROONEY. It's a little more serious than that, Miss Brewster.

MORTIMER. [*Easing* AUNTS *to* WITHERSPOON *who is above table where he has opened his brief case and extracted some papers.*] And you haven't met Mr. Witherspoon. He's the Superintendent of Happy Dale.

ABBY. Oh, Mr. Witherspoon—how do you do?

MARTHA. You've come to meet Teddy.

ROONEY. [*Somewhat harshly.*] He's come to *take* him.

[*The* AUNTS *turn to* ROONEY *questioningly.*]

MORTIMER. [*Making it as easy as possible.*] Aunties—the police want Teddy to go there, today.

ABBY. [*Crossing to* R. *of chair.*] Oh—no!

MARTHA. [*Behind* ABBY.] Not while we're alive!

ROONEY. I'm sorry, Miss Brewster, but it has to be done. The papers are all signed and he's going along with the Superintendent.

ABBY. We won't permit it. We'll promise to take the bugle away from him.

MARTHA. We won't be separated from Teddy.

ROONEY. I'm sorry, ladies, but the law's the law! He's committed himself and he's going!

ABBY. Well, if he goes, we're going too.

MARTHA. Yes, you'll have to take us with him.

MORTIMER. [*Has an idea. Crosses to* WITHERSPOON.] Well, why not?

WITHERSPOON. [*To* MORTIMER.] Well, that's sweet of them to want to, but it's impossible. You see, we can't take *sane* people at Happy Dale.

MARTHA. [*Turning to* WITHERSPOON.] Mr. Witherspoon, if you'll let us live there with Teddy, we'll see that Happy Dale is in our will—and for a very generous amount.

Arsenic and Old Lace

WITHERSPOON. Well, the Lord knows we could use the money, but—I'm afraid—

ROONEY. Now let's be sensible about this, ladies. For instance, here I am wasting my morning when I've got serious work to do. You know there are still *murders* to be solved in Brooklyn.

MORTIMER. Yes! [*Covering.*] Oh, are there?

ROONEY. It ain't only his bugle blowing and the neighbors all afraid of him, but things would just get worse. Sooner or later we'd be put to the trouble of digging up your cellar.

ABBY. Our cellar?

ROONEY. Yeah.—Your nephew's been telling around that there are thirteen bodies in your cellar.

ABBY. But there are thirteen bodies in our cellar.

[ROONEY *looks disgusted.* MORTIMER *drifts quietly to front of cellar door.*]

MARTHA. If that's why you think Teddy has to go away—you come down to the cellar with us and we'll prove it to you. [*Goes* U. S.]

ABBY. There's one—Mr. Spenalzo—who doesn't belong here and who will have to leave—but the other twelve are our gentlemen. [*She starts* U. S.]

MORTIMER. I don't think the Lieutenant wants to go down in the cellar. He was telling me that only last year he had to dig up a half-acre lot —weren't you, Lieutenant?

ROONEY. That's right.

ABBY. [*To* ROONEY.] Oh, you wouldn't have to dig here. The graves are all marked. We put flowers on them every Sunday.

ROONEY. Flowers? [*He steps up toward* ABBY, *then turns to* WITHERSPOON, *indicating the* AUNTS *as he speaks.*] Superintendent—don't you think you can find room for these ladies?

WITHERSPOON. Well, I—

ABBY. [*To* ROONEY.] You come along with us, and we'll show you the graves.

ROONEY. I'll take your word for it, lady—I'm a busy man. How about it, Super?

WITHERSPOON. Well, they'd have to be committed.

MORTIMER. Teddy committed himself. Can't they commit themselves? Can't they sign the papers?

WITHERSPOON. Why, certainly.

MARTHA. [*Sits in chair* L. *of table as* WITHERSPOON *draws it out for her.*]
Oh, if we can go with Teddy, we'll sign the papers. Where are they?
ABBY. [*Sitting* R. *of table.* MORTIMER *helps her with chair.*] Yes, where are they?

[WITHERSPOON *opens brief case for more papers.* KLEIN *enters from kitchen.*]

KLEIN. He's coming around, Lieutenant.
ABBY. Good morning, Mr. Klein.
MARTHA. Good morning, Mr. Klein. Are you here too?
KLEIN. Yeah. Brophy and me have got your other nephew out in the kitchen.
ROONEY. Well, sign 'em up, Superintendent. I want to get this all cleaned up. [*He crosses to kitchen door, shaking his head as he exits and saying:*] Thirteen bodies.

[KLEIN *follows him out.* MORTIMER *is to the* L. *of* ABBY, *fountain pen in hand.* WITHERSPOON *to* R. *of* MARTHA, *also with pen.*]

WITHERSPOON. [*Handing* MARTHA *pen.*] If you'll sign right here.

[MARTHA *signs.*]

MORTIMER. And you here, Aunt Abby.

[ABBY *signs.*]

ABBY. [*Signing.*] I'm really looking forward to going—the neighborhood here has changed so.
MARTHA. Just think, a front lawn again.

[EINSTEIN *enters through arch and comes down stairs to door* D. R. *carrying suitcase. He picks hat from hall tree on way down.*]

WITHERSPOON. Oh, we're overlooking something.
MARTHA. What?
WITHERSPOON. Well, we're going to need the signature of a doctor.
MORTIMER. Oh! [*He sees* EINSTEIN *about to disappear through the door.*] Dr. Einstein! Will you come over here—we'd like you to sign some papers.
EINSTEIN. Please, I must—

*Arsenic and Old Lace*

MORTIMER. [*Crosses to him.*] Just come right over, Doctor. At one time last night, I thought the Doctor was going to operate on me. [EINSTEIN *puts down suitcase and his hat just inside the door.*] Just come right over, Doctor. [EINSTEIN *crosses to table,* L. *of* ABBY.] Just sign right here, Doctor.

[*The* DOCTOR *signs* ABBY'S *paper and* MARTHA'S *paper.* ROONEY *and* KLEIN *enter from kitchen.* ROONEY *crosses to desk and dials phone.* KLEIN *stands near kitchen door.*]

ABBY. Were you leaving, Doctor?
EINSTEIN. [*Signing papers.*] I think I must go.
MARTHA. Aren't you going to wait for Jonathan?
EINSTEIN. I don't think we're going to the same place.

[MORTIMER *sees* ELAINE *on window-seat and crosses to her.*]

MORTIMER. Hello, Elaine. I'm glad to see you. Stick around, huh?
ELAINE. Don't worry, I'm going to.

[MORTIMER *stands back of* MARTHA'S *chair.* ROONEY *speaks into phone.*]

ROONEY. Hello, Mac. Rooney. We've picked up that guy that's wanted in Indiana. Now there's a description of his accomplice—it's right on the desk there—read it to me. [EINSTEIN *sees* ROONEY *at phone. He starts toward kitchen and sees* KLEIN *standing there. He comes back to* R. *of table and stands there dejectedly waiting for the pinch.* ROONEY *repeats the description given him over phone, looking blankly at* EINSTEIN *the while.*] Yeah—about fifty-four—five foot six—hundred and forty pounds—blue eyes—talks with a German accent. Poses as a doctor. Thanks, Mac. [*He hangs up as* WITHERSPOON *crosses to him with papers in hand.*]
WITHERSPOON. It's all right, Lieutenant. The Doctor here has just completed the signatures.

[ROONEY *goes to* EINSTEIN *and shakes his hand.*]

ROONEY. Thanks, Doc. You're really doing Brooklyn a service.

[ROONEY *and* KLEIN *exit to kitchen.*]

[EINSTEIN *stands amazed for a moment then grabs up his hat and suitcase and disappears through* R. *door. The* AUNTS *rise and cross over, looking out after him.* ABBY *shuts the door and they stand there* D. R.]

WITHERSPOON. [*Above table.*] Mr. Brewster, you sign now as next of kin.

[*The* AUNTS *whisper to each other as* MORTIMER *signs.*]

MORTIMER. Yes, of course. Right here?
WITHERSPOON. That's fine.
MORTIMER. That makes everything complete—everything legal?
WITHERSPOON. Oh, yes.
MORTIMER. [*With relief.*] Well, Aunties, now you're safe.
WITHERSPOON. [*To* AUNTS.] When do you think you'll be ready to start?
ABBY. [*Stepping* L.] Well, Mr. Witherspoon, why don't you go upstairs and tell Teddy just what he can take along?
WITHERSPOON. Upstairs?
MORTIMER. I'll show you.
ABBY. [*Stopping him.*] No, Mortimer, you stay here. We want to talk to you. [*To* WITHERSPOON.] Yes, Mr. Witherspoon, just upstairs and turn to the left.

[WITHERSPOON *puts his brief case on sofa and goes upstairs, the* AUNTS *keeping an eye on him while talking to* MORTIMER.]

MARTHA. Well, Mortimer, now that we're moving, this house really is yours.
ABBY. Yes, dear, we want you to live here now.
MORTIMER. [*Below table.*] No, Aunt Abby, this house is too full of memories.
MARTHA. But you'll need a home when you and Elaine are married.
MORTIMER. Darlings, that's very indefinite.
ELAINE. [*Rises and crosses to* L. *of* MORTIMER.] It's nothing of the kind—we're going to be married right away.

[WITHERSPOON *has exited off balcony.*]

ABBY. Mortimer—Mortimer, we're really very worried about something.
MORTIMER. Now, darlings, you're going to love it at Happy Dale.
MARTHA. Oh, yes, we're very happy about the whole thing. That's just it—we don't want anything to go wrong.
ABBY. Will they investigate those signatures?
MORTIMER. Don't worry, they're not going to look up Dr. Einstein.
MARTHA. It's not his signature, dear, it's yours.
ABBY. You see, you signed as next of kin.
MORTIMER. Of course. Why not?

Arsenic and Old Lace    363

MARTHA. Well, dear, it's something we never wanted to tell you. But now you're a man—and it's something Elaine should know too. You see, dear—you're not really a Brewster.

[MORTIMER *stares as does* ELAINE.]

ABBY. Your mother came to us as a cook—and you were born about three months afterward. But she was such a sweet woman—and such a good cook we didn't want to lose her—so brother married her.
MORTIMER. I'm—not—really—a—Brewster?
MARTHA. Now, don't feel badly about it, dear.
ABBY. And Elaine, it won't make any difference to you?
MORTIMER. [*Turning slowly to face* ELAINE. *His voice rising.*] Elaine! Did you hear? Do you understand? I'm a bastard!

[ELAINE *leaps into his arms. The two* AUNTS *watch them, then* MARTHA *starts* U. L. *a few steps.*]

MARTHA. Well, now I really must see about breakfast.
ELAINE. [*Leading* MORTIMER *to* R. *door; opening door.*] Mortimer's coming over to my house. Father's gone to Philadelphia, and Mortimer and I are going to have breakfast together.
MORTIMER. Yes, I need some coffee—I've had quite a night.
ABBY. In that case I should think you'd want to get to bed.
MORTIMER. [*With a sidelong glance at* ELAINE.] I do. [*They exit* R., *closing door.*]

[WITHERSPOON *enters on balcony, carrying two canteens. He starts downstairs when* TEDDY *enters carrying large canoe paddle. He is dressed in Panama outfit with pack on his back.*]

TEDDY. One moment, Witherspoon. Take this with you! [*He exits off balcony again as* WITHERSPOON *comes on downstairs to sofa. He puts canteens on sofa and leans paddle against wall.*]

[*At the same time* ROONEY *and the two cops with* JONATHAN *between them enter. The* COPS *have twisters around* JONATHAN'S *wrists.* ROONEY *enters first and crosses to* R. C. *The other three stop* D. L. *of table. The* AUNTS *are* R. *of the table.*]

ROONEY. We won't need the wagon. My car's out front.
MARTHA. Oh, you leaving now, Jonathan?
ROONEY. Yeah—he's going back to Indiana. There's some people there want to take care of him for the rest of his life. Come on.

[ROONEY *opens door as the two* COPS *and* JONATHAN *cross to* R. C. ABBY *steps* D. S. *after they pass.*]

ABBY. Well, Jonathan, it's nice to know you have some place to go.
MARTHA. We're leaving too.
ABBY. Yes, we're going to Happy Dale.
JONATHAN. Then this house is seeing the last of the Brewsters.
MARTHA. Unless Mortimer wants to live here.
JONATHAN. I have a suggestion to make. Why don't you turn this property over to the church?
ABBY. Well, we never thought of that.
JONATHAN. After all, it *should* be part of the cemetery.
ROONEY. All right, get going, I'm a busy man.
JONATHAN. [*Holding his ground for his one last word.*] Good-bye, Aunties. Well, I can't better my record now but neither can you—at least I have that satisfaction. The score stands even, *twelve* to *twelve*. [JONATHAN *and the* COPS *exit* R., *as the* AUNTS *look out after them.*]

[WITHERSPOON *crosses above to window-seat and stands quietly looking out the window. His back is to the* AUNTS.]

MARTHA. [*Starting toward* R. *door to close it.*] Jonathan always was a mean boy. Never could stand to see anyone get ahead of him. [*She closes door.*]
ABBY. [*Turning slowly around* L. *as she speaks.*] I wish we could show him he isn't so smart! [*Her eyes fall on* WITHERSPOON. *She studies him.* MARTHA *turns from door and sees* ABBY's *contemplation.* ABBY *speaks sweetly.*] Mr. Witherspoon? [WITHERSPOON *turns around facing them.*] Does your family live with you at Happy Dale?
WITHERSPOON. I have no family.
ABBY. Oh—
MARTHA. [*Stepping into room.*] Well, I suppose you consider everyone at Happy Dale your family?
WITHERSPOON. I'm afraid you don't quite understand. As head of the institution, I have to keep quite aloof.
ABBY. That must make it very lonely for you.
WITHERSPOON. It does. But my duty is my duty.
ABBY. [*Turning to* MARTHA.] Well, Martha—[MARTHA *takes her cue and goes to sideboard for bottle of wine. Bottle in* L. *cupboard is empty. She puts it back and takes out full bottle from* R. *cupboard. She*

Arsenic and Old Lace

*brings bottle and wine-glass to table.* ABBY *continues talking.*] If Mr. Witherspoon won't join us for breakfast, I think at least we should offer him a glass of elderberry wine.

WITHERSPOON. [*Severely.*] Elderberry wine?

MARTHA. We make it ourselves.

WITHERSPOON. [*Melting slightly.*] Why, yes . . . [*Severely again.*] Of course, at Happy Dale our relationship will be more formal—but here—[*He sits in chair* L. *of table as* MARTHA *pours wine.* ABBY *is beside* MARTHA.] You don't see much elderberry wine nowadays—I thought I'd had my last glass of it.

ABBY. Oh, no—

MARTHA. [*Handing him glass of wine.*] No, here it is.

[WITHERSPOON *toasts the ladies and lifts glass to his lips, but the curtain falls before he does. . . .*]

[*For a curtain call it is suggested the 12 elderly gentlemen file out of the cellar entrance, stand in a line across the stage, and bow.*]

# APPENDIX

## HOW TO READ A COMEDY

The first thing to keep in mind when reading a comedy is that it *is* a play, and that a play is meant to be performed. One factor alone distinguishes drama from other literary types: only plays are written to be interpreted by others for us and to us. In other words, only drama is written with an outside interpreter as an integral part. Those normally doing the interpreting are the director and the actors, the director being the primary interpreter and the actors the instruments through which his interpretation is portrayed. When reading a play we should try to place ourselves in the role of director-actor rather than looking at the play strictly from the point of view of the reader-audience as we do in narrative works. Since *drama* means *action*, we must become participants rather than observers. Empathy is the key to dramatic response—emotional identification with the character and the situation. In a live performance we identify easily with the actors playing the roles. Failure to "see" the action as you read is the primary reason for the common complaint, "I laughed much more when I saw it than when I read it."

Now let us approach the play as a director would. First, we must search out the *theme*: what does the play have to say? That is, what idea is the playwright trying to put across? This idea might be a simple comment about life in general, man's behavior, or his reaction to a specific predicament. On the other hand, the playwright may have a very strong statement to make concerning issues, foibles, or attitudes. For example, *Twelfth Night* suggests that love is a bittersweet experience of joy and melancholy. *Arsenic and Old Lace* looks at madness with a quizzical shrug: "appearances are deceiving." Every great play has something serious to say. In addition to the major theme there are often secondary themes expressed by the author.

The second consideration is *plot*. Comic plots usually consist of a major situation and several minor predicaments. These become increasingly more complicated before being resolved.

The plot consists of a preliminary situation, rising action, climax, falling action, and conclusion. The *preliminary situation* opens the play and sets the time, place, and mood, and serves to bring the audience up to date. This usually includes *exposition*, the background information essential to the establishment of the plot. The plot itself really begins with the *initial incident*. This is an event that sets off the basic conflict which must be resolved. The *rising action* usually introduces all of the important characters, determines all major situations of conflict, proposes solutions to those conflicts—usually by the protagonist—and builds suspense toward the *climax*. The climax is the turning point, the point of action where a choice is made—directly, unconsciously, or accidentally—which determines the direction in which the play will go. In a comedy, the climax is most often highly amusing, but, at the same time, the major predicament seems impossible to resolve. Before and after the climax may come a *crisis* or series of crises. A crisis is a severe challenge to the protagonist, often a decision-making challenge. Most crises in comedies force some characters to take inappropriate actions. These are comic in nature. The *falling action* releases the tensions of the play, resolving the conflicts, unifying the comic society, and leaving the audience with a feeling of general well-being. Within the falling action there may be a *denouement*, a revelation in which previously concealed information is made known to the audience. Some plays, especially comedies, may have a *deus ex machina* in the falling action. A deus ex machina is a device which is brought into a literary work to settle a seemingly unresolvable problem—legacies, missing relatives, and hidden identities such as we find in *The Importance of Being Earnest*. Such an escape for the playwright weakens serious works, but seldom bothers audiences in a comedy, especially in farces, where they often occur. The falling action may also include a *catastrophe*. Usually a catastrophe is some ill-fated event which befalls the protagonist. It can also be a painful experience for some other character with whom the audience has empathized. Finally, there is the *conclusion*, the end of the action. Most conclusions are brief, serving only to indicate the outcome of the conflict. In a comedy the conclusion shows the protagonist achieving his goals after having overcome the forces opposing him and ends with the unification of the "new society." There are some contemporary plays which sardonically question the victory of the protagonist. However, audiences have sometimes questioned the comic success of such "dark comedies."

The third element for study is that of *character*. Much of the humor depends upon the establishing of a character. Most comic characters have a dominant personality trait which, in its exaggeration, makes us laugh. Often this dominant trait is suggested by the character's name—Belch, Hardcastle, Lumpkin. The reader must determine the interrelationships of the characters. The *protagonist* is the principal character. Opposing him in conflict is the *antagonist*; the antagonist is usually another character, although it may be an idea, or something within the protagonist himself. There are *foils*, characters who are used for purposes of comparison. In most instances the foils are compared to the protagonist for degrees of similarity and difference. There are numerous other comic characters whose primary function is to amplify the comic situation. We learn about characters by what the author says about them, what other characters say about them when they are present and when they are not, and by what the character says in his own lines, especially in monologues and asides.

The fourth dramatic element is *dialogue*, frequently the most difficult facet of comedy to appreciate when reading. Words on paper often do not read as well as they play. Ironies, wordplay, and inflections are hard to "hear" when a play is read. We must read carefully to catch the "plants," the repetitions, the "setups," and the subtle character idiosyncrasies which are so important to comedy.

The fifth element is *style*. The style of a play is determined by the historical period in which it was written, the acting style in which it is presented on the stage, and the predilections of the author. Such stage conventions as the *aside* (a line spoken directly to the audience but inaudible to every one else on stage) must be understood in order to fully appreciate the comic technique. The fact that the Elizabethan stage was practically devoid of scenery makes the hiding behind boxwood trees in *Twelfth Night* an even more obvious "setup" than it would be on our stages, where we are used to a great deal of scenery. The use of masks, unusual makeup, or special props such as slapsticks, fans, and canes are essential to some plays but are difficult to imagine as you read the play.

The sixth element of drama is the author himself. Some knowledge of the author's style, technique, subject matter, and theme may help you understand and enjoy his works. Many authors have very distinct themes which dominate their plays. Once in a long while, something in the playwright's personal life may throw some light on the play. For example, before we challenge too skeptically the possibility of Marlow and Hastings' mistaking Hardcastle's manor house for an inn, we might be amused to discover that Goldsmith based the play on his own "mistakes of a night."

Finally, as we read comedies, we should remember that many experiences of life that would ordinarily make us cry out in despair, bitterness, or pain can become the objects of laughter. It is man's ability to laugh that enables him to smile at today and hope for tomorrow.

# SUGGESTED READING LIST

| | |
|---|---|
| Anouilh, Jean | *Thieves' Carnival, Time Remembered* |
| Aristophanes | *The Birds, The Clouds, The Frogs, Lysistrata* |
| Barrie, James M. | *The Admirable Crichton, Dear Brutus, Peter Pan, What Every Woman Knows* |
| Beaumont, Francis and Fletcher, John | *The Knight of the Burning Pestle* |
| Chase, Mary | *Bernardine, Harvey, Mrs. McThing* |
| Clark, Perry | *Cheaper by the Dozen* |
| Congreve, William | *Love for Love* |
| Coward, Noel | *Blythe Spirit, Hay Fever* |
| Crichton, Kyle | *The Happiest Millionaire* |
| Davenport, Gwen | *Belvedere* |
| Dekker, Thomas | *The Shoemaker's Holiday* |
| Farquhar, George | *The Beaux' Stratagem* |
| Fry, Christopher | *The Lady's Not for Burning* |
| Giraudoux, Jean | *The Madwoman of Chaillot* |
| Gordon, Ruth | *Years Ago* |
| Ionesco, Jean | *Rhinoceros* |
| Jonson, Ben | *The Alchemist, Every Man in His Humour* |
| Kaufman, George S. and Hart, Moss | *George Washington Slept Here, The Man Who Came to Dinner, You Can't Take It With You* |
| Lawrence, Jerome and Lee, Robert E. | *Auntie Mame* |
| Levin, Ira | *No Time for Sergeants* |
| Lindsay, Howard and Crouse, Russel | *Life with Father* |
| Molière | *The Doctor in Spite of Himself, The Imaginary Invalid, The Misanthrope, The Miser* |
| Nash, N. Richard | *The Rainmaker* |

| | |
|---|---|
| O'Neill, Eugene | *Ah, Wilderness!* |
| Patrick, John | *The Curious Savage, Everybody Loves Opal, The Teahouse of the August Moon* |
| Segall, Harry | *Heaven Can Wait* |
| Shakespeare, William | *As You Like It, A Midsummer Night's Dream, The Comedy of Errors, The Taming of the Shrew, The Tempest* |
| Shaw, G. B. | *Androcles and the Lion, Arms and the Man, Caesar and Cleopatra, Man and Superman, Major Barbara, Pygmalion* |
| Sheridan, Richard B. | *The Rivals* |
| Simon, Neil | *Barefoot in the Park, Come Blow Your Horn, The Odd Couple, Star-Spangled Girl* |
| Skinner, Cornelia Otis and Kimbrough, Emily | *Our Hearts Were Young and Gay* |
| Spewack, Sam and Bella | *My Three Angels* |
| Spigelgass, Leonard | *A Majority of One* |
| Synge, John M. | *The Playboy of the Western World* |
| Stoppard, Tom | *Rosencrantz and Guildenstern Are Dead* |
| Taylor, Samuel | *Sabrina Fair* |
| Thomas, Brandon | *Charley's Aunt* |
| Thurber, James | *Thurber Carnival* |
| Thurber, James and Nugent, Elliott | *The Male Animal* |
| Ustinov, Peter | *Romanoff and Juliet* |
| Van Druten, John | *Bell, Book, and Candle, I Remember Mama* |
| Vidal, Gore | *Visit to a Small Planet* |
| Wilde, Oscar | *Lady Windemere's Fan* |
| Wilber, Thornton | *The Matchmaker, Our Town, The Skin of Our Teeth* |
| Wycherly, William | *The Country Wife* |